Martin Riedelsheimer
Fictions of Infinity

Buchreihe der Anglia/ ANGLIA Book Series

Edited by
Lucia Kornexl, Ursula Lenker, Martin Middeke,
Gabriele Rippl, Daniel Stein

Advisory Board
Laurel Brinton, Philip Durkin, Olga Fischer, Susan Irvine,
Andrew James Johnston, Christopher A. Jones, Terttu Nevalainen,
Derek Attridge, Elisabeth Bronfen, Ursula K. Heise, Verena Lobsien,
Laura Marcus, J. Hillis Miller, Martin Puchner

Volume 71

Martin Riedelsheimer
Fictions of Infinity

Levinasian Ethics in 21st-Century Novels

DE GRUYTER

ISBN 978-3-11-099524-4
e-ISBN (PDF) 978-3-11-071240-7
e-ISBN (EPUB) 978-3-11-071242-1
ISSN 0340-5435

Library of Congress Control Number: 2020943149

Bibliographic information published by the Deutsche Nationalbibliothek
The Deutsche Nationalbibliothek lists this publication in the Deutsche Nationalbibliografie; detailed bibliographic data are available on the Internet at http://dnb.dnb.de.

© 2022 Walter de Gruyter GmbH, Berlin/Boston
This volume is text- and page-identical with the hardback published in 2020.
Printing and binding: CPI books GmbH, Leck

www.degruyter.com

Acknowledgements

My profound and heart-felt thanks are due to many people: First of all, to my parents, Martin and Gerlinde, for giving me their unconditional love and support. Without you, none of this would have been possible and I'm eternally grateful to you for always being there for me.

Next, I owe a great deal to those people at Augsburg University who helped me develop an interest in the study of literature and in Levinas's ethics: in particular to Martin Middeke, who not only supervised the PhD thesis that eventually turned into this book, but also has supported me from an early stage in my studies and continues to do so. Martin first brought me into contact with some of the central theoretical concepts in this book, particularly with the work of Levinas, but also, by letting me participate in his research seminars over the years, helped me hone the understanding necessary for a theory-informed discussion of literature. Before I met Martin, it was Christina Wald who first kindled my interest in the academic study of literature and Christoph Henke who in his many excellent classes acquainted me with so many facets of English literature. Christoph would also have been co-supervisor of my PhD thesis, but sadly passed away far too soon – I miss him dearly, not only as an academic influence and wonderful teacher, but above all for his human warmth. I am grateful to Hubert Zapf for stepping in at short notice and taking up the role of co-supervisor as well as to Mathias Mayer for his advice and for joining my board of supervisors.

I am no less grateful to all my friends and colleagues – in particular Christian Attinger, Georg Hauzenberger, Stefan Mordstein, Eva Ries, Korbinian Stöckl and Leila Vaziri – for their support, their openness to discuss all matters infinite and for their readiness to every now and then share a drink and forget about infinity for a while.

Finally, I want to thank Georg Hauzenberger, again, for meticulously proofreading the manuscript of this book and Nicole Held, Victoria Müller and Carolin Steinke for diligently helping me with style sheet issues. Needless to say that all remaining errors or inaccuracies are entirely mine.

List of Abbreviations

All references to the four novels that are my primary case studies are abbreviated as follows:

CA Mitchell, David. 2012 [2004]. *Cloud Atlas*. New York: Random House.
TI Banville, John. 2009. *The Infinities*. London: Picador.
S McEwan, Ian. 2006 [2005]. *Saturday*. London: Vintage.
SG Winterson, Jeanette. 2008 [2007]. *The Stone Gods*. London: Penguin.

Contents

1 **Introduction: Towards Infinity** —— 1
1.1   Properties and History of the Infinite: A Brief Overview —— 3
1.2   Fictions of Infinity —— 18

2 **Narrative Infinity: Aesthetics and Conceptualisation** —— 31
2.1   Conceptualising the Infinite: The Basic Metaphor of Infinity —— 33
2.2   Aesthetic Configurations of Narrative Infinity —— 38
2.2.1   Narrative Repetition, Circularity and Infinity —— 39
2.2.2   Mise en abyme and Infinite Embedding —— 43
2.2.3   Infinite Intertextuality —— 52
2.2.4   Infinite Perspective and Narrative Omniscience —— 58
2.3   Catachresis: Infinite Textuality —— 61

3 **Levinas and the Ethical Aporia of Infinity** —— 66
3.1   Infinity and Alterity —— 67
3.2   Saying and Said —— 71
3.3   Levinas and Literature —— 76
3.4   Catachresis: Levinas's Ethics and Infinite Aesthetics —— 84

4 **Infinitely Encountering the Ineffable: David Mitchell's *Cloud Atlas*** —— 96
4.1   "An Infinite Matryoshka Doll of Painted Moments": mise en abyme in *Cloud Atlas* —— 97
4.2   "The Ever-Constant Ineffable": Ethical Encounters —— 109

5 **Infinitely Repeating: Jeanette Winterson's *The Stone Gods*** —— 124
5.1   "Doomed to Repetition"? Circularity and Textual Infinity —— 124
5.2   "More Than One Reading": Re-Reading *The Stone Gods* —— 133
5.3   "Love Is an Intervention": Queering the Circle —— 142
5.4   "The Universe Is an Imprint": The Ethics of Infinite Reading —— 151

6 **Infinite Intertextuality: Encountering Alterity in Ian McEwan's *Saturday*** —— 156
6.1   "Literary Education": Encountering Intertextuality in *Saturday* —— 157

6.2		"The Professional Reductionist": Perowne's "Metaphysics of Comprehension" —— **160**
6.3		"A Yearning He Could Barely Begin to Define": Infinite Injections of Alterity —— **168**
7		**Infinite Perspective: John Banville's** *The Infinities* —— **184**
7.1		"The Mystery of Otherness": Encounters with Perspective —— **186**
7.2		"Another Kind of Elsewhere": The Metafictional Multiverse Narrative —— **191**
7.3		"This Voice Speaking Out of the Void": Narrative Totality and the Protean Narrator —— **200**
7.4		"Essence is Essentially Inessential": Reading Alterity —— **210**
8		**Coda: And Beyond?** —— **217**

Works Cited —— **226**

Index —— **243**

1 Introduction: Towards Infinity

Infinity is an elusive phenomenon. By its very nature it appears as too vast an idea to be fully understood. This is what has led to a fascination with the infinite pervading various academic disciplines, such as mathematics, physics, philosophy and theology, as well as the arts and literature – not to mention the ample exploitation of the buzzword 'infinity' in consumer culture and advertising, where it is used as a placeholder promising, more or less, that the sky is (not) the limit. In short, infinity is everywhere. The infinite, it would seem, captures the imagination precisely because it implies an inexhaustible 'more' beyond the here and now, beyond the finite constraints of our daily lives. Literature, of course, as all art, can be viewed as an exploration of what goes beyond the ordinary. In this widest possible sense, all fiction is itself then a gateway to infinity, if only because nothing, no content matter or perspective seems to be beyond the reach of fiction. David Winters in his essay collection *Infinite Fictions* takes this argument a step further and, quoting the American writer Gordon Lish, describes fiction as a "'bounded infinity' – an object which seems circumscribed on all sides, but which contains a limitless internal world" (Winters 2015: 2). As such a paradoxical container, any book spells out and opens up a world that "might exceed that outside it" (Winters 2015: 3). The pages of a book, this argument goes, contain more than the finite space between the covers may logically contain – and since storytelling conjures up concrete images this is not a result of extreme abstraction either. Fiction thus can store entities far larger than the physical space the text itself takes up.

In the following, I am focussing on a somewhat narrower understanding of 'infinite fiction' than suggested by Winters, namely on narrative fiction that thematises infinity. Although the infinite is not exclusively and perhaps not even primarily a mathematical concept, what Brian Rotman has to say about the presence of mathematics in literature equally holds true for any such thematisation of infinity in literature: it can occur at the content level of any fictional text, when a text is 'about' infinity – but it can "also, less obviously and more interestingly, enter and impinge on literature through its form" (Rotman 2011: 157). My interest in this study is above all in the latter, in fictional narratives that make the infinite an integral part of their aesthetic structure – not through the description of a large world or a possibly infinite universe, but through the thematisation, explicit or implicit, of infinity in the aesthetic form of the text so that ultimately the text itself appears to become infinite. The kind of text that achieves such a self-identification as infinite – and whose infinity is hence no longer "bounded" – is what I am calling in the following a 'fiction of infinity'.

Beyond the questions of representation and of the aesthetics of the infinite such fictions of infinity must inevitably pose, by thematising infinity they are also invested in another property of the infinite: its tendency to challenge, and even overawe, our thought. Among the many attempts by various philosophers at approaching the infinite, my focus will be on the key role infinity takes in the work of Emmanuel Levinas, who can be considered one of the foremost thinkers in the field of ethics in the twentieth century and whose works have proved a crucial influence on the so-called ethical turn in literary theory (see e.g. Madison and Fairbairn 1999; Critchley 2002; Womack 2015). For Levinas, infinity is closely connected to the radically unknowable other and it is in the encounter with others that, because of their very otherness, an ethical demand is imposed on us. Alterity, and hence infinity, is therefore central to Levinasian ethics. If there is a connection between infinity and ethics that stems from the way in which we, as thinkers, readers or human beings in general, approach the infinite (or fail in this approach), then this should also be traceable when infinity becomes textual in fictions of infinity and so endow these texts with an ethical dimension.

It is thus the aim of this book to answer the question of how and why fictions of infinity become infinite, that is, to analyse the aesthetic properties that may endow a text with infinity as well as their function. My claim is (1) that certain aesthetic configurations of narrative texts have the capacity to endow texts with infinity; (2) that a central function of the infinite in such contemporary fictions of infinity is the breaking open of both ontological and epistemological certitude; and (3) that as a consequence these texts attain a forceful ethical dimension. I want to show that readers may understand texts as infinite entities due to a conceptual metaphor identified by George Lakoff and Rafael E. Núñez (2000), the Basic Metaphor of Infinity. Such infinite texts are necessarily paradoxical, both because their physical extensions remain finite and because an infinite text inevitably transcends itself, challenging established notions of understanding and interpretation. It is in this latter sense that fictions of infinity reveal their ethical potential in the context of Levinas's ethics of alterity: in their textual self-transcendence they develop a disruptive potential and may thus function as ethical appeals to their readers. This will be illustrated in detailed readings of four novels I consider exemplary fictions of infinity: David Mitchell's *Cloud Atlas* (2004), Jeanette Winterson's *The Stone Gods* (2007), Ian McEwan's *Saturday* (2005) and John Banville's *The Infinities* (2009). All four novels in their own different ways create infinite texts in which textual infinity is complexly coupled with an ethical forcefulness these texts attain.

1.1 Properties and History of the Infinite: A Brief Overview

Before turning to these examples of fictions of infinity, a brief overview of the history of the infinite in mathematics, theology, philosophy and the arts seems helpful to begin with, since such an overview makes it possible to trace some of the key properties of the infinite and ways in which these properties have preoccupied humankind over the past several millennia.[1] The two properties of infinity that will prove most important to my study of the ways in which infinity may appear as an aesthetic feature in literature and of what impact such fictions of infinity may have on readers are the following:
(1) The infinite is beset by paradox and resists, or at least challenges, human understanding.
(2) As a result, infinity likewise resists its own representation, at least where this representation is anything else but highly abstract.

It seems clear that these two properties (and certainly representation and understanding in general) are closely connected – for all practical purposes, when it comes to literature, an art form rooted in representation, they imply each other. As a consequence, both have influenced the ways in which infinity has been thought and talked about and both continue to influence the ways in

---

[1] This overview must necessarily be incomplete and can only highlight some of the most important developments (or those I deem important as a background to my study) in the history of thought on the infinite. There are countless books and articles that look at infinity from various different angles. The following list represents the vantage points of various academic disciplines: Oppy's *Philosophical Perspectives on Infinity* (2006), Zellini's brief history of infinity (2010), Jori's overview of the philosophy of infinity (2010) and A. W. Moore's monograph and collection on the topic (2001; 1993); Mückenheim's account of the history of infinity in mathematics (2011); Maor's brilliant *To Infinity and Beyond: A Cultural History of the Infinite* (1986) and Rucker's excellent take on "the science and philosophy of the infinite" (1982), both also with a mathematical focus, just like Stewart's *Infinity: A Very Short Introduction* (2017); Heller and Woodin's cross-disciplinary compilation of articles on "new research frontiers" of infinity with contributions from the fields of mathematics, the sciences, philosophy and theology (2011); Barrow's *Infinite Book* (2005) with its wide ranging survey of questions and challenges of the infinite; as well as the similarly interdisciplinary approach by Brachtendorf et al. (2008); and Neidhart's theological study that contrasts the theology and the mathematics of the infinite (2007). In addition, there are a number of books on the infinite that aim to make the oftentimes complicated mathematics of the infinite accessible to readers who are not mathematicians, for example the already mentioned works by Maor (1986) and Barrow (2005), but also those by David Foster Wallace (2010), Brian Clegg (2003) and, of course, Douglas Hofstadter's famous *Gödel, Escher, Bach: An Eternal Golden Braid* (1979).

which texts approach the infinite and, not least, in which we as readers approach such texts.

Attempting a definition of the infinite is in itself a difficult endeavour in the first place, since any definition is, as Wolfgang Schoberth observes, a demarcation and so imposes a boundary on the concept defined (2016: 85) – a definition of the infinite deprives it of infinity (the first and in many ways central of plenty of paradoxes of the infinite), or, conversely, the definite is also finite. There is, in this view, no meta-level at which infinity may be safely contained. Bernhard Waldenfels has described this as the 'basic aporia' of infinity: how is it possible to think infinity without rendering it finite?[2] Rather, infinity is fundamentally at odds with our – necessarily finite – *experience* of infinity, resulting in an antagonism between what we experience (the infinite) and how we experience it (Waldenfels 2012: 53).

It is little wonder, therefore, that most properties that are commonly associated with the infinite are themselves negative properties, characterised by the absence of boundaries. The infinite is endless, unbounded, or unlimited. Beyond this endlessness, the mathematician and writer Rudy Rucker names "indefiniteness and inconceivability" as key characteristics of infinity (1982: 1) and so adds two further defining aspects that are likewise marked by absence. Infinity, at least as far as an everyday understanding of the term goes, primarily *is not*. Indeed, in many languages, the morphology of the word for infinity implies a definition *ex negativo* of the concept behind it: that which encompasses all there is (and more) within the logic of language is understood as *not* that which is finite or bounded, *the in-finite, l'in-fini, das Un-endliche, in-finitum, to a-peiron*, etc. (see Hart 2011: 255).[3] Since conceptualising the absence of a quality necessarily is less concrete than conceptualising its (physical) presence, this negative understanding of the infinite is already an abstraction of sorts and therefore indicates a difficulty with conceptualising infinity as a 'thing' – a problem that surfaces time and again in the history of thinking about the infinite.

---

2 "[E]s gibt eine Grundaporie, die dem Denken des Unendlichen ihren Stempel aufprägt. Sie lautet: Wie kann man Unendliches denken, ohne es zu verendlichen?" (Waldenfels 2012: 53).
3 This pattern seems to run through languages from all over the world, including languages from non-Indo-European language families. As far as I could verify by asking speakers of various global languages and checking with online translation programmes, there are very few exceptions (see also Rauff 2013 for further examples). One interesting case is mentioned by Wilfred Kaleva: in the Buin language that is spoken in Papua New Guinea, the term for infinity is a – clearly metaphorical – phrase that translates as "the chicken went into the bush and never came back" (Kaleva 1995, qtd. in Rauff 2013: 98–99). Although this is a much more tangible image for the infinite than the abstract absence of an end, it is likewise grounded in negativity, since the chicken never returns.

It is curious that infinity should be so elusive to the grasp and so mired in negativity of expression although it is – quite literally – ubiquitous. Infinity surrounds us in many guises: There is the infinity of numbers in mathematics, where a largest countable number does not exist – in trying to count to infinity, "we run out of names before we run out of numbers" (Stewart 2017: 22). There is the infinity of time, eternity, as well as that of space (or the universe) – and the actual physical existence of both is open to debate. Conversely, there is infinity in divisibility, resulting in the infinitely small or infinitesimal. Blaise Pascal in one of the fragments in his *Pensées* even describes all of nature as "an infinite sphere, the centre of which is everywhere, the circumference nowhere" (1958: 16; II.72). This adds a spiritual or religious dimension to infinity, since Pascal takes this hypostasised infinity of nature to be a proof of God's grandeur. Despite this omnipresence of the infinite, its exact nature does not become any clearer.

While this curious case of the elusiveness of the infinite is closely linked to the problem of its representation – as evidenced in the negative linguistic concepts for infinity – the reason for this elusiveness seems to be that infinity is associated with a number of self-contradictory and seemingly incongruous features that make it difficult to pin down a clearly delineated notion of infinity. On the one hand, the infinite is tied up with various logical paradoxes and challenges to understanding that have been discussed by mathematicians and philosophers alike.[4] On the other hand, and more pertinent to fictions of infinity, as Ian Stewart stresses, "infinity *is* paradoxical" (2017: 1).[5] There is a paradox at the heart of the infinite, then, and this paradox is engendered by our attempts to grasp the phenomenon. Writing about infinity, David Foster Wallace has pointed out that "[i]t is in areas like math and metaphysics that we encounter one of the average human mind's weirdest attributes. This is the ability to conceive of things that we cannot, strictly speaking, conceive of" (2010: 22). Thinking something that cannot be measured means attempting to apply a framework of reason to something that exceeds this framework; it means to "think the unthinkable" (Clegg 2003) – this is the aporia of the infinite.[6]

---

[4] The most famous among these paradoxes of infinity are probably Zeno's paradoxes and the paradox known as Hilbert's Hotel. These and many others are discussed by Graham Oppy (2006; for further examples of paradoxes connected to infinity see also Stewart 2017: 8–18, 36–42).
[5] Unless indicated otherwise, all emphases in quotations are also there in the original.
[6] As chapter 3.1 will show, this aporia is central to Levinas's thought. Bernhard Waldenfels discusses this and other aporias of the infinite and contrasts the role of the infinite in Levinas with that it has in the works of other philosophers (Waldenfels 2008).

It is this underlying aporia that perhaps best explains – and the notion that an aporia might explain something is just another paradox – the way in which humans have reacted to infinity. Rudolf Freiburg asserts that there is a "dialectics of fascination and fear" inherent in any encounter with the infinite – a fascination with the grandeur of the infinite and a fear at being dwarfed and rendered insignificant in comparison (2016: 7–8, my trans.; see also Waldenfels 2008: 4–8). In evidence of this claim, Freiburg quotes Pascal:

> Car enfin qu'est-ce que l'homme dans la nature? Un néant à l'égard de l'infini, un tout à l'égard du néant, un milieu entre rien et tout. Infiniment éloigné de comprendre les extrêmes, la fin des choses et leur principe sont pour lui invinciblement cachés dans un secret impénétrable, également incapable de voir le néant d'où il est tiré, et l'infini où il est englouti. (Pascal 1976: 66; qtd. in Freiburg 2016: 7)[7]

Although the infinite is infinitely beyond human understanding, an "impenetrable secret", Pascal writes, it 'swallows up' humans. This is why the infinite impacts on humans in this duplicitous way: like a secret or riddle that cannot be solved it provokes curiosity, interest or fascination; like the unknown often does, it may also provoke fear in the beholder.

These qualities of the infinite – the difficulty of representing it or defining it in any other way than *ex negativo*, its multi-faceted and inherently aporetic nature and the frequently ambivalent reaction to it – have all shaped the way infinity has been thought and spoken about, as the following short, and again necessarily eclectic, overview of the history of thinking infinity will show.

Most accounts of the history of the infinite begin with the Pre-Socratic philosophers of the seventh and sixth centuries BCE. Theirs is the first systematic, scientific approach to the infinite, but thinking about infinity goes further back and can be traced in myths from India and Iran of the second millennium BCE, which tell the story of a battle between the finite and the infinite (see Vilenkin 1995: 1–2). These myths in fact form the basis from which the Greek Pre-Socratic philosopher Anaximander's notion of the *apeiron*, the 'unbounded', is derived (Vilenkin 1995: 2; for a thorough discussion of Anaximander's *apeiron* see Gregory 2016: 85–102). As the chaotic, uncontrollable source of all being, "*apeiron* need not only mean infinitely large, but can also mean totally disordered, infinitely complex, subject to no finite determination" and as a result of

---

[7] "For in fact what is man in nature? A Nothing in comparison with the Infinite, an All in comparison with the Nothing, a mean between nothing and everything. Since he is infinitely removed from comprehending the extremes, the end of things and their beginning are hopelessly hidden from him in an impenetrable secret, he is equally incapable of seeing the Nothing from which he was made, and the Infinite in which he is swallowed up" (Pascal 1958: 18; II.72).

this disorderly quality it was by later Greek thinkers mostly considered a "negative, even pejorative, word" (Rucker 1982: 3, 2). The reason is that in classical Greek thought – particularly for the Pythagoreans, who believed that the entire world could be described with proportions of whole numbers, but also for Plato – the finite and definite, in the sense of a "finite perfection" or "perfect unity" (Badiou 2011), was seen as a governing principle and associated with the good. The *apeiron*, of course, is almost the exact opposite of such rational order and as a consequence, where it interferes with rational determination and the commensurability of actions (e.g. when it leads into infinite regress), the infinite is considered 'bad', as opposed to (ethically) good finitude (see Waldenfels 2008: 5).[8]

This notion of a 'bad' infinity is also behind the most influential position on infinity in classical antiquity: Aristotle's distinction in his *Physics* between 'potential' and 'actual' infinity shaped mathematical and philosophical thought on the infinite over the following centuries. Interestingly, for Aristotle, the question of infinity is one of (modes of) being and hence an ontological one.[9] First he considers whether infinity can be an actual thing that may exist in nature and firmly rules out the existence of an infinite body in actuality (see 1961: 49–52; 204a8–206a8; for a summary of the argument, see Jori 2010: 17–23). However, he concedes that the infinite must exist in potentiality. In this potential sense it has "the kind of being which a day has [...], the kind of being which does not belong to a concrete primary being that has come into being, but the kind of being which consists in continually coming to be and passing away, which is finite on each occasion, but which even so is different" (1961: 53; 206a 32–36). This potential infinity has then the character of a process that attains infinity 'by implication'. The most accessible example of this potentiality of the infinite is the counting of integers: each integer is finite and there is no largest

---

[8] In this context it should be noted that whereas *apeiron* is usually translated as 'unlimited', deriving from *peras* ('limit'), Paul Tannery gives *peira* ('knowledge'/'experience') as the root of the word, which would then mean the 'unknowable' (Tannery 1904, qtd. in Zellini 2010: 12; for a discussion of the etymology of *apeiron*, see Gregory 2016: 86). This is in itself telling because it contributes to the pattern that humans frequently label that which is alien or beyond their grasp as bad or negative – unless the unknowable is identified with the outright supernatural or the divine, as is the case in many religions.

[9] David Bentley Hart points out that infinity has been investigated as both a physical concept (in mathematics and the sciences) and a metaphysical or ontological concept (predominantly in philosophy and theology). However, the ancient Greek notion of the *apeiron* does not strictly distinguish between these two domains and over the centuries discussions of the physical and metaphysical sides of the infinite have overlapped (see Hart 2011: 255–257). For this reason, this short overview does not explicitly distinguish between these two sides of the infinite.

number, since in counting upwards a new, larger integer is created by simply adding one to any hitherto 'largest' integer. As a process, this could go on forever and hence the sequence of integers is infinite; yet it is also finite in every step – as soon as the process of counting stops, the result is a finite number, if possibly a very large one.[10] As in the process of 'adding one', potential infinity thus depends on the possibility of always finding a next item, on a principal unendingness, and so is an early example of thinking the infinite *ex negativo*. Since this is the only kind of infinity whose existence Aristotle accepts, infinity then is perpetually deferred into a potentiality. Crucially, for Aristotle the potentiality of the infinite is itself different from 'ordinary' potentiality, because it can never be realised in actuality – in this it differs, for example, from "the bronze which is potentially a statue [and] may become an actual statue" (1961: 53; 206a 20–21).[11] The infinite is therefore primarily characterised by incompletion: "[T]he infinite is contrary to what is usually described as such: there is an infinite, not when there is nothing left over and beyond, but when there is always something over and beyond!" (1961: 54; 206b 34–207a 3). Since infinity only exists in potentiality, but not in actuality, Aristotle then attributes a 'lesser' ontological status to the infinite (Jori 2010: 45).

In terms of how the infinite has been thought ever since, Aristotle's distinction between the actual infinite, where infinity is conceptualised as a complete, all-encompassing entity, and the potential infinite, which is characterised precisely by the absence of such completion and a perpetual deferral of the end to a beyond that never materialises, has proved pathbreaking. By rejecting the existence of the actual infinite, Aristotle moved infinity into a "virtual world" (Clegg 2003: 32) – or, in a sense, designated the entire notion of infinity a fiction of sorts. For mathematicians, the potential infinite turned out to be a pragmatic solution that allowed them to work with infinity and remained unchallenged for over two thousand years.

---

10 The largest numbers that have names are the googol – 10^{100}, a 1 with 100 zeroes – and the googolplex – 10^{googol}, a 1 with googol zeroes –, but already the googol dwarfs the estimated number of atoms in the universe (see Maor 1986: 16). As the protagonist of Ian McEwan's children's book *The Daydreamer* muses, "If you asked someone for a googol of chocolate-covered toffees, there wouldn't be nearly enough atoms in the universe to make them" (McEwan 1995: 20). In a way that shows the workings of potential infinity, exponentially larger numbers have been named googolplexplex ($10^{googolplex}$), googolplexplexplex ($10^{googolplexplex}$), etc.

11 It is this 'unnatural' potentiality of the infinite that makes it very difficult, if not impossible, to grasp infinity and that has led classical philosophers in the tradition of Aristotle, in particular Boethius, to denounce the infinite as disgraceful monstrosity (see Zellini 2010: 22).

In mathematics and related 'rational' disciplines, actual infinity then lay largely dormant, considered non-existent, until in the second half of the nineteenth century the German mathematician Georg Cantor reintroduced the notion of the actual infinite into mathematical thought and in doing so founded modern set theory and triggered a paradigm shift in the way mathematicians thought of the infinite.[12] Cantor criticised what he called the "*Horror Infiniti*" (1966: 374), the fear of actual infinity as uncontrollable and ungraspable that had dominated the philosophy and mathematics of the infinite ever since antiquity, and above all he rejected the relegation of infinity to the virtual existence of potentiality. Instead, Cantor's approach to set theory was to view any set, including infinite sets, as a totality, a thing that is whole (see Maor 1986: 54). With regard to an infinite set like, for instance, that of the natural numbers (i.e. the positive integers), this means that the set of natural numbers {1, 2, 3, ...} in Cantor's sense is a complete, or whole, object and hence not merely potentially infinite, but actually infinite. By looking at one-to-one correspondences between different infinite sets, Cantor could further prove that there are different classes of infinity. For example, there is a one-to-one correspondence between the set of square numbers and that of positive integers – in other words, square numbers are countable, so there is a first (1), second (4), third (9), etc. square –, just as there is one between the positive integers and the rational numbers (all fractions of two integers, where the denominator may not be zero); however, no such one-to-one correspondence exists between the positive integers and the real numbers, which means the infinity of the real numbers is of a different magnitude than that of the integers.[13] Cantor named the number of elements, or cardinality, of the set of integers $\aleph_0$ (aleph-null) and was able to show that infinitely many such 'transfinite' numbers, i.e. cardinal numbers of infinite sets, of different orders exist. As a consequence, as Eli Maor puts it, "There exists [...] an entire *hierarchy* of infinities, and in this

---

[12] Of course this does not mean that there were no major developments in the way infinity was thought in these disciplines in the 2200 years separating Aristotle and Cantor. In mathematics, the development of calculus by Leibniz and Newton made use of (potentially) infinite divisibility and the convergence of infinite series and mathematicians became increasingly comfortable in calculating with infinity, as can be seen by the introduction of the lemniscate (∞) as a symbol for infinity by the seventeenth-century English mathematician John Wallis. The existence of actual infinity continued to be rejected, with only few exceptions, such as the work of Giordano Bruno, who in his *De l'infinito, universo e mondi* (1584) posited the infinity of the universe – which would then be an actually infinite entity (see Jori 2010: 45–55). For a detailed account of the development of thought on infinity up to Cantor's days, see for example Zellini (2010) or Achtner (2011). On Cantor's theory of the transfinite, see also Brits (2018: 27–36).
[13] Annotated versions of Cantor's proofs can be found in Maor (1986: 53–65; see also Clegg 2003: 157–187; Rucker 1982: 64–78; Kline 1972: 994–1002).

hierarchy one can speak of infinities that are greater than other infinities!" (1986: 54–55). Cantor's outstanding achievement then was the recovery of actual infinity for mathematics and so the overcoming, at least within mathematics, of the *horror infiniti* he had diagnosed.

Further, Cantor's finding that there is a hierarchy of transfinite numbers of different orders of magnitude allows for a nuanced view of the infinite. At least mathematically speaking there is now not just one monolithic notion of infinity, but there are "degrees of infinity" (Rucker 1982: 9). However, as soon as one accepts that there is a hierarchy of infinities, the question follows of what is at the top of this hierarchy. Is there an ultimate, largest infinity, or is there merely a never-ending (potentially infinite) sequence of ever larger infinities? While there is no largest transfinite number, just as there is no largest integer, Cantor still gives a different answer to this question by claiming that the actual infinite exists in several domains (see Barrow 2005: 73–76):

> The actual infinite arises in three contexts: *first* when it is realized in the most complete form, in a fully independent other-worldly being, *in Deo*, where I call it the Absolute Infinite, or simply Absolute; *second* when it occurs in the contingent, created world; *third* when the mind grasps it *in abstracto* as a mathematical magnitude, number, or order type. I wish to make a sharp contrast between the Absolute and what I call the Transfinite, that is, the actual infinities of the last two sorts, which are clearly limited, subject to further increase, and thus related to the finite. (Cantor 1932: 378, qtd. and trans. in Rucker 1982: 9)

Beside the abstract mathematical infinities of the transfinite numbers, there is then physically existing infinity (for examples of such physical infinities see Rucker 1982: 9–35; Barrow 2005: 97–109) and the absolute infinity of the divine.

What this passage also shows is that Cantor still faces similar problems as Aristotle in that beyond any epistemological problem of 'grasping' the infinite, there is always also the ontological, or metaphysical, problem of its existence. This becomes clear in his description of the Absolute Infinite, which is at the top of his hierarchy of infinities, in a way that, as Rucker (1982: 44) has pointed out, is similar to the notion of 'the One' in Plotinus's Neoplatonism. If the Absolute Infinite is truly "fully independent" and "other-worldly", then there is no way of accessing it from within this, the empirical, world without at least partly erasing the 'full' independence – the absolute, and certainly the all-encompassing Absolute Infinite, by definition cannot be connected to experience but must be cut off from it. In other words, "[i]n terms of rational thoughts, the Absolute is unthinkable. There is no non-circular way to reach it from below. Any knowledge of the Absolute must be mystical, if indeed such a thing as mystical knowledge is possible" (Rucker 1982: 47; for a more detailed discussion of the Absolute Infinite, see 44–51). Ultimately, the question whether or not the actual infinite exists in any of Cantor's three guises remains unresolved.[14]

It is little surprising that Cantor's association of the Absolute Infinite with the divine should establish a direct link to the one place where a version of the actual infinite had lived on over the centuries, to theological considerations of the infinity of God. Perhaps the fascination that comes with encountering something that is so elusive to any understanding as the infinite explains why infinity is associated with the divine in many religions. In Hinduism, the divine powers and knowledge are infinite and the cosmos itself exists in an endless cycle of universal destruction and rebirth (see Neidhart 2007: 505–510). Buddhism's goal, nirvana, is a status of transcendental, infinite consciousness (see 2007: 512). Christianity – and in a very similar fashion Islam (see 2007: 546) – considers God to be infinite in various ways, in particular omnipotent, omnipresent and omniscient, as well as infinitely good. There is, however, no direct declaration of God's infinity in the bible: the closest to that, as Ludwig Neidhart argues, is a psalm that says "his greatness *is* unsearchable" (Ps. 145.3), which has also been translated in the Vulgate as 'his greatness has no end' (Neidhart 2007: 521) – as the original Hebrew can also be rendered as 'inscrutable', 'unfathomable' or 'inexplorable', the infinite's transcendence of human understanding is foregrounded again.

Although the bible is not explicit on the subject of the infinity of God, early Christian philosophers gradually arrived at the conclusion that God must indeed be an infinite, all-encompassing being, a thought that was continued by the mediaeval scholasticists and well into the Enlightenment period (see 2007: 533–545; 552–599). For example, in the fifth century CE, Augustine in his *City of God* argues that "all infinity [...] is in some ineffable way finite to God because it is not incomprehensible for his knowledge" and, more specifically, that god knows all numbers (1966: 91; bk. 12, ch. 19). The ineffability of this divine understanding – certainly closely connected to the problem of representing infinity – becomes clear when Augustine goes on to claim that God's "wisdom, which is simple in its multiplicity and uniform in its multiformity, comprehends all incomprehensible things with a comprehension so incomprehensible" that he is incapable of escaping his own foreknowledge (1966: 93; bk. 12, ch. 19). This description again neatly illustrates the paradoxical nature of infinity: the qualities

---

14 The existence of Cantor's transfinite numbers as mathematical entities has been accepted almost universally by mathematicians, but since they remain abstract mathematical objects, this simply shifts the question of existence to asking whether or not such purely mathematical entities exist in actuality or whether they remain a mathematical fiction of sorts (see Rucker 1982: 51).

Augustine attributes to God here are a veritable concatenation of logical and linguistic opposites, implying a *coincidentia oppositorum*, the coinciding of incompatibles in the infinite. Similar conceptions can still be found in the records of the First Vatican Council, where God is described as "almighty, eternal, immeasurable, incomprehensible, infinite in will, understanding and every perfection" (1869–1870: session 3, ch. 1; see Neidhart 2007: 677–682) – 'infinite perfection' in this context points towards completion in infinity and hence actual infinity. However, Wolfgang Achtner argues, "identifying infinity as an important aspect of God is nearly abandoned in contemporary theology" and since the Enlightenment has increasingly only entered theological discourse in the context of religious self-transcendence (2011: 47; see also Hart 2011: 270–274 and Waldenfels 2008: 4–8; for a current take on the infinity of God, see Oppy 2011). Nevertheless, there is a religious tradition of the infinite in which the qualities of incomprehensibility and, equally frequently, ineffability that are associated with divine infinity – and certainly with infinity in general, whether or not it is connected to a deity – attain a mystic quality (Neidhart 2007: 678), which again indicates that the infinite is foreclosed to strictly rational apprehension.

What seems to be central to the religious manifestations of infinity is that it is associated with what cannot be known or understood because it is in excess of what humans can grasp (see also Böttigheimer 2018: 172). This is a problem that haunts all thought on the infinite: while Aristotle's solution, followed by most philosophers and mathematicians until Cantor, was to deny actuality to the infinite and relegate it to the virtuality of potentiality, religious thought embraces this ungraspability as a sign of the divine. In this, the religious or mystic approach to the infinite associates itself with fascination and reverence for, rather than the fear of the infinite that over the centuries sprang up in the strictly rational discourses on infinity.

A further strand of philosophical thought that is associated with the infinite is the enquiry into the aesthetic ideal of the sublime that takes its beginning with Longinus in the first century CE and is central to the aesthetics of Edmund Burke and Immanuel Kant in the eighteenth century. Infinity is closely connected with the sublime because of problems the infinite causes to both understanding and representation. Thus, for Burke the infinite is a source of the sublime, as "[i]nfinity has a tendency to fill the mind with that sort of delightful horror, which is the most genuine effect, and truest test of the sublime" (1792: 109; pt. 2, sect. 8). Burke's famous phrase of the "delightful horror" caused by the infinite here seems to conflate the two main reactions that over the centuries humans had shown towards the infinite. Similarly, Kant writes in the *Critique of the Power of Judgment* that the sublime "is to be found in a formless object insofar as **limitlessness** is represented in it, or at its instance, and yet it is also thought as a totality" (2000: 128, emphasis original; pt. 1, par. 23). Again, a link between the sublime and infinity seems to emerge when Kant describes the mathematically sublime as what is **"great beyond all comparison"**, or as that "which even to be able to think of demonstrates a faculty of the mind that surpasses every measure of the senses" (2000: 132, 134, emphasis original; pt. 1, par. 25). However, Kant also stresses that aesthetic judgement is limited by a maximum of aesthetical estimation, an "absolute measure, beyond which no greater is subjectively (for the judging subject) possible" (2000: 135; pt. 1, par. 26). In this way, for Kant, the boundlessness of the sublime is contained within a totality of aesthetic judgement (see Waldenfels 2008: 18). It is then clear that for both Kant and Burke the sublime is intricately linked with the infinite, as it evokes similar affective reactions and is similarly overwhelming to the cognitive faculties.

This also becomes clear in Jean-François Lyotard's twentieth-century philosophy of the sublime. As Lyotard makes clear in his reading of Kant and Burke, the mixture of pleasure and pain that is the feeling of the sublime ensues when representation itself proves inadequate in view of the grandeur of its object and fails (1991: 98). Again, a direct connection to the infinite emerges, since "[w]e can conceive the infinitely great, the infinitely powerful, but every presentation of an object destined to 'make visible' this absolute greatness or power appears to us painfully inadequate" (1984: 78). This is the fundamental problem of the representation of infinity, the impossibility of finding an expression in representation for the infinite. For Lyotard, it is particularly the art of the avant-garde, that is, modern and postmodern art, that is the art of the sublime. There, "the art-object no longer bends itself to models, but tries to present the fact that there is an unpresentable; it no longer imitates nature, but is, in Burke, the actualization of a figure potentially there in language" (1991: 101). In this, Lyotard's notion of the sublime bears a certain proximity to what I describe as fictions of infinity, as it relies on the representation of what, strictly speaking, cannot be represented. Overall, whether in Burke, Kant or Lyotard, as a theory of representation and reception – the feeling of the sublime is a reaction to the occurrence of the sublime in nature or art – the philosophy of the sublime then straddles the "dialectics of fascination and fear" the infinite evokes.

Finally, in the context of twentieth-century phenomenology a 'third way' of approaching the infinite beyond these two main attitudes – one that finds in infinity divine perfection and fascination whereas the other sees infinity as incomplete, ungraspable and fearful – has emerged. Waldenfels points to the possibility of thinking about infinity as a mode of excess or hyperbole (2008: 18–21; see also 2012: 71–74).[15] In this sense, the infinite is complete, but cannot be contained in any totality; it is an infinity that transcends thought itself. This view of the infinite is central to the ethics of Emmanuel Levinas that forms the backbone of my study and as such is key to the way in which I understand fictions of infinity. Incidentally, its conceptual divergence from the two major philosophical approaches towards infinity might explain why although infinity plays a central role in Levinas's philosophy, his work is not usually part of philosophical accounts of the history of infinity. For example, neither Zellini (2010), nor Moore (2001) or Oppy (2006) mention Levinas in their broad overviews of the field. This is likely because Levinas does not make infinity an object of his investigation, but uses the infinite as a cipher of alterity – the sense in which it will also become relevant to my reading of fictions of infinity (for Levinas's notion of infinity, see ch. 3.1). Levinas's phenomenological approach to the infinite thus rejects the existence of a meta-level from which the infinite can be explained or categorised. It is this phenomenological view of the infinite as excessive or, as Waldenfels calls it, as a hyperbolic mode that will prove most important for my readings of fictions of infinity.

* * *

In view of the wide-ranging intellectual history of the infinite it is almost unnecessary to say that infinity in its various guises has long been an area of interest for literature and other arts. However, more so than the more abstract theoretical disciplines of philosophy, mathematics or theology, the arts face a dilemma when they thematise the infinite: it is the clash between the infinite object and the finite medium of representation. Since to a substantial degree art *is* representation, this conflict touches the very core of what artistic expression may achieve.

The finitude of the artistic form itself is a given. Whichever way one looks at it, there must be an actual end to a work of art – a picture frame, a last page with a last word in a literary text, a last note that resounds in a piece of music. It is ultimately physical restraints that dictate this finitude: the work of art is confined both by the medium through which it is conveyed, or, expressed with a metaphor that acknowledges the digital age, by the size of its storage medium, and by the physical limitations of the moment of its production and reception. Humans, artists and their audiences alike, are "metaphysically finite", spatio-

---

[15] For Waldenfels, this is distinct from the sublime, which – at least the Kantian notion, to which he explicitly refers – belongs to the group of approaches that sees perfection in infinity, since it imposes the totality of aesthetic judgement on the infinite and so delimits or 'completes' it.

temporally limited beings (Moore 2001: 218) and this finitude must transfer to the creation of art as well as to its consumption. While there may be examples of intergenerational efforts, such as in architecture the building of many of the great European cathedrals that could take several hundred years, at the level of the individuals involved in the process, the timespan to create or consume art remains limited by a human's lifespan.

Yet art has always sought to overcome this metaphysical finitude and frequently thematised its own attempts at doing so. For example, there is the *topos* of art being capable of transcending human life and so endowing it with eternity. Thus, Shakespeare's Sonnet 18 ends (!), "So long as men can breathe or eyes can see / So long lives this, and this gives life to thee" (2007: 147, ll. 13–14) – where "this" refers to the sonnet, or perhaps to Shakespeare's entire poetic work or even art in general. This is a notion frequent in the poetry of the Renaissance (for very similar ideas, see for example Shakespeare's sonnets 17, 19, 55, 60 and sonnet 75 from Spenser's *Amoretti*), but much older than that, as evidenced in Horace's Carmen 3.30, which begins by stating "exegi monumentum aere perennius" ("I have completed a monument more lasting than bronze"; 2002: 258/259) – a self-referential acknowledgement of the poet's work. Still, neither of these poetic aspirations to the transcendence of art strictly speaking can realise art's infinity. Shakespeare's version is limited by the existence of the human species, while Horace's claim to self-immortalisation – "non omnis moriar", "I shall not wholly die", he states later in the poem – finds its similar limitation in the existence of Roman culture – "dum Capitolium / scandet cum tacita virgine pontifex", "while priest / climbs the Capitol with a silent Virgin" (2002: 258/259). More importantly, both examples seek infinity outside themselves; they do not pretend to 'contain' the infinite, but seek to be indefinitely delivered to posterity and so to achieve 'infinity' in reception.

In the context of this study, however, the focus will be on art, specifically literature, that seeks to represent or express and so to 'contain' infinity, that seeks to actually *be* infinite. It is in such cases that a fundamental tension between the necessarily finite form of the work of art and its infinite content must arise. This is the reason for my initial claim that infinity resists its own representation. That tension, which essentially is the source of the aesthetic power of the sublime, can be traced across centuries and various branches of the arts. Thus, in his brief discussion of what he calls the "art of immensity" (2011: 207–210), Marco Bersanelli points to repetitive patterns in pre-historic cave paintings and much later in architecture but also in visual art – specifically he mentions the repetitive character of Andy Warhol's pop art and of many of the prints by the Dutch artist M. C. Escher – as instances where art may capture or evoke the infinite. He goes on to mention poems and paintings that thematise gazing beyond the horizon, in particular by Edward Hopper and Caspar David Friedrich – incidentally, both Friedrich's *Monk by the Sea* (*Der Mönch am Meer*) and *The Wanderer above a Sea of Mists* (*Der Wanderer über dem Nebelmeer*), the two paintings Bersanelli cites, can be considered prime examples of the Romantic sublime (see also Zimmermann 2018). Paradoxically, it is the presentation of limitation, of "a human figure, small and apparently insignificant" (Bersanelli 2011: 210), that allows an intimation of infinity in these paintings. Here the finite work of art through the thematisation of finitude – that of gaze in the horizon and that of the human being depicted – seems to be able to embrace the infinite.

As a way of concluding my brief history of infinity with further examples of infinity in the arts in the twentieth and twenty-first centuries, I would like to add to this overview the works of two more artists, Roman Opałka and Yayoi Kusama, as well as a brief glance at the music of John Cage. Opałka, a French-born Polish artist, under the title *OPALKA 1965/1-∞* created a series of paintings in which he wrote down numbers, beginning with 1 and continuing on towards infinity, in white paint against initially dark, but increasingly whitening canvas background. Opałka began his work in 1965 and when he died in 2011 the last number he had painted was 5,607,249 (Opałka 2017). He complemented his paintings with photographs he took of himself at the end of each day of working on these canvasses and began recording himself reading out the numbers he painted, creating a multimedial experience that, in the artist's own words, was intended to show that "[t]ime as we live it and as we create it embodies our progressive disappearance; we are at the same time alive and in the face of death – that is the mystery of all living beings" (Opałka 2017: "Method: Approach"). The impossibility of ever coming to an end is thus an integral part of Opałka's project: it is a performance of what the silhouette of Friedrich's monk against the receding horizon insinuates, of the finitude of the human against the immensity of nature or the infinite. In Opałka's case, this consideration is transferred to the genesis of art itself, which illustrates the problem of representing infinity in a finite medium particularly well. Although the artist's mortality must put an end to his endeavour and although, even if he were immortal, due to the potential infinity of the integers he could never arrive at an end, at some level infinity is represented in Opałka's work. In what is yet one more paradox of the infinite it seems that it is only in the failure to represent infinity that infinity can be represented.

Concerns very similar to Opałka's, yet expressed at an even grander scale and in a different medium, this time combining music and performance, are addressed in the *Organ²/ASLSP* project.[16] The project (www.aslsp.org) is the rendi-

---

[16] As in art, in music likewise the infinite may take many different shapes. It can be found in

tion of an organ piece by John Cage that comes with the instruction to performers to play it "As SLow aS Possible". Taking this instruction to heart, the project's performance of *Organ²/ASLSP* in a church in the German town of Halberstadt began in 2001 (with a seventeen-month pause) and is scheduled to last 639 years in total, ending in 2640. At the time of writing this (which any reader with time at their hands may calculate for themselves), the countdown on the project homepage is at 19,733,784,841 seconds to go till the end of the final sound and the next note changes are due in September 2020 and February 2022. In this way the performance explores the limits of the work of art and of human existence. The monotonous drone of the organ (sound samples can be heard on the project homepage) as well as the sheer time scale represent a counterpoint not just to the acceleration of life in a globalised world, but to the fleetingness of human life.[17] Although the project may offer a glimpse of eternity – and even attempt to 'contain' the eternal –, it too, in a similar way to Shakespeare's Sonnet 18, Horace's ode 3.30, or Opałka's series of paintings, is limited by the durability of the organ and by political and economic circumstances that make the performance possible in the first place (see *Organ²/ASLSP*).

Returning to visual art, another example of the art of infinity can be found in the Japanese artist Yayoi Kusama's work. Kusama has gained considerable public attention with her pop art that prominently features so-called infinity mirror rooms. Visitors to Kusama's exhibitions enter these rooms, whose walls, floor and ceiling are clad in mirrors and which usually contain light installations, sometimes including lanterns or the colourful inflatable balloons, polka-dotted phalli or pumpkins that are characteristic of Kusama's work, and find themselves in an infinitely mirrored world. The mirror rooms "invite viewers to experience a myriad of dualities and challenge preconceived notions of autonomy, time, and space" (Chiu 2017: 7; see Yoshitake 2017 for critical essays on her work and for

---

the frequently repetitive structures of minimal music, but in music as in painting (or literature, for that matter) also in the Romantic period, in the desire, or *Sehnsucht*, expressed in German Romantic music (see Brillenburg Wurth 2009). Kiene Brillenburg Wurth's study of the musically sublime, which covers music from the eighteenth century to the present, is a good starting point for further research into infinity and music, particularly so given the close connection between infinity and the sublime.

17 The last point is corroborated not only by the sacral setting of the project, but also by the possibility to purchase on the project's homepage, against a sizeable donation, a "Klangjahr" ("sound year") – sponsorship of one of the 639 years the performance is intended to last, for which then a commemorative plaque is installed in the church (including a photograph of the plaque on the homepage). Most of the plaques that have already been installed bear the names and birthdates of their sponsors, as well as quotations or individual artwork, all of which captures a snapshot of life around the project's incipience.

photographs of the mirror rooms). The infinite mise en abyme effect thus created (see Sutton 2017: 138; see also ch. 2.2.2) has a decentring effect that contrasts infinity with the finitude of human existence (see Dumbadze 2017: 122). Her work – not just the mirror rooms, but also a series of paintings called Infinity Nets, is, as Mignon Nixon observes, "defined by economies of excess, both material and psychic, and the reciprocities between them" and it is the "hyperbolic gesture, repeated ad infinitum", of accumulation that lets Kusama's works transcend their frame of representation (2012: 180). While Kusama's career as an artist began in the late 1940s and she was an integral part of New York's art scene in the 1960s, it is perhaps telling that public interest in her work is currently at a peak, to the extent that she was named among *Time* magazine's list of "The 100 Most Influential People" in 2016 (Chiu 2017: 7). The mirrors are frequently linked to the narcissism of the 'selfie culture' of the early twenty-first century, either as an expression of or as an antidote to it (see Dumbadze 2017: 118; Sutton 2017: 138–140) – with their potential to serve as critique of forms of totalitarianism (see Nixon 2012), they can, however, also be interpreted in a similar way as I will read the fictions of infinity in this study, as disruptive of the audience's viewing habits and so as infinitely posing questions to the audience.

In conclusion of this eclectic history of the infinite, the question remains whether such a thing as 'understanding' infinity is possible at all, or whether the infinite must remain an insoluble puzzle. Given the number of thinkers that over the course of three millennia have grappled with the problem of infinity – with reactions ranging from the fear of the uncontrollable to the reverence for the unfathomable and the feeling of the sublime caused by an awareness of the infinite perched somewhere between these two poles – it seems safe to say that a final answer is not possible. What makes the infinite so tough to handle is its inherently paradoxical nature. Even the thought of the infinite in a finite mind amounts to thinking the unthinkable. This paradox continues in attempts at representing infinity, and hence in art and literature, where infinity is likewise made an object of a finite medium. In a way, such representations of the infinite must then be in excess of themselves – they must contain infinity in finitude. It is this excessive representation and its aesthetic and functional consequences that particularly interest me in my study of the fictions of infinity.

1.2 Fictions of Infinity

It is clear that the discussion of infinity in literature one way or another must reflect this complex history of the infinite. Above all the basic aporia of thinking the infinite and the difficulty of representation which it entails are central to fictions of infinity. As already mentioned, I use this term to refer to texts that (attempt to) (re-)present the infinite, texts in which the infinite is ingrained, which make it a central part of their aesthetics, texts which themselves become infinite. In this, the term 'fictions of infinity' itself alludes to the over two millennia old debate over the epistemology of the infinite and implies the impossibility of representing infinity: any such representation that aims to take a concrete shape and go beyond the highest form of abstraction must inevitably rely on some form of make-believe, a fiction.

In analysing such fictions of infinity, this study then has two main areas of interest: the first is a question of aesthetics and the second one of ethics. The question infinity invariably raises when it comes to aesthetics is that of (the impossibility of) its own representation. Since a positive definition of infinity is impossible without resorting to transcendental concepts such as God, which then likewise are impossible to understand or represent, any literary representation of the infinite must be a presentation of the absent, finding words that frame a concept that cannot be framed. This points to the difficulty of finding a theoretical framework that might be able to encompass such representations of infinity: such theoretical frameworks necessarily depend on descriptions of what is there in the text and it seems to be logically impossible to describe something that cannot be represented – description after all requires representation. When it comes to the narratological question of how a text might contain infinity by means of its narrative aesthetics, its structure etc., this becomes clear immediately. While the structuralist frameworks of classical narratology can explain how a text can have a structure that *could* (in theory) go on infinitely, i.e. while they may help to describe how a text is, using Aristotle's distinction, potentially infinite, they do not explain how a text may actually *be* infinite. One conclusion to be drawn from this would be to discard the notion that a text can ever be infinite in any other way than potentially, in the sense that it can imply its possible continuation along some pattern of textual creation that could go on *ad infinitum*.

Yet my claim is that it is possible to think of certain texts as infinite texts, that is, to see these texts as infinite things, as actually infinite entities. I hope to show this by combining the classical approaches of structuralist narratology and (post-)structuralist intertextuality theory with conceptual metaphor theory.[18]

---

18 In this my approach differs from that of Baylee Brits, who in her recent study of *Literary Infinities* (2018) traces actual infinity, or more precisely Cantor's notion of the transfinite, in the works of three modern writers, Borges, Beckett and Coetzee. While Brits also suggests that an actually infinite text is possible, she claims that "the only way to compose a literary infinity

According to George Lakoff and Rafael E. Núñez (2000), it is a conceptual metaphor, the Basic Metaphor of Infinity, that allows us to conceive of entities as actually infinite. Originally developed by Lakoff and Núñez in the context of an investigation into mathematical understanding, this conceptual metaphor can equally be applied to describe how literary texts are conceptualised as infinite. Thus, the Basic Metaphor of Infinity provides the link between a structuralist, text-based analysis and the infinite, which is necessarily missing from texts and therefore seems to elude such structuralist approaches. It is then through this conceptual metaphor – strictly speaking, catachresis, or 'illogical metaphor', seems a more apposite term, since a text understood as complete but infinite thing is the conjunction of opposites, an 'infinity in finitude' – that narratives become actually infinite. The textual basis, or source, for this conceptual metaphor may take different shapes. In three of the four novels on which I focus my reading of fictions of infinity it is mise en abyme structures, textual circularity and intertextuality respectively that are instrumental in injecting infinity into the narrative structure and so make the texts themselves infinite, while in the fourth, *The Infinities*, the choice of an unlimited narrative perspective that seeks to transcend all boundaries has a similar effect.

The second question, linked to the first but also to the idea of infinity itself, is that of the function of such an infinite aesthetics in narrative texts. Infinity has a transcendental quality in that it overflows all possible boundaries and is in excess of rational categorisation. This is quite likely the reason why in religious contexts it has been associated with the divine or conceptions of bliss such as the nirvana. In these contexts, the infinite is closely associated, or perhaps itself has become, what Jacques Derrida has called a transcendental signified. However, due to its radical negativity and plurality, infinity can express the very opposite and become a cipher for extreme unknowability. This is the dimension of the infinite that is at the heart of Emmanuel Levinas's ethics and it is in this context that I want to answer the question of the function of infinite textuality.

Infinity plays a central role in Levinas's ethical philosophy because it characterises the ethical relation to the other. The other, in Levinas, is always infinitely other, someone who cannot ever be understood in the categories of

---

is via allegorical form", where allegory is understood as a "perpetual dialectic of reader and writer" (2018: 43), i.e. as a mode that is double and relies on a reader finding meaning beyond the text (see 2018: 46). Brits's method is thus different from my own, a difference that may partly be explained by the different choice of primary texts and partly by Brits's focus on literary realisations of Cantor's mathematics of the transfinite. In particular, Brits's notion of the "transfinite allegory" (2018: 43) is in the tradition of Paul de Man's rhetorical analysis of allegory and thus different to my approach, which is based on conceptual metaphor theory.

thought available to the self. The relation to the other is thus similar to the infinite in its being in excess of all such categories. In encountering the radical, infinite alterity of the other, an encounter that is pre-ontological and so must take place outside any categories of thought that are already ontological categories, the self is confronted with an ethical demand that springs from the extreme vulnerability of the other: it is a call to responsibility, to being awake to the precariousness of the other (see Levinas 1996a: 167). Since the relation to alterity closely resembles the relation to infinity, my argument is that infinity in literary texts then fulfils a similar function as a call to responsibility, an ethical appeal. However, this parallel is not as straightforwardly clear as it might seem: since any text already forms part of an ontological system of knowledge, namely of the language in which it is communicated – or written to be understood –, fiction cannot assume alterity in Levinas's sense, as this alterity is precisely outside any ontology. What it can do, however, is to become, through its poetic language, a force that is critical and disruptive of ontological structures that obliterate alterity. This is where, again, the paradoxical nature of the infinite and its representations comes into play: fictions of infinity derive their ethical appeal precisely from disrupting the fixed categories of thought that underlie their discourse.

This disruption is achieved through its infinite textuality, where the text exceeds itself, and hence its own ontology. Such an impulse to break open the ontological is always directed at the language of literature – poetic language itself, as understood by Levinas, aims to prise open its own ontological condition – but, I suggest, also at its theme. The novels that serve as my examples all construct ontological frameworks at the story level, as those discourses that rule the characters' interactions and shape their society as depicted in the novels. These ontologies are then questioned and broken open in the course of the narrative and, crucially, because the texts are infinite, this questioning never stops. Because of the textual infinity this questioning also transcends the boundaries of the text and becomes an immediate form of address to the reader, an address that structures the act of reading. This is then the ethical appeal fictions of infinity may develop due to their aesthetics of the infinite. The content of this appeal is above all a call to responsibility, but it is, as my examples will show, also linked in some way to the concrete topics of the texts in question.

In this it is important to note that the aesthetic and the ethical dimensions of such texts are mutually dependent. To the extent that an ethical appeal derives from the infinite textuality of fictions of infinity, the ethical outlook of such texts also suggests its 'translation' into an aesthetic that pays heed to infinite alterity – and textual infinity would seem to be one way of achieving this. This is then a perspective complementary to the view that an infinite aesthetics implies an ethical appeal. Neither of these two perspectives, however, should be privileged over the other. It is therefore perhaps best to say that the infinite aesthetics coincides with the ethical dimension of such texts.

My thesis on the four novels that as fictions of infinity form the backbone of this study is then the following: These novels make use of various aesthetic strategies to transcend the confines of the text and so break open the ontological structures that govern the text in the first place. In doing so, they develop an ethical appeal, intricately connected with their textual infinity, or, in other words, they demand a form of responsibility from their readers. Since such infinite texts, which transcend the ontological norms of their structure, refuse closure at the level of epistemic enquiry, their demand of responsibility is likewise one that does not come to an end – it is in this sense an infinite responsibility, as envisaged by Levinas's ethics, that is imposed on readers. This is how such fictions of infinity reflect on and introduce an ethical moment into the reading process itself.

This study is thus, as its two-pronged approach would suggest, indebted to both ethical criticism and a form of rhetorical criticism. It makes use of a rhetorical approach – in a wide sense of the word that as an umbrella term seeks to bring together the various theoretical traditions of classical structuralist narratology, conceptual metaphor theory and (post-)structuralist intertextuality theory – where the aesthetics of the infinite are analysed. This approach, in itself multiplicious, seems appropriate given the protean nature of the infinite. The way in which I read the function of these aesthetics is more straightforwardly in the tradition of ethical criticism in the wake of the so-called 'ethical turn' of the 1980s[19] – or at least in the strand of ethical criticism informed by Levinas's ethics, or of what has been called by Simon Critchley *The Ethics of Deconstruction* (1992). Among the various strands of ethical criticism[20], Levinas's ethics of

---

[19] Although the term 'ethical turn' has been widely used to refer to a renewed interest in ethical criticism as a response to perceived shortcomings of deconstructivist criticism, and in particular as a response to the 1987 revelations about Paul de Man's past writing anti-semitic articles in a collaborationist newspaper during World War II, the term in itself is perhaps an unfortunate turn of phrase. To speak of a 'turn' to ethics, as Swantje Möller rightly points out, "harbours the risk of distorting the fact that thinking about the connection between literature and ethics is not a particularly recent phenomenon, but rather refers to a tradition that can be traced back to antiquity" (2011: 39).

[20] The ethical criticism that forms part of the ethical turn itself is not uniform in its understanding of ethics or of the role it allocates to literature in the negotiation of ethics, as can be seen for example from the contributions to Garber, Hanssen and Walkowitz's compilation *The Turn to Ethics* (2000; for an overview of various currents in ethical criticism see in particular Buell 2000) or from those to Davis and Womack's collection *Mapping the Ethical Turn* (2001). For a

alterity is perhaps unique in that it unites a critique of language that is typical of deconstructivist approaches with the acknowledgement of a concrete ethical responsibility for the other. This argument is made by Robert Eaglestone (1997), who for this reason sees Levinas's ethical thought as an alternative situated somewhere between Martha Nussbaum's humanist ethics and J. Hillis Miller's more strongly text-centred deconstructivist ethics of reading. Following a distinction by Denis Donoghue, Eaglestone distinguishes between an "epi-reading" that sees literature largely as example, as a 'projective space' for morality (as Nussbaum does), and a "graphi-reading" (as offered by Miller) that "concentrates on the language, but seems unable to offer anything apart from the actual language of a text which might be considered ethical" (1997: 5; see 3–6). Levinas's thought, on the other hand, considers both the concrete thought for the other that is deeply rooted in moral philosophy and the dimension of language that is crucial to any reading of literature that is willing to consider its aesthetics, which is why it "shows how the ethical, beyond being, appears in literature" (Eaglestone 1997: 170). It is precisely for this reason that Levinas's thought offers itself to any reading of fictions of infinity – or rather, more precisely, reading fictions of infinity takes place almost inevitably in a Levinasian tradition: as a reading that must acknowledge the aesthetics of the infinite text, it is one that must take heed of the language that engenders this aesthetics; at the same time, since the infinite text overflows its own boundaries, reading fictions of infinity is always also a reading beyond the text. As my reading of four examples of fictions of infinity intends to show, this reading beyond the text is one that becomes intensely aware of the reader's ethical responsibility and that is perpetually disrupted and refigured by the infinite text; in this process of disruption it is also a reading that continues *ad infinitum*. All in all, my approach forms part of an ethical criticism in a Levinasian tradition, but differs from a tendency in such Levinasian ethical criticism to focus on encounters with alterity at the plot level of a narrative because it also actively seeks to take into account the aesthetic structure of texts. This is because it seems to me that neglecting the aesthetic dimensions of a text means neglecting a central part of its signification, of the way a text speaks to its readers.

As far as my choice of four particular novels as examples of fictions of infinity and their ethical appeal is concerned, it seems almost unnecessary to say that making such a choice when writing about the topic of infinity in literature comes with its own problems. As always, there is the question of which texts to choose

---

good overview of the ethical turn and the problems that come with the term 'ethical turn', see Möller's chapter on the topic (2011: 36–46).

from the vast (and for all practical purposes seemingly infinite) corpus of literature and, likewise, which thematic or aesthetic focus to apply in the selection of texts to study. Making a choice and setting a focus is always also imposing a limitation and as such already is at odds with the topic of infinity. It is, however, inevitable to impose limits on any representation of the infinite and the choices made here that result in these restrictions are the result of a couple of basic considerations.

First of all, my aim is to show a variety of different aesthetic and conceptual realisations of the infinite in literature, rather than to conduct an in-depth exploration of a single aesthetic feature that may express infinity. Therefore, the texts discussed in the following represent such different approaches to infinity, while they also have some key features in common. Thus, *Cloud Atlas* uses its complex mise en abyme structure to evoke infinity, while *The Stone Gods* constructs a circular narrative to the same effect. *Saturday*, on the other hand, relies on a rampant form of intertextuality to emphasise its textual infinity, while *The Infinities* rises to its name by dissolving the boundaries of its own narrative voice. Secondly, the complexity of the topic itself and the way in which I see the infinite linked to questions of ethics and reading in general require a nuanced argumentation. For this reason I have decided to focus on a small number of case studies highlighting different ways in which the infinite is realised. These are then discussed at greater length, but, hopefully, possess enough of an exemplary character so that the central findings can be transferred to the analysis of other, conceptually similar texts.

Thirdly, in order to achieve a bare minimum of homogeneity among the texts under discussion, all four novels that serve as my case studies in the following are contemporary novels, all published in the first decade of the twenty-first century, and all written by authors from the United Kingdom or the Republic of Ireland. Infinity, of course, knows no temporal or spatial restrictions: where the mere discussion of the idea of infinity is concerned, a novel from the eighteenth century such as Laurence Sterne's *Tristram Shandy* is theoretically no different than a contemporary novel, although the latter may of course recur to a greater wealth of philosophical and scientific positions on the matter, as is the case with the discussion of the multiverse in Banville's *The Infinities*. Likewise, the perspectives a British or Irish author may offer on the infinite need not be substantially different from those of a writer who is, for instance, American, Caribbean, Indian or Nigerian, or for that matter from those of an author like Jorge Luis Borges who does not write in English. Infinity knows no nationality, race or gender and has no genuine language of its own. However, literary texts are not monodimensional and do not engage in just the discussion of a single topic, even if that topic is the infinite. For that reason choosing texts that are rooted in a similar sociocultural background seems helpful to add a further level of comparability between these texts. Thus, of my four case studies only Banville does not address problems of contemporary global politics in any direct way, while McEwan, Mitchell and Winterson share a concern for such issues.

What is more, my focus on contemporary literature is in line with what might be described as an openness towards the infinite in contemporary writing, an "unboundedness" of contemporary fiction that is a reaction to "the 'globalization' of the novel" (Eaglestone 2013: 4). Florian Kläger therefore contests that it is "no coincidence" (2014: 292) that the first chapter of Robert Eaglestone's recent *Very Short Introduction* to contemporary fiction is titled "Saying Everything" (2013: 1), a heading that implies that infinity somehow lurks beneath the surface of contemporary writing.[21] The tendency towards transcending the boundaries of traditional 'national' literatures and taking a global scope, which in itself is certainly eroding and dissolving established boundaries but still not quite 'infinite' in a literal sense, has fuelled the recent critical debate of concepts such as cosmopolitanism or cosmodernism (Kläger 2014: 291; on cosmopolitanism, see e.g. Schoene 2009 and McCulloch 2012; on cosmodernism, see e.g. Moraru 2011 and D'haen 2013). Although these concepts are not the primary theoretical fulcrum of my approach here – my focus is on the epistemological and aesthetic challenges of representing the infinite and on the ethical consequences of such representations, but based on the ethics of Levinas rather than on the (neo-)humanist ethics that form the core of many cosmopolitan/cosmodern approaches –, they nevertheless share common interests with my readings. Indeed, three of my four case studies, the exception being *The Infinities*, have been discussed as examples of cosmopolitan fiction.

At the same time, my selection of texts shows that the preoccupation with infinity through aesthetics and/or contents helps to keep the conceptual scope of a literary text as wide as possible, regardless of whether or not its story addresses truly global topics. Thus, the order in which I discuss the novels chosen as my sample texts shows a narrowing from the truly broad, global or even cosmic – at any rate cosmopolitan – dimensions of *Cloud Atlas* and *The Stone Gods*

---

21 Indeed, Eaglestone's chapter title is a reference to Jacques Derrida's claim that the "institution of fiction [...] gives *in principle* the power to say everything, to break free of the rules" (Derrida 1992: 37; see Eaglestone 2013: 2). The type of infinity that literature in this sense possesses, a potential infinity, the capability to express everything and anything, is of course located at a more abstract level than the aesthetic representations of the infinite that are at the focus of my analysis here. Nevertheless, it is a prerequisite for such representations of infinity, since "the power to say everything" includes the power to say that which cannot be said and to express that which is greater than the expression itself, the infinite.

via the somewhat more narrow setting of London – still a globalised city with global concerns – in *Saturday* to the narrow confines of an Irish country mansion in *The Infinities*. This narrowing of spatial dimensions goes hand in hand with a narrowing of temporal dimensions, from the cosmic timescales of *Cloud Atlas* and *The Stone Gods* to the single-day narratives of *Saturday* and *The Infinities*. The narrowing ostensibly continues at the political and ethical topics with which these novels concern themselves: while *The Stone Gods* and *Cloud Atlas* thematise problems that concern all of humanity – climate change, exploitation of the environment, the possible consequences of unchecked technological progress or the possible aftermath of destructive wars – *Saturday* in many ways only addresses the challenges facing relatively well-off citizens of the Western world and *The Infinities* at plot level remains an inconsequential narrative about one particular family. Yet infinity remains a guiding principle in all four novels and where it underscores the global outreach of Mitchell's and Winterson's novels, it allows McEwan and Banville to maintain an equally broad scope by pointing to the epistemological and aesthetic infinity of the literary itself. Ultimately, infinity is the structural element that allows all four novels to showcase the capacity of the literary to engage and challenge readers, to disrupt their habitual patterns of thought and confront them with the text's ethical appeal.

There are then many texts that are not included here because of these self-imposed restrictions.[22] Some of them may be mentioned in passing on the following pages, others may, undeservedly, miss out entirely. This account of infinity in literature is necessarily incomplete.

---

[22] In the twentieth and twenty-first centuries alone, there is a long list of writers and texts that could be mentioned in this context. The following are just a few choice examples: James Joyce, certainly in *Finnegans Wake*, possibly also in *Ulysses*, experiments with infinity, as do his fellow Irish writers Flann O'Brien (in *At Swim-Two-Birds*, and, in a different way also in *The Third Policeman*) and Samuel Beckett – the latter in both his prose and plays. The Argentinian Jorge Luis Borges was fascinated with all facets of the infinite, and infinity can be traced throughout his work, most famously perhaps in his story "The Library of Babel" (for a study focussing on the infinite in Beckett, Borges and J. M. Coetzee, see Brits 2018). A similar interest in infinity can be found in the work of the American postmodernist writer John Barth, and in particular perhaps in his collection *Lost in the Funhouse*. Following in the footsteps of both Borges's magical realism and a much earlier novel that thematises infinity, *Tristram Shandy*, is Salman Rushdie's *Midnight's Children*, where the multi-voicedness of the telepathic congress inside Saleem Sinai's head can perhaps be said to open a window to infinity. Towards the end of the twentieth century, David Foster Wallace's *Infinite Jest*, a novel of staggering complexity and encyclopaedic depth must be named. Then there are the novels reviewed by Winters under the label of *Infinite Fictions* (Winters 2015) and, as a fairly recent addition to this list, Alan Moore's monumental *Jerusalem*.

On its way to incompletion, then, this study is structured as follows: this introduction is followed by two theoretical chapters on the two aspects of infinity in fiction I want to focus on, the aesthetical and the ethical. Since my argument is that these two go hand in hand, they should ideally be discussed simultaneously, which the medium and narrative mode of this study make impossible. For this reason I begin with looking at the aesthetics of the infinite. Chapter 2 explains the mechanics of Lakoff and Núñez's Basic Metaphor of Infinity and introduces the strategies that the four novels pursue to attain their aesthetic infinity. It shows how mise en abyme structures, circular narrative, intertextuality and, though subject to greater restrictions, omniscient narration, all can serve as sources for the Basic Metaphor of Infinity because they construct textual patterns of iteration, implying the possibility of the continuation of the text *ad infinitum*. In this way they become the source domain for the Basic Metaphor of Infinity, which endows such patterns with metaphorical completion in infinity. The chapter then shows how both relatively simple patterns of narrative repetition and circularity and aesthetic phenomena that have long been associated with the infinite by critics – Lucien Dällenbach writes of a type of mise en abyme structure that he calls "*réduplication à l'infini*" (1977: 51) and intertextuality likewise has been described as an infinite phenomenon (see e.g. Pfister 1985), while narrative omniscience makes the same all-encompassing claims as infinity – can be conceptualised as actually infinite and so allow for texts to be understood as infinite. Lastly, the transfer of infinity from textual structure to the text itself, which I make when I speak of an 'infinite text', is shown to be an example of catachresis, an illogical metaphor. Catachresis thus becomes the central rhetorical and aesthetic figure of fictions of infinity.

Having explained, in theory, how texts may become infinite, I turn to the function of the infinite in such texts in the third chapter, which focuses on the role of infinity in Levinas's ethics of alterity and traces the uneasy relationship between such an ethics and fiction. After outlining the idea of infinity and its connection to the face of the other that is central to Levinas's ethics, I turn to his later work on language, in particular to the distinction between the saying and the said in an utterance. This highlights the problem of writing about the ethical relation if it is, as Levinas argues, grounded in a radical alterity that is obliterated as soon as the other is integrated into any ontological system of understanding, including language. Levinas in this context acknowledges that writing philosophy, a writing about ethics, is already a betrayal of the ethical relation. Fiction would seem to be particularly problematic since, due to its 'made up' status, it does not have any relation to concrete alterity – yet Levinas also concedes that a poetic language may exist that can break open totality. In this poetic language, a possibility to bring together the aesthetics of the infinite discussed in the second chapter and Levinas's ethics may be found, as infinite textual structures may introduce a disruptive moment into the process of reading. The link between the infinite text and ethics in a Levinasian sense is, I argue, the phenomenon of catachresis itself. In their catachrestic genesis such texts put into question their readers' spontaneity. This is how fictions of infinity may, despite Levinas's reservations towards the literary, tentatively develop an ethical appeal.

The fourth chapter presents the first detailed analysis of an example of a fiction of infinity in my reading of David Mitchell's *Cloud Atlas*. The most prominent feature of this novel is without doubt its complex narrative structure, a mise en abyme structure that has been strangely turned inside out, resulting in what has been variously called a "Russian doll" structure (Mitchell 2004), a "boomerang trajectory" (Parker 2010: 202) or a "recursive cycle" (Mezey 2011: 13). I read this structure as what allows the novel to become infinite in a catachrestic identification via the Basic Metaphor of Infinity. This infinite structure is a vehicle for the encounters with alterity that structure the plot of *Cloud Atlas*. In these encounters, the protagonists are met with the plea that an awareness of the vulnerability of the other constitutes, which leads them to an ethical response in their interactions with these others. Thus, the novel becomes, as one of its characters describes its eponymous atlas of clouds, "a never-changing map of the ever-constant ineffable" (*CA* 373), of the relation to alterity. The moment of ethical address that shapes the novel's encounters with alterity extends through the way in which its narrative levels are embedded in each other in instances of reception and ultimately, because of the novel's textual infinity, exceeds the textual structure and opens up, in the process of reading *Cloud Atlas*, a level of address to the reader that goes beyond the literal signification of the novel.

The next fiction of infinity I look at, in chapter five, is Jeanette Winterson's *The Stone Gods*. Winterson's dystopian novel is riddled with repetition and in its plot suggests that humankind over millions of years has kept and will keep repeating the same mistakes and stick to the same practices of exploitation of the environment and of fellow human beings in totalitarian systems. This cycle of destruction, a negatively connoted form of infinity, is, however, punctured by intrusions of love and the literary. The queer love relations between the protagonists of the novel's three main narrative strands are all catalysed by or reflected in poetic language and moments of storytelling. Importantly, these love relations are a counterweight to the novel's underlying destructive patterns – they are a turning to the other in what Levinas calls the lover's caress and so counter the 'bad' infinity of the destructive cycle with the 'good' infinity of the ethical relation with alterity. At the same time, the novel's textual infinity transfers this disruption into the reading process and in a meta-hermeneutic fashion questions habits of reading, suggesting that there is no end to interpretation, but that reading is a process that itself must go on infinitely.

Although the aesthetic strategy that Ian McEwan's *Saturday* pursues in order to become infinite is very much different from that of Mitchell's and Winterson's novels, it achieves a similar effect, as the sixth chapter will show. Here it is the unbridled intertextuality omnipresent in the novel that implies the infinity of the text. In *Saturday*'s climactic scene, the recital of a poem irrupts into a moment of violence, and it is the inscrutability of poetic language that seems to be able to challenge not only the home invader Baxter's outburst of violence, which it at least briefly halts, but also the scientist protagonist Henry Perowne's schematising thought patterns. What is more, the novel's intertextuality also infinitely repeats at the discourse level the textual encounter that is at the centre of McEwan's story and, as it were, throws this encounter back at the reader. Above all, *Saturday* uses these encounters with poetic language to disrupt discourses of sameness – those dominating the worldview of its scientist protagonist and, where the fiction of infinity is in excess of its fictional frame, those of McEwan's readers. In this sense, the novel thematises the way in which fiction may engage readers, or what Derek Attridge has called the "workness" of the literary text (see 2016).

Chapter seven presents my last example of a fiction of infinity. John Banville's *The Infinities* has its place at the end of my study as it is a reflection at a meta-level of the relation between fiction, or art in general, and infinity and so marks the end point of a movement in the order in which my four sample novels are discussed towards increased reflection of the status of literature itself. The central question of Banville's novel is one of perspective, as evidenced not only in the paradoxically infinite perspective of its narrator-god Hermes, but also in the way *The Infinities* presents "the mystery of otherness" (*TI* 8) in a series of gazes at others, a form of visual mise en abyme. At the same time, perspective is reflected in the novel's thematisation of the multiverse in the formulae of its protagonist Adam Godley, another scientist character. Since this multiverse can only be accessed by the novel's divine narrator, it doubles for narration, or fiction itself, and so in conjunction with the unlimited narrative perspective raises the question whether there is a privileged position of observation, that of the author or possibly that of the reader involved in narrative worldmaking. While the existence and accessibility of the multiverse seems to suggest such a notion in the first place, the infinite plurality of the multiverse simultaneously denies the existence of any such privileged position – if only because its infinity of worlds is beyond comprehension. In its thematisation of narrative infinity, *The Infinities* thus also inadvertently demonstrates a feature of poetic language: it oscillates between totality, the ontology of linguistic categorisation, and infinity. To read fictions of infinity means to follow this oscillation and hence to break open ontological frameworks that govern the reading – this is their disruptive power.

Lastly, since this study of infinity underlies similar restrictions as any representation of the infinite, it ends not in a conclusion, but in a coda, in which I sum up its central findings: all four novels are examples of how texts may become actually infinite through a number of different aesthetic features and in all four, one way or another, the aesthetic representation of infinity is tied to an ethical impulse. In the end, I ask what comes beyond fictions of infinity.

2 Narrative Infinity: Aesthetics and Conceptualisation

The question of infinity has always been an epistemological question as much as an ontological one. The *horror infiniti* that dominated research into the infinite from antiquity to Cantor's 'revolution' in the nineteenth century was a fear of infinity as an actually existing entity, that is, a fear pertaining to its ontological status, fuelled by a fear of its ungraspability, or of the epistemological limitations humans experience when encountering the infinite. At infinity, it would seem, epistemology and ontology are even more closely intertwined than elsewhere. With regard to fiction, this becomes apparent in the aesthetic form of a text as a work of art: if a text can ever *be* infinite then its aesthetics must be key to that, since it is through its form that any text must approach the impossible task of grasping infinity in representation. It seems clear that infinity may occur at the story level of narrative texts when a narrative directly thematises the topic of infinity, for example when a character works as a scientist or mathematician on questions of the infinite, as is the case with Old Adam Godley in *The Infinities*. This type of infinity at the story level is not my main concern here, and in the four novels I analyse below, it only features prominently in *The Infinities*, while it plays a minor role in the stories of *Cloud Atlas* and *The Stone Gods* and does not appear at all in *Saturday*. The other aspect in which infinity may enter into a narrative is at the discourse level, in the aesthetics of the narrative itself. It is this kind of narrative infinity that I am particularly interested in, as it is here, at the level of formal representation, that a narrative faces the challenge of containing infinity within the finite medium of representation. Specifically, I want to look at how aesthetic features may function to let a text become infinite.

This raises a number of questions: First, if infinity may be somehow 'encoded' in finite narrative discourse, how do readers become aware of this infinity, how may infinity be detected within the finitude of the narrative? Second, closely connected to the question of perception – which is a question of the epistemology of the infinite – is the question how a narrative may then 'escape' the limitations it is subject to: how can a text that is necessarily limited to the space between the covers of a book become infinite and so transcend its own limitations? This is a question of aesthetics proper – it might be rephrased to ask what textual forms or narrative techniques exist that may create the impression in a reader that the text at hand is infinite. What tacitly links these two questions is the further question of what kind of infinity a text may take on. Is it a potential infinity – a text that could go on *ad infinitum* but due to the restrictions of the medium must break off at some point, much in the same vein as Aristotle viewed the integers – or can a text attain actual infinity, i.e. can it be viewed as a complete, infinite thing? A third question, namely what the function of such textual infinity then might be, is no longer one of aesthetics and will be discussed in detail in the next chapter.

The first question is, in fact, one of how infinity is conceptualised and thus 'understood'. Conceptual metaphor theory provides a compelling answer, which, as I hope to show, also applies to infinity in narrative texts. As narratives patently are finite – they have a first and a last page, a beginning and an end –, if a narrative might indeed be somehow understood as infinite, this would be an identification of a finite entity (the narrative) with infinity, resulting in a hypostasised infinite narrative. Such an identification of one thing with another which it is not is a metaphor. In a way, such an identification of finite entities with infinity underlies all instances in which infinity is conceptualised: there is a case to be made that "since we do not encounter actual infinity directly in the world, since our conceptual systems are finite, and since we have no cognitive mechanisms to perceive infinity, [...] metaphorical thought may be necessary for human beings to conceptualise infinity" (Lakoff and Núñez 2000: xii). This is why in the following I am looking to conceptual metaphor theory to explain how a text may become actually infinite through a process of metaphorical identification.

An answer to the second question would then be to find textual structures that serve as a source for the metaphor that endows a text with infinity. Although there undoubtedly are many structures that may have such an effect, my focus will be on four frequent examples that also are central to the four novels I discuss below – narrative repetition and circularity, mise en abyme structures, intertextuality and narrative omniscience. Textual structures that heavily rely on these features may be metaphorically understood to be infinite. This identification, which metonymically extends to the entire text, not just its narrative structure, then results in the paradoxical, or at least counter-intuitive, infinity of a finite text. Therefore, strictly speaking, understanding a text to be infinite is the result of a catachresis. Fictions of infinity in this sense are catachrestic fictions.

2.1 Conceptualising the Infinite: The Basic Metaphor of Infinity

The suggestion that the way we conceive of infinity is always metaphorical originates in conceptual metaphor theory.[23] Established in the 1980s by the linguists George Lakoff, Mark Johnson and Mark Turner, conceptual metaphor theory looks for underlying metaphors that structure the way we perceive the world (see Lakoff and Johnson 1980; Lakoff and Turner 1989). In conceptual metaphor theory, a metaphor is not merely, as in classical rhetoric, a shortened comparison without comparative particle (thus Quintilian; see Lausberg 1990: 285) – an understanding that lives on in most modern concepts of metaphor that focus on its rhetorical status, for example in Christine Brooke-Rose's definition of metaphor as "any replacement of one word by another, or any identification of one thing, concept or person with another" (Brooke-Rose 1958: 23–24; see Berger 2015: 4). While such a shortened comparison would "suggest some common quality shared by the two [elements compared]" (Baldick 2001: 153), conceptual metaphor theory frames this comparison in rather more specific terms. According to Lakoff and Johnson, "*The essence of metaphor is understanding and experiencing one kind of thing in terms of another*" (1980: 5). It is, in this view, not just one particular quality, but at least parts of the conceptual framework of the source domain that is transferred onto the target domain. In other words, such a conceptual metaphor is "a *grounded, inference-preserving cross-domain mapping* – a neural mechanism that allows us to use the inferential structure of one conceptual domain [...] to reason about another", and in particular to "conceptualize abstract concepts in concrete terms" (Lakoff and Núñez 2000: 6, 5).

In *Where Mathematics Comes From* (2000), a study that seeks to explain processes of mathematical understanding in terms of conceptual metaphor theory, Lakoff and Rafael E. Núñez argue that infinity – certainly an abstract concept – is indeed conceptualised by means of a conceptual metaphor that is rooted in concrete perception. They posit the existence of a Basic Metaphor of Infinity, which "originates outside mathematics, but [...] appears to be the basis of our understanding of infinity in virtually all mathematical domains"

---

[23] Following Eckard Rolf, who argues that the characteristic element of the work of Lakoff, Johnson and Turner is the notion that and the exploration of how metaphors are instrumental in the conceptualisation of experience I use the term 'conceptual', rather than 'cognitive' metaphor theory throughout (Rolf 2005: 235; see 235–41).

(2000: 8). The extra-mathematical origin of the concept of infinity, according to Lakoff and Núñez, is to be found in indefinitely continuing processes[24]:

> Outside mathematics, a process is seen as infinite if it continues (or iterates) indefinitely without stopping. That is, it has imperfective aspect (it continues indefinitely) without an endpoint. This is *the literal concept of infinity* outside mathematics. It is used whenever one thinks of perpetual motion – motion that goes on and on forever. (2000: 156).

It would seem, then, that this 'literal' concept of infinity comes into being as a conflation of potential infinity – as mentioned above, this is Aristotle's term for entities (such as the integers) that derive the quality of infinity from their endless continuability – and the indefinite. The difference between the two is that whereas with the potentially infinite, we *know* that there is no end to it, with the indefinite, we do *not* know whether it ever comes to an end, since the certainty of a (lack of) ending would be definite. Indeed, in this literal concept of infinity, there already is a conceptual metaphor at work that allows for this blending. As Lakoff and Núñez argue, endless, or imperfective, processes can be divided into continuative, i.e. continuous, uninterrupted or 'fluid' processes, and iterative processes that are made up of an endless number of discrete, unconnected (or 'interrupted') single elements. This distinction, however, is more of a logical one than one that seems to be made in everyday discourse, since "[i]n languages throughout the world, continuous processes are conceptualized as if they were iterative processes" (2000: 156).[25] Lakoff and Núñez's examples are sentences like *"John said the sentence over"*, which indicates a single repetition, as opposed to *"John said the sentence over and over and over"*, which, they claim, implies the indefinite continuation (and not just a threefold repetition) of the process described, i.e. of John saying the sentence (2000: 157).[26] Crucially, here the syntax

---

[24] In the following, my explication of the Basic Metaphor of Infinity is based on Lakoff and Núñez (2000: 155–180).

[25] The connection between repetition, or iteration, and infinity is not very new at all. For example, Edmund Burke writes that "[w]henever we repeat any idea frequently, the mind, by a sort of mechanism, repeats it long after the first cause has ceased to operate" (1792: 110; pt. 2, sect. 8). Indeed, Burke reflects on some of the qualities of the "artificial infinite", namely "succession and uniformity of parts" (1792: 111, see 111–114; pt. 2, sect. 9), that are also central to the conceptual metaphors Lakoff and Núñez associate with the infinite. Thus, when Burke states that "uninterrupted progression [...] alone can stamp on bounded objects the character of infinity" (1792: 112; pt. 2, sect. 9), this is akin to Lakoff and Núñez's claim that indefinitely iterating processes are seen as infinite outside mathematics.

[26] Kenneth Holmqvist and Jarosław Płuciennik in their study of the conceptualisation of the sublime look at a number of similar examples of accumulation that express 'infinity' and find that "[r]epetition [...] is a sign that the speaking subject has no adequate instrumentality of

of iteration – the conjunction 'and' suggests the 'adding up' of discrete steps – is used to express continuation. This means that a conceptual metaphor is at work, namely "Indefinite Continuous Processes Are Iterative Processes" (Lakoff and Núñez 2000: 157). The source domain of this metaphor is to be found in the concrete action of perpetual motion, such as the indefinitely repeated saying of a sentence – Lakoff and Núñez also give the examples of continuous walking or swimming, which both can be segmented into an indefinite number of repetitions of finite steps or strokes (2000: 157). The key idea is that a process that is infinitely continuous is metaphorically conceptualised as an "infinitely iterating step-by-step process[]", i.e. as an infinite series of "discrete and minimal" elements (2000: 157). This is then how potential infinity is conceptualised: its continuative aspect is understood in terms of a conceptual metaphor that segments the continuum that is infinity into an infinite number of iterated finite steps.

In a next step of metaphorical conceptualisation – and only this step is where the Basic Metaphor of Infinity proper comes into play – Aristotle's potential infinity proves to be the source for a metaphorical understanding of the actual infinite, i.e. the infinite understood as one complete thing, realised in its totality. It is important to note that the resultant state, that is, its perception as completed but infinite entity, is the characteristic feature of actual infinity. Lakoff and Núñez explain this understanding of actual infinity by claiming that the idea of actual infinity is already metaphorical, since it is understood as the result of an endless process – an image which is strictly speaking illogical (2000: 158). What happens here is that "the mechanism of metaphor allows us to conceptualize the 'result' of an infinite process – in the only way we have for conceptualizing the result of a process – that is, in terms of a process that does have an end" (2000: 158). It is this metaphor, which adds completion to endless processes so as to conceptualise them as infinite complete 'things', as the actual infinite, which Lakoff and Núñez call the Basic Metaphor of Infinity (BMI).

---

representation" (2008: 57; see 55–62) – which chimes in with the paradox of representing the infinite. The linguistic potential to infinitely (or, more precisely, indefinitely) expand a given action by simply repeating the verb with an interspersed 'and' was, as Viveca Füredy mentions, already described by Leo Spitzer, who gave the example "It rains and rains" (1957: 205; see Füredy 1989: 750). For Füredy, this type of repetition which insinuates infinity is distinct from recursion and weaker than recursion in its effect of creating a sense of infinity (see Füredy 1989: 750).

> The source domain of the BMI consists of an ordinary iterative process with an indefinite (though finite) number of iterations with a completion and resultant state. The source and target domains are alike in certain ways:
>
> – Both have an initial state.
> – Both have an iterative process with an unspecified number of iterations.
> – Both have a resultant state after each iteration.
>
> In the metaphor, the initial state, the iterative process, and the result after each iteration are mapped onto the corresponding elements of the target domain. But the crucial effect of the metaphor is *to add to the target domain the completion of the process and its resulting state.* (2000: 158)

The Basic Metaphor of Infinity thus marks the conceptual transition from an indefinitely iterating process to the understanding of this process as resulting in an infinite state, i.e. in actual infinity. While the source domain and the target domain are very similar in that they are iterative processes consisting of discrete steps – that is, steps that are in themselves complete (have an initial and resultant state) and distinct from one another – the Basic Metaphor of Infinity endows the entire process as a whole with completion, assigning it the status of the actual infinite.

As Lakoff and Núñez stress, this Basic Metaphor of Infinity is "a general cognitive mechanism", which is not restricted to mathematical understandings of the infinite, but indeed is at the heart of understanding "'the infinite' as a thing", as happens, for example, in the contexts of philosophy and, with divine infinity, theology (2000: 161). As they go on to show, the Basic Metaphor of Infinity does indeed operate outside mathematics as well – their example is the structure of categorical thought in ancient Greek philosophy, where the category of Being is the all-encompassing end that subsumes all other categories of existence and hence contains a potentially infinite number of categories.[27] This structure can only be thought by employing the Basic Metaphor of Infinity to arrive at the category of Being as the 'container' of all the other infinitely many categories, and hence as an instance of the actual infinite (see 2000: 161–163). This is precisely what the Basic Metaphor of Infinity does: it adds metaphorical completion to indefinitely continuous phenomena and thus converts infinity "from an open-ended process to a specific, unique entity" (2000: 160).

---

27 For a thorough explication of the conceptual categories of ancient Greek metaphysics from the Pre-Socratics to Aristotle in terms of conceptual metaphor theory, see Lakoff and Johnson (1999: 346–390).

The Basic Metaphor of Infinity may then come into operation whenever there is an indefinitely iterating process that is then understood as a complete infinite thing. Since it is not restricted to mathematical use, it should likewise apply to the understanding as infinite of a literary text whose structure is one of iteration. However, two *caveats* remain when it comes to the application of this conceptual metaphor in the context of literature and specifically as a methodological tool for analysing a text as infinite. First, it is important to note that the process of metaphorical identification happens unconsciously, that is, while the result of the use of the Basic Metaphor of Infinity (an entity is understood to be actually infinite) is conscious, the way of getting there (the application of the metaphor) is not consciously experienced (Lakoff and Núñez 2000: 180). With regard to infinity in literary texts, this means that a reader does not have to make a willing and conscious *interpretive* effort to read a text as infinite, but that the texts still make use of a conceptual metaphor that triggers a reader's understanding of them as infinite. In other words, when a reader understands a text to be infinite, this is the result of the unconscious use of the Basic Metaphor of Infinity and not of a conscious interpretation of a textual feature.

Second, the Basic Metaphor of Infinity should not be interpreted in such a way that any occurrence of an iterative pattern automatically triggers the identification of a text (or, for that matter, any other entity) as infinite. Lakoff and Núñez describe this conceptual metaphor in order to show how understanding a thing as (actually) infinite works at a cognitive level. They look at cases, mostly from mathematics, but as mentioned above also from other disciplines, in which certain entities are already assumed to be infinite and then make a case for how this happens through the use of the Basic Metaphor of Infinity. This does not mean that every instance of an indefinite iteration is necessarily conceptualised as infinite. Thus, the sequence 123 in the context of an enumeration – commonly written down as 1, 2, 3, ... in mathematical contexts; a distinction that vanishes as soon as it is spoken rather than written – is conceptualised as (the beginning of) an infinite enumeration via the Basic Metaphor of Infinity (see Lakoff and Núñez 2000: 164–167), while the same sequence 123 on the licence plate of a car will not be understood as infinite. Context matters in this case – as do, of course, the elliptical dots in the enumeration sequence that serve as indicators that something is missing. The application of the Basic Metaphor of Infinity, it seems, depends on the context in which the source domain is perceived.

For my project of finding and then interpreting textual structures of infinity this means that it is difficult to base an argument on the structural features of a text alone. If, say, in a text a multiple repetition of a major structural feature (or any of the other possible ways in which a text may contain elements of indefinite iteration) occurs, but there is no further connection to infinity, then this text will likely not be conceptualised as infinite – otherwise any series of detective stories, which usually share the plot structure that the detective in the end catches the murderer, would already evoke a sense of the continuation *ad infinitum* of this process. If, however, as I hope to show in my examples below, such a multiple structural repetition is either clearly marked as potentially infinite, for example through an excessive use of the structural feature within the text, or is presented alongside with more or less clear references to infinity in one of its guises (eternity, omnipresence, etc.) at the content level of the narrative, then there is a case to be made that the entire textual structure may be understood as infinite, and this happens through the Basic Metaphor of Infinity. In the following chapters that give detailed analyses of fictions of infinity, my focus therefore will be on textual structures that may serve as a source domain for the Basic Metaphor of Infinity, but also on how they are marked as infinite through other textual features.

2.2 Aesthetic Configurations of Narrative Infinity

What can be inferred from Lakoff and Núñez's description of the Basic Metaphor of Infinity is that for a text to be conceptualised as an infinite thing there must be some sort of indefinitely iterating structure underlying it. Such structures may take on a number of different forms, of which only those that occur prominently in the four novels I focus on in this study will be discussed in detail below: narrative repetition and circularity, mise en abyme structures, intertextuality and narrative omniscience. Beyond these four, any other narrative techniques or structures that combine iteration with indefiniteness, or indeterminacy, in theory should fulfil a similar function. In particular devices that suspend or avoid closure – understood in H. Porter Abbott's sense as the resolution of conflict in narrative and the answering of any open questions (see 2008: 56–61) – may create such indefiniteness and, where they are coupled with iterative elements, provide the source domain for the Basic Metaphor of Infinity.[28]

---

[28] Although necessarily related to the question of textual infinity, closure is not at the centre of this study. For critical discussions of the concept, see Abbott's overview (2008: 55–66) and, among others, the works on aesthetic techniques of closure by Barbara Korte (1985) and Hektor Haarkötter (2007), studies of endings and closure by David H. Richter (1974; with a focus on twentieth-century literature) and Marianna Trogovnick (1981), as well as Frank Kermode's more far-reaching investigation of apocalyptic narrative in *The Sense of an Ending* (1967). For a feminist study of closure, see Rachel Blau DuPlessis, for whom "[w]riting beyond the ending begins when authors, or their close surrogates, discover that they are in fact outside the terms of

2.2.1 Narrative Repetition, Circularity and Infinity

The simplest and probably most frequent types of iteration to be found at the structural level of a text are repetitions. Such repetitions need not be verbatim repetitions of longer phrases or entire passages of a text – these tend to be relatively rare, presumably because a text consisting of a small number of ever-repeating phrases would make for a rather tedious read –, but can be motifs that occur again and again throughout a narrative, repeating plot patterns or character constellations. However, as these are all fairly common features of many fictional narratives, in order for a text to be understood as infinite there must be further clear markers of an association of the text with infinity.

One example can be found in the last chapter of Julian Barnes's *A History of the World in 10½ Chapters*, a chapter called "The Dream". The narrator in this chapter has died and finds himself in a paradisiacal afterlife in heaven, where all his wishes are granted, it seems, in eternity. The temporal infinity of the eternal is underscored by a formal structure of repetition governing the narrator's actions. This begins with the narrator waking up in heaven, having the best breakfast he has ever had and deciding to have the same breakfast again for lunch, and again for dinner, and, of course, again the next morning. This begins a series of repetitive actions that occupy his days initially: breakfast, going shopping, having sex, playing golf, meeting famous people – all undertaken in the best form he has ever experienced them. The indefinite repetition of these pastimes – both at the story level and at the discourse level, through repeated enumeration of them – already could serve as the source domain for the Basic Metaphor of Infinity: the narrator's activities have a beginning and an end and can be compartmentalised into discrete and minimal but indefinitely repeating steps. If this was all that happened in Barnes's story, together with the obvious context of eternity, it might already be enough to understand the text as infinite.

However, Barnes's narrative does not stop there, precisely because for the narrator there is a problem with infinity. The problem is that it does not get better than that, that there is nothing beyond infinity. This heaven is a heaven of infinite standstill – paradoxically, despite the temporal infinity of the entire setup, "[t]here aren't an infinite number of possibilities" (Barnes 1990: 288) for what the narrator can do: enjoyment, it turns out, lies in the possibility of improvement, and implicitly also in the risk of failure. After a while this is no longer possible in Barnes's heaven. The narrator's options, one after the other, are exhausted. As he

---

this novel's script, marginal to it" (1985: 6), that is, it is founded on a rejection of the frames that govern the conventional understanding of, in this case, gender roles.

ponders the impossibility of improving on eighteen shots in an eighteen-hole golf course – *"My game has improved no end*, I thought, and repeated the words *no end* to myself" (1990: 297) – his predicament becomes clear. Since the narrator cannot find an unlimited number of activities that he is interested in and that will not eventually lose their fascination through indefinite repetition, the story ends with him considering to 'die off' into absolute non-existence. There are then in Barnes's narrative plenty of references to endlessness or infinity that in conjunction with the repetitive elements of the narrative would seem to allow for an identification of the text's repetitive structure as infinite via the Basic Metaphor of Infinity.

The last chapter of Barnes's *History* is instructive since it illustrates how the fairly simple narrative device of repeating plot elements may already be enough to create structural infinity. What is more, in terms of narrative frequency, Gérard Genette's category that describes the "relations of frequency (or, more simply, of repetition) between the narrative and the diegesis" (1980: 113), a narrative like Barnes's, due to its infinity, marks an interesting exception from Genette's framework.[29] Genette has distinguished four cases of narrative frequency (see 1980: 113–160): singulative (*"[n]arrating once what happened once"*; 1980: 114), anaphoristic (*"[n]arrating n times what happened n times"*; 1980: 114 – a case that, as Christoph Bode argues, is identical with the singulative; see Bode 2011: 92), repeating (*"[n]arrating n times what happened once"*; 1980: 115) and iterative (*"[n]arrating once [...] what happened n times"*; 1980: 116). If events happen an infinite, or at least indefinite, number of times, the anaphoristic mode is impossible because of the representational paradox of infinity. There is simply no medium in which an act of telling could happen an infinite number of times and if the event takes place an indefinite number of times, the telling of it is an act of representation and as such renders it no longer indefinite. Similarly, for infinitely repeating events neither the singulative nor the repetitive mode are appropriate, while the iterative mode entails a necessary abstraction[30] of the specific multiply occurring events and besides seems inadequate for a story like Barnes's in which it is arguably more important how often things happen than what happens – something that would be emphasised precisely through the repetition of instances of telling. Indeed, in Barnes's chapter the relation between the number of times the events take place and the number of times they are reported in the nar-

---

29 Unless otherwise stated, all narratological terminology in this study is used as in Gérard Genette's *Narrative Discourse* (1980) and *Narrative Discourse Revisited* (1983), respectively.
30 This is a claim that Genette makes about repetition in general: what we conceptualise as the "'recurrence of the same event' is a series of several similar events *considered only in terms of their resemblance*" and thus an "abstraction" (1980: 113).

rative does not fit any of Genette's categories particularly well. Most of the narrator's activities are told several times (playing golf, for example, is mentioned on at least six different occasions), but it is clear that they happen an indefinite, or (near-)infinite, number of times, being repeated over several centuries (Barnes 1990: 307). 'Narrating n times what happened in(de)finitely often' is not a mode of narrative frequency offered by Genette and constitutes a curious mix of his repetitive and iterative modes. It is, however, precisely what makes possible the metaphorical identification of a text as infinite – an identification that in this case is specifically constituted in the interrelation between elements of its story and discourse – because it allows for both the indefiniteness and the iterating structure of a repeated telling (as opposed to the single act of telling of Genette's iterative narration) that form a source domain of the Basic Metaphor of Infinity. In this way the unusual frequency of Barnes's narration, together with the story's focus on endlessness, contributes to the infinity of its text.

At the same time, Barnes's chapter is also an example of a second iterative feature, closely connected to simple repetition, namely circularity.[31] Since texts are not actually physically circular and the reading process is, broadly speaking, linear, the notion of a 'circular' narrative is itself already metaphorical. Circles, although they are finite in that they take up only finite space (their diameter must be a finite length), are symbols of infinity and eternity or eternal recurrence (see Cirlot 1971: 46–48, 123; Brogi 2008) because moving along the circle line they can be run through potentially infinitely. The key qualities of a circle that become relevant to a 'circular' narrative are thus the iterability of the rotations of the circle, that is, the repetition of structural or plot elements, its non-linearity and the coinciding of starting and end point. As the possibilities for a genuinely (not metaphorically) non-linear text are somewhat limited[32], and the mere repe-

---

[31] Circularity, or cyclicality, of literary texts is linked to infinity, but may develop its own aesthetic paradigm and can also be associated with a long socio-cultural and literary tradition of its own. For a more detailed discussion of circularity in literature, see Henke and Middeke (2009).
[32] A notable exception that transcends the common restrictions of the book as medium is John Barth's "Frame Tale" (1988: 1–2). This very short experimental postmodernist text comes with the instructions to cut out a strip of paper upon which the words "once upon a time there was a story that began" (the narrative in its entirety) are printed, to twist the paper strip once and glue it back together, creating a Möbius strip. Due to the geometrical properties of the Möbius strip this results in a text that seems to be independent of its original medium of publication and complete in and of itself – a Möbius strip does not have an 'inside' and 'outside' but is a surface with just one side – and whose readers despite the linearity of their reading process itself will inevitably be returned to their starting point in circular fashion. This can only be achieved by breaking open the ontological restrictions of the linearity of a printed page as the result of an uncommonly incisive act of reading. While this subversion of the text's ontology is very effective

tition of parts of the text alone seems insufficient to mark it as circular, the latter quality, the coinciding of beginning and end, seems to me to be the most pertinent to a circular narrative. Again, this needs to be qualified: on a circle line, there is no beginning or end, and no otherwise privileged point. Narratives, on the other hand, almost inevitably have such privileged points as a result of their medium – a book offers the natural starting point of the first page and the natural end point of the last page, which both stand out as privileged even if the narrative does not actually begin or conclude there – and plot structure. Since most narratives can be said to develop their story one way or another, a point later in the story cannot usually be readily chosen as the starting point of the narrative, unless the missing elements of the preceding story are then provided, for example, in analepses.

As such privileged points in narrative seem to exist either way, the most clearly marked form of narrative circularity therefore seems to be one in which beginning and end of the narrative discourse coincide or are strongly linked. Most famously, perhaps, this is the case in James Joyce's *Finnegans Wake*, which begins mid-sentence with the second part of the sentence whose first part ends the narrative several hundred pages later. Barnes's "Dream" does something similar: its first sentences, "I dreamt that I woke up. It's the oldest dream of all, and I've just had it. I dreamt that I woke up" (1990: 283), already form a miniature version of a circular structure due to the repetition of "I dreamt that I woke up" and so foreshadow the repetitive nature of what is to follow. On the scale of the entire narrative, this circle closes when the last two sentences of the story are identical repetitions of the first two (see 1990: 309). As a consequence, beginning and end of Barnes's text become interchangeable and the impression of a circular, eternally repeating text is created, which adds to the ways in which "The Dream" can be understood as infinite.

Overall, narrative repetitions and circular structures – themselves already metaphorical in nature – are closely linked with the source domain of the Basic Metaphor of Infinity. They lead to textual structures that are both iterative and indefinite, as can be seen in Barnes's story, and so make it possible for the texts to be metaphorically identified as infinite. Since such repetitions make for the most basic cases of indefinitely iterating textual structures, they can be found in all four novels discussed below, with circularity featuring in both *Cloud Atlas* and, particularly prominently, in *The Stone Gods* (see ch. 5).

---

at the scale of Barth's narrative experiment, it is hardly practicable for longer texts that remain tied to the restrictions of their narrative medium. For such longer narratives, particularly in print media – digital media and hypertexts may provide new opportunities here – circularity can essentially only be achieved through metaphor.

2.2.2 Mise en abyme and Infinite Embedding

Besides such narrative repetitions and the special case of narrative circularity, mise en abyme structures are a further example of textual elements that may lead to the identification of a text as infinite. Here the indefinite iteration takes place at the structural level of a narrative. The term 'mise en abyme', commonly used by narratologists to refer to stories within stories, was coined by the French writer André Gide at the end of the nineteenth century. In the diary entry in which Gide first uses the term, it is in the wider sense of a work of art containing its own subject transposed to a smaller scale:

> J'aime assez qu'en une œuvre d'art, on retrouve ainsi transposé, à l'échelle des personnages, le sujet même de cette œuvre. Rien ne l'éclaire mieux et n'établit plus sûrement toutes les proportions de l'ensemble. Ainsi, dans tels tableaux de Memling ou de Quentin Metzys, un petit miroir convexe et sombre reflète, à son tour, l'intérieur de la pièce où se joue la scène peinte. Ainsi, dans le tableau des *Meniñes* de Velasquez (mais un peu différemment). Enfin, en littérature, dans *Hamlet*, la scène de la comédie; et ailleurs dans bien d'autres pièces. Dans *Wilhelm Meister*, les scènes de marionnettes ou de fête au château. Dans *la Chute de la Maison Usher*, la lecture que l'on fait à Roderick, etc. Aucun de ces exemples n'est absolument juste. Ce qui le serait beaucoup plus, ce qui dirait mieux ce que j'ai voulu dans mes *Cahiers*, dans mon *Narcisse* et dans *la Tentative*, c'est la comparaison avec ce procédé du blason qui consiste, dans le premier, à en mettre un second "en abyme". (Gide 1951: 41)[33]

Gide's intuitive description of the phenomenon has since been subject to much critical discussion with the aim of systematising the concept.[34] It seems clear that the function of clarifying the proportions within a work of art that Gide identifies first of all applies to visual art, while in literature the concept of proportionality between the 'levels' of the mise en abyme is already based on metaphorical

---

33 "In a work of art I rather like to find transposed, on the scale of the characters, the very subject of that work. Nothing throws a clearer light upon it or more surely establishes the proportions of the whole. Thus, in certain paintings of Memling or Quentin Metzys a small convex and dark mirror reflects the interior of the room in which the scene of the painting is taking place. Likewise in Velázquez's painting of the *Meniñas* (but somewhat differently). Finally, in literature, in the play scene in *Hamlet*, and elsewhere in many other plays. In *Wilhelm Meister* the scenes of the puppets or the celebration at the castle. In 'The Fall of the House of Usher' the story that is read to Roderick, etc. None of these examples is altogether exact. What would be much more so, and would explain much better what I strove for in my *Cahiers*, in my *Narcisse*, and in the *Tentative*, is a comparison with the device of heraldry that consists in setting in the escutcheon a smaller one 'en abyme', at the heart-point" (Gide 1967: 30–31, qtd. in Ron 1987: 418).
34 For the history of the term 'mise en abyme', see in particular Dällenbach (1977) and Moshe Ron's response (1987); see also Ricardou (1967: 171–190) and Scheffel (1997: 71–85).

transfer. In visual art, the proportionality highlighted by the mise en abyme may still be one of scale, where the mirror shows a smaller version of the subject of the entire painting; however, the use of a mirror to achieve this already implies an inversion of perspective introducing a reflection that deviates from Gide's ideal of an escutcheon containing a miniature version of itself.

In literature, the focus of a narrative mise en abyme structure shifts from proportionality to the aspect of mirroring. Thus Lucien Dällenbach in his study of 'mirror narratives', which focuses on mise en abyme as a literary phenomenon, finds that mise en abyme is above all a "modality of *reflection*" ("une modalité de la *réflexion*"; 1977: 16) in which the work of literature turns back to itself, because it contains another text that is similar to the overall work (1977: 18). Mirroring here becomes all but inevitable. This is because the literary equivalent to the perfect (and potentially infinite) self-containment of an escutcheon contained within the very same escutcheon (which would then have to contain yet another, smaller version of that escutcheon, and so on) is hardly relevant for pragmatic narrative purposes. It is the type of narrative embedding which can be found, for instance, in the nonsense song about the bread-stealing dog, sung by Vladimir in *Waiting for Godot:*

> A dog came in the kitchen
> And stole a crust of bread.
> Then cook up with a ladle
> And beat him till he was dead.
>
> Then all the dogs came running
> And dug the dog a tomb –
> [*He stops, broods, resumes.*]
>
> Then all the dogs came running
> And dug the dog a tomb
> And wrote upon the tombstone
> For the eyes of dogs to come:
>
> A dog came in the kitchen
> And stole a crust of bread.
> Then cook up with a ladle
> And beat him till he was dead.
>
> Then all the dogs came running
> And dug the dog a tomb –
> [*He stops, broods, resumes.*] [...] (Beckett 2006: 53)

It is clear that in such cases the focus of the narrative does not primarily lie on the contents – since the narrative form makes the furthering of any plot, which of course is a, or perhaps *the*, central feature of narratives, well-nigh impossible –

but on the narrative form itself (Vladimir's song makes a point about repetition, a central motif of the entire play). In this sense, even such a 'perfect' literary mise en abyme is not merely an illustration of the 'proportions' of the text, but always already a reflection of the narrative form, of textuality itself.[35]

The same, of course, holds true for the less 'perfect' (and far more common) types of literary mise en abyme. The broadest definition of the phenomenon given by Dällenbach is that "est mise en abyme toute enclave entretenant une relation de similitude avec l'œuvre qui la contient" (1977: 18; "mise en abyme is any enclave entertaining a relation of similarity with the work which contains it"; trans. in Ron 1987: 421). In his typology, Dällenbach identifies three types of such nested narratives: in a *"réduplication simple"* (1977: 51), a text shows only one instance of self-containment – a frequently cited example is the play within the play in *Hamlet*, which is already mentioned in Gide's diary. Meanwhile, in a *"réduplication à l'infini"* (1977: 51) the fragment contained in and similar to the overarching structure contains itself another structurally similar fragment that contains yet another one and so on *ad infinitum* – this is the case with the coat of arms mentioned in Gide's diary that contains a miniature copy of itself, or with Vladimir's 'dog song'. Dällenbach's third type is the *"réduplication aporistique"*, described as "fragment censé inclure l'œuvre qui l'inclut" (1977: 51; "[a] fragment supposed to include the work which includes it"; trans. in Ron 1987: 421) – a type that is closely related to narrative metalepsis (see Pier 2016: par. 34) and includes (but is not restricted to) cases in which the diegesis appears as a narrative contained in the metadiegesis.[36]

---

[35] This is underpinned by the fact that, as Scheffel points out, the self-containment in such 'perfect' mise en abyme structures creates a narrative metalepsis, as the metadiegetic narrative, i.e. the inscription on the tombstone, is identical with the intradiegetic narrative, which means that frame narrative and framed narrative become interchangeable (see Scheffel 1997: 75–76; for the use of intradiegetic narrative for the first narrative level and metadiegetic narrative for the subsequent level, see also John Pier's explication (2014: par. 2)). This interchangeability of narrative levels questions the ontological stability of the narrative order and hence is in turn a reflection on the narrative form itself, developing a metafictional potential that has been described as typical of narrative metalepsis (see Pier 2016: par. 32).

[36] One example can be found in Flann O'Brien's 1939 novel *At Swim-Two-Birds*, in which the homodiegetic narrator composes a novel about a novelist (already at the metadiegetic level) who freely interacts with his characters (populating the meta-metadiegetic level) and even rapes one of his own creations, fathering a child with her in the process (so far, in narrative terms, this is still only an elaborate metalepsis) and prompting his characters to take revenge by telling a story of their own in which they put their own author to trial, torture him and eventually decide to sentence him to death – a logical conundrum that can only be solved through the accidental burning of the entire manuscript and hence the destruction of those diegetic levels that have contributed to the aporetic structure in the first place. The aporia of the mise en

In the context of fictions of infinity, the *réduplication à l'infini* for obvious reasons is particularly interesting. Dällenbach clearly has cases like Vladimir's song from *Waiting for Godot* in mind, when he describes this type of narrative duplication as "fragment qui entretient avec l'œuvre qui l'inclut un rapport de similitude et qui enchâsse lui-même un fragment qui ..., et ainsi de suite" (1977: 51; "a fragment which entertains a relation of similarity to the work that includes it and which itself frames a fragment which..., and so forth"; my trans.). However, there is a problem with the label 'infinite' duplication here, since a text featuring an 'infinite' mise en abyme encounters the same difficulties that any attempt at representing infinity must run into, namely its own finitude and the paradox that any representation of the infinite must restrict it to the finite space of the medium of representation and hence deprive infinity of its one defining quality (that of not being finite). Indeed, in his description Dällenbach has to break off and relegate the 'infinite' aspect to the elliptical dots and (perhaps appropriately redundant in this case) to the expression 'and so forth', both indicating the possibility of an indefinite continuation. What is this continuation supposed to look like, though? There is strictly speaking no binding rule, no natural or empirical law, that the next level, the one that is just cut off by the ellipsis, would have to look just like the preceding one. While our understanding of seriality and recursive processes certainly suggests such a continuation – the next bread-stealing dog, having met his sorry end, to be interred and receive a tombstone telling the story of one just like him and so on, eventually enforcing the next ellipsis –, fiction is not bound by such laws. Is it really unthinkable that the dogs at the tenth (forty-second? four-hundred-and-fifty-first?) level of the narrative, on the ninth tombstone, perhaps having finally tired of what went before, should come up with a different inscription, perhaps even one that provides closure without taking recourse to the semiotic crutch of the three dots? In fiction, it is not. In a narrower, more literal-minded, or simply more sceptical sense, then, since any mise en abyme must have its last level that is still represented – in the case of the escutcheon containing a smaller version of itself, the restriction is again of a physical nature, since the infinitesimal versions of ever smaller inescutcheons can be inferred but cannot be actually represented – Dällenbach's *réduplication à l'infini* is necessarily finite.

---

abyme in this example consists in the doubling of the meta-diegetic level (in which the fictional author abuses his characters) as the meta-meta-metadiegetic level (in which the characters take revenge on their author) through which it becomes entirely unclear which narrative level is the superordinate. For further examples of this aporetic type of mise en abyme structures – called 'strange loops' by Douglas Hofstadter (1979) –, see McHale (1987: 119–124).

Yet Dällenbach's label of the *infinite* duplication is not entirely unjustified. It would seem that any alternative ending to Vladimir's endless song is as elusive as Godot himself – it is just not there in the text and there is no indication that it should arrive at all. Instead, the ever same opening up of a new narrative level on a new gravestone lets the audience intuitively assume that this is just the way the song goes on forever.[37] The crucial aspect here is the potential for iterability in the process of narrative embedding: if the embedding is repeated a number of times – in particular, if the act of storytelling itself is repeated over and over, since "only by the narrating, the act that consists precisely of introducing into one situation, by means of a discourse, the knowledge of another situation" (Genette 1980: 234), can subsequent levels of the mise en abyme come into being at all – and if the possibility for further repetitions can be inferred, then an indefinite continuability is implied and the mise en abyme structure indeed takes on a sense of the infinite. As Brian McHale observes, "The specter of infinite regress haunts every recursive structure in which narrative worlds have been 'stacked' beyond a certain depth of embedding" (1987: 114). But what is the "certain depth of embedding" that is required for the "specter of infinite regress" to rear its head and how can a structure be identified to be "recursive"?

Recursion may be defined as "the determination of a succession of elements (as numbers or functions) by operation on one or more preceding elements according to a rule or formula involving a finite number of steps" (*Merriam-Webster*) or, similarly, as "a repeated procedure such that the required result at each step is defined in terms of the results of previous steps according to a particular rule (the result of an initial step being specified)" (*OED*, 3rd ed.). Crucially, the number of defining steps is what is finite here, not (necessarily) the number of elements produced through recursion.[38] If a mise en abyme structure is to be

---

37 This endless continuation can be seen as the self-referentiality of literature taken to its extreme: The difference between the inscription on the canine tombstone in the song and an ordinary epitaph is that the former thematises its own genesis, the process of writing itself. Once the question of how the inscription was created is raised, i.e. once the writing is written about, one is already trapped in the logic of a *regressus ad infinitum*, for the same question must then be raised at the next level, and so on, to infinity. On the importance of self-referentiality, recursivity and circularity in Beckett, see for example Connor (1988) and Breuer (2002), on self-reflexivity in literature see the contributions in Huber, Middeke and Zapf (2005).

38 Thus, to give a simple example, in mathematics, where recursion is used as a standard means of defining sequences of numbers, the sequence of natural numbers, i.e. of positive integers (1, 2, 3, ...), can be recursively defined by giving an initial value ($a_1 = 1$) and a rule by which all the other elements (all the other positive integers) can be derived from this initial value. In this case the rule is to simply add one to each preceding number ($\forall i \in \mathbb{N} : a_{i+1} = a_i + 1$). While the num-

read as infinite, this is only possible by way of such a recursive definition: the levels of the mise en abyme that are actually present in the text, a necessarily finite number of levels, must then provide the 'rule' that implies its infinite, or at least indefinite, continuability.[39] In the case of Vladimir's song, this rule is easily derived: The first time the dog's story is recounted presents the initial step in the recursion; from the subsequent repetitions a rule can be inferred that could read like this: 'from the second tombstone onwards, each tombstone bears the story of the dog that died for this tombstone to be erected, up until where his dog friends decide to erect and inscribe his tombstone, telling us the contents of the epitaph'. By analogy, similar rules of recursion must be deducible in more complex literary texts that have a mise en abyme structure. This means that an infinite mise en abyme structure seems possible after all. It would require two ingredients: (1) An at least implicit, and hence deducible, textual recursion, that is, the establishing of a rule of (textual) progress based on the features of the accessible narrative levels. As McHale points out, there have to be several levels stacked "beyond a certain depth" in order to achieve this – the number of levels actually required would seem to depend on the overtness of the recursive principle; at least in the very simple case of Vladimir's song (where the recursion is clearly marked as a matter of identical repetition) as few as two narrative levels appear to be sufficient. (2) Further, a general narrative openness is required to ensure that a continuation of textuality beyond the confines of the physical text is not ruled out. In the simplest case this openness is represented by the three elliptical dots Vladimir's song has to recur to, but in general it is perhaps best described as the absence of narrative closure – for, assuming the last dog was finally buried and through an iconoclastic mishap of his canine companions the stone tablet of his tombstone shattered into pieces, thereby effectively ruling out the continuation of the narrative, then even the infinite dog song might come to an end by an act of narrative closure. These two features, recursivity and narrative openness (in the sense of a lack of narrative

---

ber of steps needed to arrive at a rule that produces all natural numbers is hence finite, the product created, the sequence of positive integers, is infinite.

39 Similarly, in generative linguistics recursion is seen as a "fundamental *property* of grammar, permitting a finite set of rules and principles to process and produce an infinite number of expressions" (Christiansen and MacDonald 2009: 127; see Mezey 2011: 15). By inserting linguistic constructions that adhere to (a finite number of) language rules, a sentence can be expanded potentially to infinity (see Christiansen and MacDonald 2009 for examples). This indefinite continuability becomes apparent once the underlying recursive rule can be ascertained.

closure), must be identifiable, one way or another, in all narrative structures deserving of Dällenbach's *réduplication à l'infini* label.[40]

This can be directly linked to the understanding of these structures as infinite through the Basic Metaphor of Infinity. The iterability and indefiniteness required in the source domain can be found in the recursivity and openness of such structures. In this regard it seems clear that the basis of each mise en abyme structure is an iteration of narrative levels. In practically all cases (save perhaps in radically experimental texts[41]) these narrative levels have a concrete beginning, a point at which they are narrated into being, and likewise a clear-cut ending, even though this need not mean narrative closure. This means each narrative level forms a discrete unit. In addition, in the vertical layering of levels that is typical of mise en abyme structures, each narrative level is also 'minimal', in the sense that a narrative level forms a basic structural unit that cannot be segmented into further narrative levels. This is the case as the levels of narrative are in such 'vertical' mise en abyme structures characterised by the "change of both (diegetic) level and speaker and/or addressee" (Pier 2014: par. 1). By definition, then, in such structures a new level requires and is brought into existence by a new speaker or addressee, that is, by an ontological shift in the communicative process. As a consequence, a narrative level cannot contain within itself such an ontological shift (which would already create the next narrative level) and is therefore minimal.

Since the narrative levels that constitute mise en abyme structures are both discrete and minimal, they form ideal stepping stones for the first conceptual metaphor identified by Lakoff and Núñez, "Indefinite Continuous Processes Are Iterative Processes". This conceptual metaphor accounts for the fact that a narrative structure that, as McHale puts it, stacks narrative levels "beyond a cer-

---

[40] Indeed, when Wolf uses the terms 'frequent' and 'endless' mise en abyme without further distinction and states that Vladimir's 'dog song' *insinuates* its own endless continuation (2008: 503), this can be explained by the presence of both a principle of recursion and narrative openness in most such 'frequent' mise en abyme structures.

[41] Again John Barth's "Frame Tale" (1988: 1–2) is an example of such an experimental text (see footnote 32 above). Due to the narrative's physical shape as a Möbius strip, which comes with an essentially circular form, there is no logical necessity and no clear indicator (other than habit conditioned through reading fairy tales) that suggests to begin the reading process with 'once upon a time'. Any beginning or ending of Barth's "Frame Tale" is wholly extratextual: it exists only in the reader. In other words, there is nothing in the physical reality of the medium of the narrative that tells a reader where to begin the story. Nevertheless, if a reader of "Frame Tale" begins reading with "once upon a time", then a potentially infinite self-recursive narrative is constructed that, just like Vladimir's 'dog song', is self-similar at every level (see Füredy 1989: 751; Breuer 1976: 228–229).

tain depth" is metaphorically understood as an indefinitely continuing structure of stacked levels. Indeed, upon closer scrutiny, from the point of view of conceptual metaphor theory the aspect of recursion identified by critics such as McHale or Füredy (1989: 750) as central to infinitely regressing narratives is relegated to the structural level – that is, recursion need not necessarily be identifiable at content level (as it would be in the case of Vladimir's song from *Waiting for Godot*); it suffices if the narrative structure, by virtue of the stacking of narrative levels, can be understood as a recursive pattern. The principle is just the same as in the sentence *John said the sentence over and over and over* or *It rained and rained*: instead of using syntactic means, such as the conjunction 'and', to allow a repetition that reduplicates a part of the preceding sentence, it is now repeated acts of narrating that conjoin narrative levels to create the Chinese box structure of diegetic levels that is commonly associated with mise en abyme structures, where the first-level diegesis contains the metadiegesis, which contains the meta-metadiegesis, and so on.[42] It is clear that the acts of narrating that engender such structures need not be identical at each level (as in Vladimir's song), but may vary considerably in their scope. The crucial function of the acts of narrating is the engendering of new narrative levels. Since the acts of narrating are discrete and iterated, so are the narrative levels themselves, and for this reason they form the initial stepping stone for Lakoff and Núñez's conceptual metaphor. In other words, the iteration of narrative levels in such cases is already a metaphor for the infinite continuation of the narrative process, transferring onto the mise en abyme structure potential infinity.

At this point the Basic Metaphor of Infinity in a further step of metaphorical conceptualisation then leads to the understanding of such mise en abyme structures as complete, but infinite entities, that is, as possessing the qualities of the actual infinite. This is because the "iterative step-by-step process" (Lakoff and Núñez 2000: 160) that is the source domain of the Basic Metaphor of Infinity is, as has been shown, already given in a mise en abyme structure. According to Lakoff and Núñez, the metaphorical process that finally arrives at actual infinity works as follows: "From a given state, produce the next state. From an initial state, the process produces intermediate resultant states. The metaphorical process has an infinity of such intermediate states and a metaphorical final, unique, resultant state" (2000: 160). This is precisely what happens in Dällenbach's *rédu-*

---

[42] There is no reason why this process of containment should break off after the meta-metadiegetic level (and in many 'Chinese box narratives' it does not break off this soon); indeed, it could continue potentially infinitely. The only thing needed at each (but the last) level is an act of narrating that engenders the subsequent diegetic level and thus induces an ontological shift in the communication.

plication à l'infini: the iteration of a finite number of discrete and minimal narrative levels is conceptualised through a first conceptual metaphor as indefinitely continuous sequence of narrative levels, and hence as potentially infinite narrative structure. This structure then consists of the "infinity of intermediate states" required as a basis for the addition of a resulting state through the Basic Metaphor of Infinity – the resulting state being, of course, actual infinity. Since Lakoff and Núñez stress that "the nature of the process is unspecified in the metaphor", and indeed the metaphor "covers any kind of process" (2000: 160), the transfer of the Basic Metaphor of Infinity from a mathematical understanding of infinity onto the understanding of narrative structures as infinite would seem perfectly acceptable. This is then, finally, how Dällenbach's infinite mise en abyme structure is conceptualised as actually infinite by a reader.

There remains, however, one last question that needs to be addressed in this context: Are then not all mise en abyme structures inherently infinite by these standards, since all of them allow for the construction of at least one iterating step (in the case of what Dällenbach calls *réduplication simple*) and all of them could then serve as the initial state that allows the two conceptual metaphors identified by Lakoff and Núñez to operate? If this were the case, the play within the play in *Hamlet* would lead into infinity in just the same way as Vladimir's 'dog song', or as any other instance of a narrative within a narrative. This seems counter-intuitive and is indeed at odds with all research into the phenomenon of mise en abyme. This is because such an approach would fail to distinguish between the fairly simple structure of a sentence like *John said the sentence over and over and over* and the by comparison much more complex narrative structure of a novel that stacks several narrative levels. However, since in conceptual metaphors the target domain is understood in the conceptual terms of the source domain – in this case, the iterating sequence of narrative levels provides the source for the entire textual structure to be understood as actually infinite –, these conceptual terms of the source domain need to be in some way marked so as to provide the basis for the conceptual transfer. It follows that if the stacking of narrative levels cannot be seen to be of an overtly repetitive kind (a narrating equivalent to *over and over and over*) then the conceptual metaphor, as it were, cannot gain traction. I therefore suggest that the content dimension of the narrative is always taken into account whenever its structure is understood to be infinite. The watershed here consists in textual markers that point towards a reflection of endlessness: a weak type thereof is the lack of narrative closure that implies the possibility of meaningful narrative progress beyond the textual boundaries; a stronger type is the thematisation of infinity at one or more of the narrative levels themselves. The *réduplication simple* of the play within the play in *Hamlet* possesses neither type, whereas Vladimir's 'dog song' may not contain any overt thematic references to infinity – it does, however, thematise death and a particular kind of textualised or narrativised afterlife, and hence immortality –, but due to its insistence on opening up ever new narrative levels incessantly refuses to grant narrative closure. This is the reason why, even though both constitute just a single embedding, "The Murder of Gonzaga" in *Hamlet* is not usually understood to imply the infinite continuation of fictional levels and therefore cannot serve as source for the Basic Metaphor of Infinity, whereas Vladimir's 'dog song' is immediately understood to do precisely this.[43] It is thus by virtue of conceptual metaphors, in particular the Basic Metaphor of Infinity, that a textual *structure*, namely a narrative mise en abyme structure, can be understood to be infinite, provided that structural recursivity can be inferred and textual openness prevails.

Although such *réduplications à l'infini* are structurally much more complex than simple repetitions of plot elements, they then fulfil a similar function in the context of fictions of infinity. They provide a basic pattern that may underlie such texts and allow for the Basic Metaphor of Infinity to come into operation in any reading of these texts, leading to understanding the texts themselves to be infinite. A clear example of this can be seen in my analysis of *Cloud Atlas* below (see ch. 4).

2.2.3 Infinite Intertextuality

An altogether different way in which infinity may enter a text through its structural properties is by means of intertextuality. As a critical concept, intertextual-

---

43 Another reason might be found in their respective functions: Genette (1980: 232–234) distinguishes the relationships between different diegetic levels according to the function the embedded narrative takes on in the context of the text as a whole. However, his distinction seems rather blunt. According to Genette's classification, not only the main action in *Hamlet* and its play within the play, but in fact the entirety of all mise en abyme structures feature a "thematic" relationship, i.e. "a relationship of contrast [...] or of analogy", between their diegetic levels (1980: 233). I suggest that there is a key difference, however. Whereas the thematic relationship in *Hamlet* is noticed by the characters and actively used – "The Murder of Gonzaga" is the catalyst that propels Hamlet into action after his uncle's reaction to the play finally convinces him of the latter's guilt – such an active impact on the action of the preceding diegetic level is certainly not the case with Vladimir's 'dog song'. In the case of infinite mise en abyme structures, the thematic relationship above all seems to fulfil the function of alerting the reader to the textual structure itself, and not to specifics of content – here it is then the structural analogy between the levels that stands out and points towards the overall potential infinity of the mise en abyme structure.

ity goes back to Julia Kristeva, who coined the term in her discussion of Mikhail Bakhtin's work on the dialogicity of the novel, which is generally seen as a precursor of theories of intertextuality (see Allen 2011: 2–3).[44]

While Bakhtin's notion of dialogicity focuses on the plurality of voices that find expression *within* a given novel and is therefore above all intratextual, Kristeva extends her concept of intertextuality to the interrelations between different texts (see Pfister 1985: 4–6). In her 1969 essay "Word, Dialogue and Novel", Kristeva argues that literary communication takes place along two axes, a 'horizontal' one, for the communication between writer and reader (or, to use Kristeva's term, "addressee"), and a 'vertical' one, along which a text establishes a communicative relation with other texts (Kristeva 1986 [1969]: 36–37). Crucially, these two axes intersect in each single literary word, since the addressee "is included within a book's discursive universe only as discourse itself" (1986: 37).[45] The addressee

> thus fuses with this other discourse, this other book, in relation to which the writer has written his own text. Hence horizontal axis (subject-addressee) and vertical axis (text-context) coincide, bringing to light an important fact: each word (text) is an intersection of word [sic] (texts) where at least one other word (text) can be read. [... A]ny text is constructed as a mosaic of quotations; any text is the absorption and transformation of another. The notion of *intertextuality* replaces that of intersubjectivity, and poetic language is read as at least *double*. (1986: 37)

Clearly, this doubleness, or multi-dimensionality, of literary texts implies their potential infinity along Kristeva's two axes of literary communication (see also Kristeva 1980). If along the vertical axis each word is in relation with other words in other literary texts, then these other texts themselves are 'absorptions and transformations' of (a further set of) texts, which themselves are 'mosaics of quotations', and so on. Since this holds true for "any text", the ensuing pattern of intertextuality is one of iteration and, grounded in the abstract 'rules' of the intertextual relation, recursion: each text, or even each word in each text, becomes a 'basis' that points toward the intertext it has absorbed; in this 'absorbed' text likewise each word functions as such a basis. The result is a *"regressus ad*

---

[44] For a good introduction to intertextual theory, see in particular Allen (2011) and Pfister (1985).

[45] In the context of an ethical reading inspired by Levinas, this notion of the discursivity of the reader seems problematic. In a reversal of the critique that can be levied against the act of reading or interpretation – that any reading is an appropriation of what is read, incorporating it into the reader's own horizon of sameness – one might criticise that, from this Kristevan perspective, any text devours its own readers and absorbs all readings into one textual horizon of sameness.

infinitum" of textual referentiality (Pfister 1985: 9). This doubleness of poetic texts implies the indefinite continuability of such texts, both where the deep structure – the 'strings' of relations to other texts along Kristeva's vertical axis – and the lateral structure – in the sense that each text may accommodate several intertexts and even each word may be an intersection of multiple 'parallel' intertexts – are concerned; metaphorically speaking this allows for width in depth.

Indeed, it becomes clear that again Lakoff and Núñez's Basic Metaphor of Infinity may serve to explain how intertextuality may be understood as an actually infinite textual phenomenon. The intertextual relation between any two texts constitutes a relation of embedding that fulfils Lakoff and Núñez's requirement of being a "discrete and minimal" basic unit (2000: 157). In fact, this relation of embedding that can be repeated *ad infinitum* is an "ordinary iterative process with an indefinite (though finite) number of iterations", has an initial ('text A') and a resultant ('text A intertextually refers to text B') state, and hence can constitute the source domain of the Basic Metaphor of Infinity (2000: 158). What follows, then, is that the conceptual mapping of infinity onto such structures is possible and that intertextual structures may be understood as actually infinite, as infinite texts, by virtue of the Basic Metaphor of Infinity.

However, just as with the understanding of mise en abyme structures as infinite, there are some reservations about the universal applicability of this process of metaphorical identification: to what extent do the intertextual references have to be marked in a text in order for the text to be understood as infinite by means of the Basic Metaphor of Infinity? Or is such an understanding of a text as infinite not even needed, because infinity is a quality all texts have? The latter position seems to follow from Kristeva, for whom intertextuality is a feature of all literary texts, which then implies that inherently all texts already possess the infinity of the intertextual. This view is echoed in the work of Roland Barthes, who distinguishes between the (graspable, monological, doxical, closed) 'work' and the 'text' and claims that "the Text cannot stop", i.e. its process of signification is unlimited, and that it accomplishes "an *irreducible* [...] plural" of meaning through its situatedness in an endless network of intertexts (1977a: 157, 159). For Barthes, then, the text is "taken up in an *open* network which is the very infinity of language, itself structured without closure" (Barthes 1977b: 126), and this again is a feature of all texts (but not of all works), since all texts are located in this network of intertextuality.

While this view has been widely accepted and is consistent with a poststructuralist philosophy of language, it raises the question what impact this has on the reading of a text. Infinite intertextuality may indeed be a quality of all texts, but this then also suggests that it does not stand out as something to be *read*, unless it were somehow emphasised within a text. This means that in order for the (inter)textual feature of infinity to attain meaning of its own (for the infinite to be understood as infinite), it needs to be marked, that is, a text needs to draw attention to its own plurality. For this reason structuralist and hermeneuticist approaches in the wake of Kristeva and Barthes have tended to narrow the scope of intertextuality to those cases that are (more or less) overtly traceable.[46] In this vein, Michael Riffaterre has pointed out that the meaning that a text acquires through its intertextuality is predominantly dependent on the reader's awareness of the intertextual relation (see Riffaterre 1978: 124–150; see also Middeke 2005a: 213). It follows that textual infinity attained through intertextuality as a structural feature implicated in the text's projection of signification is likewise dependent on readerly awareness. This means that in the context of a text attaining 'infinity' via the Basic Metaphor of Infinity, first and foremost the reader's identification of the initial state and its openness to repetition, the source domain of the conceptual metaphor, is required. In order to achieve this, a first intertextual relation and then, building on it, the principle of intertextual construction underlying the overall text must be identified. In other words, for the intertextual doubleness of the poetic text to serve as a source domain for the Basic Metaphor of Infinity – or far more generally for it to develop any impact on a reader rather than to merely exist as theoretical structural feature that is only accessible to a reader familiar with literary theory and its positions on intertextuality – it must first be perceived, if not actively recognised as a structural feature that permeates the text and is potentially iterable.

The intertextual relation thus needs to draw a certain measure of attention to itself and overtly present itself as a connection within the given text to other texts. Although it seems difficult to determine the precise degree of perceptibility various types of intertextual relations have, some basic patterns can nevertheless be established. Gérard Genette in his *Palimpsests* has provided a detailed overview of the varieties of transtextuality, a term which he defines as "all that sets the text in a relationship, whether obvious or concealed, with other texts" (1997: 1) and which he prefers over the term intertextuality. Transtextuality, then, ranges from the direct quotation, as an intertext with a (more or less) clearly identifiable source, to the architextual relationship that stems from genre ex-

---

[46] The overtness or degree of intertextuality can never be determined absolutely, but there are a number of textual indicators that may serve to foreground an intertextual relation (see below). For an overview of the differences between the broad textual theory of intertextuality as propagated by poststructuralists like Kristeva and Roland Barthes and the more descriptive approaches of the structuralists, see e.g. Kerler (2013: 23–46).

pectations and is rather more indirect and implicit in most cases. Between these two poles (in terms of the overtness of the intertextual relation) Genette places paratextuality, which establishes a relation in the text's marginalia, such as headings, epigraphs, footnotes, etc.; metatextuality, where a text is a comment on another text that may or may not be explicitly mentioned; and hypertextuality, in which a text is modelled on another text without being a commentary on it, as is the case with Virgil's *Aeneid* and Joyce's *Ulysses*, which Genette both describes as hypertexts of Homer's *Odyssey* (see 1997: 1–7). An example of the former types of transtextuality would be Levinas's essay "Ethics as First Philosophy" discussed in chapter 3 below. Here the translators Seán Hand and Michael Temple by changing the original French title "Justifications de l'éthique" (Levinas 1989a: 75) into "Ethics as First Philosophy" have added a paratextual reference to Descartes' *Meditations on First Philosophy*, a work that is both explicitly (intertextually) referenced by Levinas (1989a: 77) and a metatext on which Levinas comments. Genette's work on transtextuality, then, provides a framework to establish the type and overtness of the transtextual (or in Kristeva's sense 'intertextual') relation.

To determine the degree of intertextuality a given text showcases, Genette's types of transtextuality may be complemented with more general parameters, such as those suggested by Martin Middeke, who introduces the following six parameters of intertextuality (2005a: 216–217; see 2005b: 234–235): (1) self-reflexivity, or the overtly self-conscious, even metafictional use of intertextual references; (2) alteration, or the extent to which the intertext is transformed; (3) explicitness, i.e. the question whether intertextual traces are overt or whether they are "covered up" (2005a: 217); (4) reader-understanding, which asks whether readers are "meant to identify the intertextual relations opened up by the text and whether the meaning of a text varies according to the degree of reader-understanding" (2005a: 217); (5) density in/of adaptation, or the question of how frequent intertextual references are in a given text – the underlying understanding of intertextuality here is, in line with Riffaterre, a more pragmatic, reader-oriented one than Kristeva's, since rather than assuming each word to be intertextually linking to other texts, it requires a certain degree of reader-understanding; and (6) (lack of) structural limitation, which looks at whether or not, or perhaps rather to what degree, the text is part of a superstructure (a series, genre, publication format, etc.) that imposes rules on it. It is the realisation of these parameters in a text that contributes to the reader's identification of intertextuality as a central textual feature. Only if a text possesses a reasonably high degree of intertextuality can it serve as the source domain for the Basic Metaphor of Infinity. A text would then be understood as infinite on account of its intertextuality precisely when it possesses a degree of intertextuality (to be established in critical discourse with the help of Genette's work on transtextuality or parameters such as those suggested by Middeke) that has the potential to point beyond the text's own boundaries and towards its being part of an endless (inter)textual universe.

At the same time, in seeking to critically trace how precisely a text may emerge as source domain of the Basic Metaphor of Infinity careful treading is required. For, somewhat paradoxically, trying to establish the degree of intertextuality any given text possesses may lead to readings that tend to neglect the infinity of the intertextual and instead focus too unilaterally on the uncovering and study of (inter)textual sources. This has been pointed out by Jonathan Culler, who warns that

> [t]heories of intertextuality set before us perspectives of unmasterable series, lost origins, endless horizons; and [...] in order to work with the concept [of intertextuality as a term in literary criticism] we focus it – but that focusing may always, to some degree, undermine the general concept of intertextuality in whose name we are working. (1981: 111)

In attempting to 'focus' the concept of intertextuality, or a text's intertextual entanglements – and establishing a text's degree of intertextuality certainly is a type of such focusing –, there is then a risk of 'losing sight' of the overarching infinite structure that is created precisely through the focused intertext, but also necessarily lost in this single text at focus. This risk is entrenched in the critic's attempt to master the unmasterable. Crucially, this is the very same problem, only mirrored to the domain of the literary critic, that arises from attempting the representation of the infinite. The series of intertexts are unmasterable precisely because they are infinite. As such any search for textual origins, for an arché-text of sorts, or merely for the definitive scope of an intertextual reference, must end in a *regressus ad infinitum*, in a wild goose chase for a first text that the very notion of intertextuality, as understood by Kristeva or Barthes, renders absurd. This is not an approach I would like to take when looking at the ethical potential of intertextual infinity. What interests me is the link between intertextuality and literary representations of infinity that consists in the very unmasterability emerging from both, a quality that will be central to my reading of the phenomenon in terms of the ethics of the infinite (see also ch. 3.4).[47]

---

[47] Incidentally, "unmasterability" is a term Culler uses to describe literary theory: theory's unmasterability, for him, is grounded in its forever questioning nature, which "painfully" resists our "desire [for] mastery" (1997: 16). In their own way, as I hope to show, fictions of infinity are also forever questioning and for this precise reason ethical. Paraphrasing Levinas, one might say that they call into question the reader's spontaneity and their certainties (Levinas 1969: 43).

Overall, as far as the understanding of intertextuality as an aesthetic configuration of the infinite is concerned, then, it should be noted here that, while the original Kristevan poststructuralist notion sees intertextuality as a phenomenon that is *per se* infinite, for a text to be identified as infinite on account of its intertextuality requires an explicit marking of this intertextuality in the manner that has been discussed by structuralist scholars in the wake of Kristeva. Since the process of referring to other texts is always iterable (which is precisely the poststructuralist point about the infinity of intertextuality), and indefinitely so, as far as intertextuality is concerned in principle any text may serve as the source domain for the Basic Metaphor of Infinity. As generally speaking most readers will not think of every text they read as an infinite assemblage of quotations spanning the entire textual universe, intertextuality seems to be a good example of a case where the Basic Metaphor of Infinity only comes into operation when the context is clearly marked, for example through a plethora of overt references to other texts or an explicit thematisation of the phenomenon in the story. If this is the case, then intertextuality may turn out to be another aesthetic device that can lead readers to identify the structure of a text (in this case the referential structure) as infinite. My analysis of *Saturday* (ch. 6) may serve as a concrete example of how this can be achieved.

2.2.4 Infinite Perspective and Narrative Omniscience

A last example of the diverse ways in which infinity may enter the structure of a narrative is through an unlimited narrative perspective, specifically in some cases of heterodiegetic narration with zero focalisation or variable focalisation. While in principle the way in which such a narrative perspective may be understood as infinite is very similar to my other examples of structural features that may endow a text with infinity, the requirements as to the contextual markedness of infinity that are needed for the Basic Metaphor of Infinity to come into operation, are perhaps stricter in the case of what has been called omniscient narration: in order for a narrative perspective to be understood as infinite, I suggest, the narrative voice must be identified at the story level as transcendent, divine or following some principle of limitless construction.

What is commonly known as 'omniscient narration' in narratological terms is often described as the absence of restrictions on the narrator's perception, that is, as "aperspectivism" (Stanzel 1984) or narrative with "zero focalisation" (Genette 1980: 189). Since the narrator's perspective in these cases is then unlimited and being unlimited in turn is one of the key qualities of the infinite, the proximity of omniscient narration and infinity seems straightforward. Indeed, the basic conditions for the identification of such a narrative situation as infinite through the Basic Metaphor of Infinity can almost always be found: the perspectives of different characters that an omniscient narrator may occupy are minimal and discrete building blocks of an iterating pattern. The iteration in this pattern is precisely the 'jumping' from one perspective to another. If – and this is the point on which the infinity of omniscient narration hinges – there are enough indicators to point to an indefinite continuability of this changing of perspectives on to ever *new* perspectives, then such a text may indeed appear to have an infinite narrative perspective due to the Basic Metaphor of Infinity.

This can be seen, for example, in Alan Moore's *Jerusalem*, parts of which are narrated by a homodiegetic omnipresent and omniscient angelic narrator. In these parts, the narrator's omniscience and omnipresence is emulated by the narrative perspective quickly changing back and forth between a number of different focal characters, who live centuries apart and are shown at different stages of their lives (see Moore 2016: 807–826). The frequent rapid changes between different perspectives clearly constitute an iterative pattern that may serve as the source domain for the Basic Metaphor of Infinity. The understanding of *Jerusalem* as an infinite text is further corroborated by the nature of its narrative world, which thematises its infinity for example by its suspension of temporality in the world of the novel's heaven-like Upstairs. Even more pertinently, the narrative voice begins this passage by stressing its own omnitemporality and omnipresence – the voice describes its own status as "[n]ow always, even when it's then. Here always, even when it's there. Me always, even when I'm you" (2016: 807) – as well as its omniscience and immanence – "Seeing and being everything, never detached and never distant", it continues (2016: 807) – and even self-consciously reflects on its status as a text: "I know I am a text made only of black words. I know you are observing me. I know you, and I know your grandmother. I know the far threads of your family line reading me in a hundred years, reading me now, from left to right, from Genesis to Revelation" (2016: 808; see also 824). What the narrative voice is telling the reader here is then shown in the crossing between the perspectives of a plethora of different characters over the subsequent pages. This is the structural feature that renders the narrative perspective in this part of Moore's novel infinite. In this, the decisive aspect for the identification of the perspective as infinite is the narrative changing between a number of different perspectives against a backdrop, at the story level, that explicitly thematises infinity in some way.

In principle, this can not only be achieved through zero focalisation, but also through variable internal focalisation – i.e. the switching of perspective between characters without the presence of an overarching 'omniscient' perspective that encompasses more at once than any single character may see or know (see

Genette 1980: 189–190) –, as both make the switching between perspectives possible. As this switching is an integral part of the aesthetic configuration of narratives that are presented in this way and as in particular heterodiegetic narration with zero focalisation is a very common phenomenon in novels throughout the eighteenth and nineteenth centuries – and, after appearing to be out of fashion for most of the twentieth century, is making its return, as Paul Dawson (2013) argues – it seems to me that in the case of narrative perspective, the context of infinity needs to be particularly clearly marked in order for this structural feature of a narrative to be understood as infinite. For it seems clear that despite the intuitive connection between omniscience and infinity, there is no reason to think of a text like Fielding's *Tom Jones* as infinite only because of its omniscient narrator. The key ingredient to understanding a narrative perspective as infinite, rather than just a form of multiperspectivity within limits, is then the context of the story that is presented in this way.

In fact, this strikes at the heart of the critical debate around narrative omniscience: the term 'omniscient narration' has been in use for a long time, but has come under scrutiny for a number of perceived shortcomings. Jonathan Culler claims that the concept "conflates and confuses several different factors that should be separated if they are to be well understood" (2004: 22).[48] Central to Culler's critique is the "analogy between God and the author", which he identifies as the "basis of 'omniscience'" and rejects on the grounds that divine omniscience, provided that such a thing exists, is of a different kind than the knowledge of an author about their work (2004: 23). This is also pertinent to the understanding of 'omniscience' as a kind of infinite perspective: if the perspective that is provided to readers by a heterodiegetic narrator with zero focalisation is taken to be the author's – Stanzel's term 'authorial narrator' for what is essentially this type of narrative perspective certainly suggests as much –, then the author may perhaps know all about her narrative (and be omniscient with regard to the diegesis), but there is no reason why her knowledge should extend beyond that (see Culler 2004: 23–25). The all (*omni-*) of omniscience in this sense is very much a finite rather than an infinite quantity.

Most narratologists have tended to agree to at least some extent with the view expressed by Culler and it is a point of considerable contention in accounts of omniscient narration to what extent such narrators are in fact limited and how limitations may be motivated. Limitation here not only applies to the author's or

---

[48] Giving a comprehensive account of the state of the debate would go far beyond what is possible here. For an overview of Culler's criticism and Meir Sternberg's (2007) defence of the concept of narrative omniscience, see Dawson (2013: 49–54), who takes up an intermediary position, but wants to revive rather than discard the concept.

narrator's knowledge, but also to the extent to which they choose to publicise this knowledge in the literary text – knowing it all does not necessarily entail telling it all, or telling it all at once, and there are numerous examples of supposedly omniscient narrators imposing restrictions on what information they provide in the narrative. Thus, Wilhelm Füger has argued that the limitations on omniscient narrators are so frequent that "there is no such thing as a fully omniscient narrator and that this spectral figure may only be a construct invented by literary theorists" (2004: 287; see Dawson 2013: 31).

All of this seems to make the concept of narrative omniscience very problematic when it comes to structural infinity in narrative. Even if a number of different perspectives are presented in an iterating fashion, the number of theoretically possible perspectives the narrator might occupy is severely limited by the parameters of the fictional world. Unless, that is, there are clear indicators that the scope of the narrative perspective goes beyond the perspectives of a limited number of focaliser characters. This can only be established at the story level, for example through a narrator who is a transcendental or divine being, as is the case in both Moore's *Jerusalem* and Banville's *The Infinities* (see ch. 7), or through the self-conscious thematising of multiperspectivity and the infinity of the narrative universe, which can also be found in *The Infinities*. Compared with my other examples of structural features that may be identified as infinite, the narrative perspective then seems to require a relatively high degree of contextual charging, that is, a markedly 'infinite' element at story level that pertains to the narrative voice or to the narrative world, for such an identification to be feasible. Any reading that seeks to understand a text's narrative perspective as infinite in this fashion would need to pay heed to these elements at story level particularly carefully. Despite this restriction, I have decided to include this phenomenon here since it is relevant to my discussion of *The Infinities* and beyond that, as my reading of Banville's novel will show, may unfold a powerful performative potential in texts that engage in critical epistemic self-reflection.

2.3 Catachresis: Infinite Textuality

All of the above examples then are cases where a text's structure contains an indefinitely iterating element and so, given an apposite context, may be understood as infinite through the conceptual mechanism that Lakoff and Núñez have called the Basic Metaphor of Infinity. This structural infinity in a next step can be said to be transferred from a text's structure to the text itself – only then is it possible to speak of an infinite text. It is the metonymic relationship between textual structure and textuality, similar perhaps to the metonymic relation between container and contained, that allows for this transfer of the quality of infinity onto the text itself. A text with an infinite structure thus metonymically is also an infinite text.[49]

To be more precise, this is not just a metonymic relation but in this particular case, where infinity comes into play, a catachrestic one. In rhetoric, catachresis is understood as the use of an inappropriate term in lieu of another – in the words of Renaissance grammarian John Hoskins, it is "the expressing of one matter by the name of another which is incompatible with it, and sometimes clean contrary" (Hoskins 1935: 11, qtd. in Berger 2015: 126n4). This semantic 'abuse' – this is how the term catachresis literally translates – can take on different forms: firstly, there is a fairly common type of catachresis that is caused by the lack (*inopia*) of an exisiting term in language for a new, as yet unnamed, concept. For lack of a better name, as it were, this new concept is then described with an existing but strictly speaking improper term, as for example in computer 'mouse' (see Chrzanowska-Kluczewska 2011: 39; Neumann 1998; Lausberg 1990: 288–291). Secondly, catachresis also denotes a poeticised rhetorical device, namely the yanking together in one image of strongly conflicting or discordant source and target domains, as in the phrase "blind mouths" from Milton's *Lycidas* (see Chrzanowska-Kluczewska 2011: 41–42). Going beyond these two traditional definitions of catachresis, Elżbieta Chrzanowska-Kluczewska identifies a third type of catachresis that operates as a metatrope at the level of the entire text (see 2011: 47–49).

When it comes to the catachrestic genesis of an infinite text, all three types of catachresis are pertinent. In a broad sense, the identification of a text as infinite is a catachresis caused by *inopia*, by the lack, indeed the impossibility, of an already existing mode of representation of the infinite. Textual structures that may elicit the identification of a text as infinite via the Basic Metaphor of Infinity thus are images for the infinite, for something that does not, *cannot*, have an image. Since the 'image', that is, the textual structure, and the represented, infinity, are also obviously and necessarily discordant to the extreme – the structure is *de facto* finite, but represents that which it can never be, the infinite –

---

[49] This relationship is metonymic not just in the conventional sense of metonymy, but also as propounded by conceptual metaphor theorists, who see metonymy as "a cognitive process in which one conceptual entity, the vehicle, provides mental access to another conceptual entity, the target, within the same domain [...]" (Kövecses 2002: 145). In this case the infinite textual structure is the vehicle providing access to the understanding of the text itself, the target, as infinite; vehicle and target here both belong to the domain of the work of literature.

such a structure is a combination of incompatibles, of polar opposites, and hence clearly catachrestic.

The most interesting aspect of this catachresis of infinity is, however, the metatropical. Chrzanowska-Kluczewska distinguishes tropes, including catachresis, according to their textual scope into microtropes, macrotropes and metatropes (see 2004; 2011). She describes as microtropes those typical objects of traditional rhetorical analysis that are locally operating at sentence level – for example, Robert Burns's "my Luve's like a red, red rose" is a simile operating as a microtrope. Macrotropes are "big semantic figures" that "are capable of organizing considerably longer fragments of a text" (2004: 67), such as extended similes or extended metaphors. Finally, a metatrope is

> a 'self-aware' and auto-reflexive figure, a figure that distances itself in relation to a particular text or particular texts, a figure that is capable of 'talking about itself', about figures subordinate to it, about the language whose part it is but which it can transcend in its own way, and finally about all that exists beyond the boundaries of language: both in reality and in the sphere of the imaginary. (2004: 72)

As opposed to macrotropes that are identifiable as structuring devices at the level of the text itself, metatropes characterise entire genres or periods and hence a larger body of texts: "Figures achieve their metatropological status the moment they recede into the tacit metalevel, at which they have to be processed by a sort of rhetorical inferring mechanism, part of which can be dubbed the **stylistic/literary competence**" (2004: 78). Chrzanowska-Kluczewska lists fourteen metatropes altogether, one of which is catachresis (see 2004: 73–77; 2011: 47–49). As a metatrope, catachresis is "based on various kinds of logical deviance", leading to a "cleavage in discourse (marked by areas of incongruity, clashes of ideas, etc.) [that] reveals the essence of catachresis to be that of a *fundamental incoherence*" (2011: 48, 49).[50]

---

[50] For this reason, as Chrzanowska-Kluczewska points out, metatropical catachresis is closely associated with Michel Foucault's concept of heterotopia. Foucault first uses the term heterotopia in his preface to *The Order of Things*, where, after reading a passage from Borges, he discovers "a worse kind of disorder than that of the *incongruous*, the linking together of things that are inappropriate" (1970: xviii; see Chrzanowska-Kluczewska 2011: 48–49). He goes on to describe heterotopias, the sites of this inappropriate linking, as "disturbing, probably because they secretly undermine language" (1970: xix), which indeed echoes the qualities of catachresis. Interestingly, Foucault elsewhere speaks of the mirror as a link between utopian and heterotopian sites, for the mirror is both a utopian "placeless place" and a heterotopian place exerting "a sort of counteraction on the position that I occupy", since it makes it possible to "discover my absence from the place where I am since I see myself over there [in the mirror]" (Foucault 1984). This evokes Dällenbach's description of the mise en abyme as 'mirror narrative': it is pre-

Catachrestic representation, then, essentially touches on problems very similar to those of the representation of the infinite: it is mired in the incompatibility, the "fundamental incoherence", of its constituents. Where representations of infinity are concerned, this incompatibility is one that arises between the object and the medium of representation. In the case of catachresis, the scope the incompatible elements may take on is considerably wider, since catachresis as a rhetorical device means the yanking together of two conflicting images, or objects of representation, into one image, allowing for a broad range of constituent images to make up the catachresis. Nevertheless, if the finitude of any medium of representation and its inevitable clash with any attempt at representing the infinite within this finite medium is considered, representations of the infinite, and particularly all instances where a text itself may be identified as 'infinite', are necessarily catachrestic. In fact, I would like to suggest that in 'infinite' texts, catachresis is at work in two ways: In single novels catachresis operates as a macrotrope that consists in the identification of the finite text as infinite, while across what I call fictions of infinity catachresis is a metatrope that is constituted in the allocation of infinite textuality to the finite medium of any given literary text and in the unattainability and/or impossibility of the ensuing textual status.

* * *

As far as the questions asked at the beginning of this chapter are concerned, I can then give the following preliminary answers: First, the way in which a reader may become aware of infinity as a structural feature in narrative is, I contend, not substantially different from the way in which infinity is conceptualised elsewhere. Following George Lakoff and Rafael E. Núñez's take on conceptual metaphor theory in connection with the conceptualisation of mathematical entities, infinity is generally conceptualised as an indefinitely iterating process. With regard to a narrative structure, this means that a structure that breaks down the continuum of the infinite into an indefinitely iterating sequence is precisely the kind of structure that Lakoff and Núñez have identified as the source domain of a conceptual metaphor that realises the metaphorical completion of such indefinite iterations as actually infinite entities, the Basic Metaphor of Infinity. It is only through such metaphorical identification that a text's structure may be considered infinite.

---

cisely in the *réduplication à l'infini* that the aporetic, simultaneously heterotopian and utopian textual encounter with alterity may be found.

In answer to the second question, if indefinite iteration is the central feature of the source domain of the Basic Metaphor of Infinity, then any narrative whose structure contains an indefinitely iterating element may theoretically lead to the understanding of a text as infinite via this conceptual metaphor. Such indefinite iterations at a structural level can be achieved by relatively simple devices, such as the repetition of plot elements or mere phrases, but, as the examples discussed above (and in greater detail in the following chapters) show, also through more elaborate structural features. Importantly, the mere presence of an element of iteration in a text is generally speaking not enough for its structure to be understood as infinite. For this identification via the Basic Metaphor of Infinity to be triggered, I argue, such structures must be marked as infinite in the first place, that is, there must be some further indication of the infinity of the structure. Such an indication can be the occurrence of infinity at the story level or simply an excessive accumulation of the structural features that create the indefinite iteration within the text. If coupled with such indicators, structural elements of indefinite iteration within a text may indeed account for the identification of the structure as infinite.

A final step is that from textual structure to text itself. The aesthetic elements discussed in this chapter all contribute to the structure of a text and, given the right context, may lead to the text's structure being perceived as infinite. Since there is, I argue, a close metonymic relationship between a text and its structure, the structural infinity may then be transferred onto the text itself, resulting in infinite textuality. Finally, as this is strictly illogical, resulting in an impossible entity – the infinite text – the entire process of understanding a text to be infinite should best be described as catachresis. It is through this conceptual catachresis that readers may understand certain texts to be actually infinite entities.

3 Levinas and the Ethical Aporia of Infinity

Fictions of infinity then comprise texts that are perceived as actually infinite as the result of a metaphorical understanding of their structure as infinite. Since this is a central element of the aesthetics of such texts, the question arises of what further function(s) such textual infinity may have. It is my suggestion that infinity endows such texts with an ethical dimension and gives them a particular ethical appeal that disrupts any reading of these texts. How exactly do fictions of infinity become ethical, though, and why should they exert a particular ethical appeal in the first place? An answer to this question may be found in the work of Emmanuel Levinas, whose philosophical writing continues to have a strong influence on the European strand of ethical criticism (see Womack 2015). Infinity plays a crucial role in his ethical philosophy, to the extent that it appears in the title of his first major work, *Totality and Infinity* (Levinas 1969 [1961]). It is precisely because of this central role of the infinite in Levinas's work, I suggest, that a tentative link from Levinasian ethics to fictions of infinity can be established. This chapter seeks to outline this connection: after tracing Levinas's thoughts on ethics and representation as well as on the structure of the ethical encounter it attempts to reconcile Levinas, who at least in his earlier work expressed great scepticism towards art, with fiction and its aesthetic power – which, I will argue, in the case of fictions of infinity is also an ethical power. Ethical language in Levinas's sense, the argument goes, is a catachrestic language, which establishes a link to the catachrestic structure of fictions of infinity.

As Simon Critchley points out, the dominant idea in Levinas's work is "his thesis that ethics is first philosophy, where ethics is understood as a relation of infinite responsibility to the other person" (2002: 6). This notion is defining for Levinas, because when he describes "ethics as first philosophy" (1989a), this is in opposition to the tradition in Western philosophy to presuppose Being, that is, to consider the question of Being, or ontology, as the fundamental question of philosophy, and in particular it is in opposition to Heidegger's fundamental ontology (see Critchley 2002: 6–12; Levinas 1996d; see also Bergo 1999: 37–54). For Levinas, it is then not Being that is fundamental and thus gives structure to all philosophical thought, but ethics. As a consequence, ethics is prior to, not part of, the ontological relation. Crucially, ethics for Levinas is tied to alterity. In *Totality and Infinity*, he defines ethics as the "calling into question of my spontaneity by the presence of the Other" (1969: 43) – importantly, the French term *autrui* used by Levinas for 'the other' exclusively refers to another person (see Critchley 2002: 11). This means that the presence of the other, from which the ethical relation arises, is prior to ontology – a somewhat puzzling notion that has to be seen in the light of the role of the other in Levinas and of his understanding of ontology: for Levinas, ontology is the "general term for any relation to otherness that is reducible to comprehension or understanding" (Critchley 2002: 11); in this sense, ontology may be best described as "metaphysics of comprehension" (Eaglestone 2004: 184). As a process, cognition, or knowing and understanding, ineluctably erases alterity, because through cognition all otherness is assimilated into terms of sameness, into the terms of what is already known and therefore into an ontological relation of totality (see Levinas 1969: 42). Simply put, "If one could possess, grasp, and know the other, it would not be other" (Levinas 1989d: 51). Knowing the other thus would mean grasping, and hence appropriating and ultimately erasing, all their[51] alterity.

3.1 Infinity and Alterity

Such an erasure of alterity cannot, however, happen with regard to the human other whom we encounter in the ethical relation. As ethics for Levinas is an exposure to the other that is prior to any ontology, the other here is *not* reducible to comprehension. The alterity of the other is absolute, opening a gap that cognition cannot bridge, or creating a "'curvature' of intersubjective space [... that] expresses the relation between human beings" (1969: 291; see Robbins 1999: 5). It is in Levinas's attempt to describe this absolute alterity that infinity comes into play. For Levinas the relation to the other – of whom we can think and write, but whose otherness we cannot comprehend because we meet it before ontology can make it into the same and thus accessible to cognition – has precisely the same structure as the idea of the infinite that Descartes outlines in his third meditation (2013: 48–73).

There, the idea of the infinite is key to Descartes's proof of the existence of God. The argument runs as follows: Based on the premise that no effect can be greater than its cause, Descartes posits that every idea must ultimately derive

---

[51] Levinas consistently uses the masculine pronoun forms when referring to the other in the ethical relation. This, however, does not mean that the other must be male – in fact, one might argue that categories of masculinity or femininity are ontological categories of sameness and for this reason simply do not apply to the pre-ontological encounter with the other. Nevertheless, Levinas's practice of gendering the language of his ethics has attracted feminist criticism. Indeed, it undeniably seems to suggest that "the crucial ethical experience is that of the male subject" (Gibson 1999: 29). To avoid giving this impression, I will use the gender-neutral 'they' here. For an overview of gender roles in Levinas and feminist responses to Levinas, see for example Sandford (2002).

from a cause that has formal reality equal to or greater than the reality of the idea (see 2013: 59). Thus, every idea must have a 'real' antecedent that causes it. However, as I can through cogitation establish my own reality, is it not possible that I, or my mind, then be the cause of all my ideas? Descartes concedes that such a solipsistic universe is thinkable with regard to most ideas, and certainly with regard to all "ideas of corporeal things", which crucially are all limited in all of their properties (2013: 61). The only idea that does not fall into this category is the idea of "a substance that is infinite" (2013: 63) and whose qualities have no bounds – the name Descartes gives to this substance is 'God'. As the idea of the infinite must originate from a cause that is equal to or greater than this idea, it cannot originate from a finite human being, for "it is in the nature of the infinite not to be grasped by a finite being" (2013: 65). Descartes' proof, then, relies on the tenet that the infinite is entirely alien and inconceivable to human thought, but, as the idea of the infinite does exist in human beings, it must originate from elsewhere, an elsewhere that is itself infinite (for its formal reality must be equal to or greater than the idea it causes) – and this infinite other being is God.

The reason for the relatively great attention given to this proof here is that Levinas points to the Cartesian idea of the infinite in order to explain our relation with the other (see 1987b: 53–54; 1969: 48–49; 1985: 92).[52] As Levinas argues,

> the idea of infinity is exceptional in that its ideatum surpasses its idea. In it the distance between idea and ideatum is not equivalent to the distance that separates a mental act from its object in other representations. The abyss that separates a mental act from its object is not deep enough for Descartes not to say that the soul can account for the ideas of finite things by itself. The intentionality that animates the idea of infinity is not comparable with any other; it aims at what it cannot embrace and is in this sense the infinite. [... W]e can say that the alterity of the infinite is not cancelled, is not extinguished in the thought that thinks it. In thinking infinity the I from the first *thinks more than it thinks*. Infinity does not enter into the *idea* of infinity, is not grasped; this idea is not a concept. The infinite is the radically, absolutely, other. (1987b: 54)

The movement of thought which, paradoxically, exceeds itself in engaging in the idea of infinity is thus a way of knowing without grasping, for the idea of infinity is possible to be thought without grasping its *ideatum*. It is hence an *incomplete* knowing of that which is other: in the idea of infinity, it becomes possible to think alterity without 'cancelling' it in the act of cognition, that is, without subjecting it to the ontology of sameness. This is crucial as it gives a structure to the

---

[52] It should be noted that the analogy between Levinas and Descartes and the way the latter uses infinity to prove the existence of God is a strictly formal one, where "Levinas *transforms* the argument by substituting the Other for God" (Critchley 2007: 59).

pre-ontological ethical encounter with alterity, which must equally be irreducible to comprehension and therefore resist ontological appropriation in/through knowledge. Hence, the ethical relation to the other is described by infinity because in Levinas's ethics that precedes ontology the alterity of the other, just like the Cartesian infinite, cannot be grasped, and yet we encounter the other, just like infinity, in our thought. Infinity here describes the absoluteness of alterity – both are equally ungraspable. It is in this way that one of Descartes' *Meditations on First Philosophy* provides Levinas with the idea of the infinite and its unique structure that is the key to his conception of *ethics* as first philosophy.

This abstract structural affinity does not, however, do justice to the other we meet in the ethical encounter. It might even cause alterity to be hidden behind a cloud of abstraction. For this reason, Levinas introduces the concept of the face, which can be understood as "the deformalization or concretization of the idea of infinity" (Levinas 1969: 50), or variously as "the concrete figure in which the notion of alterity acquires its meaning" (Robbins 2001: 115). It describes "[t]he way in which the other presents himself, exceeding *the idea of the other in me*" (Levinas 1969: 50). In particular, we first encounter the alterity of the other in beholding their face. Levinas poignantly describes the face as naked skin, unprotected and uncovered, which is why the revelation of the face is the revelation of the other as vulnerable and destitute (see 1989a: 83) – an outright "epiphany" (1987b: 55) that coincides with an appeal that goes forth from the face of the other to the I. This appeal, or rather demand, cannot be evaded; it consists in a becoming aware of the vulnerability and of the "extreme precariousness of the Other" (Levinas 1996a: 167), a 'recognition without cognition' that demands a response. For this reason, as it cannot be left unattended, Levinas even calls it an imposition (see 1986: 352; see also Robbins 1999: 9). It is an encroaching of the other on the I that takes on the form of a pure expression or exteriority – to an extent that Levinas indeed proclaims, "[t]he epiphany of the face is wholly language" (1987b: 55). This is not to be understood as a language that "receive[s] a signification by relation to something", but as a "first instance of signification", as the face's plea that comes before any categories and transcends any categories by which it could be understood or within which it might signify (1969: 261) – it is "wholly language", but a language that precedes ontology, and hence not a language anyone can actively speak to communicate.[53] It is a language of

---

[53] In the way in which Levinas describes both the face and the idea of infinity, the structural parallel between infinity and the face can again be seen. Where in *Totality and Infinity*, he writes that "[t]he face signifies by itself; its signification precedes *Sinngebung*" (1969: 261), he uses an almost identical formulation to describe the idea of infinity in "Transcendence and Height", a paper he gave shortly after the publication of *Totality and Infinity* and in which he argues

passivity, in which the face expresses itself in its destitution. In this epiphanic moment, the face "speaks" to me, addressing me with the clear imperative "thou shalt not kill" (1985: 87).

An ethical relationship is established that is marked by its asymmetry: in it, the other is at my mercy, calling for my responsibility, calling into question my spontaneity, and it is I who am yielding to the demands of the other I encounter in beholding their face. In this epiphanic encounter, the face reveals itself, paradoxically, in its commanding destitution as a vulnerable master, for the "thou shalt not kill" is a powerful command spoken from a position of nakedness and destitution (see Levinas 1985: 89). It is then through this imposition that emerges from the face of the other that the ethical encounter with the other presents itself to us as the "ethical exigency to be responsible for the other" (1995: 189). Since the other is infinitely other, in encountering them, "the subject relates itself to something that exceeds its relational capacity. This is what Levinas calls *'le rapport sans rapport'*, the relation without relation" (Critchley 2007: 57). Such a 'relationless relation' is precisely the structure of the idea of infinity: it allows the self "to think more than it thinks", to respond to the demand the other makes without grasping and so effacing their alterity. As the responsibility this relation calls for is not one I can choose to forgo, the encounter with alterity imposes restrictions on my freedom and spontaneity (see Claviez 2008: 117). This is why for Levinas ethics is a "putting into question of the ego" (Critchley 2002: 15) and of its attempts to absorb alterity. The face of the other is the concretised figure in which the enigma of the ethical encounter is encapsulated.

Crucially, the meaning of the face is again not to be grasped in ontological categories. The reason is that the face as the concrete idea of infinity is infinitely other, and from its infinite alterity it must follow that the face is irreducible to cognition (see 1985: 85–86). When Levinas describes the face as "signification without context" (1985: 86), he means that the face is removed from ontological, or, for that matter, ontic, relations: its pure signification transcends such categories which are only "plastic forms" obscuring the face (1989a: 82; see also Duncan 2001: 19). In fact then, the meaning of the face is the "proximity of the other" and the "extreme exposure" to the vulnerability of the other (1989a: 82, 83). Awareness of the face's expression coincides with awakening to the face's demand not to kill, a radical call for peace. Notably, the peace demanded by the face is one that relies on alterity, or rather on the unquestioning, untotalising acceptance of alterity, as an act of murder, forbidden by the "thou shalt not kill", is

---

that when "the Infinite unseats its idea", it does so through "a signification that precedes any *Sinngebung*" (1996b: 19). Both the face and the idea of infinity exceed the scope of thought.

the most extreme way to eradicate alterity (see Levinas 1996a: 165–166). The proximity of the other and the concomitant imposition of their destitution on the I result in a call for peace that characterises the ethical relation according to Levinas: "The face as the extreme precariousness of the other. Peace as awakeness to the precariousness of the other" (1996a: 167). Infinity is central to this ethical vision as it is the only idea that allows for thinking and embracing – but, crucially, not assimilating into an ontology of sameness – the radical alterity of the other.

It should be seen in this context when Levinas states that the "thought that is awake to the face of the other human is not a thought of …, a representation, but straightaway a thought for …, a nonindifference for the other" (1996a: 166). The other in the ethical relation does not become an object of thought or of representation, but through the dejection of their face elicits an unrepresentable responsibility. The problem with representation here is that it is intrinsically tied to ontology, as any act of representation is not just an act of signifying, but must also have a signified rooted in an ontological order.

For this reason, Levinas's ethics raises pertinent questions with regard to literature and literary criticism, but certainly also with regard to philosophy as a system of thought and exchange of ideas – the interrelations between these modes are complex and their boundaries are fuzzy: philosophy may be seen as one kind of literature, while literary criticism may take on the form of one kind of philosophy, and all three modes often enough engage in self-critique. If, now, the ethical response to encountering the face of the other, as indeed the encounter itself, is one that cannot be captured in representation – which is also one of the key properties of infinity – then Levinas's own work is in the paradoxical situation that it addresses (and thus represents) precisely this unrepresentable encounter. The same holds true for literature, criticism or any philosophical text that attempts to approach the alterity inherent in the ethical encounter. How can these systems of thought that must necessarily establish discourses reliant on representation and that can themselves only exist in and through representation ever express alterity? Would not any such expression of alterity immediately subject it to the diktat of ontological sameness required by the semiotics of representation?

3.2 Saying and Said

In Levinas's second major work, *Otherwise than Being* (1981 [1974]), the question of language and its ramifications with regard to the ethical relation is given greater attention (on Levinas and language, see for example Wyschogrod 2002 and Llewelyn 2002). This is a reaction to Jacques Derrida's discussion of Levinas's ethics in "Violence and Metaphysics", a long "essay on the thought of Emmanuel Levinas" in which Derrida addresses the problem of language in Levinas (2005 [1967]; see Critchley 1994 and 2002: 17). Derrida points out that, while writing about the ethical relation that precedes ontology and so refuting the primacy of Heideggerian ontology, Levinas still employed language and that this language of Levinas's, the formal discourse of philosophy, is necessarily a language of ontology – it seeks to be understood, establish propositions, etc. (for an outline of Derrida's argument, see Eaglestone 1997: 130–136; on the similarities and differences between Derrida and Levinas, see also McNally 2014: 87–105). As Derrida puts it,

> the attempt to achieve an opening toward the beyond of philosophical discourse, by means of philosophical discourse, which can never be shaken off completely, cannot possibly succeed *within language* [...] except by *formally* and *thematically* posing *the question of the relations between belonging and the opening*, the *question of closure*. (2005: 138).

The fundamental problem with Levinas's ethics identified by Derrida is then the apparent impossibility to escape the framework of language, which is already an ontological frame. Notably, the way out of this dilemma Derrida suggests is posing a question – not giving an answer, which would merely reaffirm the ontological frame or at best replace it with a new one – and it is a question about closure, and hence finitude. The notion of closure, as used by Derrida here, is precisely the thematisation of this problem of a 'self-defeating' language in Levinas's ethics, for it "is the double refusal both of remaining within the limits of the tradition and of the possibility of transgressing that limit" (Critchley 1992: 20). Closure thus describes the problem of Levinas's language.

Levinas reacted to Derrida's critique by introducing the distinction between 'saying' and the 'said' that is central to *Otherwise than Being*. The said is a content, establishing meaning through identification: in the said of a word, the identification of "'this *as* that'" (Levinas 1981: 35) takes place. It is the signified in a process of signification, that which carries the meaning for communication to meaningfully function. As such it is an expression of ontology, "a statement, assertion or proposition of which the truth or falsity can be ascertained" (Critchley 2002: 18). In contrast, saying is the act of address itself that constitutes the communicative act; it is signifying, but a signifying of a pure form that comes without signification, as Levinas stresses (see 1981: 48).[54] At its core, "Saying is com-

---

[54] There may be a certain affinity between saying and what linguists term phatic communication, but saying goes beyond phatic speech acts since it is a prerequisite for all communication.

munication, [...] but as a condition for all communication, as exposure" (Levinas 1981: 48). This exposure, the exposure the I experiences when responding to the other, is described by Levinas in extreme terms – as a "denuding of denuding", as suffering and vulnerability, as "an exposure to expressing, and thus to saying, thus to giving" (1981: 49, 50) –, which is reminiscent of Levinas's description of the destitution of the face of the other. In my response to the other, the saying is "my inability to resist the other's approach" (Critchley 2002: 18). As such, saying is not subjected to the ontology of the said, as it forms part of the pre-ontological ethical relation. Saying is the unconditional opening up to the other, "the performative stating, proposing or expressive position of myself facing the other" (Critchley 2002: 18; see 1994: 649). In fact, saying *is* Levinas's eponymous 'otherwise than being', as its "disinterestedness" in the essence of that which is thematised in the said leads to an opening up towards the other, because the saying is a reduction of signification's "'one-for-the-other'" into a "'for-the-other'" (Levinas 1981: 50) and so moves beyond the essence of being, as Levinas's title further suggests.

However, in language that is removed from this primordial ethical situation, the saying is drowned out by the ontological facticity of the said. This is due to the primacy of ontology in our everyday discourse, where the saying is reduced to the "enunciation of the said" (1981: 43). Indeed, it is difficult to imagine any utterance in which the saying dominates over the said, in which the address, or the fact that it is uttered, is more important than the content, particularly in written language, where through the setting down in writing of a text an ontological object is created and the saying loses much of its immediacy of address. Nevertheless, the saying as the turning to the other, the signifying in language, is a constitutive element of speech and cannot be wholly effaced by the said. It remains, as Critchley puts it, as the "nonthematizable ethical residue of language that escapes comprehension, interrupts ontology and is the very enactment of the movement from the same to the other" (2002: 18; see also 1992: 7).

In distinguishing between the saying and the said as elements of speech, the problem of the representation of the ethical encounter in literature, criticism and philosophy takes on a clearer shape: in these modes of written discourse, the said quite naturally prevails. But as the said establishes ontological identification and the ethical encounter with the other is pre-ontological and therefore in its originary state not yet a theme in language, writing about the ethical relation endows its pure saying with a said and thus subjects it to the ontological relation. Alphonso Lingis describes this an act of dissimulation of the pre-thematic ethical encounter in the thematic philosophical discourse that in attempting to lay it bare must necessarily veil it in thematic language – an irresolvable dilemma (see Lingis 1981: xxxvii). In other words, a "betrayal" (Levinas 1981: 6) takes place in any such act of representation, as the structure of ethical responsibility can only ever be found in the saying, but the nature of representation must turn the saying into a said in the very instance of representation (see Lingis 1981: xxxvii; Claviez 2008: 128). As Lingis puts it in his introduction to *Otherwise than Being*,

> The very sentences of this book – thematic, synchronic time, systematic language, constantly making the verb *to be* intervene in phrases that profess to express what is antecedent to the work of being – can only be a continual transposition, and dissimulation, of the prethematic alterity [...] which these phrases mean to put forth. What they mean to translate into a text is always betrayed, in a translation always unfaithful to the pre-text. But it is only thus that they can be said. And the saying cannot be utterly obliterated under the said. It is also conveyed nonetheless in this unfaithful text. (Lingis 1981: xxxvii)

Once more, then, the problem of the representation of infinity emerges as the root of this betrayal: The pre-thematic infinite alterity is made a theme of in the necessarily finite philosophical discourse that hence attempts to contain that which cannot be contained, to become a frame to the infinite. This can only be achieved through a process of abstraction – 'the alterity of the other' is an abstract term, not a concrete figure, and likewise when Levinas describes the face, this is just an abstract term for the concrete epiphany of alterity. It is this abstraction that is the betrayal identified by Levinas, as such an abstraction gives up the saying that is characteristic of the ethical encounter and thematises it, coagulating it into the said.

In fact, only with such a betrayal is representation possible at all, which means that whenever we speak of the ethical, of the unsayable responsibility for the other that is 'beyond essence', we already betray the saying. As Thomas Claviez finds, "Language [...], qua representation, can never represent the Other, can never capture the very epiphany of the face that made it possible" (2008: 128). The instance the epiphany of the face, which is saying, were captured, it would turn into a said and lose its epiphanic quality. This impossibility is the aporia, the irresolvable paradox, of ethical representation. It follows that as Levinas's philosophical work itself constitutes discourse on this very topic it must necessarily be such a betrayal of the saying through its thematisation, a problem that all philosophy shares:

> But there is no way to construct a key, whereby the systematic unfaithful text could be systematically translated into a direct and univocal discourse. There is no metalanguage in which one could establish oneself so as to control the meaning and the evidence of the text and the pre-text. All one can do is live this effort to reduce the said to the saying, and be confounded by the ever-unfaithful text that that yields. Philosophy has to exist

> in this ambivalence, between the intelligibility of system and synchrony and the intelligibility of signifyingness itself which is assymetry [sic!] and diachrony. (Lingis 1981: xxxvii)

Philosophy itself, then, cannot escape the aporia of the representation of the infinite. The recognition of the absence of a metalanguage of philosophy is a decidedly poststructuralist move. Levinas's reason for this move is that any metalanguage, by virtue of its endeavours to 'control the meaning' of a text, would impose itself as ontological totality, limiting and so subduing the infinite alterity of the other. In Levinas's words, "The Infinite resists the univocity of an originary or a principle" (Levinas 1981: 156). This is why philosophy *has to exist in this ambivalence:* The philosophical text performs the betrayal to simultaneously disavow it; it is an ever failing effort at expressing the saying, at salvaging it from being drowned out entirely by the said.

This is the parallel in thought between Levinas and Derrida that has been so convincingly traced by Critchley in his *Ethics of Deconstruction* (1992). For Critchley,

> the philosopher's effort is to enact within language a spiralling movement between the Saying and the Said, an ethical writing that Levinas performs in *Otherwise than Being*. The reduction uses the unavoidable language of the Said, and attempts to avoid, or unsay, that Said by finding the Saying within it. Yet – and this is crucial – *this reduced Said retains a residue of the unsaid Said within the Saying. The reduction is never pure or complete.* This leaves philosophy in a spiralling movement between two orders of discourse, that of the Saying and that of the Said, whereby the ethical signifies through the oscillation, or alternation, of these orders. It is precisely this alternation that constitutes, for Levinas, the enigma of philosophy. (1992: 165)

The ethical faculty of philosophy thus springs from the indeterminacy of discourse, of the process of signification and hence of representation. This is then how what Derrida terms the question of closure can be posed: by the oscillation between saying and said that lets the language of philosophy as used by Levinas in his later work enter the intermediary space between the facticity of systematic thought and the ethical moment that is beyond expression in language – such a language then neither 'remains within the limit of tradition' nor transgresses it entirely.

In this once more the idea of infinity becomes pertinent as a structural analogy. In a formulation that highlights not only the aporetic nature of the idea of infinity but also shows its connection to this oscillation between saying and said, Levinas claims that "[t]he idea of the infinite consists in grasping the ungraspable while nevertheless guaranteeing its status as ungraspable" (1996b: 19). Since saying itself must remain ungraspable to discourse, the language of philosophy that allows for the spiralling between saying and said is also a language of infinity. What the infinite signifies in its excess of categories of thought is the residual saying that breaks open the ontology of the said (see Levinas 1996c: 138).

3.3 Levinas and Literature

At this point it is time to turn to literature. Since ethics, as first philosophy, is inescapably mired in the aporia of representation, there emerges a tentative parallel to literature. As fictional discourse, literature may face the same problems of representation, yet due to its fictional nature the relationship between literature and ontology is arguably more complex. At the heart of the matter the question arises whether that "indiscretion with regard to the unsayable, which is probably the very task of philosophy" (Levinas 1981: 7), is not also a task that can be performed by certain literary texts. Cannot the same ethical impetus arise from a work of literature that may be engendered in the performance of the betrayal at the core of a philosophical text on ethics? It is my intention in this book to show how literature *can* work as such an ethical form of betrayal, as an attempt, failed from the beginning, and yet indispensable, to express the saying. For this purpose, it is necessary to re-examine the structure of the betrayal Levinas identifies in the discourse of philosophy and weigh it against Levinas's reservations against literature in order to see whether the same structure may apply to a work of literature.

Levinas himself is surprisingly reluctant when it comes to conceding ethical potential to art.[55] On several occasions he expresses his scepticism towards the totalising tendency of, in particular, the aestheticised representation of arts, including literary or fictional representation. His aversion takes on two forms: that of a rejection of the allegedly 'mythopoetic' qualities of art and that of a deep-rooted mistrust in the ethical potential of representation per se (see Claviez 2008: 116–154). In an early essay entitled "Reality and Its Shadow" (Levinas 1987a [1948]), Levinas expresses a – as the title itself suggests – Platonic scepticism of art in general and of the image in particular, be it visual or linguistic.[56]

---

[55] For a more extensive overview of Levinas's complex relationship with art and literature than can be given here, see for example Robbins (1999); Eaglestone (1997: 98–128); Claviez (2008: 143–154); Staehler (2010: 164–179) and Kearney (1995).
[56] See Eaglestone (1997: 104–111) and Staehler (2010: 165–168) for longer discussions of Levinas's essay. Staehler's book-length study (2010) is the most comprehensive work available that compares Plato and Levinas.

There the image is described as a mere caricature, the eponymous shadow to the reality of the face (Levinas 1987a: 6). This analogy, as Jill Robbins points out, "suggests that no aesthetic approach to the face could also be ethical", because the face after all is irreducible to the plasticity of the image it inevitably takes on in representation (Robbins 1999: 84). With regard to literature, as opposed to philosophy, but also other arts, Levinas's scepticism is rendered in rather stark terms in another early essay, "The other in Proust" (1989b [1947]):

> The theory put forward by a scholar or philosopher refers unequivocally to the object that stands as its theme. The theory put forward by a poet, like everything he says, harbours an ambiguity, for it is concerned not to express but to create the object. Like images or symbols, reasoning is called on to produce a certain rhythm in which the reality that is sought will appear by magic. The truths or errors articulated are of no value in themselves. (Levinas 1989b: 161)

Again, this understanding of literature – rightly criticised by Claviez as a "too reductive definition" that causes Levinas's "disdain" of the aesthetic (2008: 114) – reveals a Platonic mindset: The presumptive 'unreality' of poetry devalues it, making it a mere play of signification devoid of meaning, which is also a reason for Levinas's denouncement of "rhetoric as violent and unjust" (Robbins 1999: 76).[57] Literature and art in this sense are merely constructing the unreality of the "plastic forms" (1989a: 82) that obscure the face of the other and hence

---

57 In the long history of the debate over the truthfulness and therefore implicitly the moral value of literature, the compelling counterargument has been made for example by Sir Philip Sidney, who in his *Apology for Poetry* famously defends literature against such Platonist criticism by stating that the poet "nothing affirms, and therefore never lieth" (Sidney 2012: 1068). In Levinasian diction, this would mean that as literature is aware of its own fictional status, its mythopoetic qualities are openly marked as such and its dissimulation is directly acknowledged in the first place. In this sense, the poet is no less unequivocal than the philosopher. Aesthetic mediation is not moral devaluation.

Similarly, when Levinas claims that "the truths or errors articulated [in literature] are of no value in themselves", this is certainly true in the sense that if, say, in a crime novel character A murders character B, this has no direct connection to the real world. The characters are just that, signs on a page, and what happens to them is a mere figment of the imagination. Sidney's answer to this likewise Platonic critique of art is that literary representations of "truths or errors" may still attain 'value' once they are encountered by others – by the real-life readers. After all, literature, and art in general, does not exist independent of reality and can be seen to have an exemplary function. (Indeed, Levinas himself repeatedly falls back onto literature and art in the search for examples; see Eaglestone 1997: 100–103). Far beyond Sidney's classical line of defence, it would seem to me that the aesthetic itself has a potential to question its own process of creation of the object of the work of literature rather than simply create it and in doing so it possesses a quality that is inherently sceptical of ontology.

cloud the responsibility to which it commands me (see Wyschogrod 2002: 199). It is in such profound Platonic scepticism that what has been described as "Levinas's exclusion of the work of art from the possibility of ethicity" (Robbins 1999: 77) is grounded.

Beyond his general Platonic disparagement of art and literature, it would seem that Levinas's more fundamental concern with art is the one that is shared with philosophy: art's dependence on cognition, and hence on ontology, make it susceptible to the same representational aporia philosophy faces. Art, or the aesthetic, can only exist in representation; meanwhile, others are bereft of their alterity in representation, as they are rendered an object of representation that is 'grasped', i.e. made a part of the ontological order, in the act of representing. This would seem to make art per se unethical, unable to do justice to the ethical encounter with alterity. In literature, like in philosophy, it is the unsayable unicity of the face that poses perhaps the greatest problem in this respect. As Claviez asks: "How can there appear, on the written pages of a book, a face which would not be reduced to a bloodless image, robbed of its expression and synchronized into a story [...]?" (2008: 143–144). Indeed, it would appear that literature must inevitably fail at the prospect of presenting a (quite literally) fleshed out face, as both the literary discourse and the medium[58] in which it is presented serve as what Levinas describes as masks that cover over the face (see Levinas 1989a: 82–83; 1996a: 167). It does not become clear, however, why this predicament of the literary should be any different from that of philosophy, which itself is after all dependent on representation and therefore on the said, betraying the saying of the face. Claviez's question could then equally be asked of a book of philosophical writing – as has been done by Derrida in "Violence and Metaphysics" (2005). Should there then be a difference between philosophy and literature? Does the fictional nature of literature as opposed to the supposedly pure reasoning of philosophy mean that literature dissimulates and betrays somehow more or in a different, inherently worse way than philosophy?

---

[58] The question of the medium, as well as that of literary genre, offers interesting areas of research for literary criticism informed by Levinas's ethics. It may not be purely coincidental that in recent years the theatre, which after all relies on the (relative) immediacy of performance, has emerged as a fruitful field for ethical criticism, frequently with an emphasis on spectatorship (see e.g. Aragay and Monforte 2014; Aragay and Middeke 2017; Ridout 2009), whereas there seem to be few such scholarly endeavours with regard to the traditionally more subjective genre of poetry. A systematic study as to whether and how literary genre and the medium of representation influence the 'ethical potential' of a text has to my knowledge not been conducted yet.

This seems at least questionable, as there is no obvious reason why one form of betrayal (in philosophical discourse) should be superior to another form of betrayal (in fictional discourse). As Bettina Bergo has claimed, philosophy for Levinas

> can only be the questions that a consciousness, which is capable of inquiring into itself, asks itself. But this questioning is not the act of a consciousness that has never itself been put into question. Some other questioning, as some interruption, must give consciousness occasion to falter in its certainty about the beings it regards. (1999: 39)

This interruption, Bergo continues, must come from outside the consciousness itself, from the other, which is how philosophy is generated in the encounter with alterity (see 1999: 39). Why should then not literature be able to respond to the other's interruption in its own way, or even become irruptive itself and challenge readers to the kind of self-questioning that Bergo associates with Levinas's ethics? Indeed, literature is a mode of communication or address and, as Robbins points out, "reading alters – or interrupts – the very economy of the same that the other interrupts" (1999: xxiv). In this sense, literature can maybe even be understood to carry the potential to be a more direct way of turning towards the other than philosophy or, for that matter, literary criticism, as the latter two are instances of metacommunication, already at a remove from the address of the other.[59]

In fact, Levinas himself, his sceptical attitude towards literature notwithstanding, seems to be strangely drawn towards literature and its aesthetics (see Claviez 2008: 151–152) – and in his later works partly reneges on his earlier fundamental opposition towards the literary: he both relies on examples from literature and, centrally, falls back on its aestheticised language. In a passage in which he seeks to describe the face – the pitfalls of the non-representability of the ethical encounter again become apparent –, Levinas invokes a literary description: In "Peace and Proximity" (1996a [1984]), he quotes a passage from Vasily Grossman's novel *Life and Fate*, in which a woman queuing to visit a dissident in a Soviet prison perceives the necks and backs of the people waiting in line with her:

---

[59] Levinas's view on this is different. He suggests that "criticism [...] is the word of a living being speaking to a living being, [and] brings the image in which art revels back to the fully real being" (1989c: 148). In other words, criticism then serves as a vital connection that 'revives' the image that has been absorbed into the said of a rigid aesthetics and so keeps in check the usurpation of alterity that art constitutes (see Wyschogrod 2002: 199).

> A line is formed at the counter, a line where one can see only the backs of others. A woman awaits her turn: "[She] had never thought that the human back could be so expressive, and could convey states of mind in such a penetrating way. Persons approaching the counter had a particular way of craning their neck and their back, their raised shoulders with shoulder blades tense like springs, which seemed to cry, sob, and scream." The face as the extreme precariousness of the other. Peace as awakeness to the precariousness of the other. (Levinas 1996a: 167, quoting Grossman 1985: 683)

Levinas uses this literary description to illustrate that the concept of the face need not necessarily refer to an actual face, that it is "not exclusively a human face", but rather means the destitution, and hence the "extreme precariousness of the other" (1996a: 167). What is remarkable is that an image taken from a literary text is employed by Levinas to evoke the face. Levinas seems to suggest here that Grossman's text – literature! – is in fact able to represent, or at least provide something that approximates a representation of, the unrepresentable face. This is what Claviez calls "the uncanny dynamics of the example: an 'example' that is again designed to serve as a bridge to bring us closer to an absent center never to be reached entirely" (2008: 152) – it follows, again, from the aporia inherent in the representation of the infinite.

Another implication from Levinas quoting Grossman to describe the face as an expression appearing in the neck and back of a human being is that the Levinasian face itself is metaphorical and Levinas himself uses the language of rhetoric. This claim is no less than problematic, since it clearly conflicts with Levinas's declaration that the face appears to us "without any metaphor" (Levinas 1974: 186, qtd. in Robbins 1999: xxiv). The metaphoric quality of the face, however, seems inevitable, as becomes clear from the passage in which Levinas quotes Grossman and from a number of other examples given by Robbins (see 1999: xxiii–xxiv). It is, as Levinas stresses, not an actual face, but, as already mentioned, "the concrete *figure*" for alterity. The *tertium comparationis* between the face and alterity is, however, not immediately clear. In her reading of Levinas, Judith Butler comments on this passage in which Grossman is quoted and remarks that "[h]ere the term 'face' operates as a catachresis" (2004: 133).[60] The illogical, 'abused' *tertium comparationis* would then consist in the transferral of the actual nudity and vulnerability of a human face – as that part of the body "which stays most naked, most destitute" (Levinas 1985: 86) and that part which is not usually covered over by protective layers of clothing, or text-ile – to the vulnerability of the other that is a result of their alterity

---

[60] On catachresis see also ch. 2.3 and 3.4. For an analysis of Butler's use of the term, see Arteel (2011).

and of the subject's impulse to efface this alterity and subsume it into the ontology of sameness. To be precise, the Levinasian notion of the face is then a catachresis (see ch. 2.3). It is the use of an existing term for something that otherwise has no expression in language and in this sense makes up for a lack (*inopia*) in language. Simultaneously, the term 'face' is also a rhetorical catachresis, because the image it chooses is strictly illogical: it is the outright paradoxical choice of a figure, an *image*, for that for which no image can exist. Neither the abstraction of the word 'alterity' nor the concretisation of the figure of the 'face' can wholly signify the otherness of the other, as both abstraction and concretisation are already categories of sameness. The catachresis of the face is already an abuse of alterity. Here, the betrayal of language continues into the rhetoric of Levinas's ethical language, which by virtue of its rhetoric already has become an aesthetic language. The catachresis of the face is a rhetorical performance of betrayal.

Levinas's own use of a rhetorical language and his turn to a literary text like Grossman's in his search for examples are indicative of an ambivalence that, despite all foregrounded scepticism, permeates Levinas's attitude towards art and literature and suggests that literature may have an ethical potential after all. In *Otherwise than Being*, for instance, he describes art as "the pre-eminent exhibition in which the said is reduced to a pure theme" and suggests that the aesthetic has a somewhat seductive quality that "supports Western ontology" (1981: 40).[61] At the same time, he concedes that art's continuous "search for new forms [...] keeps awake the verbs that are on the verge of lapsing into substantives" (1981: 40), that is, it prevents the saying from becoming entirely fossilised into the said. It becomes clear that the aesthetic – in literature, "the evocative

---

[61] In even stronger tones of condemnation, in "Reality and Its Shadow" Levinas claims that "[t]here is something wicked and egoist and cowardly in artistic enjoyment. There are times when one can be ashamed of it, as of feasting during a plague" (Levinas 1987a: 12). I agree with Tanja Staehler's assessment that this general caution, or even mistrust, towards the aesthetic might be tied to Levinas's own experience as a European Jew living through the catastrophe of the twentieth century, Nazism and the Holocaust (see Staehler 2010: 168). The Nazi ideology was of course fuelled by the devious rhetoric and aesthetic of fascism – an aesthetic that nevertheless managed to exert its seductive influence over all kinds of people, intellectual and non-intellectual, philosophers (Heidegger), critics (de Man) and poets (Pound) alike. At the same time, Levinas's criticism is directed against any form of aestheticisation of suffering – of turning the horrible into the beautiful – that art may be prone to (Staehler 2010: 168). As Staehler has convincingly argued, Levinas's position in this context is, however, problematic with regard to commemoration and cultural memory: "How shall we memorize the horror if nothing other than the present expression of a living person, coming to the aid of his or her own speech, counts?" (2010: 168–169). This problem was later addressed by Lyotard in his work on the differend (1988 [1983]). For a discussion of Levinas's positions towards history and temporality, see Staehler (2010: 180–198).

powers" of the language of poetry (1981: 40) – has a potential to question, perhaps even transcend the ontological.

But what might such an evocative language be? Levinas suggests that it would have to constantly renew and exceed itself, going beyond any limits that discourse might impose:

> Language would exceed the limits of what is thought, by suggesting, letting be understood without ever making understandable, an implication of a meaning distinct from that which comes to signs from the simultaneity of systems or the logical definition of concepts. This possibility is laid bare in the poetic said, and the interpretation it calls for ad infinitum. (1981: 169–170)

There is then the possibility of a "poetic said" that exceeds the limits of what is thought, and hence its own limits. This kind of evocative language thus assumes the properties of the Cartesian infinite. For the infinite, like the face of the other, transcends the possibilities of representation, rendering any attempt at representing it already a betrayal. In Levinas's words, "In re-presentation the Infinite would be belied without ambiguity, as though it were an infinite object which subjectivity tries to approach but misses. The plot of the Infinite is not elaborated according to the scenario of being and consciousness" (1981: 154). The representation of the infinite, then, is entirely inadequate, since it resorts to the language of being in order to represent what is beyond being. It must be catachrestic, a 'belying'/betrayal or abuse of what it seeks to express. This is Levinas's answer to the paradox of the impossible representation of the infinite: it is possible only in betrayal. As Butler puts it, "Any finite representation betrays the infinity represented, but representations do carry the trace of the infinite" (2005: 96; see McNally 2014: 17). In this way, then, the evocative language of poetry becomes the language of a fiction of infinity.

The aesthetics of literary texts may then, in some cases, create this resoundingly evocative language of the infinite and result in literature that is one way or another ethical. Such an ethical literature, Richard Kearney points out, "refuses the consumerist status of imaging as imitation without depth or reference" (Kearney 1995: 111). The aesthetic condemned by Levinas is one that indulges in "artistic idolatry" (Levinas 1987a: 13) by using (or perhaps rather abusing) the power of imagination "to incarcerate the self in a blind alley of self-reflecting mirrors" (Kearney 1995: 110), in an excess of those masks and plastic forms that veil the face and therefore impede the ethical relation. There is then the possibility that "[m]an can give himself in saying to the point of poetry – or he can withdraw into the non-saying of lies" (Levinas 1995: 194).

It would thus seem that there is indeed a way in which literature, like philosophy, through a particular use of poetic language and hence through its aesthetic form, can become ethical. Such an aesthetics is the aesthetics that can be found in fictions of infinity. It is a disruptive aesthetics that goes beyond the self-mirroring and endless repetition of ontological fixity and breaks open, in the contemporary novel (but not only there), a path to alterity. It is an aesthetics that Levinas has found in the work of authors such as Proust, Blanchot, Celan and Leiris (see Kearney 1995: 112–117; 1999). When Levinas considers the work of these (and other) writers, an alternative, more positive view of literature emerges in his essays. In particular, he celebrates the 'bifurcations' and 'erasures' Leiris creates in his autobiographical novel *Biffure* and so hints at a possible aesthetics that may allow literature to perform the betrayal any act of representing alterity entails without in the process obliterating the face in the act of representation (see Levinas 1989c). It follows then from Levinas's own reading of literature, as Kearney compellingly argues, that the face is in fact not per se threatened by representation, as long as poetic imagining "remains answerable to an ethics of alterity" (1995: 114; see 1999: 18), that is, as long as the aesthetic does not lay claim to its own absoluteness, or totality – bifurcations and erasures are just one way in which a text delegitimises itself.

Perhaps the clearest description of an aesthetics that maintains its ethical responsibility can be found in Levinas's essay on the literary work of Maurice Blanchot, "The Servant and her Master" (1989e [1966]). Here, poetic language is described in terms of a rupture. Considering Blanchot's novel *L'attente l'oubli*, where a couple find themselves stuck with each other in the narrow confines of a hotel room, Levinas writes: "Poetic language will break through the wall while preserving itself against the rubble from that very breakthrough, which threatens to bury and immobilize its advance by breaking it down into projects and memories that are synchronous and eternally contemporaneous in significance" (1989e: 154). This kind of poetic language is then a language that disrupts, that breaks through the metaphorical wall of totality. However, it is not just a counter-discourse directed against one particular concept or structure. Such a counter-discourse would merely replace one ontological structure with another and in this sense become buried under the rubble of its own breakthrough. Instead, poetic language is the language of a perpetual openness, the language of saying:

> A discontinuous and contradictory language of scintillation. A language which can give sign (*faire signe*) above and beyond all signification. A sign made from afar, from beyond and in the beyond. Poetic language gives sign without the sign being a bearer of signification through relinquishing signification. [...] Poetry can be said to transform words, the tokens of a whole, the moments of a totality, into unfettered signs, breaching the walls of immanence, disrupting order. [...] No novel, no poem – from the *Iliad* to *Remembrance of Things Past* – has thus perhaps done anything else. To introduce meaning into Being is

> to go from the Same to the Other (*Autre*), from Self to Other (*Autrui*), it is to give sign, to undo the structures of language. Without this, the world would know only the meanings which inspire official records or the minutes of the board meetings of Limited Companies. (1989e: 156–157)

In this dense and again metaphorically charged passage, Levinas likens such an ethical poetic language to the sudden and unpredictable flash or sparkle of scintillation. It is a language that is anything but limited, that transcends even the bounds of signification itself. At the same time, it is still representational language and therefore must "still solidify into a narrative, still envelop itself in the totality of the *said*" (1989e: 157). This ethical poetic language is thus subject to the same restrictions as the language of philosophy and must likewise obliterate the saying in its manifestation as said, while at the same time trying to prise open the very rigidity of the said it engenders in the first place.

Levinas's attitude towards the literary is thus ambiguous. While he resoundingly rejects any 'empty rhetoric' and in his early work seems to conflate the literary as a whole with such empty rhetoric, his position later shifted towards accepting the possibility of a poetic "language of scintillation" that transcends such rhetoric. This is what he finds in his analysis of Blanchot (1989e), where he is interested in Blanchot's "use of images as ciphers of infinity" (Kearney 1995: 114). The use of an image for the unsayable, as 'cipher of infinity' is also what Levinas himself does in his use of the term "face". The basic mode of this ethical poetic language is, I suggest, following Butler's analysis of the Levinasian face, that of catachresis. The cleavage of discourse that is catachresis thus becomes the site of scintillation, the site of ethics in the literary.

3.4 Catachresis: Levinas's Ethics and Infinite Aesthetics

It is precisely here, in catachresis, that the link – itself then a necessarily catachrestic, 'broken' link – between the structural infinity that can be found in fictions of infinity and Levinas's ethics emerges. Here the two threads of enquiry that this study follows, the enquiry into the aesthetic means by which a text may 'become' infinite and that into the ethics of an infinite text, come together. By introducing infinity into the discourse of a narrative, aesthetic features such as the ones already discussed may indeed invest a text with the disruptive quality of the kind of poetic language envisioned by Levinas. This ethical "language of scintillation" may take widely diverse concrete shapes, as I hope to show in the following chapters. In fact, although this seems to be at odds with Levinas, I want to show that the *structure* of a narrative can become instrumental in creating such a disruptive text.[62] In one more paradox of the infinite, this is achieved through the use of aesthetic forms and narrative structures that would at first seem to lead into precisely the "postmodern crisis of endless self-mirroring" (Kearney 1995: 111) Levinas condemns – indeed, mise en abyme structures have been explicitly described as 'mirror narratives' by Dällenbach (1977). However, my argument is that such textual structures of infinity already engender the cleavage of catachresis and in this way become disruptive in themselves. It is through this disruption that such texts develop an ethical moment that extends itself in the addressing of their readers.

The reason for this disruptive quality is that at its core catachresis is a figure of alterity. This follows if one accepts that catachresis is indeed essentially constituted in a "fundamental incoherence" (Chrzanowska-Kluczewska 2011: 49). For such fundamental incoherence must necessarily resist the ontological totality of knowledge criticised by Levinas, for the simple reason that, were it knowable in its entirety, it would form part of a coherent system of thought and the figure of catachresis would lose its defining feature. In this sense, catachresis must remain irreducible to complete comprehension. In the case of fictions of infinity that rely on the catachrestic identification of infinite textuality, this textual macrotrope of catachresis leads on to a likewise catachrestic metatrope that runs through all these texts. In such texts, the realisation of the 'infinity' of these texts entails the aporia of an incessant textual self-withdrawal: the understanding of the text as infinite is dependent on its status as finite artefact that merely provides the 'building blocks' of textual infinity. Conversely, in a different way a text gains finitude the very instant it is understood as infinite, since this understanding (or grasping) delivers closure to a process of understanding (in the terms of the Basic Metaphor of Infinity, this is the completion added to an endless process with the resulting state of infinity): once understood as infinite, the text can no longer be understood as finite – it cannot possibly be both at the same time, and yet it is precisely that – and there is nothing beyond infinity, no 'meta-infinity' the text may aspire to, that would lend itself to relativise the nature of textual understanding. As such, the textual status of any fiction of infinity is undecidable, or, hearkening back to Descartes's analysis of the idea of infinity, truly unknowable. This is what the structure of catachresis has in common with alterity: it resists any fixed ontological grasp.

---

62 This is not to say that the structure of a text alone can make it ethical. Since there is no ethical relation in pure abstraction, in the 'ontology' of the narrative structure, the somewhat more concrete elements of the story level must be taken into account as well. However, the aesthetics of a text can in themselves already create some of the 'sparks' of the scintillating language of the literary that transcends the totality of ontology.

It seems little surprising therefore that those structural features that are particularly prone to being identified as infinite can also be most directly linked to a form of alterity. This is above all true for the mise en abyme and intertextuality, but can be applied to all other cases in which texts attain textual infinity. As far as mise en abyme structures, at least those that Dällenbach has called *réduplications à l'infini*, are concerned, their 'scintillation' can be found in their "abyssal indeterminacy" (Elam 1994: 28). Diane Elam's interpretation of the mise en abyme[63], which she sees as a representational structure of "infinite deferral" (1994: 27), also applies in the context of an ethical language:

> The *mise en abyme* [...] opens a spiral of infinite regression in representation. Representation can never come to an end, since greater accuracy and detail only allows us to see even more [...]. This is rather odd since we are accustomed to think of accuracy and detail as helping us to grasp an image fully, rather than forcing us to recognize the impossibility of grasping it. (1994: 27–28)

The aesthetic structure itself thus already implies the "impossibility of grasping" what is represented in it. Like alterity in Levinas's philosophy, the object of representation in such a mise en abyme eludes any grasp – as Elam puts it, "the object cannot be grasped by the subject; it slips away into infinity" (1994: 28). This is how the abyss of the mise en abyme manifests itself in reception or interpretation, in reading.

It is a consequence of the ungraspability of the representation that reading itself is broken open in such structures. In a similar manner, Andrew Benjamin has described the mise en abyme as "the moment when interpretation can be seen as taking itself as its own object within the practice of interpretation, thus giving rise to a state of affairs in which any straightforward distinction between subject and object is called into question" (1991: 16). It follows that the mise en abyme is inherently self-reflexive at the level of interpretation. The calling into question of the subject/object distinction is the result of the reading subject being drawn into ever new levels of infinite textual signification, which not only means that the object is forever withdrawn from the grasp of representation but also that the subject's gaze is turned back onto itself. It is in this infinite back and forth movement that such texts, because of their structure, may 'scintillate' and resist ultimate cognition. As Elam has it, "The subject thus is faced with its

---

[63] In her argument, in which she suggests the representational structure of the mise en abyme as a way of rethinking feminism that avoids the problem of essentialism (see 1994: 27–35), Elam seems to presuppose that the 'mirroring' in a mise en abyme structure is always infinite. Although I do not think that this is necessarily the case, her analysis still applies to the mise en abyme structures I am interested in here, which can indeed be understood as infinite.

inability to know what it knows, to see what it sees. In this sense, the subject becomes the subject of a representation that exceeds it" (1994: 28). This representation that is in excess of itself as well as of the beholder breaks open the ontological structure of representation and reception – it signifies infinitely and thus demands infinite reading. In this way, such infinite mise en abyme structures certainly "exceed the limits of what is thought", just like Levinas's ethical language (Levinas 1981: 169).

It is for this reason that the "cleavage in discourse" (Chrzanowska-Kluczewska 2011: 49) of catachresis can be found in 'infinite' mise en abyme structures in two ways: both as the cleavage between finite representation and infinite represented discussed above (see ch. 2.3) and as the cleavage between a reading that seeks to grasp the text in its entirety and so to delimit it on the one hand and the text's infinite deferral of any such grasping on the other. These two dimensions of the catachresis inherent in infinite mise en abyme structures – one might call them representational and interpretive catachresis, respectively –, like the two sides of a coin, coincide in the structural phenomenon itself. As a consequence of the latter, the interpretive catachresis inherent in the infinite mise en abyme, there is no final reading of a text with such a structure – something that is simultaneously also achieved through the infinite textuality created in the representational catachresis. It would thus seem that the abyss of the mise en abyme is tantamount to the cleavage in discourse of catachresis. It is due to its denial of an end to reading, due to its refusal to impose a limit on interpretation, that an infinite mise en abyme structure calls into question the reader's spontaneity – in other words, their spontaneity to decide on a finite, definitive reading, to arrive at an end, to delimit the text, is challenged by the text itself. This is then how the textual structure of a *réduplication à l'infini* in the mise en abyme unfolds its ethical potential.[64]

There is a similar link between catachresis, ethics and intertextuality, a link that is encapsulated in Kristeva's notion of a poetic logic based on the doubleness of poetic language (see ch. 2.2.3). According to Kristeva, its doubleness makes poetic language incompatible with the logic of the binary, of 0–1 or true and false, which is inherently monological and "dogmatic", as 'true' is always preferred over 'false' and one pole of the binary attains the dominance

---

[64] For a different way of linking the structure of the mise en abyme to Levinas's thought, see Dickmann (2015). In his critique of Levinas's ethics, Dickmann sees the structure of infinite responsibility for the other that is at the heart of Levinas's work as a mise en abyme. Dickmann is, however, critical of this structure both because of its central lacuna, or abyss, and because, he claims, in this structure the other is reduced to a "'wall' from which the act of responsibility 'bounces off'" (2015: 137).

of totality (1986: 41). Instead of entering into such systems of signification, "poetic language", Kristeva repeats, "is at least *double*, not in the sense of the signifier/signified dyad, but rather, in terms of *one and other*" (1986: 40). For this reason she identifies a "*poetic logic*" that transgresses any binary logic and, rooted in Bakhtinian dialogism, is "a logic of the 'transfinite'" (1986: 41, 42). Kristeva, then, directly associates her poetic logic, which relies on the intertextual doubleness of literature, with the infinite and the contradictions and complexities arising from formal preoccupations with infinity.[65] So infinity enters the intertextual equation, which really rather is an equivocation, both at the level of the infinitely sprawling intertextual relations and, inextricably linked to it, at this more abstract level of the poetic logic identified by Kristeva.

Because of its close connection with the infinite, structurally this poetic logic of the intertextual, just like infinite mise en abyme structures, corresponds to the poetic metatrope of catachresis (see also ch. 2.3). One might even go so far as to say that if catachresis is "based on [...] logical deviance" and rooted in "fundamental incoherence" (Chrzanowska-Kluczewska 2011: 48, 49), then the doubleness created by the intertextual poetic is always a catachrestic doubleness.

---

[65] Kristeva borrows the notion of the transfinite from Georg Cantor, who in the nineteenth century laid the foundations of set theory and of the modern mathematical understanding of the infinite (see also chapter 1.1). While Cantor's new take on the infinite revolutionised mathematical set theory, it also left mathematics with one of its most famous problems. Cantor had proven that different orders of the infinite exist and that, in particular, the cardinality (or number of elements) of the set of all integers, a number Cantor named $\aleph_0$ (aleph null), is smaller than the cardinality c of the real numbers – transfinite numbers was the name he assigned to cardinal numbers of infinite sets, such as $\aleph_0$ and c. What Cantor was unable to prove is whether or not there exist intermediate transfinite numbers between $\aleph_0$ and c. This problem, the Continuum Hypothesis, which states that there is no intermediate cardinal number between $\aleph_0$ and c, was soon considered to be so important to mathematics that it became the first problem on David Hilbert's famous programmatic list, published in 1900, of 23 problems to be solved by mathematics in the twentieth century. In the context of Kristeva's use of the term transfinite, it is revealing that the Continuum Hypothesis was finally, in 1963, proven to be unsolvable with the methods and axioms of contemporary mathematics (see Maor 1986: 64–65; for an overview of the history of the Continuum Hypothesis and new approaches to extend the scope of mathematics and find a solution to it, see Kennedy 2011). It is perhaps with the somewhat baffling answer to the Continuum Hypothesis in mind that Kristeva uses the term transfinite in connection with her poetic logic: the Continuum Hypothesis was shown to be "both true and false", or simply "independent of the axioms of set theory" (Maor 1986: 65). In this sense, conceptually speaking transfinite numbers may perhaps be identified with the doubleness or resistance to the monological Kristeva associates with her poetic logic. In her work on the "literary transfinite", Baylee Brits argues that a "'doubling' process" or "linguistic bifurcation" is crucial to creating a mode of the transfinite in literature (2018: 45). Although Brits does not refer to Kristeva in this context, the parallels to the doubleness of poetic language in Kristeva are striking.

After all, its resistance to the (mono)logical follows from Kristeva's claim that each word is already the location of an intersection of a multiplicity of texts. Necessarily these texts do not only co-signify but also, as it were, signify 'against' each other, inevitably creating "cleavages" that are then instrumental in establishing the "logic of the transfinite" that Kristeva associates with intertextuality and that in itself constitutes a deviance from the monological. At the same time, much in the same vein as infinite mise en abyme structures, texts that overtly foreground their intertextuality and as a consequence can be understood to be structurally infinite are also cases where catachresis operates as a macrotrope. In such texts, there is also the representational rift between the finitude of the representation and the infinite (inter)textuality they display so that their overall structure can again be described as catachrestic.

What follows is that intertextuality is another dimension in which literary texts are permeated by alterity. Not only does it open texts up to the potential of infinite signification, allowing the unknowability of the infinite to enter into discourse, but crucially, the doubleness or dialogism at the heart of the poetic logic envisioned by Kristeva springs from the encounter with otherness: it is, as Kristeva herself writes, a doubleness "in terms of *one and other*" (1986: 40). Intertextuality implies, after all, that in each text, in each word even, elements of other texts are present and influence our reading. As Graham Allen puts it,

> If intertextuality stands as the ultimate term for the kind of poetic language Kristeva is attempting to describe, then we can see that from its beginning the concept of intertextuality is meant to designate a kind of language which, *because of its embodiment of otherness*, is against, beyond and resistant to (mono)logic. Such language is socially disruptive, revolutionary even. Intertextuality encompasses that aspect of literary and other kinds of texts which struggles against and subverts reason, the belief in unity of meaning or of the human subject, and which is therefore subversive to all ideas of the logical and the unquestionable. (2011: 44–45; my emphasis)

In other words, poetic language, and specifically its intertextual dimension, resists textual totality. Following Culler, one may add that it equally resists any critic's attempts at (metatextual) totalisation, as the unmasterable, infinite quality of intertextuality disavows the critic's attempts at 'focusing' it (see 1981: 111). The reason for this resistance to totality that is ingrained in the entire concept of intertextuality is, it would seem, that intertextuality is to some extent an expression of alterity. If the language of intertextuality is an "embodiment of otherness", this is the case precisely because the very notion of intertextuality refers to texts containing other texts. In fact, 'containing' seems to be the wrong word here: it is more of a 'hosting', a text opening itself up to other texts signifying through it.[66] In this sense, intertextuality is always an encounter with textual otherness.

It is thus in this textual resistance to totality of the infinitely intertextual text that the clearest parallel between the textual otherness ingrained in intertextuality and Levinas's radical ethical concept of alterity emerges. Just as the other resists being known, resulting in an infinite gulf in apperception and making alterity an inherently aporetic notion – a notion that cannot be had or expressed without obliterating itself to some extent (in what Levinas terms a 'betrayal') –, so as a concept intertextuality becomes unmasterable, resists 'focusing', on account of its infinity. As such, it is a textual expression of openness, or a refusal of closure. Therefore, where the infinity of intertextuality is concerned, it falls within the domain of Levinas's saying, which after all is the part of language that expresses "an ethical openness to the other" and resists the "ontological closure to the other" of the said (Levinas 1995: 194). This is precisely what intertextuality does at the textual level in that it resists closure and indeed provides space for (textual) otherness within a text. In this sense, intertextuality constitutes an encounter with otherness at the level of texts that is at least as far as the underlying structure of a radical, infinite unknowability is concerned, similar to the ethical encounter described by Levinas.

At this stage, it seems necessary to point out that the alterity inherent in the catachresis of infinite textuality is of a different quality to the alterity of the other in Levinasian thought. Levinas makes clear that a text – steeped, as any representational form, in the plasticity of images – simply cannot possess a face, a site where the vulnerability and precariousness and at the same time the absolute alterity of a flesh-and-blood human other manifests itself. This form of radical alterity is only inherent in the ethical encounter with human beings. The radical alterity of the ethical relation cannot be contained in any narrative, as Levinas makes explicit: "The unnarratable other loses his face as a neighbour in narration. The relationship with him is indescribable in the literal sense of the term, uncontrovertible into a history, irreducible to the simultaneousness of writing, the eternal present of a writing that records or presents results" (1981: 166). Texts do not possess a face and cannot, for example in the intertextual encounter with other texts, take up responsibility for other texts or for humans in the same way a human being is responsible for the other in the ethical relation, and conversely the reader's responsibility towards a text cannot be the

---

[66] Indeed, the complex interrelations between intertexts are strangely reminiscent of the way Derrida describes the concept of hospitality as a liminal construct at the threshold between opening up and appropriation, between the amicable and the inimical – hence Derrida's term "hostipitality" (see Derrida 2000).

same as that for a human other. Whatever alterity may be engendered in texts through their infinite textuality is therefore different from Levinas's notion of the absolute, extremely vulnerable alterity of the other.

Nevertheless, there are two dimensions in which the infinite textuality that can be found in fictions of infinity may overcome this deficit and create in the encounter with the text an ethical moment that is spurred by the 'alterity' – better understood as the disruptive force – of the text. First, there is the "fundamental incoherence" of catachresis. Just like Levinas in his use of the term 'face' (see Butler 2004: 133), these texts use an image for something that cannot have an image, for infinity, and therefore they are necessarily catachrestic.[67] Indeed, this incoherence of catachresis seems to be none other than that which arises in language between the saying and the said, between the pure signification of the silent plea of the face and its thematisation the very instance it is given an image. It is an incoherence that in this case is constitutive of what Levinas has described as the betrayal any philosophical utterance about ethics must perform. In a wider sense, then, the language of Levinas's entire work might be considered catachrestic, where catachresis is merely another term – admittedly more technical and less suggestive of the deep ethical conflict inherent in the genesis of Levinas's work – for this betrayal. Indeed, the betrayal, which consists in giving a language and hence an ontology to that which cannot be expressed, essentially is a – however necessary – abuse (catachresis).[68] Both in the catachresis of

---

[67] It should be noted that here the text in its entirety is the 'image'. In a way, their use of structural features, of a structure of scintillation rather than a direct linguistic image of scintillation, achieves a more indirect way of representing what cannot be represented and so perhaps preserves more of the characteristic ungraspability of the infinite and of alterity.

[68] At this point the proximity between philosophy and literature becomes apparent, or at least between philosophy and literature that both attempt to resist ontological totality. Asked by Richard Kearney about the links between philosophy and literature, Derrida answers: "I have always tried to expose the way in which philosophy is literary, not so much because it is *metaphor* but because it is *catachresis*", and goes on to describe catachresis as "a violent production of meaning, an abuse which refers to no anterior or proper norm" (Derrida 1995: 172). The violent potential here seems to be derived precisely from a rejection of the ontology of metaphysics. Derrida's aim in writing philosophy is, he continues, "to produce new forms of catachresis, another kind of writing, a violent writing which stakes out the faults (*failles*) and deviations of language; so that the text produces a language of its own, in itself, which while continuing to work through tradition emerges at a given moment as a *monster*, a monstrous mutation without tradition or normative precedent" (1995: 172). This is then the potential of the catachrestic representation of infinity in literary texts: they resist the normative and so give a text a "language of its own", testifying to that which is infinitely other.

the face and in the catachrestic betrayal, this abuse is structurally akin to the catachresis of infinity that is instrumental in fictions of infinity.

Second, there is the dimension of the reader being addressed by a text. Even though alterity may not be caught between the covers of a book, it may still enter this moment of reception. While literature is, at best, just one kind of the betrayal that ensues from attempting to find words for otherness, Levinas acknowledges that "books have their fate; they belong to a world they do not include, but recognize by being written and printed, and by being prefaced and getting themselves preceded with forewords. They are interrupted and call for other books and in the end are interpreted in a saying distinct from the said" (1981: 171). There is, then, an openness to the process of interpretation, or reading, that results from the text's status in the world, from its context of production (visible, for example, in the paratext) and, crucially, reception.[69] Books, literature as a whole, do not exist independently, they do not form a closed space of their own because they are interrupted – and at least partly the interruption seems to consist in their "call for other books", that is, in their intertextuality. This interruption allows for their reading "in a saying distinct from the said", as a form of address that transcends the rigidity of totalising meaning, and as Lisa McNally points out with regard to this passage from *Otherwise than Being*, "the saying might become apparent *only* in this interruption" (2014: 19). This is particularly prominent in the infinite textuality of fictions of infinity, which keeps interrupting itself and any reading.

In this sense, ingrained in their infinite openness there is a way in which fictions of infinity are ethical in a Levinasian sense in that they put into question the reader's spontaneity. That is to say that inherent in the aesthetic structures that contribute to the texts attaining their textual infinity is a form of alterity that has surreptitiously invaded the literary text and makes not just the monolithic understanding of literature impossible, but by virtue of its presence serves as a constant reminder of the plurality inherent in all texts and encountered in the process of reading. This is at the very core of fictions of infinity: through their infinity, which is always tied up with a resistance to closure, these texts one way or another become ethical. At least they do so if the ethical is, as in Critchley's reading of Levinas, "the critical *mise en question* of the liberty, spontaneity, and cognitive emprise of the ego that seeks to reduce all otherness to itself" and hence is "a point of alterity, or what Levinas also calls 'exteriority' (*extériorité*), that cannot be reduced to the Same" (Critchley 1992: 5). As textual infinity pre-

---

[69] For an excellent discussion of Levinas and Derrida in the context of reading and reception theory, see McNally (2014).

cisely resists the reduction of otherness to sameness, or the closure of any reading *process*, it must inevitably become such a calling into question.

What happens, then, in fictions of infinity is the catachrestic opening up of an endless form of address and it is through this infinite address that the text calls into question the reader's spontaneity and becomes ethical. Since this endless address results from the infinite textuality that can be found in fictions of infinity, in principle this can be seen in all types of aesthetic structures that endow a text with infinity. In the infinite mise en abyme this is achieved through the structural abyss that renders impossible any grasping of the represented in its entirety. It is in the infinite deferral of meaning, which in a similar way can also be found in some of the texts that use simpler structures such as repetition and circularity to attain infinity, that the infinite address comes into being. When it comes to intertextuality, since a text along what Kristeva describes as its horizontal axis is an act of address, with the reader being the addressee, and since its infinite extension along the vertical axis of intertextual relations coincides with the simultaneous extension of its horizontal structure of address – for every word constitutes an intersection of words/texts both horizontally and vertically; if one is expanded, the other must follow – the text's underlying structure of address likewise becomes infinite. This means that a text never stops in its address of the reader, that it does not settle for a single, ultimate meaning, but instead ceaselessly offers new perspectives – something that can also be said about the narrative infinity that is created in an entirely different way through the infinite perspective of narrative omniscience. It is this very process of ever decentring the prevalent perspective that has the potential to put into question a reader's spontaneity.

In this way what I have called fictions of infinity avoid what Levinas criticises as "artistic idolatry" (1987a: 13), or empty play of signification, as here, by means of their infinite structure, the texts transcend – and so undermine – themselves in an act of aesthetic self-critique. This self-transcendence takes place as soon as a text is perceived as infinite and so eludes any final or definitive understanding. It is in this fashion that the "bad infinity of the text" (Greisch 1991: 68) and its endlessly meaningless mirroring is overcome in the realisation that the text itself represents the idea of infinity.

At the same time and as a central part of their aesthetics, these texts reflect what Levinas already acknowledges as the effect of poetic language on readers: they pose the question of an infinite reading. The possibility of such an infinite reading is what Levinas seems to suggest when he writes of "the poetic said, and the interpretation it calls for ad infinitum" (1981: 170). In fictions of infinity, this call is perhaps most clearly constituted in the way in which these texts, through their infinity, transcend their boundaries and so in a way stay with the reader after the first reading, encouraging further, multiple and multiplicious readings. In calling for infinite interpretation they resist any fixity of meaning and so make reading likewise an open-ended endeavour. As every interpretation, every reading, is an act of grasping or appropriating that which is read and interpreted, reading must also inevitably establish the said. Every reading is thus necessarily already a betrayal of the ethical signification of saying (see McNally 2014: 21; Robbins 1999: 13). Encouraging an unending reading process is then one more sense in which fictions of infinity form part of the interruption that is ethical language. In this case, it is an interruption of the finality of interpretation, that is, an opening up for the saying allowing for an interpretation "in a saying distinct from the said" (Levinas 1981: 171; see McNally 2014: 19).

In all of this it must, however, remain clear that the text (or work of art) itself cannot, ultimately, possess alterity in the same way a human other does – and yet it can affect a reader through an appeal that is ethical. Literature itself, understood as a grouping together of signifiers on the written page (or in the spoken word), does not possess a face and cannot exude the extreme vulnerability and precariousness with which the human other speaks to me and makes their ethical demand, the entreaty not to kill. At least a text cannot do so with the same urgent immediacy as the other, as the pure saying of the face is necessarily betrayed and obliterated in the said of the text. Nevertheless, in the act of betrayal there must be contained a however faint echo of the saying, and indeed, while the literary text cannot *be* the other, it may bring us closer to the other, create proximity, or even just the acute awareness, in the reader, of the vulnerability of the other in the world beyond the text. After all, literature is not entirely unconnected to the extra-literary reality: literary texts are recognised by their readers and so directly impact on the world beyond literature in which they elicit a response. Narratives that appear to their readers as infinite may be particularly prone to doing so, since they have the capacity to go beyond their textual boundaries – or rather they do not have such boundaries, since infinity cannot be contained. When J. Hillis Miller writes that the ethics of reading "begins with and returns to the man or woman face to face with the words on the page" (1987: 4), one might add that the ethics of reading an infinite text does not end with a return to the original situation of reading – because here the text transcends the words on the page; and because it never ends. It is in this reaching beyond the text that an infinite text may speak to its reader, that the text's appeal may become ethical. It is for this reason that "[f]or Levinas [...] the best poetry is unfinished poetry" (Kearney 1995: 111). Fictions of infinity can then indeed lay claim to having a particular ethical appeal.

Again it is the peculiar structure of the infinite, its inherently paradoxical nature – resistant to the rationality of thought – and the impossibility to adequately represent it in language, that emerges as the key mechanism of an ethical dimension of fictions of infinity. As has already been established, the infinite is un(re)presentable, perpetually defying its own representation in literature, art, or indeed any form of thought. Crucially, in the thought of the infinite the discrepancy between idea and *ideatum* engenders an aporia: it is the irresolvable discrepancy between a finite medium and an infinite mediated, irrespective of whether the medium is one of representation or, figuratively speaking, an act of thought as a medium for that which is thought. Infinity in this sense is a perpetual, unanswerable challenge to its medium (language or thought), a challenge that nevertheless demands a response. Such is the challenge of the catachresis that the thought of infinity presents: it attempts a conceptual representation of that for which there is no image. Just as with the face as figure for alterity, the idea of infinity must turn to images to represent (even if just mentally) its *ideatum*. Such a (re-)presentation of the un(re)presentable cannot but result in a catachresis. It is this catachrestic aesthetics of the infinite that prises open the structure of thought and rends the totality of sameness that governs understanding. The resulting gulf in thought is its challenge to whoever encounters such aesthetics to engage with alterity, with what ruptures the ontology of sameness. In this way this questioning of totality is the imposition of responsibility on the recipient. This is the aporia of the infinite and its representation – it is an aporia that makes infinity the structural cipher for the ethical relation according to Levinas. If, as Simon Critchley argues, "[e]thics should be infinitely demanding" (2007: 69), these catachrestic texts certainly are just that. This is how fictions of infinity develop their ethical appeal. This is then the aporetic ethics of the infinite and of fictions of infinity.

4 Infinitely Encountering the Ineffable: David Mitchell's *Cloud Atlas*

David Mitchell's 2004 novel *Cloud Atlas*[70], probably the author's best-known novel to date, is my first example of a novel whose structure lets the text become infinite and which as a consequence develops a strong ethical appeal. Shortlisted for the Man Booker Prize in 2004, the novel was adapted for the screen in 2012 and made into a film that was directed by Tom Tykwer and Lana and Lilly Wachowski and had a star cast including, among others, Halle Berry, Tom Hanks and Hugo Weaving. The novel's broad scope, spanning several centuries and regions of the globe, and its focus on transhistorical ethical challenges of human cohabitation has led to it being hailed as "pioneer [of] a new cosmopolitan modus operandi for twenty-first-century British fiction" (Schoene 2009: 97). It brings together different narrative styles and distinct storylines, all complexly interwoven in its narrative structure and so takes its readers onto a veritable "tour du monde" (Schoene 2009).

As an example of a fiction of infinity, *Cloud Atlas* serves to highlight both the epistemological question of how to represent infinity in a text and the ethical potential of such 'infinite' texts. In the novel, infinity is ingrained in several ways: firstly, the mise en abyme structure in *Cloud Atlas* insinuates an endless iterability of textual embeddedness, and hence an emerging infinite textuality; secondly, the novel's cyclically recurring themes suggest the infinite iterability of the narrative structure is mirrored at the content level; thirdly, all narrative levels are characterised by a distinctive lack of closure, which again implies an infinite narrativity; and lastly, although not at the centre of my analysis for this novel, the extraordinarily high degree of intertextuality self-consciously sit-

---

[70] Due to complications in the editing process, there are substantial differences between the US and UK editions of the novel, particularly in the section entitled "An Orison of Sonmi~451". As Martin Paul Eve has pointed out, these differences include entire passages of text that only appear in one of the two editions; the choice of edition therefore "must change any close reading of the text" (Eve 2016: 3). These changes do not primarily affect the level of the story (or syuzhet, to remain with the terms Eve prefers to use), but have a strong impact on the discourse (or fabula), to the extent that "the narrative has been almost totally re-written in nearly every sentence" (Eve 2016: 11). For an overview of the differences between the editions and of some of the effects created by the differences, see Eve (2016). Although these differences do not have any major impact on my reading of the novel and although, Eve stresses, neither version should be considered "definitive" over the other (2016: 9), it should be pointed out that the edition used for my analysis is the US market edition (Mitchell 2012).

https://doi.org/10.1515/9783110712407-006

uates *Cloud Atlas* in an infinite textual tradition.[71] The novel's infinite textuality can be seen as an aesthetic device that creates textual alterity, that is, as the text's self-conscious marking of its performance of a 'betrayal' in the Levinasian sense. Together with the focus on encounters with the other that occupy central positions in the plot, this is instrumental in creating the strong ethical appeal that *Cloud Atlas* exudes and that can be found at every level of the text.

4.1 "An Infinite Matryoshka Doll of Painted Moments": mise en abyme in *Cloud Atlas*

What is perhaps the most characteristic feature of *Cloud Atlas* is its complex narrative structure. It is also the feature that situates the novel most firmly within the context of fictions of infinity. In fact, the complex mise en abyme structure itself can be considered a structural approach to the infinite, as it can be identified as infinite via Lakoff and Núñez's Basic Metaphor of Infinity. The novel's various narrative strands are related through moments of reading or reception that create the recursive embedding at the heart of the narrative structure. The indefinite continuability of this process is suggested by the sense of openness that permeates the endings of all the novel's narrative episodes. At the same time, the text's temporal structure and its (onto)logical structure are partly inverse, which creates a 'strange loop' and so gives the text an element of circularity that echoes its central principle of Nietzsche's eternal recurrence. Infinity is thus ingrained in the novel's structure not only through the *réduplication à l'infini* of its mise en abyme but also through the circularity that is created by the way in which the narrative levels are arranged.

In *Cloud Atlas* six episodic narratives that are set in different places at different times and feature different characters are intricately interlinked through the novel's complex narrative structure. In analogy to the six voices of the novel's eponymous Cloud Atlas Sextet, a (fictional) piece of modern music composed by Robert Frobisher, one of the novel's protagonists, *Cloud Atlas* can be seen as the composition of its six distinct storylines into a whole. The six episodes, comprising eleven sections altogether, present six individual stories that are all fashioned in the style of different distinctive literary genres and, at first glance, seem to have little in common. The novel begins with the nineteenth-century "Pacific Travel Journal of Adam Ewing", an American notary who while

---

[71] For an exemplary reading of a novel that links intertextuality and infinity, see chapter 6 on Ian McEwan's *Saturday*.

crossing the Pacific on his way home is slowly poisoned by the trickster Dr Henry Goose and saved from his deathbed by the freed slave Autua. The second narrative episode, "Letters from Zedelghem", is set in Belgium in 1931 and presents letters written by Robert Frobisher, aspiring composer and amanuensis to the famous composer Vyvyan Ayrs, whose wife he has an affair with and whose daughter he falls in love with; neither of the relationships turns out too well and Frobisher eventually commits suicide. In "Half-Lives: The First Luisa Rey Mystery", 1970s California sees investigative journalist Luisa Rey uncover a corporate conspiracy to run a nuclear reactor despite drastic safety risks. The fourth episode, "The Ghastly Ordeal of Timothy Cavendish", set in Great Britain in the 2000s, tells of its hapless protagonist's escape from a nursing home for the elderly, where he finds himself trapped against his will at the behest of his treacherous brother. The last two episodes are set in the near and far future respectively – there are no clear textual markers for the precise temporal settings, but the twenty-second century and a distant future may be assumed (see Mezey 2011: 14). "The Orison of Sonmi~451" is an interview between Sonmi~451, a clone worker who has developed an independent consciousness and joined the rebellion against the autocratic capitalist regime ruling Korea, and an archivist working for that regime; the interview is conducted after Sonmi's arrest and prior to her execution. The last episode, "Sloosha's Crossin' an' Ev'rythin' After", set in the Hawaii of a post-apocalyptic world, revolves around the relationship between the protagonist Zachry and Meronym, a member of the technologically advanced Prescients and ends in the two having to flee Big Isle together after Zachry's peaceful tribe is conquered and enslaved by the neighbouring Kona tribe.

All these different stories do not only share a number of key motifs,[72] but, crucially, are embedded in each other as texts – variously in the form of a futuristic video/hologram recording called "orison", the film version of a memoir, the manuscript of a crime novel, one half of a letter exchange between two friends and lovers, and a travel report – that are received by characters on the subsequent story level. Like Frobisher's sextet, *Cloud Atlas* thus "unfolds as the orchestrated interplay of a range of intimately entwined tunes, played in different modes on a variety of instruments, yet invariably chiming as one" (Schoene 2009: 114; see *CA* 445 for a description of the sextet's structure, which mirrors

---

[72] Apart from textual traces such as the comet-shaped birthmark shared by characters across all episodes and recurring motifs such as the hydra – used in connection with a company producing clones, a nuclear reactor, the London-based criminal Hoggins brothers, or humanity as a whole – it is above all acts of betrayal, cannibalism and exploitative relationships that occur again and again in all narrative episodes (on the latter, see especially Ng 2015), but also, although this may be easily forgotten, acts of kindness that counter them.

that of the entire novel). The delicate complexity of this narrative melody arises in part because its episodes are first presented in chronological order, but interrupted about halfway through to be followed by the next episode, in which, as is only belatedly revealed, the protagonist then encounters the narrative of the previous episode in some way or other. The action of embedding the narratives in each other thus remains unobtrusively casual: in none of the initial six sections does it become clear from the beginning how the section is linked to the preceding one and it only gradually emerges that the protagonists of the 'later' (with regard to the chronology of the diegesis) episodes are recipients, that is, readers or viewers, of the texts that contain the episode immediately preceding their own. Only the sixth episode is presented in full, after which the remaining five sections, containing the second halves of the other five episodes follow in reverse chronological order, resuming from the point where they were cut off.[73]

This disruption of the narrative's 'natural' sequence through the embedding of new narrative levels results in a complex mise en abyme structure and creates what Heather J. Hicks describes as the narrative's characteristic "boomeranging arc" (Hicks 2010; see also Parker 2010: 202). The narrative structure has frequently been likened by critics, and not least by Mitchell himself, to a "Russian doll" (Mitchell 2004; see also Ng 2015: 107; Hopf 2011: 109; and, for critical discussions of the appropriateness of this term, O'Donnell 2015: 75–79 and Wiemann 2017: 512–514). Indeed, the arrangement of the diegetic levels could be described as a linear narrative path following a transverse section through the centre of a Russian doll, as can be demonstrated by the use of brackets indicating narrative levels:

(AE 1 (RF 1 (LR 1 (TC 1 (S 1 (Z) S 2) TC 2) LR 2) RF 2) AE 2)[74]

---

[73] Structurally, this alludes to Italo Calvino's postmodernist masterpiece *If on a Winter's Night a Traveller*, acknowledged by Mitchell as one of his influences in the genesis of the novel (see Mitchell 2005). Calvino opens up ever new narratives for his protagonist, the Reader, addressed in the second person, to peruse, but these narratives are denied their conclusions by a number of mishaps, such as faulty print editions, and once interrupted, they are never returned to. In *Cloud Atlas*, this principle of narrative disruption is emulated, but the interrupted narratives are returned to and given conclusions, albeit not closure. For a comparative reading of *Cloud Atlas* and *If on a Winter's Night a Traveller* with particular regard to their fragmented structures, see McMorran (2011). For an overview of the narrative levels, their settings and narrators and how they are nested, see also Mezey (2011: 14–15).

[74] The sections of narrative are represented by the initials of their protagonists with the numbers indicating part one or two of the respective episodes. As can be seen immediately, only the innermost 'doll', the "Sloosha's Crossin' an' Ev'rythin' After" episode, represented by the letter Z for its protagonist Zachry, is presented in its entirety.

What makes this narrative arrangement unusual despite its neat symmetry is that these narrative levels are not presented in their ontological order from 'lowest' (i.e. the first diegetic level) to 'highest' (i.e. the sixth diegetic level), but in reverse order for the first half of the novel.[75] The typical narrative order of mise en abyme structures – as for example in One Thousand and One Nights, where a similar amount of nested narrative levels are presented, but beginning with the (intra-)diegetic level and then following through with stories-within-stories of the intradiegetic narrator Scheherazade's narratives – is thus turned inside-out (see also Parker 2010: 206–207).

This narrative setup is instrumental in the novel's infinite aesthetics: it lets the narrative appear to extend *ad infinitum* because it lends it the infinite 'depth' of a potentially endless stacking of narrative levels coupled with a circular temporality. On the one hand, the novel's structure is both recursive and characterised by a lack of closure on all narrative levels and therefore can be understood as infinite by virtue of the Basic Metaphor of Infinity, making it a *réduplication à l'infini* in Dällenbach's sense (see ch. 2.2.2). On the other hand, this strangely inverted mise en abyme structure impacts both on the temporal and the logical structure of the novel, which both are twisted to create a "strange loop" (Hofstadter 1979), bending the narrative progress into a circle and thus reflecting in the narrative structure the novel's central topic of Nietzschean eternal recurrence.

As far as the mise en abyme structure is concerned, it is clear that the narrative levels lead to textual recursion: storytelling, or, given the novel's emphasis on moments of reception, the moment of being confronted with stories, forms a structural principle in *Cloud Atlas*. As already mentioned, due to the inverted mise en abyme structure the connection between the various narrative episodes only presents itself belatedly to the reader. Again, the typical order of storytelling – that of a narrator signalling more or less directly the beginning of a narrative that is about to follow – is inverted, for only after they have read the first parts of the various narrative episodes, readers discover in the subsequent section that the preceding was already read (or viewed) by the narrator on the next diegetic level and therefore has the status of a narrative within another narrative. The focus thus shifts from the narrating to the receiving, the being told, because

---

[75] My use of highest/lowest here follows Genette, who writes that "*any event a narrative recounts is at a diegetic level immediately higher than the level at which the narrating act producing this narrative is placed*" (1980: 228). In *Cloud Atlas*, then, the lowest narrative level is the "Sloosha's Crossin'" episode: it contains the narrating act (watching the orison recording) that (retroactively) 'creates' the next episode, "The Orison of Sonmi~451", which in turn contains the narrating act (watching a film) that 'creates' "The Ghastly Ordeal", and so on, up to the 'highest' level, which is "The Pacific Travel Journal of Adam Ewing".

this is the new information readers get when they find out that the protagonist of one level is also a reader of the preceding protagonist's tale (see also Mezey 2011: 16–17; Currie 2009: 361–362). In the process of reading *Cloud Atlas*, then, the reader's expectations as to the structure of the novel are subverted time and again: upon picking up the novel a common expectation would be that the first episode, "The Pacific Journal of Adam Ewing", constitutes the primary (lowest level) diegesis, with Adam Ewing as its homodiegetic and extradiegetic narrator, when in fact it is the highest level diegesis. When the journal is interrupted mid-sentence (*CA* 39) and Robert Frobisher's first letter from Zedelghem follows on the next page, its link to what went before in the novel is entirely in the dark, because the "Letters from Zedelghem" episode is set not only about 80 years after Adam Ewing's travels, but also at the other end of the world – in fact, the two settings form almost exact antipodes – and it presents an entirely different cast of characters. Only at the end of Frobisher's third long letter does the connection to Ewing's travel journal, and hence the nature of the narrative embedding, become clear, as Frobisher now mentions how he has found a battered and incomplete copy of the journal. The protagonist Frobisher at this point becomes a reader, asking in his letter questions and making assumptions similar to those that any reader of *Cloud Atlas* might already have asked or made: he is curious about setting, provenance and authenticity of the journal, speculates about the continuation of its plot and draws literary parallels (*CA* 64), all of which places a firm emphasis on the aspect of reception in the process of embedding. In similar ways, this type of reception-oriented 'belated' embedding is repeated for the other episodes, leading to what Mark Currie identifies as a "relation of reading" between the novel's characters (2009: 362): Rufus Sixsmith, the ever-absent recipient of Frobisher's letters, becomes a character in "Half-Lives: The First Luisa Rey Mystery" – the only instance in the novel of a character making an appearance 'in the flesh' in more than one episode[76] – and after his murder, Frobisher's letters pass on to the protagonist Luisa Rey, who reads them avidly (*CA* 116, 120); in the next episode, "Half-Lives" itself is sent as a manuscript to publisher Timothy Cavendish (*CA* 156), who overcomes his initial reluctance to become an avid reader of the manuscript; Cavendish's own "Ghastly Ordeal" mem-

---

[76] It could be argued, however, that Sixsmith does not really appear in "Letters from Zedelghem" in any other way than as the passive addressee of Frobisher's letters, even though Frobisher in the letters mentions things done by Sixsmith, such as the writing of a telegram (*CA* 52) or even a failed attempt at finding Frobisher in person, shortly before the latter's suicide (*CA* 468). Sonmi~451 retains a similarly passive role in "Sloosha's Crossin' an' Ev'rythin' After", where she is revered as goddess by the tribespeople – something that can ultimately be explained by a narrative tradition again.

oir, as becomes clear at the end of the first half of "An Orison of Sonmi~451", has been turned into a film that is then watched with fascination by Sonmi (*CA* 234); and, lastly, Sonmi's own orison has been preserved and is watched by Zachry's descendants at the end of the "Sloosha's Crossin' an' E'vrythin' After" episode (*CA* 309). This retrospective embedding with its "intensified sense of readership" (Mezey 2011: 17) brought about by the clear focus on moments of reception rather than on the actual telling of the story, then, is the recursive principle underlying the mise en abyme structure of *Cloud Atlas*. It regularly recurs throughout the novel and is instrumental in creating the mise en abyme structure.[77]

An equally recurring principle is the conspicuous suspension of closure on a narrative meta-level, perhaps best described as lack of textual (as opposed to narrative) closure. While in *Cloud Atlas* each of the six episodes seems to follow a conventional plot that leads it to some sort of narrative closure, it emerges upon closer examination that all these closures must appear as fragile, since they are all both subverted by the overall structure of the novel and by elements specific to the particular narrative episodes. As Jo Alyson Parker observes, already the splitting up of the narrative episodes in two halves leads to a deferral of closure in which readers are being made to wait for the endings of all the episodes except "Sloosha's Crossin'" (see 2010: 204). However, even when these endings finally arrive, the closure they provide remains provisional. The six episodes that make up the narrative of *Cloud Atlas* find their respective conclusions when Adam Ewing survives the attempt to poison him and, inspired by his travels and his friendship with the freed slave Autua, takes resolve to campaign for the abolitionist movement; Robert Frobisher commits suicide; Luisa Rey, in typical crime novel fashion, solves the mystery and unveils the corporate conspiracy; Timothy Cavendish escapes from his 'ghastly ordeal' at Aurora House to retire peacefully; Sonmi~451 awaits her execution; and Zachry escapes the Kona on Big Isle to start a family elsewhere and die as an old man. Taken by themselves, these would be typical, almost over-conventionalised, stock conclusions, but given the context of the narrative structure of *Cloud Atlas*, the closure that is implied in each of these conclusions is instantly denied: The closures that seem to be achieved on the level of each single narrative episode are undercut by the fact that the episodes end with the opening up of another narrative level of the mise en abyme structure. Thus, on a meta-level – in the sense of bringing the narrative itself, or the act of narrating, to an end – the very opposite of closure is enacted: a strong sense of incompletion ensues, something that is already implied in the

---

[77] For a similar line of argumentation, albeit with a focus on the recursiveness of textual constructedness in *Cloud Atlas*, see Front (2015: 79–80).

sudden interruption of the narratives throughout the first half of the novel. As Peter Childs and James Green observe, "Although the nested structure of *Cloud Atlas* does satisfy the readerly desire for the closure of each of its interrupted stories, the concepts of narrative transmission and the transmigration of identity underpinning the novel's architecture suggest that endings are always provisional and arbitrary, germinating new beginnings" (2013: 157).

These new beginnings are to be found precisely in the reception of the stories at the superordinate diegetic levels, which points to the narratives transcending themselves as they continue to exist on a different diegetic (and hence ontological) level beyond their actual textual boundaries.[78] This holds true particularly for the middle episodes that are framed by other episodes and themselves are narrative frames to other diegetic levels, which they present, as mentioned above, with a strong focus on the mode of reception: Sonmi's orison ends in her last wish of being allowed to finish watching the filmic version of Timothy Cavendish's memoirs (*CA* 349) and so defers closure by opening up another narrative. Cavendish's "Ghastly Ordeal" likewise defies the apparent closure of its plot in ending on the protagonist's comparison of himself with Alexander Solzhenitsyn, whose place of exile, the Vermont town of Cavendish (see Rimer 1994), likely served as inspiration for Timothy Cavendish's name. "Like Solzhenitsyn, I shall return, one bright dusk" (*CA* 387), Cavendish announces in his final words, not only spurring a chain of intertextual associations[79],

---

[78] For an opposing reading, see Hopf, who from the fact that "every protagonist in the novel shares the desire to complete the narrative they began reading in the first half" infers that "the desire for narrative closure is a constant for these diegetic readers as well as for the external reader" (2011: 115).

[79] Solzhenitsyn's perhaps best-known work, *The Gulag Archipelago*, does not only thematise forced labour in Soviet labour camps and is thus aligned with the central topic of slavery in *Cloud Atlas*, but its title also establishes a connection to the topicality of islands in *Cloud Atlas*. Not only do islands, or rather groups of islands, form the geographical and temporal scope of the novel (see Ng 2015: 108), beginning with Adam Ewing departing from the Chatham Islands and ending with his arrival on Hawaii, which is also the location for the novel's other temporal endpoint, the post-apocalyptic world of "Sloosha's Crossin' an' Ev'rythin' After", but they are also settings in other parts of the text: Luisa Rey's mystery takes her to Swannekke Island, Timothy Cavendish's ordeal is set on the British Isles, and Sonmi~451 lives on the Korean peninsula. This ubiquity of islands in the novel perhaps points to another intertext that is alluded to in *Cloud Atlas* through several parallels: the seventeenth meditation from John Donne's *Devotions upon Emergent Occasions* (on this intertext, see also Wallhead and Kohlke 2010: 224). Firstly, this meditation famously contains the line, "No Man is an *Iland*, intire of it selfe; every man is a peece of the *Continent*, a part of the *maine*" (Donne 2015: 299), which is conceptually echoed in Mitchell's concluding image of a human life being a drop in the ocean (*CA* 509; discussed at greater length below). Secondly, a link to the comet-shaped birthmark in *Cloud*

but also pointing to the novel's topic of eternal recurrence and so immediately questioning the finality of the narrative. Like Sonmi's orison, Luisa Rey's narrative ends in a moment of reception: after she obtains from Sixsmith's daughter Frobisher's final letters addressed to her father – the letters that make up the subsequent section, that is, part two of the "Letters from Zedelghem" episode –, she inhales the scent of one of the old letters and wonders, *"Are molecules of Zedelghem Château, of Robert Frobisher's hand, dormant in this paper for forty-four years, now swirling in my lungs, in my blood?"* (*CA* 436). This suggests an extreme form of reception, incorporation – as if indeed the transmigration of souls, an idea the novel repeatedly toys with, were also possible through the materiality of the written word –, and in placing a focus on the impact Frobisher's letters have on Rey, the continuity of narrative beyond its boundaries is implied once more. Such a continuity is also, despite all appearances to the contrary, implicit in the last of the "Letters from Zedelghem". Although Robert Frobisher in the letter announces his imminent suicide, a most definitive form of closure to the fate of a protagonist and his story, he does so not without emphasising his firm belief in Nietzsche's theory of eternal recurrence, stressing (with an echo of Timothy Cavendish's last words) that "[w]e do not stay dead long" (*CA* 471). As can be seen from Frobisher's influence, through his letters, on Luisa Rey, "[i]ndividual demise in Mitchell's novel does not spell an end but, rather, a reigniting of life through the transpositional links with other central characters" (McCulloch 2012: 161). Closure here is thus again subverted before it can be attained, something that is reinforced by Frobisher's signing of his suicide letter with a Latin quotation: "Sunt lacrimae rerum" (*CA* 471). This overt intertextual reference to a half-line from Vergil's *Aeneid* (1900: 1.462) opens up an entirely new textual horizon that, crucially, is also rooted in a moment of reception, as the words are uttered by Aeneas when in distant, foreign Carthage he encounters mural depic-

---

Atlas emerges when Donne asks, "who takes off his *Eie* from a *Comet* when that breaks out?" (2015: 299). Finally, in this meditation Donne describes the entirety of humankind as a book authored by God, a conventional trope that sees the extra-linguistic world as a kind of "hyper-text" (Chrzanowska-Kluczewska 2004: 79). Donne's extended metaphor – "*All mankinde is of one Author, and is one volume; when one Man dies, one Chapter is not torne out of the booke, but translated into a better language; and every Chapter must be so translated; God emploies severall translators; some peeces are translated by Age, some by sicknesse, some by warre, some by justice*" (2015: 299) – is, of course, full of metafictional potential and seems to provide yet another image for the narrative structure of *Cloud Atlas*, where the various chapters cover the lives of several protagonists and translate central motifs across the novel's vast spatio-temporal distances. For a similar reading, see also Celia Wallhead and Marie-Luise Kohlke, who also link Donne's 'book of the world' metaphor to the connections between the characters of *Cloud Atlas* (2010: 225).

tions of the Trojan War on the walls of the temple of Juno.[80] Thus, the novel's textual scope is augmented to include the reception of two classical epic poems, Vergil's *Aeneid*, invoked by Frobisher, and its pre-text, Homer's *Iliad*, as represented in the mural Aeneas encounters, an intertextual allusion that mirrors the novel's overarching principle of recursive reception and so again suspends closure on a textual meta-level.

In the two episodes that can be considered as frames to the entire novel, "Sloosha's Crossin' an' Ev'rythin' After" and "The Pacific Journal of Adam Ewing" – one is the diegetic frame in that it presents the lowest diegetic level, the other is the 'physical' frame in that it opens and closes the novel – textual closure is overcome in yet another way. It is clear that both episodes constitute in one way or another an end to reception: the "Sloosha's Crossin'" episode cannot be read at another diegetic level in the novel, as there simply is no lower level, and the "Pacific Journal" does not contain another diegetic level of the novel to be read by Adam Ewing, as this episode is the highest diegetic level represented in the novel. Nevertheless, both end in similar openness as the other episodes of *Cloud Atlas*. As these two frame episodes are of particular relevance to my argument and contribute perhaps the most to the novel's ethical appeal that ensues from its textual alterity, they are discussed in detail below.

What follows both from the novel's textual openness and from its recursive mise en abyme structure that is built on the principle of foregrounding processes of reading is that the narrative structure of *Cloud Atlas* can indeed serve as the source domain for the Basic Metaphor of Infinity. The narrative embedding both

---

80 This is "one of the most quoted and controversial utterances" in the entire *Aeneid*, as David Wharton states at the beginning of his detailed discussion of the line, a controversy which arises because the semantics are "perceptibly and intentionally ambiguous" (Wharton 2008: 259, 260). The plethora of scholarly interpretations collected and contrasted by Wharton range between the phrase expressing belief in universal sympathy with human suffering and it referring to the mural's, i.e., in a more general reading, art's, depiction of human compassion. The to my knowledge only other reading of *Cloud Atlas* that pays attention to this particular intertextual reference is Jason Mezey's. Mezey analyses the quotation of Aeneas's encounter with his own past as an "act of reading [that] is recursive" and that in the encounter with a traumatic past implies the potential for (self-)renewal, as an individual's story may lead to universal compassion and hence serve as an example that effects change (2011: 30). In the context of Mitchell's novel, one might add, this reading gains particular traction because "lacrimae", the Latin word for "tears", establishes a connection to the conclusion of Adam Ewing's "Pacific Journal", where the multitude of drops of water – after all, tears are nothing else than this – that make up an ocean is evoked: It is this concluding image (for a more detailed analysis, see below) that most clearly advocates the individual's responsibility before history. I agree with Mezey that "Sunt lacrimae rerum" would seem to highlight how this responsibility can be evoked by the texts that make up our (hi)stories.

creates a clearly iterating textual pattern and, due to the rejection of closure at every level, a strong element of the indefinite, resulting in precisely the kind of indefinitely iterating structure on which the Basic Metaphor of Infinity may come into operation. As some of the central motifs the novel repeatedly returns to, such as the "atlas of clouds" (*CA* 373) or the Nietzschean concept of eternal recurrence – both will be returned to below –, are associated with the infinite, both in its spatial and its temporal dimension, and as infinity is thus also present at the story level, it seems clear that the mise en abyme structure in *Cloud Atlas* may indeed be understood as infinite through the Basic Metaphor of Infinity.[81]

This sense of infinity prevalent in the narrative structure is reinforced by the 'strange loop' that ensues from the disparity between the temporal arrangement of the novel and its logical sequence of narrative levels. A strange loop, according to Douglas Hofstadter, who coined the term, "occurs whenever, by moving upwards (or downwards) through the levels of some hierarchical system, we find ourselves right back where we started" (1979: 10).[82] In the case of *Cloud Atlas*, the inversion, or turning inside-out, of the mise en abyme structure creates such a strange loop as far as both the novel's temporal and its logical structure are concerned. In terms of the temporal dimension, the strange loop results from the fact that a linear reading progress through the novel in terms of the story time takes the reader from the nineteenth-century travels of Adam Ewing to the post-apocalyptic future setting of "Sloosha's Crossin' an' Ev'rythin' After" and back to the outset. In other words, the disjointed chronology of story time is at odds with the linearity of discourse time. While story time and discourse time run parallel, both progressing in a linear way, until the mid-section of the novel, the chronological progress of story time then changes and for the second half of the novel – by means of a series of leaps back in story time as discourse time progresses – the chronological order of the narrative episodes is reversed.[83] This temporal arrangement results in what Lynda Ng calls the "confounding [of] linear time by positing an interrelationship of past and future configurations of human society" (2015: 107).

---

[81] This central status of infinity in the novel was acknowledged by David Mitchell in an interview in which he cited a story "about an Egyptian Goddess who gave birth to a pregnant daughter, whose embryo in turn was already pregnant and so on to infinity" as inspiration for the narrative structure (Mitchell 2004).

[82] On strange loops as aesthetic devices in postmodern fiction, see also McHale (1987: 119–121).

[83] Jo Alyson Parker describes the narrative structure of *Cloud Atlas* in a very similar way and provides an insightful chart (see 2010: 207) that illustrates what she calls – with reference to Timothy Cavendish's statement "Time's Arrow became Time's Boomerang" (*CA* 147), jocularly referring to his state of inebriation – the "boomerang trajectory" (2010: 202) of the narrative.

At the same time, the inverted mise en abyme structure also means that the (onto-)logical order of the narrative episodes is first presented in inverted order, starting with the highest diegetic level, Adam Ewing's travel journal – which incidentally also is the 'lowest' level in the ontological hierarchy of the narrative since it depends, through relations of embedding, on all the other levels –, and working its way to the lowest diegetic (and 'highest' hierarchical) level – the "Sloosha's Crossin'" episode is "the container of all the stories 'below' it" (Hopf 2011: 116) –, while in the second half of the novel this order is then restored. The effect created by these contrary chronologies is that each 'frame' narrative is framed by the narrative it in turn frames: the primary diegesis of "Sloosha's Crossin'" may contain all the other episodes in the ontological order of the narrative levels, but is itself contained by all the other episodes in the order of discourse time. Conversely, "The Pacific Journal of Adam Ewing", which constitutes the frame containing all other episodes in the discursive order of the novel, is contained by all other stories in terms of its ontological status. Likewise, this paradoxical situation holds true for all the other narrative episodes: they all contain those episodes in the ontological hierarchy in which they are contained in the order of discourse time, and vice versa.[84] When Isaac Sachs, a minor character in "Half-Lives", in an intensely metafictional moment muses on time as *"an infinite matryoshka doll of painted moments, each 'shell' (the present) encased inside a nest of 'shells' (previous presents)"* and concludes that *"[t]he doll of 'now' likewise encases a nest of presents yet to be [...]"* (*CA* 363), this is a precise description of the temporal structure of *Cloud Atlas* (see Parker 2010: 206; Mezey 2011: 14).

The effect of this strange loop created by the narrative structure is the establishing of a circularity or cyclicality in the narrative that reflects the topic of Nietzsche's eternal recurrence the novel toys with, most prominently in the "Letters from Zedelghem" episode, in which Vyvyan Ayrs wants to name a piece of music "Eternal Recurrence in honor of his beloved Nietzsche" (*CA* 84), whose *Also sprach Zarathustra* Frobisher describes as "Ayrs's bible" (*CA* 63).[85] Nietzsche

---

[84] Another analogy, related to the strange loop, to describe this property of the narrative is the Möbius strip. Parker, whose analysis of the relation of framing and embedding in the novel is similar to mine, concludes that "[f]rame narrative and embedded narrative change places depending on perspective so that the outside (frame) and inside (embedded narrative) are one and the same [...]" (2010: 206). In other words, there is no real 'inside' and 'outside' left, but just a logically twisted narrative band possessing one side only – a topological characteristic of the Möbius strip. On the similarity between the framing structure and a Möbius strip, see also Fiona McCulloch (2012: 147).

[85] The strength of Nietzsche's presence in the novel, and in particular in the "Letters from Zedelghem" episode is attested to in the novel's Acknowledgements, where Mitchell points out that "Vyvyan Ayrs quotes Nietzsche more freely than he admits". For a more thorough dis-

posited that the universe is temporally infinite, but spatially finite and hence only contains a finite number of atoms, and deducted from this that "the number of the configurations of these atoms must be finite" and hence that all states of being (all combinations of atoms) are bound to recur, not once, but eternally (Front 2015: 73–74). Crucially, in *Also sprach Zarathustra* this eternal recurrence is associated with a series of circular images:

> Alles geht, Alles kommt zurück; ewig rollt das Rad des Seins. Alles stirbt, Alles blüht wieder auf, ewig läuft das Jahr des Seins.
> Alles bricht, Alles wird neu gefügt; ewig baut sich das gleiche Haus des Seins. Alles scheidet, Alles grüsst sich wieder; ewig bleibt sich treu der Ring des Seins.
> In jedem Nu beginnt das Sein; um jedes Hier rollt sich die Kugel Dort. Die Mitte ist überall. Krumm ist der Pfad der Ewigkeit. (Nietzsche 1968: 268–269)[86]

The images of circularity (the wheel, the ring and the ball) evoked by Nietzsche seem to inform the circular temporal structure in *Cloud Atlas*. Indeed, the notion of a "crooked" – another translation would be "curved" – "path of eternity" is emulated by the 'path' the narrative in *Cloud Atlas* takes because of the novel's inverted mise en abyme structure. This is the reason why Hicks's and Parker's descriptions of the narrative structure as "boomeranging arc" (Hicks 2010) or "boomerang trajectory" (Parker 2010: 202) respectively, acknowledging the return, or recurrence, inherent in the structure, is so appropriate. Since this narrative structure "embed[s] the future inside the past" (Currie 2009: 361), it is instrumental in creating the strange loop the narrative takes in Mitchell's novel. Ng cites the disruption of linear concepts of time by the achronological embedding when she claims that "a more apt analogy for the novel's structure is that of the ouroboros – the snake eating its own tail" (2015: 118). Of course, the ouroboros is also a symbol for infinity, especially in a temporal sense, as eternity, as well as for reincarnation and eternal life (see Rösch 2010: 325; Ferber 2007: 189)[87], which

---

cussion of Nietzsche's eternal recurrence in *Cloud Atlas*, see Front (2015: 73–95) and Hicks (2010). As both Front and Hicks point out, in particular Frobisher's last letter before his suicide is rife with his belief in the eternal return of human history, both on an individual level and on a collective level (see *CA* 471).

[86] "Everything goeth, everything returneth; eternally rolleth the wheel of existence. Everything dieth, everything blossometh forth again; eternally runneth on the year of existence. Everything breaketh, everything is integrated anew; eternally buildeth itself the same house of existence. All things separate, all things again greet one another; eternally true to itself remaineth the ring of existence. Every moment beginneth existence, around every 'Here' rolleth the ball 'There.' The middle is everywhere. Crooked is the path of eternity" (Nietzsche 1891: 120).

[87] Somewhat contrary to these meanings, Ng sees the ouroboros realised above all in the "narrative self-cannibalization" performed by the narrative structure, which she then links to the

brings the argument concerning the temporal structure of *Cloud Atlas*, as it were, full circle. Indeed, perhaps the best metaphor for the novel's cyclical temporal structure is one provided by Robert Frobisher, who ironically refers to the theory of eternal recurrence as "Nietzsche's gramophone record" (*CA* 471). This image complements the novel's musical sextet structure that is mirrored in the six interwoven narrative levels of its narrative structure with its own mechanical reproduction, the circle-shaped, eternally re-playable gramophone record, and so unites in one image the polyphonic progress of the narrative with its cyclical temporality. Infinity, then, is not only to be found in the *réduplication à l'infini*, but also (and, of course, closely connected) in the circular temporal structure of *Cloud Atlas:* together, they form the "recursive cycle" (Mezey 2011: 13) that is characteristic of the novel's narrative.

4.2 "The Ever-Constant Ineffable": Ethical Encounters

The identification of the novel's narrative and temporal structure as infinite coincides, I suggest, with the catachrestic identification of the text itself as infinite. Both imply that the novel somehow transcends its own physical boundaries, signifying *ad infinitum* and so, at a structural or textual level, creates what Levinas has called the scintillation of poetic language. What is more, such an infinite process of textual signification must reverberate in the reading process. It means that the text's addressing of the reader, which mirrors the countless moments of address and encounters with otherness at the story level of the narrative, is unlimited, even though the physical presence of the text is limited. Ultimately in this way the text becomes infinitely demanding and endows *Cloud Atlas* with a strong ethical impetus.

One particular consequence of the catachrestic identification of the novel's text as infinite would seem to be that in such an infinite text, held together by

---

novel's overarching topics of cannibalism and colonisation (2015: 118). For a similar line of argumentation, see also Shoop and Ryan (2015: 97–98). This reading echoes Adam Ewing's warning that "one fine day, a purely predatory world *shall* consume itself. Yes, the Devil shall take the hindmost until the foremost *is* the hindmost" (*CA* 508). However, this seems to me a rather too negative view of the novel's structure: it neglects the narrative potential for renewal and reflection inherent both in the symbol of the ouroboros and in the narrative structure of *Cloud Atlas* as well as the overall optimistic tone of the novel's concluding image (see Edwards 2011: 194). For an altogether different reading of cannibalism in *Cloud Atlas*, see Wiemann, who describes the novel as a "highly cannibalistic text" because of its appropriation of different genres and styles (2017: 510).

moments of textual embedding and a "relation of reading" (Currie 2009: 362) between the characters, readers are always implicated in the text in a more direct way than is otherwise common. If the stacking of narrative levels is understood to be infinite, then there is no first and no last level, and automatically the question arises what comes 'before' and 'after' the levels represented in the novel. Standard models of literary communication describe the level of nonfictional communication between author and readers as the level preceding the extradiegetic communication between narrator and addressee. Therefore, once the process of narrative embedding is understood to be infinite, this level of communication comes into play as well – if a text is infinite and comprises infinitely many narrative (and hence also ontological) levels, why should the level on which the readers find themselves be exempt from the reaches of the text?

The effect of this in *Cloud Atlas* is not that the readers are sucked into a vertiginous abyss of textual self-procurement, but that a level of address beyond the literal signification of the novel opens up. This is how the text 'scintillates', how it "give[s] sign [...] above and beyond all signification" (Levinas 1989e: 156), in a self-transcending perpetual address to the readers. There is, however, no way to 'read' this next level, in which readers may suspect themselves present as 'characters', or whose timespan may cover the readers' own lifespans, simply because this level does not exist in writing. It exists only as a 'what if' implied in the aesthetic form of Mitchell's novel and is hence transposed into a form of pure address: not the (non-existent) content, but the fact that the text speaks beyond its boundaries is central here – in other words, there is a palpable sense of address, but no directly graspable subject matter. In Levinas's terms, it is saying that prevails over the said in this kind of infinite textual continuation. If, as Critchley claims, saying manifests itself only in writing, and in a kind of writing that destabilises and deconstructs the boundaries of ontological language (1994: 650), then this seems to be a literary example of such writing. In *Cloud Atlas*, not only the boundaries of ontological language, but those of the aesthetic form of the novel itself are destabilised. The result is an appeal that emanates from the infinite text in the form of its addressing of the reader that goes beyond the textual confines and so in a sense pierces the aesthetic form. This appeal constitutes the ethical centre of *Cloud Atlas*. It shows itself in particularly clarity in the novel's two framing episodes, "The Pacific Journal of Adam Ewing" and "Sloosha's Crossin' an' Ev'rythin' After", as well as in the central image of the atlas of clouds, which as the novel's leitmotif establishes a metaphorical connection between both episodes and the episodes separating them.[88]

---

[88] Gerd Bayer, without becoming more concrete, claims that "Levinasian encounter[s] with the

As the episode that constitutes the novel's frame in discourse time, "The Pacific Journal of Adam Ewing" introduces some of the key topics and, in particular, it perhaps most clearly voices the ethical imperative that reverberates throughout *Cloud Atlas*. What is key to this is the relationship between the narrator and Autua[89], a member of the Moriori people that has been colonised and enslaved by the more aggressive Maori (a situation echoed in the relationship between the Kona and the Valleysmen in post-apocalyptic Hawaii). Their first encounter comes early in the novel, when Ewing by chance comes to witness the flogging of Autua at the hands of the Maori and an intense moment of non-verbal communication takes place:

> The piteous prisoner, hoarfrosted with many harsh years, was bound naked to an A-frame. His body shuddered with each excoriating lash, his back was a vellum of bloody runes, but his insensible face bespoke the serenity of a martyr already in the care of the Lord.
>
> I confess, I swooned under each fall of the lash. Then a peculiar thing occurred. The beaten savage raised his slumped head, found *my* eye & shone me a look of uncanny, amicable knowing! As if a theatrical performer saw a long-lost friend in the Royal Box and, undetected by the audience, communicated his recognition. (*CA* 6)

In this scene, Autua's body has become the medium for a language of violence, "a vellum of bloody runes" that is being inscribed with each lash of the whip and 'read' by those attending the spectacle. At the same time, Ewing, the narrator, is addressed in a very different, more immediate, language that emanates from the vulnerability of the beaten body laid bare under the "excoriating" strokes.[90] This

---

Other [...] are exactly the kind of encounter and empathetic rapport carefully staged and celebrated in *Cloud Atlas*" (2015: 350). I think the passages analysed here may serve as examples supporting Bayer's claim.

89 Autua's palindromic name can be read as an allusion to the novel's narrative structure (see Hicks 2010). On the symbolism of the names in *Cloud Atlas*, especially those of Autua, Meronym, and Adam and Zachry, whose initials reflect their status as first and last protagonist of the novel, see Schoene (2009: 117), Shoop and Ryan (2015: 98), Wallhead and Kohlke (2010: 240, 244n14) and Hicks (2010). Moreover, the names of Adam and Zachry also carry biblical connotations of the beginning – Adam, according to the Book of Genesis, was the first man – and end – the Old Testament Book of Zechariah contains sections of apocalyptic prophecies – of time, while the name Ewing might be an oblique pun on the German word "ewig", meaning eternal, as in the German "ewige Wiederkunft" for Nietzsche's eternal recurrence.

90 In contrast, Wallhead and Kohlke claim that "Ewing's 'reading' of the victim in terms of Christian martyrdom" transforms the experience, from Ewing's point of view, into a sublime one, which means that "Ewing is relieved of the need to formulate an ethical response in the face of the other's trauma" (2010: 236). This shows, I think, how Ewing is guided by the dominant socio-political discourses of his time and only gradually over the course of the entire narrative undergoes a development that makes him leave behind the white Christian sense of

is a moment that illustrates what Levinas describes as the language of the face, which presents itself in "extreme exposure, defencelessness, vulnerability itself" (Levinas 1989a: 83). From the destitution and utter helplessness of the bound and abused man goes out a wordless call, a communicative act in which the saying is paramount. It is a silent appeal that is recognised by the narrator even before the direct eye contact between Autua and himself, when it leads to his strong visceral reaction of swooning at every lash. The saying, according to Levinas, "is the fact that before the face I do not simply remain there contemplating it, I respond to it" (1985: 88) – and respond to the face that emerges as the skin comes off Autua's mistreated back is precisely what Ewing does. Crucially, the compassion Ewing senses is not grounded in an already established relation with Autua, whom he sees for the first time and whose name he does not even know at this point. Rather, it is his response to the plea of the face. Indeed, Ng shows that this response elicits a marked shift in Ewing's attitude towards the Moriori, whom he until this encounter describes in "zoomorphic terms" (Ng 2015: 114) when he observes their "bovine torpor" (*CA* 6). Already in this brief encounter, then, wordless but by no means devoid of language, the foundations of a radical change in Ewing's thought are laid.

The irruption that the encounter with the face that emerges from the maltreated body of the other, Autua, represents for Ewing becomes clear in the further development of the plot. The next time he encounters Autua is a week later aboard the *Prophetess* somewhere in the Pacific, when Autua emerges as a stowaway in Ewing's cabin and asks for his aid to escape enslavement. Ewing's reluctance to help the stowaway (and in the process possibly endanger his own status on board) is only overcome in a second moment of absolute vulnerability, in which Autua reacts to Ewing's refusal of help by placing a dagger in Ewing's hands and asking him to kill him instantly rather than deliver him without protection to the tyrannical captain (*CA* 27). It is only after this renewed realisation of the other man's vulnerability and a clear reminder of his own responsibility for the life of the other facing him that Ewing can bring himself to help the freed slave by persuading the captain to give Autua a chance to prove himself as a crew member. This act of being there for the other is of course later reciprocated, as Autua saves Ewing's life when the fraud and murderer Dr Henry Goose attempts to poison him. In the end, his relationship with Autua, founded on that moment of the silent plea of the face, leads Ewing to the resolve to

---

entitlement. The foundations for this change, I suggest, are laid precisely in this encounter with the pained and beaten Autua. Ewing's swooning shows that he is *not* free from any response to the suffering he witnesses.

"pledge [himself] to the Abolitionist cause" (*CA* 508) and fight slavery to make the world a better place for his son to inherit. Aware of the difficulties in achieving the goals of his newly found convictions, Ewing ends his travel journal (and the entire novel) by imagining his father-in-law criticising him for his naïvety in taking up what seems a futile fight against human nature and answering that criticism:

> "[...] Naïve, dreaming Adam. He who would do battle with the many-headed hydra of human nature must pay a world of pain & his family must pay it along with him! & only as you gasp your dying breath shall you understand, your life amounted to no more than one drop in a limitless ocean!"
> Yet, what is any ocean but a multitude of drops? (*CA* 508–509)

Mezey, who describes this passage as the "ethical climax of the novel", sees in it the "ethical rebirth" of Adam Ewing (2011: 27, 12), and it is certainly true that a profound change in Ewing's attitude, from being enshrouded in racist discourse (see Ng 2015; Mezey 2011: 23–24) to becoming a champion for abolitionism, has been effected by his relationship with Autua. This concluding image of the infinity of the ocean that is made up of singular drops neatly encapsulates not only Ewing's transformation but the performative ethical power of the entire narrative. While I agree with Mezey that this final tableau creates a "sharp sense of ethical clarity about the individual's obligations to a global totality" (2011: 12), I would like to add that, with the context of Adam Ewing's journey, even prior to that stand the obligations to the other in his or her infinite alterity: ethics is dependent on the encounter with the other and only based on this can any ethical 'totality' (if such a thing exists – the word choice seems unfortunate here given Mezey's reliance on a Levinasian ethics; see 2011: 22–23) come to pass. In the end, in the image with which Ewing presents readers, it is the multitude of singular drops that prevails over the totality of the ocean, just like the totality of human society, whose entrenched rules and sense of status represent the main obstacles to Ewing's new-found cause, ultimately consists of a multitude of others.

With regard to the overall aesthetics of the novel, this concluding image fulfils a further purpose: it reinforces the lack of textual closure and the sense of an address transcending the text's boundaries. When *Cloud Atlas* ends in an image of limitlessness and openness, this is also a last metafictional commentary. The relation to alterity presented in "Adam Ewing's Pacific Journal" is first and foremost that of Ewing to his other, Autua, but at the same time also another instance of the "relation of reading" pervading the novel. This becomes clear in Ewing's son Jackson, who, symbolic of generations to come, is not only the journal's addressee, but also its editor (see *CA* 501), and so takes on the role of a reader who is addressed by and responds to a text. In fact, the narrative construction of *Cloud Atlas* means that "every character in this novel is encountered by other characters as a textual artifact" (Mezey 2011: 27) and that therefore otherness is frequently met through narrative. In its resistance to textual closure, which is reinforced in the image the novel leaves its readers with, the novel implies a wariness of the finality of the said and of the predicament of the betrayal inherent in any text. Continued signification, textual address continuing *ad infinitum*, is a performative textual strategy, necessary but necessarily failing, of deferring the betrayal. This conclusion also implies an awareness of the novel's own status as such a textual artefact that will be encountered by readers and must address those readers, with the address taking on the form of an appeal to take on responsibility for the other, for the fragile drops that surround them in the ocean of human society. As such, the novel's conclusion continues the overall impetus of its narrative structure, which engenders a "self-conscious temporal loop between the act of reading and the act of writing which represents it" (Currie 2009: 363) and transfers it – in an instance of textual self-transcendence which simultaneously becomes a stark appeal for ethical responsibility – from the levels of the novel's protagonists to the level of the readers of *Cloud Atlas*. It is thus not just in this concluding image, but in the continuation of the text beyond its boundaries, infinitely addressing the readers and infinitely appealing to them, that the ethical power of *Cloud Atlas* can be located.

Similarly, the novel's other frame story "Sloosha's Crossin' an' Ev'rythin' After", which is the diegetic (and hence logical) frame of Mitchell's narrative universe, also presents a story of encountering alterity that ends in a scene which testifies to the appellative power of narrative. As the only one of the episodic narratives that is presented in full, without being interrupted by other narratives, and the only narrative that is not being read by another character somewhere in another of the nested narratives, "Sloosha's Crossin'" is the narrative linchpin, a structural element on which the entire novel hinges, and, crucially, presents at a little over the halfway mark of the novel its first conclusion.[91]

Its story closely echoes that of "Adam Ewing's Pacific Journal". In a post-apocalyptic version of Hawaii that is thrown back to a world of primeval tribalism, the narrator Zachry is a member of a peaceful tribe, the Valleysmen, who are under attack and eventually are enslaved by the warlike Kona. His most formative encounter with the other, an encounter he himself acknowledges as life-

---

[91] While the "Sloosha's Crossin'" episode is not *read* by other characters in the novel – its only readers are the real world readers outside the diegesis – it is still being told to and hence received by other characters. The episode represents a return to the mode of oral storytelling, as can be seen from the listeners being directly addressed, first by Zachry and then, in the 'epilogue' of the chapter, by Zachry's child (see *CA* 243, 309).

changing (see *CA* 249), comes when a (space) ship arrives with Meronym, a member of the technologically (and supposedly also culturally) advanced Prescients, who wants to stay as a guest with Zachry's family. Initially, Zachry meets her with suspicion of her advanced knowledge, identifying a "vin'gary stink o' Smart" (*CA* 251) about her, and a mutual sense of distrust, strengthened when Zachry is caught eavesdropping on Meronym and searching her belongings (see *CA* 259–265), develops between the two. It takes a moment of crisis to turn around this negative relationship: Zachry's sister Catkin is stung by a scorpionfish and lies on her deathbed – narrowly avoiding death through poisoning is another parallel between the "Pacific Journal" and "Sloosha's Crossin'" –, when Zachry in his desperation turns to Meronym for help, hoping that the advanced medications available to the Prescients may save his sister. However, she initially refuses to take action, even after she has visited Catkin and has been exposed to the dying girl's destitution, which leads to a dialogue with Zachry in which the ethical obligation she is under becomes apparent:

> The Prescient didn't move nor look at me, nay. *The life o' your tribe's got a nat'ral order. Catkin'd o' treaded on that scorpion fish if I'd been here or not.*
> Rainbirds spilt their galoshin'-galishin' song. *I'm just a stoopit goat herder, but I reck'n jus' by bein' here you're bustin' that nat'ral order. I reck'n you're killin' Catkin by not actin'.* (*CA* 267)

What is at stake here is a struggle between what Levinas would perhaps call the order of Heideggerian ontology and the demand of the other that is in opposition to this ontological order. In fact, Meronym's line of defence, invoking the "natural order" of things and thus relegating her personal responsibility to the construction of an overarching, anonymous, faceless concept, recalls what Levinas strongly criticises about Heideggerian ontology:

> Heideggerian ontology subordinates the relation with the other to the relation with the neuter, Being, and it thus continues to exalt the will to power, **whose legitimacy the other alone can unsettle**, troubling good conscience. When Heidegger calls attention to the forgetting of Being, veiled by the diverse realities it illuminates, [...] when he deplores the orientation of the intellect toward technology, he maintains a regime of power more inhuman than mechanism [...]. This is **an existence which takes itself to be natural**, for whom its place in the sun, its ground, its *site*, orient all signification – a pagan *existing*. Being directs it building and cultivating, in the midst of a familiar landscape, on a maternal earth. Anonymous, neuter, it directs it, ethically indifferent, as a heroic freedom, foreign to all guilt with regard to the other. (Levinas 1987b: 52–53; bold emphases mine)

In other words, acts like the positing of a given order of human existence as "natural", just as Meronym does with regard to the technologically less advanced

Valleysmen and their lack of life-saving medicine, are nothing but the erection of smokescreens behind which an individual may hide to shirk their ethical responsibilities. It is, Levinas claims, "the other alone" who may "unsettle" the foundations of such an order of Being, notably by "troubling good conscience". This is precisely what Zachry – and perhaps even before that, Meronym's visit to the dying girl – does: he reminds Meronym of that responsibility she has towards the human other.

Indeed, the situation Meronym finds herself in evokes Judith Butler's take on Levinas's ethics. Butler departs from Levinas's stance that radically places the other before the self and asserts that "the life of the other, the life that is *not* our own, is also our life, since whatever sense 'our' life has is derived precisely from this sociality, this being already, and from the start, dependent on a world of others, constituted in and by a social world" (2012: 140–141). In her argument, she draws on Hannah Arendt's idea of the unchallengeable nature of human cohabitation: since we cannot choose those we share our planet with without "deciding which portion of humanity may live and which may die" – an act tantamount to genocide that, crucially, would deprive its agent of his or her freedom to exercise precisely that choice – what follows is an obligation "to preserve those lives and the open-ended plurality that is the global population" (Butler 2012: 143, 144; see 142–144).[92] When Zachry tells Meronym that "by bein' here" she is "bustin'" the order of the Valleysmen's lives, this serves as a reminder of her obligation towards those she cohabits the island with. Eventually, Zachry's appeal is successful, but not until after a reciprocal act of denuding of the self in which Zachry banishes Meronym's fears of being forced into an unwanted position of healer for the entire tribe by making himself vulnerable through revealing to her his own deepest secret, his role in his father and brother's murder at the hands of the Kona (see *CA* 267–268). Inherent in this moment of vulnerability is then a plea that ultimately cannot remain unanswered: it is, once more, the "thou shalt not kill" expressed by the face of the other (see Levinas 1985: 87, 89), ensuing from the encounter with the other, an encounter that is inevitable in a shared world.

The relationship between Meronym and Zachry, which is much improved from this critical moment on – they now trust each other and as the story develops go on to save each other's lives several times –, fulfils the same function as that be-

---

[92] Reading the ethics propagated by *Cloud Atlas* in this way, with a focus on the ethical obligations arising from cohabiting the earth, is close to approaches that see the novel as cosmopolitan novel or world literature (see especially Schoene 2009, who uses Jean-Luc Nancy's notion of the inoperative community as a backdrop for his reading of *Cloud Atlas* as a cosmopolitan novel; see also McCulloch 2012; Childs and Green 2013).

tween Adam and Autua in the other frame story: It serves as a catalyst for the novel's ethical appeal, an appeal which again becomes manifest in the conclusion of the "Sloosha's Crossin'" episode. Quite fittingly in view of the resistance to closure that is so prominent in *Cloud Atlas*, the conclusion of this episode comes in two parts. After the Valley has been overrun and occupied by the Kona, Meronym frees Zachry from Kona captivity and they manage to flee together. Their dramatic escape ends when they meet a rescue party of Meronym's fellow Prescients. In a quasi-cinematic scene Zachry, lying wounded in a kayak, is watching Big Isle, the island he has spent his entire life on, recede on the horizon:

> I watched clouds awobbly from the floor o' that kayak. Souls cross ages like clouds cross skies, and tho' a cloud's shape nor hue nor size don't stay the same, it's still a cloud an' so is a soul. Who can say where the cloud's blowed from or who the soul'll be 'morrow? Only Sonmi the east an' the west an' the compass an' the atlas, yay, only the atlas o' clouds.
>
> Duophysite saw my eyes was open an' pointed me Big Isle, purple in the sou'eastly blue, an' Mauna Kea hidin' its head like a shy bride.
>
> Yay, my Hole World an' hole life was shrinked 'nuff to fit in the O o' my finger'n'thumb. (*CA* 308)

It is here that the novel's 'vertical', diachronic movement inherent in the topic of the transmigration of souls across the ages is conceptually linked to the 'horizontal', synchronic configuration of the clouds and that for the first time the title-giving "atlas o' clouds" is mentioned.[93] When it is linked to human souls, the cloud atlas – just like the comet-shaped birthmarks that link the characters across the episodes (see Wallhead and Kohlke 2010: 223–224) – becomes an image of the uncertainties inherent in all human interactions, whose impact on others, whether in the near or far future, cannot be known. In this sense, the atlas of clouds and the multitude of drops in the ocean are complementary images – what is any cloud but a multitude of drops? – and span a bridge from this 'first' conclusion of the novel to its 'last' conclusion. Both images convey a sense of unity in diversity, as Childs and Green note: "Just as clouds are ever-changing coalescences of wind-blown water molecules, *Cloud Atlas* suggests that the human species is at once infinitely protean and bound together in an inter-reliant community that spans the boundaries of ethnicity and nation" (2011: 35). The novel then ends where clouds begin and end: in their singular parts, as drops in the ocean. Together, the atlas of clouds and the multitude of

---

[93] The passage is anticipated shortly before, when Zachry uses very similar words to muse on the beliefs of his people, who revere Sonmi as a goddess: "Souls cross the skies o' time [...] like clouds crossin' skies o' the world. Sonmi's the east'n'west, Sonmi's the map an' the edges o' the map an' b'yonder the edges" (*CA* 302).

drops point to yet another circular image underlying the novel: the water cycle, which is not only essential for all life on earth, but also brings together the lives of Mitchell's protagonists in one image.[94] Here the novel itself, as Berthold Schoene observes, strives to become a map of "the sense of th[e] diachronic, multidimensional being-in-common, of human life as such, without fixing it by subjecting it to any particular teleological principle" (2009: 116).

It is this last property, the resistance to the rigidity of any teleology, that makes the image of the atlas of clouds a catachresis and so renders it parallel to the novel's narrative structure. This becomes particularly evident in Timothy Cavendish's wistful longing for an atlas of clouds as "a never-changing map of the ever-constant ineffable" (*CA* 373), a description that shows that the image is self-contradictory in at least two ways. First, the very idea of a "never-changing map" is for all practical purposes an impossibility, since maps in general depict changing entities – no matter whether the change is geological or political – and in this particular case the objects depicted – whether clouds or human relations – are highly instable and constantly shape-shifting (see O'Donnell 2015: 80). Second, what is more important is that the atlas of clouds is supposed to be a map of the ineffable and hence a representation of the unrepresentable. Herein lies the fundamental incoherence that makes the image of the atlas of clouds a catachresis. The cloud atlas is then an aptly impossible image for the ethical relation between human beings: Just as mapping the ineffable is impossible, so is the idea of delineating the ethical encounter and giving a textual representation to the other bound to end in failure and must lead to what Levinas calls betrayal the instance alterity is attempted to be clad in words or captured in any other medium. *Cloud Atlas* is an example thereof, for it, just like the cloud atlas Cavendish craves, casts in language the ineffable of the ethical encounter. While the characters seem aware of the unattainability of this cloud atlas, it would seem that the novel suggests that such a map of the ineffable, a representation of the unrepresentable ethical encounter, can perhaps be achieved in art, be it Frobisher's Cloud Atlas Sextet or Mitchell's *Cloud Atlas*.

Clearly, the novel attempts to perform this very task, to become an aesthetic artefact that testifies to human otherness and the obligations that arise from it. It does so on the one hand by repeatedly using images and describing situations that are symbolic of these ethical obligations and on the other by transferring this ethical appeal into a direct address of its readers conveyed through its infinite textuality. The former is achieved in the many passages that describe decentring encounters with otherness – meeting Autua ultimately makes Ewing ques-

---

[94] On this topic, see also McCulloch, who links the clouds of the titular image to a "repetitive water cycle that mirrors the rebirth motif of the novel" (2012: 163).

tion the order of the world he believes in, just as Zachry's reservations against foreigners are challenged after he meets Meronym, who likewise gives up her reliance on the 'natural order' when she is faced with the dying girl Catkin – and in the central images of the atlas of clouds and the multitude of drops. These passages and images emphasise both alterity, thus constituting an "empathic ethical 'opening up to otherness'" (Wallhead and Kohlke 2010: 225), and the obligation to respond to this otherness. Zachry's final words, "my Hole World an' hole life was shrinked 'nuff to fit in the O o' my finger'n'thumb", encapsulate this process of decentring. They describe a change of perspective which results in the island that has harboured Zachry's entire life being reduced to the size of a tiny O, a drop in an ocean of narrative – the only difference to the changes in attitude that Ewing, Meronym and Zachry undergo is that this time the change of perspective is physical, a rowing away across a multitude of drops from the previous foundations of everything known. Encountering others, then, may lead to radical changes of perspective (after all, Zachry's escape in the kayak is a direct consequence of his having met and befriended Meronym) and, when an ocean is seen as a multitude of drops, and an island as an O, may perhaps even result in the insight that the supposedly taboo ontological order may not be quite as untouchable. At the same time, due to the ostentatious ambiguity of Zachry's minimalistic language, comes the insight that no perspective can be definitive: the world is always a 'Hole World' incomplete in its completeness and can, depending on the point of view, fit into an 'O' formed by fingers – the figure zero, and a symbol for nothingness, but also a circle, and hence emblematic of the novel's theme of eternal recurrence, circularity and its structural infinity. As such, this putting into perspective represents a fitting end to Zachry's narrative.

It is not, however, the end of the "Sloosha's Crossin'" episode. As if to underscore the novel's overall resistance to closure and as if to prospectively echo Robert Frobisher's end, this diegetic frame episode continues beyond its narrator's death. For immediately upon the first conclusion quoted above, separated only by three asterisks, follows a second conclusion of this episode. It comes as a brief epilogue-like coda set after Zachry's death, in which one of his children (it does not become clear whether the first-person narrator here is a son or a daughter), born after the events described in his narrative, comments on Zachry's credibility.[95] Hence another temporal leap to a future presumably several decades

---

[95] A notable change was made in the 2012 film version of *Cloud Atlas*. In an attempt to return to a more (chrono)logical temporal sequence (and probably to keep up suspense in all the episodes), the episodes were all split up into several parts, interspersed with the other narrative episodes, creating the impression of a parallel narration, or perhaps of the different narrative strands being braided together to create a narrative 'plait'. The conclusions of the episodes

after the main action of the "Sloosha's Crossin'" episode has taken place, comparable to the temporal leaps that are brought about by the transitions between the various episodes of the novel. This is where the novel perhaps most clearly insinuates its own infinite textuality. The hint that an indefinite, or even infinite, continuation of the narrative from this point is implied is already contained in the title of the episode: in "Sloosha's Crossin' an' Ev'rythin' After", the "Ev'rythin' After" is – after all – not just a reference to Zachry's adventures after surviving the attack at Sloosha's Crossin', but to an indefinite, all-encompassing amount of narrative that potentially is to follow upon the second conclusion of "Sloosha's Crossin'", distinctly echoing a fairy tale's formulaic 'ever after'. This is reinforced by the prominence of children, symbols of the future, of times to come and narratives to be told and heard/read. According to Schoene, this "can hardly be described as proper ending[]" but rather "stands as a potential recommencement marking the curve of a never-ending spiral of narration" (2009: 121). As an act of communication, narrative is by definition pointed in two temporal directions: the past (recent or distant) conventionally serves as the temporal location of the story itself, while the present and the future are the temporal locations of reception. The narrative structure of *Cloud Atlas*, which once more draws attention to itself here, implies that the process of producing, addressing and receiving narrative is infinite.

The focus in all this is on narrative encounters, on moments of addressing and being addressed, rather than on the facticity of the narrated, as becomes obvious from the coda of "Sloosha's Crossin'". Zachry is here described as "wyrd buggah" whose stories, or "yarnin's", mostly were "jus' musey duck fartin'" (*CA* 308) while Zachry's preceding narrative is, not exactly reassuringly, assessed as "mostly true" (*CA* 309), all of which of course must cast doubt on Zachry's reliability as a narrator. For readers, there is no way of finding out which parts of the story are true and which are not, and neither is this entirely relevant. When the accuracy of Zachry's account is questioned, this highlights a property of all storytelling and all writing of history: In the process of capturing life in text, inevitably certain aspects are lost, glossed over or exaggerated as a consequence of the choice of (the narrator's) perspective. In Levinasian diction, the question of reliability, in Zachry's words, of how much "true" there is in a

---

are presented one after the other, following the novel's order, with the exception of the second conclusion of the "Sloosha's Crossin'" episode, which now marks the end of the entire film. It was notably changed to show Zachry himself, as an old man, in what is likely a bow to popular taste now married to Meronym, gathering his grandchildren round a fire and showing them the Orison. While putting a clearer emphasis on the aspect of oral storytelling, this conclusion also does not thematise the doubts cast in the novel over the narrator's reliability.

yarnin', is one of ontology and belongs to the category of the said. The indifference displayed by Zachry's child towards whether or not his story is entirely true – as well as the fact that in the minimalistic language of the post-apocalyptic world of "Sloosha's Crossin'" the words 'tell' or 'narrate' seem to have been completely replaced by 'yarn' with its connotations of the tale being "of a marvellous or incredible kind" (*OED*, 3rd ed.) – suggests that the ontological categories of truthfulness or falsehood are not the most important elements of the narrative. Instead, the act of address integral to the telling itself, what Levinas calls saying, takes centre stage in a novel that is composed precisely as a succession of narrative encounters across centuries.[96] This focus on the saying, the act of address as quintessential part of narration, is underlined in the final paragraph of the "Sloosha's Crossin'" episode, when Zachry's child produces the device that contains Sonmi's "Orison":

> See, after Pa died, my sis'n'me sivvied his gear, an' I finded his silv'ry egg what he named *orison* in his yarns. Like Pa yarned, if you warm the egg in your hands, a beautsome ghost-girl appears in the air an' speaks in an Old-Un tongue what no un alive und'standds nor never will, nay. It ain't smart you can use 'cos it don't kill Kona pirates nor fill empty guts, but some dusks my kin'n'bros'll wake up the ghost-girl jus' to watch her hov'rin'n'shimm'rin'. She's beautsome, and she 'mazes the littl' uns an' her murmin's babbybie our babbits.
>
> Sit down a beat or two.
> Hold out your hands.
> Look. (*CA* 309)

The fact that the language of the orison itself is no longer understood but still has an obvious power over the addressees testifies to the power of the saying. In fact, it could be argued that this is an attempt at a description of pure saying that is removed from ontological necessities such as the need to kill for survival or even just the need to discover immediate meaning in the communication. As

---

[96] The "hyperfictionality" of Luisa Rey – and subsequently also of Robert Frobisher and Adam Ewing – discussed by Mezey (2011: 27) is another case in point. Since Rey, and hence also her subordinated 'relations of reading', Frobisher and Ewing, exists only as a fictional character in a book manuscript within the fiction that is *Cloud Atlas*, she represents a challenge to the reader's suspension of disbelief (see Parker 2010: 209n8; for a similar argument related to the process of narrative embedding in general, see Machinal 2011: 129–130). I concur with Mezey that "[b]y calling attention to Luisa Rey […] as a metatextual trace, Mitchell presents a fiction that is still in the process of its fictionalizing" (2011: 27). In *Cloud Atlas*, this process of fictionalising is, the narrative structure implies, never-ending. It is also first and foremost a process of saying, of striving to express the "ever-constant ineffable".

such, the encounter with the orison is an ethical encounter, one that is representative of the reception process of the entire novel. It is an image that conveys a readiness to be open to that which is other, that which possesses alterity that cannot be dissolved in processes of understanding, just like the language of the orison is one that "no un alive und'stands nor never will". What happens in this scene then is a turning to the infinitely other, both that of Sonmi's impermeable orison – which, of course, for the readers has already been and is about to continue to be received as a further narrative episode – and to that other which is narrative itself. Fittingly, this image of openness towards the other is the image that remains at the end of the "Sloosha's Crossin'" episode, marking the centrepiece, the first (or second?) closure-less conclusion and the narrative turning point of *Cloud Atlas*.

The final appeal in this passage is then addressed to the listeners on postapocalyptic Hawaii and to the readers of *Cloud Atlas* likewise. It comes as an invitation to the readers (see Machinal 2011: 145) to open themselves up for the demand made by the text. Jonathan Boulter identifies this moment as "the central event – both structurally and [...] philosophically – in the novel" (2011: 136; see Schoene 2009: 119 for a similar assessment) and convincingly reads it with Derrida, who in *Specters of Marx* speaks of a "principle of a radical and interminable, infinite (both theoretical and practical, as one used to say) critique" that informs deconstructive thinking, a critique that "belongs to the movement of an experience open to the absolute future of what is coming" (1994: 90). This infinite critique, Boulter argues, can be located in the "clear appeal to the listener/reader to attend, to view the orison: it is an ending that confers upon the listener/reader a burden, the burden of responsibility for what we know is the story of Sonmi~451" and an ending that is therefore "an appeal for Sonmi~451's critique of power, her critique of injustice, to continue beyond her" (2011: 137, 138). It is the groundedness in alterity paired with the directness of address of the listeners and hence also of the readers at this point that makes this appeal particularly forceful.

In this ending, then, the sense of ethical obligation that results from encountering alterity and the way it is intertwined with the novel's narrative structure presents itself in great clarity. Since here, at the narrative linchpin, the novel's aesthetic structure unfurls its full power, this appeal must transcend the text's boundaries and indeed become an infinite critique. In the coda to "Sloosha's Crossin'", the novel's cyclically recurring, infinitely continuable mise en abyme structure seems to pause, if just for "a beat or two", to allow for an instance of direct address. At the same time, the coda is a frame to the novel's diegetic frame and so reinforces, or, given its relative shortness, even 'accelerates', the sense that infinity pervades the textual structure, making the entire coda a catachrestic moment. From this catachresis, caused by the novel's infinite textuality, *Cloud Atlas* draws its strength as 'fiction of infinity'. This is where what I would like to call the textual alterity at the heart of the novel can be intuited. It is hardly surprising that this comes at another one of the novel's many moments of textual reception, a moment in which the text's infinite demand and resistance to any sort of metaphysical closure become tangible.

To conclude this reading of *Cloud Atlas*, a return to the novel's final image of the "multitude of drops" forming an ocean seems appropriate: this image not only advocates the individual's ethical responsibility, but also illustrates what the text itself performs. The six narrative episodes are like drops blending together to form a whole: individually they are received by readers at other levels in and outside the narrative and impact on them. Thus, any story may be a drop in a limitless ocean of text, while our textual universe is just a multitude of narratives we surround ourselves with. In this way, *Cloud Atlas* 'scintillates' in Levinas's sense, that is, it presents its own multiplicity and ungraspability while at the same time challenging readers to engage with and take up responsibility for this impermeable unintelligibility of alterity. As each story is an address of its reader and demands an *act* of reading, none is entirely inconsequential. This is then the closure-less conclusion of *Cloud Atlas*. As Mezey observes, "Far from being 'utterly finished', *Cloud Atlas* evokes a text that is continuously fashioned and refashioned, by its readers and even by its characters" (2011: 27). It is in particular the narrative structure with its sense of infinite textuality that leads to this perpetual (re-)fashioning. In all likelihood, the acute ethical appeal inherent in the narrative and projected by the narrative form means that this refashioning is not only one of the text by the readers, but also of the readers by the text. When the novel ends on a question mark, this is not only a sign of hermeneutic and epistemological openness, but also its final, infinite, appeal to the readers, who leave the novel behind but not its infinitely demanding text.[97]

---

[97] Bruce Robbins provides a contrasting reading of the novel when he accuses *Cloud Atlas* of being "ethically shallow" (2015: 11). Robbins argues that the novel's antagonists, notably the Maori and the Kona, lack any depth of character and are portrayed as mere barbarians whose acts of colonising and enslaving are portrayed at a par with European colonialism, whose "special moral opprobrium [...] is thereby erased" (2015: 10). This is compounded, Robbins argues, by the novel's Nietzschean emphasis on recurrence that eliminates the chance of (moral) progress. While Robbins's objection to the one-dimensional depiction of the novel's villains seems understandable, I agree with Dirk Wiemann, who in reply to Robbins points out that the "plea for the *production* of progress is itself a recurrent theme in *Cloud Atlas*" (2017: 505). Mitchell's narrative is certainly more complex than a Hollywood-style battle of good versus evil and draws its ethical depth at least as much from its structure as from its contents.

5 Infinitely Repeating: Jeanette Winterson's *The Stone Gods*

Published in 2007, Jeanette Winterson's *The Stone Gods* similarly avoids narrative closure and projects the continuation of the narrative's main concerns beyond the boundaries of the novel. Like David Mitchell's *Cloud Atlas*, *The Stone Gods* has been labelled 'cosmopolitan fiction' (see McCulloch 2012) and like Mitchell, Winterson addresses a vast range of topics, ranging from environmental destruction and climate change to themes that have long been stalwarts of dystopian fiction, when she traces the establishment of a totalitarian consumerist society or discusses the impact of technological development on the human body and on the basic question of what it means to be human. While there certainly are a number of conceptual and thematic parallels between these two novels, the aesthetic structures show considerable differences and Winterson crucially combines reading and feeling, specifically the feeling of love, as forces that have the potential to challenge and change human interactions.

At the centre of *The Stone Gods* is the notion that humanity keeps repeating its mistakes over and over, *ad infinitum*, as the cyclical structure of the narrative would suggest. Infinity here seems to develop above all the almost tyrannical effect of fixating the circular recurrence of human misery and thus endlessly prolonging it. However, this infinite repetition does not merely lead into a maelstrom of human self-destruction, but also allows for the repetition of what the novel portrays as positive qualities of humanity, namely literature and love. Both have the capacity to serve as what the novel repeatedly calls an "intervention" in the cycle of devastation and introduce an element of difference into the circular narrative of global demise. Thus, while the novel appears to suggest the infinite repetition of human greed will inevitably lead to the end of the planet, it also stakes the claim that a combination of the cognitive and affective disruptive forces of literature and love, likewise infinite phenomena, can intervene in this downward spiral, since they propagate openness towards alterity and so resist the fixed totality of the ever-same human demise. In the end it seems clear that *The Stone Gods* itself with its infinite circular text aims to become just such an intervention.

5.1 "Doomed to Repetition"? Circularity and Textual Infinity

Across its four parts, *The Stone Gods* presents fragments from three narratives, interlaced with a plethora of cross-references, resurfacing passages or expressions and recurring intertextual references. What keeps the fragments together are the protagonists Billie/Billy Crusoe and Spike/Spikkers, incarnations of whom are central to each part of Winterson's novel, as well as the repetition of the ever-same story of environmental collapse and the demise of society into totalitarian systems as a consequence of human actions. Around this structural backbone, *The Stone Gods* constructs a circular narrative whose parts are linked by literary fragments. The effect of this circularity of the narrative is twofold: on the one hand, it leads to the suspension of temporal orientation, to an odd timelessness in which the sequence of the parts becomes irrelevant. On the other hand, this circularity is instrumental in perpetually deferring the apocalyptic end the novel seems to evoke time and again and so underscores the narrative's eschewal of endings and closure. What is more, together with the way in which the narrative parts are embedded in each other, the circular narrative allows for the identification of the text as infinite via the Basic Metaphor of Infinity. In this, the paradoxical temporal structure, in which future precedes past and vice versa, underlines the catachrestic nature of such an identification of the text as infinite.

The exchangeability of past and future events and hence the circularity of the temporal order is already implied in the story of the novel's first part, *Planet Blue*. Orbus, the planet that is home to humanity, is dying after centuries of manmade exploitation of resources, wars and environmental pollution and rapidly becoming uninhabitable. Humanity therefore plans to relocate to Planet Blue, a newly discovered inhabitable planet. Billie Crusoe, a scientist working for the government and critic of the consequences of hyper-technologisation on society and on the environment, is sent on a pioneering colonising mission to Planet Blue, her only chance to escape prosecution as a dissident on Orbus. With her on the mission is Spike, a Robo *sapiens*, "[t]he first artificial creature that looks and acts human, and that can evolve like a human" (*SG* 17). As they approach Planet Blue, Billie finds out the actual purpose of their mission was to redirect an asteroid so it will impact on Planet Blue and eradicate the dinosaur population on the planet. However, due to a miscalculation they find themselves stranded on the planet when the asteroid hits earlier than expected and are once more trapped on a planet on which human-made climate change, a consequence of the atmospherical changes after the asteroid impact, makes survival impossible. While the rest of the crew set out to find a previously established penal colony, Spike and Billie, who have meanwhile fallen in love, stay behind. As dust and debris from the impact keep out the sun and temperatures drop, the first part ends with solar-powered Spike running out of energy and dying in Billie's arms. It is clear that the story already questions the strict linearity of temporal and civilisational progress, since it begins on Orbus, a planet that seems like a version of earth in a not too distant dystopian future, where nature is beyond salvage and ravaged by red dust storms, and ends on Planet Blue, a planet very much like earth 66 million years ago, when the asteroid impact happened that is likely to have led to the extinction of dinosaurs (see *SG* 207). Since the space ship's crew tells stories about Planet White, the planetary equivalent of a ghost town, where remnants of civilisation can be found but environmental conditions have made life impossible, as the planet has succumbed to its heat death (*SG* 62–64), the novel allegorically presents three developmental stages of the earth coexisting simultaneously, "a dead white planet, a dying red planet, and Planet Blue [...] just starting up" (*SG* 68), and implies that these stages form part of a destructive cycle of human development (see Reichl 2017: 258).

This cycle is continued in part two, *Easter Island*, which tells the story of one of the seamen on one of Captain James Cook's voyages. Billy Crusoe is left behind on Easter Island after an altercation with the island's natives. He witnesses conflicts among the natives and eventually is helped by Spikkers, a Dutch sailor who suffered a similar fate as Billy when he was part of an earlier expedition to the island. While Billy stays with Spikkers, he learns about the history and culture of the island and finds out that humans are to blame for its barren, wasteland-like nature, since they cut down all the trees and now lead a civil war over the remaining few resources. The same patterns of exploitation that devastate entire planets in part one are now mirrored at a smaller scale on a single island. However, repetition is not restricted to these environmental discourses, but also occurs at the level of the relationship between the two protagonists: again Billy and Spikkers fall in love and again it is a queer form of love, the relationship between a woman and a female-gendered robot now replaced by a homosexual relationship between two men. As in the first part, at the end, Billy holds dying Spikkers in his arms, after the latter has been murdered in an attempt to end the conflict on the island.

The third narrative, comprising the last two parts of the novel, *Post-3 War* and *Wreck City*, again presents a variation of the same themes and brings the narrative full circle. Set on earth in the early twenty-first century in what used to be London, but now, after the nuclear devastation of the Third World War, is part highly technologised, futuristic, consumerist Tech City and part Wreck City, polluted and beyond state control, a "carnivalesque space" (Johns-Putra 2017: 189) that is home to social outcasts and those who reject the social order of Tech City, it again presents versions of Billie Crusoe and the Robo *sapiens* Spike, now at an earlier developmental stage than in part one and as yet only a head without a body. This time round, Billie works for the governing MORE company and teaches Spike what it means to be human. Against her orders, she takes Spike to Wreck City, where Spike 'defects' to the alternative lifestyle of a community of lesbian vegans. As the government's armed forces arrive to reclaim Spike and armed conflict with the inhabitants of Wreck City ensues, Billie and Spike flee to the nearby disused Lovell Telescope where the narrative's circularity becomes clear when Spike picks up a mysterious radio signal, "one line of programming code for a Robo *sapiens*" (*SG* 240) sent 65 million years earlier by Spike's first incarnation (*SG* 100; 222–223). The novel ends when Billie decides to leave, without any clear purpose but possibly in search of her mother from whom she was separated as an infant, and is shot and killed by the government's soldiers, with the last lines presenting an Edenic vision of a return to lost origins, where a long-lost 'you' is waiting for Billie.

The circularity of the narrative is thus constructed at the level of both story and discourse: firstly, at the story level the main ingredients clearly repeat, making *The Stone Gods* "a repeating world – same old story" (*SG* 59; see Onega 2011: 292), as Captain Handsome, commander of the space ship in the first section, in a metafictional comment remarks about the origins of the books he has on board. Human history is here presented in a form reminiscent of the ouroboros, the snake or dragon devouring its own tail, as a self-destructive cycle – as Billie reflects at one point, humans "have made every mistake, justified ourselves, and made the same mistakes again and again. It's as though we're doomed to repetition" (*SG* 216). Secondly, at the discourse level, the temporal order of the three main stories does not seem fixed and beyond the order in which the parts are presented in the novel there is no indication of any part necessarily being the first or last in this sequence, just like a circle line does not have a beginning or end. In fact, chronology is suspended to an extent that the three main narrative strands could be brought into any order and their sequence would still be logical in some way. This is underlined, for example, by Billie's parting words to Spike at the end of the third section, "See you in sixty-five million years, maybe" (*SG* 244), which give the time span that separates the third narrative from the first and point to the possible recurrence of earlier events at a future date. What is more, as Susanne Reichl has observed, the changes in narrating time, which frequently alternates between simultaneous, present-tense narration and subsequent, i.e. past-tense, narration, add to the sense of an unstable chronology in Winterson's narrative (2017: 259). Temporal orientation thus indeed is suspended, just as is insinuated by Billie at the end of the novel, when she echoes an earlier similar statement of Spike's: "There are two questions: where have you come from, and where are you going? But the brain doesn't have separate regions for past and future; only the present is differentiated by the brain" (*SG* 243; see 214). Past and future are then conflated into the "not now" (*SG* 243) in Winterson's novel and time's arrow is bent into a circle, its shaft and tip forever meeting in the 'not now'.

Somewhat paradoxically, for its readers this 'not now' is precisely what the novel presents in each part – despite some obvious parallels, none of the narratives presents a world that is like the world of the early twenty-first century a prospective reader might know – and it is this perpetual deferral to the 'not now' that plays an integral part in the establishing of narrative openness and the rejection of endings. This rejection of closure becomes clear when "The End" is confidently declared for the first time after just a few pages, in this case with regard to the impending shutdown of Spike (*SG* 7), only for the narrative to continue beyond 'The End' and for Spike to survive her planned dismantling. Of course, the end that is at the heart of the novel is one at a grander scale, the apocalyptic "end of everything" humanity seems to have brought on itself time and again (*SG* 47). While the biblical apocalypse results in the construction of the utopian New Jerusalem, such utopian visions are – with the exception perhaps of pristine Planet Blue, whose state of bliss duly falls victim to the human-made impact of the asteroid – largely missing from *The Stone Gods*, or at least deferred to fleeting moments of happiness in the protagonists' love relationships, and so demoted from the social to the personal level. Winterson's novel thus denies any resolution or ending (no matter if happy or unhappy) to its destructive cycles. Instead, it presents humanity in various states of decay, with the actual end never quite coming to pass.[98] In this sense, in *The Stone Gods* the end is 'not now' but perpetually deferred, which may point to "the very fictionality of apocalypse itself – an end so much described but yet to manifest itself" (Hicks 2016: 21). The absence of such an end from the text is a clear marker of narrative openness and follows directly from the circular narrative structure.

The "structural loop" (Reichl 2017: 258) that is constructed in this fashion is underscored by the way in which the three main strands of the narrative are linked through what can be read as an aporetic mise en abyme structure. While most critics seem to interpret the novel as a sequence of three stories, or "novellas-in-a-novel" (Ellam 2010: 220), that are connected by common motifs and the characters' names but do not necessarily stand in any hierarchical log-

---

[98] As Mahlu Mertens and Stef Craps argue, the reason for the absence of any concrete ending on a planetary level – not even the asteroid impact comes close to actually putting an end to a planet; all the other destructive events either take the shape of a slow poisoning through environmental pollution or are relegated to the folklore of the ship crew's tales of Planet White – is the timescale of climate change that simply exceeds human conceptions of time, as well as the general difficulty of historicising the Anthropocene, which would involve imagining life without humans (see Mertens and Craps 2018). The end is therefore necessarily deferred, either to the level of individual characters (in the deaths of Spike, Spikkers and Billie) or to a yet-to-come but already implied point beyond the narrative present.

ical relation with each other – in the same way, again, as a circle line does not have any 'privileged' point –, Susana Onega has pointed out that "Part Two [is placed] *en abyme* with respect to Part One, thereby enhancing the repetitiveness of the two stories and the palimpsestic structure of the novel as a whole" (2011: 293). The reason given by Onega is that at the end of the first part, Billie picks up a copy of Captain Cook's *Journals* salvaged from the space ship and reads the same passage that opens part two (see *SG* 112, 117). Strictly speaking, this is then a mise en abyme structure only in the broadest sense of Dällenbach's definition, as an "enclave entertaining a relation of similarity with the work which contains it" (Dällenbach 1977: 18, trans. in Ron 1987: 421; see ch. 2.2.2), but not one based on a relation of narrative embedding, i.e. of embedding through an act of narrating that shifts the subsequent narrative to a higher diegetic level. For there is no clear indicator that Billie peruses the entire *Easter Island* section, which clearly is not narrated as a part of Cook's *Journals* but only framed by a short excerpt from them, which means that there is no clear-cut instance of narrative embedding through the telling/reception of the secondary story. However, this principle of narrative embedding through reading is implied not only here, but also in the third part, which begins with Billie finding the manuscript of *The Stone Gods* on the tube and reading it perfunctorily (*SG* 143; see Onega 2011: 293–294). Thus, according to Onega's reading, *Planet Blue* becomes a narrative contained in *Post-3 War/Wreck City* and *Easter Island* in turn is contained in *Planet Blue*.[99] Yet, since Spike in *Wreck City* picks up the radio signal sent out by Spike in *Planet Blue*, the ontological status of these narratives in relation to each other is altogether less clear and the mise en abyme structure may be considered aporetic.[100] The effect is, as Florian Kläger states, that "[i]n a

---

[99] It is unclear whether the manuscript Billie finds on the tube contains, as Kläger claims, only the story up to that point (see Kläger 2014: 298–299) or if it is indeed, as the title suggests, the manuscript of the entire novel the reader holds in their hands. In the latter case, the novel would contain itself and so allude to the classical example of a coat of arms containing a miniature copy of itself, which then leads to what Dällenbach has called *"réduplication à l'infini"* (1977: 51; see ch. 2.2.2).

[100] Characters in novels do not, as a rule, send out any signals other than those contained in the text of the novel via the narrator's discourse. Of course, this is precisely where the narrative construction of *The Stone Gods* irretrievably turns paradoxical: if the first part is a novel Billie reads in part three and hence part one constitutes the metadiegetic level of the narration, then the radio signal leads to a metalepsis, since it transgresses the boundaries of the narrative levels when it is picked up at the diegetic level. This metalepsis together with the self-inclusionary nature of the narrative suggests that the structure here can be described as a *"réduplication aporistique"* (Dällenbach 1977: 51; see ch. 2.2.2), albeit it perhaps constitutes a weaker case than a character transgressing such a narrative boundary.

Hofstadterian 'strange loop,' [...] the novel keeps writing itself, with no beginning and no end" (2014: 299). Similarly, pointing to the dense (and overtly metafictional) intertextual references in the passage, in which Billie first picks up the manuscript of *The Stone Gods* – the beginning of *Robinson Crusoe* is quoted by Billie Crusoe, who denies any connection with Robinson (*SG* 146) – as further evidence, Onega observes that "by opening the manuscript found on the tube, Billie is entering an infinite World/Book" (2011: 294). Thus, not only the sequence of temporal events and the question of what is past and what is future become blurred, but also the difference between diegetic levels, whose sequence the novel likewise seems to bend into an aporetic circular structure.

It is this circular structure, which can be found in the plot, in the temporal order of the novel's parts and in the hierarchical order of narrative levels, that makes *The Stone Gods* 'infinite' and an example of a fiction of infinity. This is because the circularity that is thus integral to the novel's aesthetics already implies the indefinite, and potentially infinite, iterability of the story and therefore allows for the identification of the text as infinite via Lakoff and Núñez's Basic Metaphor of Infinity (see ch. 2.1). To be precise, this metaphorical identification takes place in two steps, a first that allows readers to see the narrative as circular – 'the text is a circle/circular' is of course a metaphorical description of the text – and a second step in which the Basic Metaphor of Infinity proper comes into play. The 'building blocks' of the metaphorical identification that turns the text into a circle are the novel's three main narrative strands. They are discrete, since they are separated either by long time spans (65 million years between the first part and the other parts, more than 250 years between part two and parts three and four) or by relations of fictional embedding, depending on how the novel is read in this regard. As narrative episodes these three stories are also finite – each one of them even ends with the death of one of its protagonists. The presentation of three such narratives, which bear a considerable degree of similarity to each other – they are in many ways indeed the "same old story" – amounts to the presentation of an iteration of discrete steps and therefore to the understanding of the "repeating world" of *The Stone Gods* as an indefinitely continuous process, a circular structure, through the conceptual metaphor "Indefinite Continuous Processes Are Iterative Processes" identified by Lakoff and Núñez (2000: 157). The image of a circle, which lends itself as the source domain for this metaphor, is in this case conceptualised not as a set of points, but as a closed curve that can be run through an indefinite number of times and the three stories are comparable with single rotations or 'laps' on the circle.

In fact, therefore, understanding the structure of *The Stone Gods* to be circular is itself already the result of a metaphorical transfer of qualities, which then becomes the basis for the second step of metaphorical identification in which the

Basic Metaphor of Infinity endows the text with infinity. If the narrative of *The Stone Gods* is circular in the way just described, then it can also serve as source domain for the Basic Metaphor of Infinity (see Lakoff and Núñez 2000: 158–161): the narrative possesses an initial state (the first narration, *Planet Blue*), which is completed when Spike has died, and with Billie's last words, "This is one story. There will be another" (*SG* 113), the next state/narration, *Easter Island*, is already projected. If the overall narrative structure is understood to be circular, then it also expresses the indefinite continuation of this pattern, resulting in an indefinite, potentially infinite number of iterations of the "same old story", with each of the narrations leaving behind a dead protagonist and destroyed environment. The existence of an initial state and an indefinite number of iterations (as suggested by the circularity of the narrative) that all lead to a resultant state is precisely the precondition that according to Lakoff and Núñez allows the Basic Metaphor of Infinity to "*add to the target domain the completion of the process and its resulting state*" (2000: 158), the resulting state being infinity. This is then how the textual structure of *The Stone Gods* indeed suggests itself to be understood as infinite by the reader through a process of metaphorical identification.

It is thus clear that whether through the circularity or through the aporetic mise en abyme structure which the narrative implies, *The Stone Gods* makes its own textual infinity its foremost aesthetic principle. Again, the feature of infinity can be metonymically transferred from the infinite textual structure to the text as a whole, a transfer that overall results in the catachrestic identification of a finite text as infinite (see ch. 2.3). The strictly illogical nature of the catachresis is in this case underlined by the way in which the three main narratives are embedded in each other, resulting in an aporetic mise en abyme structure, or a 'strange loop', as well as by the suspension of linear temporality through the cyclical narrative. *The Stone Gods* is then a text that clearly strives to transcend its own boundaries and a text to which Adeline Johns-Putra therefore rightly attests a "seeming desire not to end" (2017: 178).

However, this textual infinity, which, as in *Cloud Atlas*, has been linked to the Nietzschean principle of eternal recurrence (see Onega 2011: 279; Bradway 2015), raises the problem that, as Johns-Putra points out, the principle of eternal recurrence with its repetition of the ever-same is fundamentally at odds with the "radical openness of narrative" (2017: 178) the novel propagates in its refusal to end, i.e. in its textual infinity. Firstly, given the novel's rather pessimistic outlook on the destructive nature of humanity, there seemingly is little hope for improvement on offer. On the contrary, the circularity of the narrative would suggest an inevitability of the perpetual repetition of the environmental destruction of planets inhabited by humanity and seems to turn *The Stone Gods* into an anti-utopia in the sense of Lyman Tower Sargent, i.e. into a sustained criticism of utopianism or "social dreaming" (1994: 9). The infinite circularity of the narrative in such a reading would underline that humanity is, to put it bluntly, rotten to the core and no change is possible, the repetition of past mistakes leading to future destruction again and again. Taken at face value, such an understanding of the circular structure then would preclude any reading of the novel as advocating political change – since change seems to be impossible in a world of eternal recurrence – or making any ethical appeal. Rather than the openness an infinite text might be expected to showcase, infinity here would seem to guarantee a closed narrative in which change is impossible.[101] Secondly, Johns-Putra argues that the "return to the beginning" that the circular structure necessarily entails and that is strongly implied in the novel's last image of Billie's homecoming, which embraces a nostalgic form of a love of origins, makes this element of repetition "more problematic than closure" (2017: 192). Ultimately, she claims, it renders the narrative structure "a closed loop, rather than an opening up" (2017: 192). The infinite repetition of the ever same ouroboros-like cycle of human self-destruction depicted in *The Stone Gods* in this sense indeed would appear to advocate for a conservative form of determinism and closed stasis rather than openness and change.

Although this notion seems to be inextricably linked with the novel's textual infinity and circular structure, in my reading of the novel I would like to show that – owing perhaps to the inherently paradoxical nature of the infinite – its infinite textuality is precisely what can overcome any fixity or determinism. If read in that way, the narrative's eternal recurrence indeed "affirm[s] the ever-present chance for a becoming that would counter the violence of the present" (Bradway 2015: 191).[102] Importantly, the infinite repetitions *The Stone Gods* insinuates are *not* repetitions of identical stories, no matter whether the plots share some similarities. Instead, the infinity of the text also allows for an infinite perpetuation of difference. The repetitions Winterson's novel presents are always already transposed, carrying forth and perpetuating an element of difference. What is more, somewhat counterintuitively, the circular structure and infinite

---

[101] This reading is in line with Ursula Heise's recent critique of the contemporary dystopian genre in general and of post-apocalyptic fiction in particular (Heise 2015). Heise arrives at the conclusion that "[c]ontemporary dystopias [...] aspire to unsettle the status quo, but by failing to outline a persuasive alternative, they end up reconfirming it" (2015: n. pag.). For an answer to Heise in defence of the dystopian and post-apocalyptic genres, see Hicks (2016: 8–9).

[102] As Onega has demonstrated in her reading of "circularity and the quest" in some of Winterson's earlier novels, eternal recurrence need not be interpreted negatively – as the 'heavy burden' Nietzsche saw in it – but may indeed be read in a more optimistic way, as offering infinitely many chances (see Onega 2009).

textuality of *The Stone Gods* are what makes change possible, not only at the level of the plot, but also beyond that, in the sense that, as I hope to show, they turn the text into a stark ethical appeal to its readers. This is effect is achieved in particular through the way Winterson has worked two main motifs, literature and love, into her infinite text: both function as elements of disruption that embrace difference and otherness and because of the infinitely repetitive structure of the novel this disruption is likewise infinitely repeated.

5.2 "More Than One Reading": Re-Reading *The Stone Gods*

Literature and reading, then, play a central role in *The Stone Gods*, both as structuring devices and as instances that introduce otherness into the prevalent discourse of sameness. "Stories abound in this novel", as Hélène Machinal observes (2015: 167), and engaging with these stories is one of Winterson's central issues. The topic of reading is introduced in a number of ways: through direct intertextual references to canonical literary texts that are most of the time clearly marked as quotations; through the absence of the literary and the reduction of language to the degree zero of inanity in the society of Orbus, a common theme of dystopian fiction; and through the encounters of characters with literary texts, most notably that of Spike with love poetry in *Planet Blue* and that of Billie and Spike with the manuscript of *The Stone Gods* in the last two parts of the novel. In all these cases, the literary serves simultaneously to underline and undermine the repetitive structure of the overall narrative by continuing the repetition whilst introducing alterity into the narrative and showing that no process of reading can arrive at a complete understanding of that which is other to the reader.

On the one hand, the many intertexts that are quoted again and again throughout the novel as well as the intratextual repetitions of some fragments of text introduce major themes, establish connections between the different parts of the novel and at the same time underscore its circular structure. For example, early on in the novel a textual fragment is presented (and later repeated several times) italicised like those passages that are directly quoted from intertexts and unconnected to the narrative at this point:

> *The new world – El Dorado, Atlantis, the Gold Coast, Newfoundland, Plymouth Rock, Rapanui, Utopia, Planet Blue. Chanc'd upon, spied through a glass darkly, drunken stories strapped to a barrel of rum, shipwreck, a Bible Compass, a giant fish led us there, a storm whirled us to this isle. In the wilderness of space we found...* (SG 8)

This list of places, real and mythical, highlights the mythopoetic nature of discovery and the promises associated with it. The same passage recurs in the middle of the tale of Planets White, Red and Blue (*SG* 62), when Captain Handsome imagines a new life with Spike as settlers on Planet Blue (*SG* 94) and twice when Billie in the last two parts thinks of her own family history and her lost origins (*SG* 150, 238). While the recurrence of the same fragment five times in the novel is a sign of repetition and circularity, it also implicitly, through the mentioning of El Dorado and the Gold Coast, introduces the novel's prominent theme of the colonisers exploiting their new environment in search of riches and already points to the continuity of such exploitative patterns, which the narrative's repetitive structure suggests are a constant of human behaviour. In a similar manner, Winterson uses intratextual self-quotations to likewise emphasise the infinite repetitiveness of the narrative, most prominently perhaps the dialogue between Billie and Spike towards the end of part one – "I said to Spike, 'Is this how it ends?' She said, 'It isn't ended yet'" (*SG* 107; see 154, 241) – which returns twice, including towards the very end of the novel (see Machinal 2015: 167– 168, who sees a somewhat tenuous intertextual reference to the end of T. S. Eliot's "The Hollow Men" in this dialogue). The clearest example of such self-referential repetitiveness is certainly the manuscript of *The Stone Gods* Billie finds in the third narrative strand, the emergence of which, as already mentioned, may point towards the *réduplication à l'infini* (in Dällenbach's sense) of the narrative structure.

However, this narrative repetition, and in particular the repetition of intertextual references, is not a case of the eternal return of the ever same. Instead, the intratextual repetitions inevitably add new contexts – and hence already a modicum of change, if only in the novel's own textual environment – to the phrases that are repeated, while the way in which the direct quotations from intertexts are introduced also subtly points to the possibility of change. For in fact, many of the lines of poetry and other texts that are quoted by the characters are minimally altered from the originals. A word may have been added or may be missing, or the word order almost imperceptibly changed. Thus, the line from John Donne's "The Sun Rising" that is quoted several times across *The Stone Gods* as "*She is all States, all Princes I, Nothing else is*" (*SG* 31, see 6, 58, 80, 100, 110, 152) in Donne's original has an additional 'and': "She is all States, *and* all princes, I, / Nothing else is" (Donne 2010: 249, ll. 21–22; my emphasis) – there does not seem to be any extant manuscript variant of the poem in which 'and' is likewise missing. The most clear-cut example of an intertext that has been modified is what is presented as an excerpt from Captain Cook's travel journal and forms the transition between parts one and two of *The Stone Gods*. Rather than the verbatim quotation from Cook's journal a reader might expect, given that Billie explicitly names this as her source (*SG* 112), the short passage that is quoted is a pastiche of the style of Cook's journals laced with some actual quotations from his entry on Easter Island in the journal of his second voyage.[103]

In a similar vein, several of the lines of poetry Spike reads out on the spaceship in the novel's first part are also changed in details: "When in silks my Julia goes" (*SG* 81) is "*Whenas* in silks my Julia goes" in Robert Herrick's poem (Herrick 1996: 323, l. 1; my emphasis), "Me she caught in her arms long and small" (*SG* 81) modifies a line by Thomas Wyatt, "and she me caught in her arms long and small" (2005: 181, l. 12), "When did your name become a charm?" (*SG* 81) is a variation on the beginning of Carol Ann Duffy's "Name" – "When did your name / change from a proper noun / to a charm?" (2005: 3, ll. 1–3) – and the last line of Andrew Marvell's "The Fair Singer", "She having gained both the wind and sun" (Marvell 1996: 438, l. 18), is rendered without 'the' by Spike (*SG* 81). Given the frequency of these minute changes, it is fitting that the first of the poems from which Spike quotes, Shakespeare's sonnet 109, is likewise misquoted in a detail, but here this is done in such a way as to reflect the story of *The Stone Gods* at this point. When Spike recites "*Nothing in this wide universe I call, save thou, my rose, in it thou art my all*" (*SG* 80), she adds the first 'in' to Shakespeare's words (see 2007: 329, ll. 13–14) and actually changes the meaning of these lines considerably: in the Shakespeare sonnet, the entire universe is considered worthless (called nothing) in the absence of the lover, whereas Spike's version seems to suggest a search (calling for) the lover, and no one/ nothing else, throughout the wide universe – a modification that chimes in with the novel's topic of Billie's search for (maternal) love, which is introduced later in part three. Apart from this instance, the changes to the intertexts that are directly quoted are all relatively minor but their frequency as well as their origin in a cosmic "bookstorm" that whirls through the universe battered editions of literary classics that are largely forgotten on Orbus (*SG* 59) – the storm itself being a

---

103 While the passage matches the contents of Cook's journal, it is more a re-telling, an adaptation, than a direct quotation. The clearest parallel to Cook's actual journal can be found in the reference to the moai, the stone statues for which the islands are famous and which inspired the title of Winterson's novel. The version in *The Stone Gods* reads, "*In stretching in for the land we discovered those Monuments or Idols mentioned by the Authors of Roggeweins Voyage which left us in no room to doubt but it was Easter Island*" (*SG* 112, 117). The account in Cook's actual *Journal* is different: "At 10 o'clock the next morning a light breeze sprung up [...] and inabled us to stretch in for the land in the doing of which we discovered people and some of those Monuments or Idols mentioned by the Authors of Roggeweins Voyage" (Cook 1772–1775: 191; image 199).

highly symbolic image of instability and changeability – suggests that these alterations form part of the aesthetics of repetition in *The Stone Gods*.

What these almost, but not quite, quotations of canonical intertexts show, then, is that despite the infinitely repeating world of *The Stone Gods* the repetitions leave room for change, even, or perhaps especially, where the written word is concerned. The changed quotations thus undermine any determinism that the narrative's repetitive structure might imply. If *The Stone Gods* presents an excerpt from the history of humankind, a glimpse of humanity as it was and/or will be, but key texts written by humans exist in altered forms, despite the repeating universe, then the implication is that change is possible after all, if only in very small quantities. Indeed, narration, or more precisely the reading of stories, is promoted as a catalyst of change in Winterson's novel:

> Every second the universe divides into possibilities and most of those possibilities never happen. It is not a universe – there is more than one reading. The story won't stop, can't stop, it goes on telling itself, waiting for an intervention that changes what will happen next.
> Love is an intervention. (SG 83)

Crucially, the novel here advocates the plurality of reading and hence of the text itself. "There is more than one reading", and every reading also entails an interpretation and hence the possibility of a change of meaning. While love is presented as the strongest possible intervention in *The Stone Gods* – it is notably an intervention in 'the story', through an irruption of feeling – acknowledging the multiplicity of readings in such a prominent way suggests that encounters with texts may have a similarly disruptive effect, resisting the totality of the ever-fixed recurrence, simply because their reading is not fixed.

When *The Stone Gods* thematises its circular story and this plurality of reading, it also addresses this question of interpretive openness. In other words, it essentially becomes a reflection on hermeneutics, i.e. on processes of understanding. Traditionally, hermeneutics as the theory of interpretation has viewed understanding as a circular process in which a back and forth movement between the understanding of the text as whole and its various parts eventually leads to a complete understanding (see Iser 2000: 52). The nineteenth-century hermeneutic conception of understanding in this context was, according to Friedrich Schleiermacher, the construction of "something finite and definite from something infinite and indefinite" (1977: 100, qtd. in Iser 2000: 52). Such a form of closure-seeking understanding would be achieved, were one to read the story of *The Stone Gods* as purely negative, inalterable and predetermined cycle of destruction. However, by underlining the inherent multiplicity of the reading process, the novel actively resists such determinism. With this emphasis on the openness of reading, the novel becomes a meta-hermeneutic comment because it couples a circular structure with this foregrounding of reading processes. Given that circularity remains at the core of any hermeneutic notion of understanding – although in the wake of poststructuralism the 'hermeneutic circle' has been criticised and re-formed into a "transactional loop" (Ricœur's term, adopted by Iser 2000: 69–81) or a "spiral" (see Bolten 1985), which must inevitably expand the larger the temporal difference between the instance of reading and the text's conception becomes (see Middeke 2009: 107–108) – the circular narrative structure may then be read as a comment on hermeneutic practice. In fact, more recent hermeneuticist approaches are more sceptical of the possibility of absolute understanding as promoted by Schleiermacher, and once a critical hermeneutics, influenced by deconstruction, is prepared to accept Derrida's concept of the iterability of the sign, it must accept that "there can never be a *full* understanding" (Middeke 2009: 112, see 110–113). Instead, as Billie has it, "there is more than one reading" and reading itself, just like the story of *The Stone Gods*, "won't stop". Reading, and as a consequence understanding, then has become the very infinite and indefinite process Schleiermacher wanted to put an end to.

It is this infinite openness of the reading process that *The Stone Gods* demands, paradoxically setting its own seemingly closed circular structure against the plurality of readings it encourages, and hence against the infinity of the text itself. In this, the narrative structure is instrumental, since its circularity allows the novel to turn back on itself and in a sense constantly re-read itself in a new and different way. The repetitive structure therefore already guarantees that there is "more than one reading" of the story. This turning back on itself, key to the novel's principle of 'repetition with a difference', becomes clearest in the central moment of narrative self-containment, when the manuscript of *The Stone Gods* is found and read by Billie. It is crucial to the way in which *The Stone Gods* envisages reading, and hence the role of literature in general, as an element of human disruption. Thus, initially it seems to be a mere coincidence that Billie finds the manuscript on the tube and on a whim starts leafing through it, thinking there's "[n]o point starting at the beginning – nobody ever does. Reading at random is better: maybe hit the sex scenes straight away" (*SG* 143). Even though the manuscript barely features directly for the rest of the novel – apart from the odd intratextual quotation of snippets of text from earlier chapters, the manuscript is pointedly absent until the very last pages of the novel, except when Billie briefly mentions its existence to Spike (*SG* 175) – the circular structure of the narrative means that the first two parts serve as blueprints for the third narrative strand, which begins with Billie finding the manuscript. The manuscript is one of the novel's many discoveries, "chanc'd upon" by Billie who in reading it enters into the meta-hermeneutic spiral of Winterson's infinite text. While her life unfolds over the last two parts of the novel, it also is a re-reading, displaced to a future turn of the spiral, of the lives of her two alter egos in the first two parts of the novel – as if the text, trapped in its infinitely spiralling structure, needed to read itself.

Clearly, this textual re-reading accommodates re-imagining and, since "reading at random is better", potentially disrupting the circular repetition. When at the end of the novel Billie drops the pages of the manuscript and picks them up again, they are "shuffled as a pack of cards" (*SG* 241), which suggests precisely such an element of contingency or randomness. The ensuing dialogue, interspersed with one of the already mentioned intratextual quotations, is not only one of the many passages in the novel that emphasise its circularity and lack of temporal orientation but also shows how literature may intervene in the circular repetition. Asked by Spike what the manuscript pages are, Billie replies:

> 'It's what I told you about, today, yesterday, when, I don't know when, it seems a lifetime ago. *The Stone Gods*.'
> 'I wonder who left it there?'
> > 'It was me.'
> > 'Why, Billie?'
> > A message in a bottle. A signal. But then I saw it was still there ... round and round on the Circle Line. A repeating world.
>
> *Is this how it ends?*
> > *It isn't ended yet.*
>
>   *
>
> 'The book isn't finished, but this is as far as I could go.'
> > 'What shall I do with it?'
> > 'Read it. Leave it for someone else to find. The pages are loose – it can be written again.' (*SG* 241–242).

The text of the manuscript is then a signal, waiting to be found, but by no means a closed story. In fact, the implication is that finding and reading a text like *The Stone Gods* always entails the possibility to 're-write' it, or even necessarily results in a 're-writing', in the sense that it resists a fixed final meaning – the pages are loose, ready to be reshuffled, and the book is not only 'not finished', but its text is infinite, resisting the imposition of any ultimate meaning.[104] An

---

[104] In this form of rewriting, the question of authorship becomes irrelevant, or even a limiting factor. While some critics have interpreted the passage quoted here to signal that Billie herself is the author of the *Stone Gods* manuscript (Kläger 2014: 299; Machinal 2015: 167), there is no clear indicator for that – in fact, this is the first indication in the entire novel that Billie was in pos-

openness to change as much as a refusal to end, even at this point, close to the very end of the novel, then again emerge as key elements of the narrative.

In this sense, the repetition in and of *The Stone Gods* is always a repetition with in-built change, eschewing the determinism of the circle line, and the implication is that the agents of this change are the readers (see McCulloch 2012: 74). Thus Reichl suggests that "[t]he 'someone else'" Billie hopes will find the manuscript "is the reader, who, it is implied, is not reading exactly the same book but a rough version of it. Therefore, it is not the exact story that is being repeated but the schema of the story, or maybe an echo of the past (or the future)" (2017: 256). In this it is crucial that there is "more than one reading", and each reading already is a re-reading with a changed perspective and therefore a re-interpretation and hence a re-writing. It is through this emphasis on the malleability of *The Stone Gods* at the hands of the reader, who may reshuffle or even write it again, that any sense of determinism on account of the eternally repeating circular structure must be called into question. Even though the narrative structure may be infinitely repeating in ever the same cycles, the reading process, the encounter with the text, is different each time.

These encounters with texts are central to challenging the characters who read them to reactions that 'change what will happen next', that is, to the kind of intervention Billie is hoping for, while conversely the most dystopian parts of the novel are dystopian precisely because of the absence of the literary and the impossibility of such encounters. Such an absence characterises particularly the first half of the *Planet Blue* section, which is set on Orbus. In the society of Orbus, writing and reading are seen as antiquated and while not exactly forbidden, they are considered eccentric pastimes. When Billie's boss Manfred spots her writing in a notebook, his reaction is to tell her that she should try to fit in better: "Nobody reads and writes anymore – there's no need", he says. "Why can't you use a SpeechPad like everybody else?" (*SG* 9). Not only is reading and writing frowned upon in the dystopian world of the first section, but language in general is reduced to its bare minimum, to single letters that explain the world as in children's books (see McCulloch 2012: 66): "S is for Solo, a single-seater solar-powered transport vehicle. L is for Limo, a multi-seater hydro-

---

session of the manuscript even before she finds it on the tube where "someone had left it" (*SG* 143). It therefore seems problematic, perhaps grounded in a realist impulse – and I agree with Onega that a realist stance is not the most satisfactory way to approach Winterson's novel (2011: 197) –, to look for authorship, and hence authority, in a novel that promotes openness in the way *The Stone Gods* does. After all, as Roland Barthes has it, "To give a text an Author is to impose a limit on that text, to furnish it with a final signified, to close the writing" (1977c: 147).

gen hybrid. [...] Single letter recognition is taught in schools" (*SG* 11). In a similar way, prompted by a street sign that indicates "Belle Vue Drive" with the picture of a bell, Billie sarcastically reflects that "[e]tymology was one of the first victims of State-approved mass illiteracy. Sorry, a move towards a more integrated, user-friendly day-to-day information and communications system. (Voice and pictures, yes; written words, no.)" (*SG* 15). As Machinal has claimed, in the absence of literacy, this reduced form of language thus comes to define the world of Orbus, and boiled down to its minimal form, the single letter, "stand[s] for a dehumanized code, deprived of any affect or sensitivity" (2015: 165). In this dystopian world, language has almost completely fossilised into what Levinas calls the said. The said, that is, that part of an utterance which establishes a proposition ('S is P' – or here, "S is for Solo") whose ontological facticity can be established (see Critchley 1994: 649), dominates discourse on Orbus, while in the inanity of "S is for Solo" language has become entirely bereft of the saying, of its disruptive moment of address and opening up to alterity. With the rejection of reading and writing and its regression to the simplistic formulaic emptiness of "single letter recognition", language on Orbus has become a tool for subjection and an integral part of Winterson's dystopia (see Machinal 2015: 165–166).

In this "intellectually infantilized" (McCulloch 2012: 66) society of Orbus, the fact that Billie still reads and writes, even though she works for the government that disapproves of such activities, makes her a "figure of resistance" and "an archetypal character of SF novels which present a dystopian and autocratic diegetic world", in the tradition of George Orwell's Winston Smith in *1984* and Ray Bradbury's Guy Montag in *Fahrenheit 451* (Machinal 2015: 166). This continues in the third narrative strand, where books are similarly absent from Tech City, but find refuge in the outlaw area of Wreck City. Tech City, governed by the MORE company – whose pre-war slogan "MORE IS MORE" (*SG* 161) echoes the simplicity of "S is for Solo" – has largely replaced books with "Digi-readers" that are "[q]uicker, cheaper" (*SG* 168) and any access to art and literature is severely restricted, with, for example, Spike having to hide that she has been given Homer's *Odyssey* to read by Billie (*SG* 175). Books as material objects hardly exist anymore, and it is only in the parallel society of Wreck City, the abject social other to the shiny world of Tech City, that Billie to her surprise comes across an actual library – and in one of the many instances of repetition the first book she picks up is James Cook's *Journals* (*SG* 193). It is telling that the existence of the books is only possible in the outlaw world of Wreck City that resists the totalitarian corpocracy of Tech City's MORE company. In these situations, language, particularly that of literature, "become[s] an artefact through which resistance to oppression and any form of restriction of individual freedom can be achieved" (Machinal 2015: 167).

The reason why literature and the act of reading may develop into resistance is that they introduce alterity into the totality of the novel's permanently recurring dystopian worlds. Whereas the "dying worlds" presented in *The Stone Gods* "have lost their connection to poetic language and art – they have forgotten how to imagine beyond the world of the present, to create new worlds through language" (Rine 2011: 82), this alternative imagination which provides "intimations of other and better worlds" (Onega 2011: 289) is precisely what literature offers. Crucially, it is above all alternatives to a computational or strictly binary logic that the encounter with literary texts offers. The novel's prime representative of this binary logic, Spike, the Robo *sapiens*, designed to give "impartial advice based on everything that can be known" (*SG* 17) is at a loss when she is confronted with literature. Thus, when she reads poetry in the *Post-3 War* chapter – she recites three lines from W. H. Auden's "In Sickness and in Health", again slightly altered, with "taught" replacing the original "showed" (*SG* 168, see Auden 1991: 319) – she "can't understand it" (*SG* 168). Billie tells her that "I can explain it, but I can't make you feel it" (*SG* 168), pointing to a dimension of poetic language that transcends what can be grasped within the parameters of even the most stringent computational logic. For example, while "[t]he sensual properties of one dear face" that Spike quotes from Auden (*SG* 168, Auden 1991: 319) are put forward in poetic language, they cannot be fully contained in Spike's binary understanding of the world. Following Levinas, it would seem that it is the saying taking precedence over the said in such utterances, that in these cases in the language of literature there is a surplus of signification beyond the ascertainable facts. It is this otherness in the language of literature that endows it with its irreducible plurality and ensures that there is "more than one reading", making it a vehicle of resistance in totalitarian worlds such as the dystopian societies depicted in *The Stone Gods*.

In fact, the passage from *Post-3 War* in which Spike reaches the limits of her understanding is, due to the novel's circular structure, an echo – or re-reading – of a moment in *Planet Blue* at which the further developed version of Spike describes her first encounter with poetry. She tells Billie about this moment of discovery, which happened aboard Captain Handsome's spaceship on the first research mission to Planet Blue, coinciding with the discovery of the planet:

> While the crew were making the film record, the first shots to be replayed back to Orbus, Handsome got out his book of poetry. Everyone laughed at him, but he insisted that only a poet could frame a language that could frame a world. Underneath the digital images of Planet Blue, he wrote, *She is all States, all Princes I, Nothing else is.*
>
> I can read several languages and I can process information as fast as a Mainframe computer, but I did not understand that single line of text. (*SG* 80)

Again, the language of poetry proves to be impermeable to the binary, computational understanding of even the most highly developed computer – and that is what Spike is at this moment after all. The reason is that the logic of poetic language is, as Kristeva has argued, a "transfinite" logic that transgresses the *doxa* of the binary true-false logic (1986: 41, see ch. 2.2.3 and ch. 3.4), which is constitutive of Levinas's said. It emerges that poetry can only function as a language that can "frame a world" in so far as poetic language itself here cannot be understood or 'framed' – it certainly defeats the information processing of Spike's Mainframe computer –, as it resists the kind of definitive, reasonable or binary meaning Spike is looking for. Indeed, after Handsome tries to explain Donne's line to her, Spike continues to remember, "I went back to my data analysis, and I thought I was experiencing system failure. In fact, I was sensing something completely new to me. For the first time I was able to feel" (*SG* 81).

The encounter with poetic language here clearly constitutes an irruption in the repetition of the ever same and allows for the experience of difference, of "something completely new". This is then the key function of the many textual encounters, whether in subtly altered intertextual references or in intratextual repetitions, *The Stone Gods* offers: they introduce difference into the novel's repetitive narrative cycles by highlighting the saying and the non-binary logic of poetic language and opposing it against the totality of identical repetition that must result in an emphasis on the said and in the fossilisation of destructive discourses. Encounters with texts here become a plot device that injects alterity into the narrative. In this process, although it may seem paradoxical, the narrative's repetitive, circular structure is essential. Despite its apparent iteration of sameness, by repeating acts of reading – and hence understanding – and ultimately falling back onto itself, conducting its own re-reading, Winterson's novel highlights the fundamental plurality of reading processes by means of its circular structure reintroduces difference at every repeated step.

5.3 "Love Is an Intervention": Queering the Circle

As Spike's reaction to Donne's poetry shows, the difference introduced into the cyclical repetition through the encounters with texts is not merely a cognitive one, but, as a result to the inherent challenge of cognition itself, an affective one – she begins to feel. In this particular case as well as on similar occasions in the novel, this new-found feeling is triggered or at least reinforced by the challenge to definitive understanding that poetic language poses, but is then transferred to interactions with others. This is symptomatic of how in *The Stone Gods* the frequent irruptions into the ontology of sameness the novel's repetitive cycle of destruction constitutes are almost all at some level directed towards others, in the sense that they result in an opening up and in what Levinas has described as the "calling into question of [...] spontaneity by the presence of the Other" (1969: 43), that is, in an increased ethical awareness. In this it is crucial that, in accordance with the disruptive nature of language, the turning towards the other that is occasioned by these linguistic encounters results in queer – in the broad sense of non-normative and hence in themselves disruptive – relationships between characters.

The turning towards the other is in these instances realised as love, the "intervention" in the totality of identical recurrence that the novel most prominently suggests (see *SG* 83, 217, 244). Given love's role as force of intervention, it is important to note that the love relationships at the focus of *The Stone Gods* are all non-totalising forms of love, where love is an ethical longing for the proximity of the other that still maintains the fundamental difference and alterity of the other. There are two kinds of love relationship presented in *The Stone Gods*, Billie's filial love towards her mother in the last two sections and erotic love, where the novel's most prominent erotic love relations, between the various incarnations of Billie/Billy and Spike/Spikkers, are all defying the heteronormative: they portray either homosexual love between two men – Billy and Spikkers in the *Easter Island* section – or between a woman, Billie, and the female-gendered Robo *sapiens* Spike in a world in which homosexual relationships seem generally accepted, but where "[i]nter-species sex is punishable by death" (*SG* 18), and so are queer also in the sense that they are at odds with and undermine the norms of Winterson's dystopian societies.[105] Crucially, all of these love relationships are tightly linked to stories and the language of literature.

When it comes to the instances of erotic love in the novel, the openness and non-totalising nature of the love relationships presented in *The Stone Gods* seems to reflect the way in which Levinas describes erotic love.[106] In "Time

---

105 Fiona McCulloch adds that "Billie's love for writing materials, in a world where writing has become defunct, marks her out as queer insofar as she is different from the mainstream, not only in her sexual and emotional desires, but also in her pursuit of wisdom" (2012: 66).
106 In the context of Winterson's non-heteronormative love relations that often provide female perspectives it is necessary to point to the feminist critique of Levinas's gendering of the love relation into an active masculine and a passive feminine part (see Sandford 2002; Critchley 2015: 96–98). Although Levinas later suggested that "the participation in the masculine and in the feminine [is] the attribute of every human being" (1985: 68) and even reads the biblical "male and female he created them" (Gen. 1.27) in this fashion (1985: 69), this remains a contentious issue. Perhaps the most compelling critique is that by Luce Irigaray (1986 [1983]), who criticises the passivity and downright infantilisation of the feminine in Levinas and advocates for an active female lover part and the sharing of responsibility among the lovers (see Critchley 2015:

and the Other", he writes of the "caress", the erotic contact between lovers, as a mode of being drawn towards the enigma of alterity in a positive, non-possessive way, without effacing that which is other (see also Critchley 2015: 101):

> The caress is a mode of the subject's being, where the subject who is in contact with another goes beyond this contact. Contact as sensation is part of the world of light. But what is caressed is not touched, properly speaking. It is not the softness or warmth of the hand given in contact that the caress seeks. The seeking of the caress constitutes its essence by the fact that the caress does not know what it seeks. This 'not knowing', this fundamental disorder, is the essential. It is like a game with something slipping away, a game absolutely without project or plan, not with what can become ours or us, but with something other, always other, always inaccessible, and always still to come (*à venir*). The caress is the anticipation of this pure future (*avenir*) without content. It is made up of this increase of hunger, of ever richer promises, opening new perspectives onto the ungraspable. It feeds on countless hungers. (Levinas 1989d: 51)

This caressing is the way in which Winterson's lovers interact. Their love is based on a fundamental "not knowing" of the other and on the acceptance of this openness, of the "pure future without content" the other offers. The "not knowing" is in these cases encapsulated in the way love is connected with stories and the fundamental plurality of reading those stories. Love in *The Stone Gods* is then not just a closed discourse, like the discourses of sameness that drive the novel's various destructive patterns of human behaviour, and neither is it a manifestation of pure affect or emotion, although Billie certainly advocates for the importance of emotion over rationalism (see *SG* 170). Instead, love is the novel's most concrete figure for opening up to difference, for turning toward the other.

Thus, in the first section, as mentioned above, Spike, the all-knowing but unfeeling Robo *sapiens*, only begins to "feel", to experience affects, after her understanding has been challenged by the reception of literature, of the (due to its 'transfinite logic') enigmatic language of poetry. This new ability to feel allows her to fall in love with Billie, who is at first reluctant because of Spike's status as a robot who, she thinks, is unable to feel and love. If Spike's riposte that "[g]ender is a human concept [...] and not interesting" and her argumentation that ultimately they are alike as far as consciousness is concerned do not quite sway Billie yet (*SG* 76), things change soon, when Spike tries to convince Billie to sleep with her, promising that "*you once voyaged would be my free and wild place that I would never try to tame*" (*SG* 82). When Billie argues that

---

96–97 and 110–119; Sandford 2002: 143–148; for further endeavours to reconcile Levinas to feminism, see Sandford 2002). The passages on love relations from Levinas's work I am referring to in this chapter do not specifically address the masculine/patriarchal and feminine. The claims they make seem to me to apply regardless of gender or sexual orientation.

"*You can't love me. You don't know me*", Spike responds by asking her, "*Can you only love what you know? [...] Or is love what you don't know?*" (SG 82–83), which suggests precisely the Levinasian understanding of love as embracing alterity without assimilating otherness into categories of sameness. Love, as envisioned by Spike, where Billie is her untamed "free and wild place", and indeed as eventually returned by Billie, who sees Spike as "unknown, uncharted, different in every way from me, another life-form, another planet, another chance" (SG 90), is then precisely the "pure future without content" of the Levinasian caress. At the same time, the affective power of this queer love is directly contrasted with the human capacity to colonise, exploit and destroy, since this conversation between Billie and Spike in which Spike emphasises the importance of 'not knowing' is conducted parallel to a speech by Handsome in which he outlines his plans for the asteroid impact and subsequent colonisation of Planet Blue (see Bradway 2015: 195). Tyler Bradway in his reading of this mutual 'non-seizing' of the two lovers, as opposed to Handsome's attempted 'seizing' of the planet, therefore states that "Spike and Billie's lover's discourse affirms the other's radical difference as a locus for change. [...] Here queer eroticism opposes exchange relations that transcend the difference of the other" (2015: 195; see also Rine 2011: 79). Love thus indeed becomes the intervention that seems able to break up the repetition of the ever-same mistakes as which it is propagated in the novel.

The way in which Spike and Billie uphold each other's fundamental difference within their love relationship is ultimately again linked to the power of stories and to the novel's own infinite narrative structure. When after the miscalculated asteroid impact they navigate the increasingly wintery world of Planet Blue and Spike is running out of battery power and being dismantled, her arms, legs and ultimately the torso being taken off her to conserve energy, they turn to storytelling (see SG 109–111). Again, the openness of narratives, the multiple readings they allow, is emphasised and now directly linked to the affective force of love. Indeed, when Spike is dying in Billie's lap at the very end of the novel's first section, Billie muses:

> Is this the universe, lying across the knees of one who mourns?
> Things dying... things new-born.
>
> There will be a story of a world held in a walnut shell, cracked open by love's finger and thumb. There will be a story of a planet small as a ball, and a child threw it, or a dog ran away with it, and dropped it on the floor of the Universe, where it swelled into a world.
>
> Your lips are moving, what is it you say? Your lips are moving over mine, what is it? [...]
>
> Snow is covering us. Close your eyes and sleep. Close your eyes and dream. This is one story. There will be another. (SG 112–113)

Even as their love is brought to an end in their deaths – it is clear that on her own Billie will not survive much longer – the "pure future" of the Levinasian caress seems to be shifted back to the mode of storytelling or reading. Love, the argument goes, will be instrumental in propelling future stories – as is already hinted at earlier, when Spike and Billie agree that once humanity will have re-created "millions of years" later, the first poem to be written will be a love poem (*SG* 110). Notably, in Billie's story it remains syntactically ambiguous whether it is the walnut shell[107], the world or the story that is "cracked open by love's finger and thumb" – in either case, love is a force that intervenes in and opens up rigid ontologies such as the walnut shell, the state of the world or any singular reading of a story. Thus in a novel full of circular structures yet another circle, the circular movement between love's intervention and literature's disruption, ensues here: to love in the non-normative, queer fashion of Winterson's lovers means to accept the other's fundamental difference and hence to read in more than one way; plural reading disrupts totalising understanding and allows for uncertainty and, ultimately, feeling; and feeling allows for love.[108] This is then the queering of the circle of destruction that *The Stone Gods* presents.

This principle also becomes apparent in the love relationship between Billy and Spikkers on Easter Island, which functions in a similar way to that between Billie and Spike. It is grounded in a strong ethical imperative. The lovers' first encounter is when, in absolute despair at being stranded on the island without food and with the natives hostile towards him, Billy is trying to commit suicide by drowning himself:

---

107 The "walnut shell" is possibly a reference to Hamlet's famous claim "O God, I could be bounded in a nutshell and count myself a king of infinite space – were it not that I have bad dreams" (Shakespeare 2006: 466). The function of the metaphor is the same in Winterson's novel: the severe spatial restrictions of a nutshell are directly contrasted with the infinite possibilities of the imagination. However, whereas Hamlet remains sceptical and points to his "bad dreams" that do not allow him to escape the rigour of the "prison" (2006: 466) that Denmark is to him after his father's murder, Billie Crusoe, perhaps true to the adventurous character of her literary namesake Robinson, upholds her optimistic prophecy of love's power to crack open any such 'prison'.

108 In keeping with the strong interrelation between love and literature in *The Stone Gods*, it is possible to reverse the direction in which this circle is run through: in Rine's reading of Winterson's novel "love makes poetry, and poetry can change the world" (2011: 83).

I was up to my chin when the shout came, and I will never forget it. Never. For it seems to me that any hope in life is such a shout; a voice that answers the silent place of despair. It is silence that most needs an answering – when I can no longer speak, hear me.

I turned. (*SG* 127)

In the terms of Levinas's ethics, Spikkers's call that stops Billy from killing himself is a response, the taking up of responsibility, to the silent plea that the utter vulnerability and destitution of the other constitutes and which in itself is already a disruption of the self's sense of ontological primacy (see ch. 3.1). It is in the wake of Spikkers's ethical act of saving Billy and subsequently giving him shelter that their love develops, but actually this saving act is already a first manifestation of love. It reflects what Levinas writes at the beginning of a section of *Totality and Infinity* titled "The Phenomenology of Eros": "Love aims at the Other; it aims at him in his frailty [faiblesse]", a frailty that "qualifies alterity itself. To love is to fear for another, to come to the assistance of his frailty" (1969: 256). Spikkers calling out to save Billy from drowning himself seems to reflect[109] this kind of love.

Although the lovers have only rudimentary means of communication, since Spikkers's English is poor (*SG* 128), they soon share common stories. The most prominent among them is the fiction Spikkers has created for himself that his father's hometown of Amsterdam is one of the stars that can be seen in the night sky (*SG* 129). This story, together with a Delft tile depicting a Dutch house with an open door (*SG* 135), becomes emblematic of the lovers' desired future together. Therefore it also provides the closing image of the chapter: When Spikkers in yet another moment of structural repetition has been rescued from the sea by Billy after being thrown off a cliff by one of the natives and he lies dying in their cave, Billy inevitably returns to the symbolism of the home

---

109 Perhaps 'prefigure' would be a more accurate way to express this, as this is the first direct encounter of the two men. Billy has only spotted Spikkers at a distance through his "Glass" earlier (*SG* 122, 127) – another example of how the novel utilises metaphors of discovery for human interactions. Furthermore, in this case there is a strong overtone of the biblical "through a glass darkly" (1 Cor. 13.12) that is one of the many frequently recurring intertexts quoted in *The Stone Gods* (see *SG* 8, 62, 94, 150, 238). This well-known passage from the First Epistle to the Corinthians addresses the topic of unconditional love in terms that bear a similarity not only to the way the queer love relationships in *The Stone Gods* are described, but also, crucially, to Levinas's notion of the caress and the infinite alterity of the other. For Levinas, approaches to alterity likewise must resist knowledge of the other, i.e. regard them, as it were, "through a glass darkly". The proximity of this bible verse to Levinasian thought can be seen from the fact that it continues by contrasting love and knowledge: "For now we see through a glass, darkly; but then face to face: now I know in part; but then shall I know even as also I am known" (1 Cor. 13.12).

among the stars, the ending of this section closely echoing that of the preceding one:

> Night comes long and straight and his breath comes in shorter bursts like an animal that has run too far.
> In the sky there is a star called Holland and the tall wooden houses called Amsterdam are clear to be seen.
> '*In my dream*,' he says, 'the island is thick-forested like fur, and green and dark and alive. [...] *Where are we going, Billy?*' he says.
> To him I say, 'We are coming by Ship to the Amstel River, and look at us now with bales of cloth and a palm tree in a barrel. A canal-boat will take us along the Singel and stop us at a house where the door is open.' I held up the Delft tile, like a mirror to his face.
> He smiled.
> 'Go in,' I say to him. 'Go in.'
> And he passes through the door. And in the house he must make ready till I have finished my business here and come back to him. (*SG* 139–140)

The story here serves as a projection of the "pure future" of the Levinasian caress. Ostensibly, this dream may not seem like a case of 'not knowing' what is sought – the vision of a common future in Amsterdam is very clear, after all – and hence at first glance it would hardly qualify as a form of caress in Levinas's sense. However, since it is clear that the story of Amsterdam-among-the-stars is a fiction, utopian dreaming, a symbol of a desired future together, which as Spikkers is on his deathbed both are aware will never arrive – or at least not in this story –, it is not so much the factual content of the promise, that is, its said, but the turning to and addressing of the other, the saying, that is foregrounded in the telling of this story.[110] In other words, Billy's promise is not so much an anticipation[111] of a future state – if anything, Billy's conviction that they will be united again in the house at the end is a spiritual, religious one, not a factual one – as it is a turning to alterity, to the "something other, always other, always inaccessible, and always still to come (*à venir*)" of Levinas's caress (1989d: 51). Just as "[t]he caress reaches towards a non-existence that is not an avatar of what is" (Critchley 2015: 101; see Levinas 1969: 259), so Billy's promise to Spikkers, presented in the mode of a story, a fiction, aims at such a never to be realised togetherness.

---

[110] Indeed, this is illustrated by Billy twice stressing that the story he is telling is addressed "to him", Spikkers. The direction of the address seems to be given priority over its content here.
[111] 'Anticipation' is, in fact, almost the exact opposite of the caress: "Anticipation grasps possibles; what the caress seeks is not situated in a perspective and in the light of the graspable" (Levinas 1969: 258).

At the same time, the lovers' caress here again constitutes an irruption into the ontology of the present, as it "juxtaposes once more the journey to and discovery of love by an enlightened pair with the destruction of ecosystems by ignorant others" (Johns-Putra 2017: 186). After all, Easter Island is a localised microcosm of the same destruction the novel shows on a global or cosmic scale in the other two narrative strands. The island's last tree has recently been cut down by the native people, who deforested the entire island in order to keep their economy going and build the novel's eponymous Stone Gods, rendering it barren and barely inhabitable (see *SG* 132–133). Not only do the two lovers then represent an alternative to the destructive metaphysics of the Stone Gods, but Spikkers's dying vision of the island as being full of forests and alive again provides a story with an alternative to the reality of devastation, again linking the intervention of love with the inherent plurality of stories.

The primary instance of love in the third narrative strand is different from the two preceding ones in that it is the non-erotic filial love Billie has towards her mother she was separated from as an infant and with whom she longs to be reunited. Indeed long passages of the chapter *Post-3 War* are Billie reflecting on and remembering – she claims (see e.g. *SG* 145) – the time she spent in her mother's womb and the twenty-eight days she spent together with her mother before she was given up for adoption as a time of wholeness and unity. The love she feels for her mother is "[l]ove without thought. Love without conditions. Love without promises. Love without threats. Love without fear. Love without limits. Love without end" (*SG* 146) – it is, then, again a love that transcends the limits of fixed ontology and so provides a counterpoint to the post-3 war society Billie finds herself in.

Above all, the search for a 'landing place' – one of the novel's central metaphors for the other's proximity and nearness, whether offered in the lover's caress or in maternal love – is the driving force in Billie's life and offers perhaps the novel's most difficult vision of love. Reflecting on her search for her mother, in yet another self-consciously metafictional moment Billie realises that "[y]ou never stop looking. That's what I found, though it took me years to know that's what I've been doing. The person whose body I was, whose body was me, vanished after twenty-eight days. I live in an echo of another life" (*SG* 149). At first glance, the mutual corporeal 'being one another' of mother and daughter Billie yearns for seems to offer an almost proto-Romantic image of unity and wholeness destroyed in a traumatic event of separation, rendering Billie's search for her mother a quest for the restitution of this lost totality. However, if this really were the case, Billie's filial love would hardly constitute the "love without promises" she sees in it – the promise of wholeness would indeed be the constitutive element of such a love relation. In this context it seems therefore necessary to point to the ambiguity of filial love Levinas has described: "Filiality is still more mysterious [than erotic love]: it is a relationship with the Other, where the Other is radically other, and where nevertheless it is in some way me" (1985: 69; see also 1969: 267). Critchley interprets this strange 'double being' of parent and child – also termed a "duality of the Identical" by Levinas (1969: 268)[112] – to indicate a "plurality [...] that ontologically structures our relation to and through the child. Also, and perhaps more importantly, because we're all children too, we're structured plurally. [...] Such is our undeniable and plural facticity" (2015: 105–106). In this sense, then, Billie's love for her lost mother would seem to speak of the fundamental plurality of her self. It is an intervention in and of the protagonist herself, eventually leading to her breaking out of the totalitarian society of Tech City.[113]

Although Billie's filial love thus has a similarly disruptive effect as the instances of love relations in the previous chapters, it appears to be more solipsistic, an inward turned search for the lost mother rather than a turning to the presence of an other. Together with the emphasis on the recuperation of wholeness in Billie's search for her mother, this may be the reason why some critics have called Winterson's conception of love "conservative" (Ellam 2010: 229) and particularly the novel's end a nostalgic and totalising vision (see Johns-Putra 2017: 192; Hicks 2016: 102). For like the Easter Island section, the novel ends with the image of homecoming – this time that of the protagonist herself. Shot by the soldiers of the MORE company, Billie opens her eyes to find herself in an idyllic scenery that is also part of an earlier memory of her mother (see *SG* 156), walking towards an old house. When she stops at the gate,

> There's a noise – the door of the house opens. It's you coming out of the house, coming towards me, smiling, pleased. It's you, and it's me, and I knew it would end like this, and that you would be there, had always been there; it was just a matter of time.

---

[112] Levinas sees filiality from the position of the parent and, as in his description of erotic love, again takes up a male-centred perspective, speaking of the father's relationship with the son. This result of a "silent substitution of son for child" has been criticised, among others, by Derrida and Irigaray (Critchley 2015: 104, see 94–110). On maternity in Levinas and its feminist critique, see Baraitser (2009: 40–45).

[113] The connection between Billie's filial love – and hence her plural being – and her decision to take Spike and run away from Tech City, a decision she never explains, lies in the imagery of the gate and its Edenic surroundings at the very end of the *Post-3 War* chapter (*SG* 176). Not only does this evoke the story Billy tells the dying Spikkers on Easter Island – this time the paradisaic "artificial rainforest" (*SG* 176) is left behind, however – but also a 'memory from the womb' Billie has of her pregnant mother standing by the gate of an idyllic house (*SG* 156), the very same memory Billie also returns to in her dying moments at the end of the novel (*SG* 245–246).

> Across the gate, your face. You can't come any further. I have to go through. The latch is light. Yes, open it. It was not difficult.
> Everything is imprinted for ever with what it once was. (*SG* 246)

Indeed, this can be read as the "essentialist" return to discourses of sameness – 'you' and 'I', or Billie and her mother, becoming one again –, or even as an indication that "Winterson herself has apparently fallen for the old (male) myth that women are 'home'" (Jennings 2010: 143), that several critics have seen in this passage. However, as Hope Jennings remarks, this homecoming (just like the one presented in Billy's narrative at the end of the *Easter Island* section) is a utopian one, present only as the possibility of the "choice of love over destruction" that allows for an "opening into the infinite possibilities of a future that is not foreclosed or doomed to repeat its past mistakes" (2010: 143). The myth of wholeness is indeed only realised in death, that is, not in existence. If anything, then, to me this final passage points to the plural structure not only of the protagonist Billie, but also of the novel as a whole. If *The Stone Gods* is perpetually re-reading itself, then the vision of Billie's homecoming is likewise both a returning and an opening up of the text to itself. At the end, the text like the gate in front of Billie remains open – as befits Winterson's novel, there is "more than one reading".

5.4 "The Universe Is an Imprint": The Ethics of Infinite Reading

The Stone Gods is then a novel that combines and contrasts the global or cosmic with the local and (inter)personal, the future with the past, destruction with love and reading with feeling. In the novel's synecdochical depiction of human development, where "the protagonists [are] a pars pro toto for humanity" (Mertens and Craps 2018: 148), its textual infinity is instrumental in more than one way. Firstly, the circular structure, like a narrative bogeyman, sets up the scenario of an eternally repeating failure of humanity to learn from its mistakes and of the perpetual destruction of human spaces of (co)habitation. In this way it sketches the very totality or ontology of sameness against which the text then turns, not least through its infinity. For, secondly, the infinity of the text is also the novel's way to ensure the openness and plurality that are Winterson's "leitmotiv" (Machinal 2015: 168), in particular since its repetitions are always repetitions with a difference and this difference, irreducible to the underlying cycle of sameness, is likewise repeated *ad infinitum*. The infinite text here seems to be another example of what Jean-Michel Ganteau, with regard to

Winterson's earlier works, has termed her "baroque" aesthetics that has a "tendency to overflow the frame and all possible margins" (2005: 203; see Onega 2011: 273; Johns-Putra 2017: 187). Thirdly, particularly due to the novel's emphasis on the plurality of reading, its infinite structure also serves to reinforce the meta-hermeneutic character of *The Stone Gods*. Ultimately, it is the infinite circularity of the hermeneutic process that is reflected in this narrative structure and so turns the reading of the novel back onto itself, in an already plural re-reading.

Beyond this, the novel's infinite textuality is also closely connected with its central force of intervention, love. Time and again, it is love that "'intervenes' in the self-enclosed story by unleashing difference" (Bradway 2015: 196). In doing so, the novel's depictions of queer love reflect its infinite textuality. On the one hand, since love is intricately connected with storytelling, and the narratives in the novel attain their openness through the text's infinite repetition of difference, the "uncontrollable difference" (Bradway 2015: 195) of queer love in *The Stone Gods* mirrors precisely the infinite textuality. As Jennings claims, when the two lovers in the first part are finally alone on Planet Blue, they are "no longer confined to the restrictions of cultural prejudice, [and so] they accept the infinite possibilities of love [...]" (2010: 140). It seems to me that, aesthetically, in the narrative of *The Stone Gods* these infinite possibilities present themselves as the infinite possibilities of literature, of the infinite text itself, which allows for the unending continuation of the disruptions that love and literature have in common. On the other hand, there is a perhaps even stronger connection between love and the infinite text of Winterson's novel. If, as Levinas writes, "Love is possible only through the idea of the Infinite – through the Infinite put in me, through the 'more' which devastates and awakens the 'less,' turning away from teleology, destroying the moment and the happiness of the end" (Levinas 1996c: 139), then the infinite structure of Winterson's novel, the actual infinity of the text, is a textual strategy to make love possible. Textual infinity is the novel's own metaphorical nutcracker that enables love to crack open the walnut shell of closed repetition – the infinite and circular text eschews teleology and ends of all sorts and is an aesthetic manifestation of the Levinasian idea of the infinite. The parallel between love relations and the infinite text is then not only constituted by the openness of the love relations that echo the infinitely disruptive text, but also by the text itself that is structured like the Levinasian caress, as an opening up directed at a pure – infinite – future.

This brings me to the last and perhaps most important function of the infinite textuality of *The Stone Gods*: in a similar way to the infinite text of Mitchell's *Cloud Atlas* (see ch. 4), it allows the novel to transcend its own boundaries and become a mode of endless address to its readers.[114] As the novel turns its reading back onto itself and keeps re-reading itself, so the readers are challenged to constantly 're-read', and so to reject the seeming inevitability of systems of totality. Since "[i]n the novel, a radical openness to others is inseparable from a radical openness of narrative" (Johns-Putra 2017: 178), and the latter is likewise inseparable from the infinite textual structure, the process of reading this open narrative is structurally akin to – one might also call it a structural metaphor for – the opening up towards others. In its infinite text the novel thus presents a demand to its readers, the demand for a response that consists in the confrontation with that which cannot be grasped, the infinite. When Onega remarks on Winterson's fiction that it uses "formal experimentation as a way to shock readers into affective participation and reflexive thought" (2011: 270), this is certainly true for *The Stone Gods*. The infinity of the text is central to this, since "[t]he Infinite affects thought by devastating it and at the same time calls upon it" (Levinas 1996c: 138), that is, since it brings the shock of devastation to the fixed ontology of thought while simultaneously demanding reflection and response. Given the novel's preoccupation with love, its textual infinity is almost like a caress the text extends towards the reader. This is highlighted by Abigail Rine, who has suggested that the figuration of love in the novel

> has the potential to intervene in the ceaseless, lethal repetition of the social order, [and] is a love that is radical enough to let the other exist fully and autonomously. This love is possible not only between two people, but between a work of literature and its reader. When this love is fertile enough, it can open an 'alternative paradigm'; it can intervene in the (re)production of the normative order. (2011: 83)

If the infinite text indeed makes possible such an extension of a lover's caress beyond the boundaries of the text towards the reader, it would seem that the response it seeks to elicit from readers is an opening up, not just in encounters with texts, but in encounters with others.

The novel's last line, "[e]verything is imprinted for ever with what it once was" (*SG* 246), is also a last metaphor that expresses the transcendence of textual boundaries through the infinite text. It is – as most of the central passages in *The Stone Gods* – an echo of an earlier, or later, conversation between Billie

---

[114] In what is either a huge coincidence or, perhaps more likely, a clever marketing exercise on behalf of the publishers, such a transgression of the novel's boundaries indeed took place when a couple of months before the novel's publication in 2007 a copy of the manuscript of *The Stone Gods* was apparently forgotten on a bench at London's Balham station, where a present-day doppelgänger of Billie's – and self-declared Winterson fan – indeed picked it up and began reading it (see Briggs 2007; Onega 2011: 294–295).

and Spike in the first section of the novel. Countering Billie's conviction that humans are incapable of learning from history, Spike replies: "It is not so simple. The universe is an imprint. You are part of the imprint – it imprints you, you imprint it. You cannot separate yourself from the imprint, and you can never forget it" (*SG* 105). Clearly, this plays with the time-tested trope of the "Book of the World" (Chrzanowska-Kluczewska 2004: 79), where Winterson's novel may quite literally be an imprint, but everything else beyond it, the reader's world, is similarly imprinted. In this sense, this answer is directed not only at Billie, but at the reader, who is thus made a part of the narrative, who becomes implicated, or imprinted. This suggests a metonymic relation between reading and living. If the universe is an imprint, then living and acting in it is a form of reading. The ethical consequences thereof are then caused by the contents of the story told as much as by the way in which it is read. This much is acknowledged by Billie. Although she is not entirely convinced by Spike's claim of the imprinted universe, it sets her thinking and reflecting on her own life, in what is yet another one of Winterson's metafictional comments:

> When I look back at my own life [...] what is it that I recognize?
> Not the stories with a beginning, a middle and an end, but the stories that began again, the ones that twisted away, like a bend in the road. [...]
> True stories are the ones that lie open at the border, allowing a crossing, a further frontier. The final frontier is just science fiction – don't believe it. Like the universe, there is no end.
>
> And this story? (*SG* 106)

The answer to Billie's question would seem to be that Winterson's story attempts to allow crossings – simply, because "there is no end" to its infinite text – and the response the novel seeks to elicit from its readers is such a crossing.

In conclusion, with its radically open, plural narrative, driven by its infinite text, *The Stone Gods* challenges its readers to an infinite reading process. This is a reading process that demands of readers to read differently, to be open to alterity and resist the closed cycle of interpretation the novel superficially seems to offer, a cycle that, although it follows a teleology – that of colonisation and the exploitation of resources – leads nowhere but to the repetition of totality and destruction. Above all, it is a way of reading that eschews finitude and therefore is always already a re-reading, that is, "more than one reading". This is achieved through the narrative structure, which can be identified as infinite due to its circularity and the countless repetitions it presents. At the story level, the openness of the textual infinity is generated through the focus on reading and the effects of encounters with poetic language, which inevitably lead to an opening up, an affective, 'feeling' reaction, which is directed towards others. Reading is what allows the "crossing" of Winterson's queer lovers from the totality of their dystopian worlds into the infinity of their non-totalising love relations and so leads to the queering of the circle of destruction that the novel depicts. In this conjunction of love and literature the infinite textuality manages to transcend the physical boundaries of the novel: readers, it is implied, should do more than merely reading singularly – ultimately what is called for is a re-reading that also becomes an active act of reshuffling the seemingly inevitable fate of humanity. This is, then, the 'infinite reading' that forms the ethical appeal of *The Stone Gods*.

6 Infinite Intertextuality: Encountering Alterity in Ian McEwan's *Saturday*

Infinite reading is achieved in an entirely different way in my next example: Ian McEwan's 2005 novel *Saturday* is a British writer's reaction to the aftermath of the terror attacks on 11 September 2001 written and published before the United Kingdom itself saw similarly motivated atrocities with the 7/7 bombings in 2005. As several critics have pointed out, elements of the novel's plot closely echo sentiments expressed by McEwan in an opinion piece published in the *Guardian* as an immediate reaction only days after the 9/11 attacks (McEwan 2001; see Lusin 2009, Schwalm 2009, Weidle 2009). With the protagonist's anxiety in the face of the threat of terror attacks and its setting against the backdrop of the demonstration against the Iraq War that took place in London on Saturday, 15 February 2003, and was "the largest political demonstration in British history" (Clark 2005), *Saturday* clearly negotiates what Judith Butler, with reference to the post-9/11 atmosphere, calls "conditions of heightened vulnerability and aggression" (2004: xi).

For Henry Perowne, the novel's protagonist, this atmosphere is constantly present, although it doesn't seem to have an immediate impact on his actions, but rather on how he perceives the world around him. As a successful neurosurgeon in his late forties with a too-good-to-be-true upper-middle-class family – his wife Rosalind is a distinguished lawyer, his daughter Daisy, who is flying in from Paris that day, is a budding poet, taking after his father-in-law, the eminent poet John Grammaticus, and his son Theo is an accomplished blues musician – he seems to have it all, when on that Saturday his life temporarily becomes disjointed. After waking up in the small hours of the morning to a false sense of alarm when he sees a burning plane over London and immediately fears a terror attack – the plane later turns out to have had a damaged engine – Perowne goes about his daily business, traversing London for chores and recreation. In this, the anti-war demonstration is promoted from a news item in the early morning news to an obstacle Perowne tries to circumnavigate on his errands (Daisy is the only one of the Perownes who actually attends the protests). While trying to steer his car through the city with its blocked-off streets, Perowne becomes involved in an accident with another car, resulting in minor damage to both vehicles. On the verge of being beaten up and coerced into paying for the damage by the other driver, an aggressive young man called Baxter, Perowne, who has observed his opponent's unsteady behaviour, reacts by diagnosing him with Huntington's disease, which takes the wind out of his assailant's sails and allows Perowne to escape the dangerous situation. This turns out to be a temporary reprieve, however, when in the evening the Perownes' family get-together is interrupted by Baxter, who together with one of his gangster friends invades the family home. Again a precarious moment of near violence ensues, when Baxter decides to rape Daisy Perowne and only desists when he realises she is pregnant. Instead he then wants her to recite a poem and is so moved by the recital – she chooses to recite Matthew Arnold's "Dover Beach" and passes it for one of her own poems – that he can again be deceived and eventually overwhelmed by Perowne, who manages to throw Baxter down the stairs. Subsequently Perowne is called in to operate on Baxter's injuries sustained during the fall and only after his returning home from the operation, Henry's day and the novel end.

In my reading of *Saturday*, the focus is on the ubiquitous intertextuality that dominates the novel and creates a 'textual infinity' within it. The consequence of this dominance of intertextuality is that textual encounters and the ethical appeal that may ensue from such encounters become the driving forces of the novel. This happens at two levels: Not only is the encounter with an intertext, Matthew Arnold's "Dover Beach" (2012 [1867]), instrumental in the resolution of *Saturday*'s climactic moment of crisis, but the entire novel is persistently and overtly structured around a plethora of intertexts whose existence it repeatedly points out. Intertextuality, an inherently infinite phenomenon (see ch. 2.2.3), is hence the key principle of McEwan's novel and from the rampant intertextuality at its core, the text attains a radical, ungraspable plurality, a sense of 'textual alterity': the aesthetic composition of *Saturday* thus performs the encounter with textual otherness that is also a major topic of the novel. At the same time, such encounters with a textual form of otherness, encounters that are necessarily tied up with acts of reading, demonstrably coincide with the ethical appeal that, according to Levinas, inheres in the encounter with alterity. Ultimately, these textual encounters, and hence the novel's boundless intertextuality, become a vital source from which *Saturday* draws its ethical potential.

6.1 "Literary Education": Encountering Intertextuality in *Saturday*

One of the more eye-catching elements of *Saturday* is that McEwan's novel is saturated with intertextual references so that these intertextual phenomena due to their (relative) overtness and pervasiveness take on a highly self-conscious and therefore aesthetically marked quality. It is this emphasis on intertextuality as an aesthetic principle in McEwan's novel that lets it act as a counter-discourse to the binary oppositions that dominate the plot, which seems to take an uneasy defensive stance against alien intruders, best symbolised by Baxter, the antagonist to the novel's protagonist and focaliser Henry Perowne. The latter's propensity to think in the simplistic black and white terms these binaries entail is undercut by the novel's aesthetic structure, and particularly by the multiplicity of perspectives inherent in the novel's ubiquitous intertextuality. Encountering intertexts becomes the novel's structural principle and serves as an injection of alterity that the plot itself lacks. This is the case most prominently when the novel finds its climax in an encounter with an intertext, Matthew Arnold's "Dover Beach", but in fact the entire novel is performing such encounters with (textual) otherness throughout. It is through these textual encounters, I suggest, that *Saturday* develops a strong ethical impulse. My reading of the novel is thus grounded in Levinasian ethics and therefore follows the overall approach taken by Tammy Amiel-Houser (2011/2012) and Swantje Möller (2011), although my focus is more on the disruptive power of the literary in the face of the totalising patterns of thought of the protagonist and therefore on the ethical potential of literary encounters themselves.[115]

It is clear that McEwan's novel is by any standards pervasively intertextual. Indeed, there is a plethora of explicitly referenced intertexts in *Saturday* that serve not just to establish a sense of the protagonist's and his family's erudition, but at the same time place the novel itself within a rich tradition of literary and cultural production. In his overview of those intertexts that are directly mentioned in the novel, Sebastian Groes compiles an impressive list with the names of around forty writers (from Sophocles to Andrew Motion), classical composers (such as Johann Sebastian Bach or Richard Wagner), blues and jazz musicians (like Eric Clapton or John Coltrane) and painters and artists

---

115 Such a Levinasian reading, as Amiel-Houser points out, goes against the grain of the "the common critical interpretation of [McEwan's] literary ethics" (2011/2012: 128), which is usually read as a humanist ethics of empathy (for such approaches to McEwan's work, see for example Puschmann-Nalenz 2009; Schwalm 2009; see also Mellet 2015: 222–227; for a critique of the "limits of empathy" in *Saturday*, see Gauthier 2013). According to such readings, "[a]t the heart of McEwan's poetology is the desire to look through the eyes of someone else. The confusion of the self and the other [...] opens up for Ian McEwan the ethical dimension of literature" (Nicklas 2009: 9). This is of course at odds with Levinas's ethics, where the absolutely unknowable alterity of fellow human beings forms the basis of the ethical relation and any attempt at 'looking through the other's eyes' constitutes a reduction of the other's alterity to categories of sameness and hence the obliteration of rather than the taking up of responsibility for alterity. While looking through the eyes of other people is certainly at the heart of Henry Perowne's ambitions to make the world a better place through scientific progress, it also implies the appropriation of the other's perspective and to some extent of alterity itself.

(for example Paul Cézanne, Piet Mondrian or Cornelia Parker) that are referenced (see Groes 2009: 102). Needless to say that despite its thoroughness, this list is not, and could not possibly be, a comprehensive account of all the intertexts in *Saturday*, where intertextuality is not just established through "direct citation and the borrowing of 'voice'", but also more indirectly through "the construction of parallels" and "echo and allusion", in particular to a number of modernist intertexts (Groes 2009: 102). In particular, the novel bears parallels to James Joyce's *Ulysses* and "The Dead" and to Virginia Woolf's *Mrs Dalloway*, among others (see ch. 6.3). There is, then, without doubt a thick layer of explicit intertextuality in *Saturday*.

However, most of the names on Groes's list are mentioned just once or twice in the novel and do not seem to immediately impact on its action. In most cases their immediate function is to provide a background that serves to situate the Perowne family in the context of what is commonly accepted as Western 'high culture'. The names of novelists and their works most frequently crop up when Henry reminisces about his daughter Daisy's first contacts with literature or about her attempts at his own "literary education" (*S* 6; see *S* 58, 66, 133 – 134); the poets mentioned predominantly fulfil the same function or appear as foils to the novel's own (fictional) acclaimed poet figure, John Grammaticus, who aspires to the same fame as Ted Hughes, James Fenton, Stephen Spender or Seamus Heaney (see *S* 130, 135); the jazz and blues musicians and the classical composers either illustrate Henry Perowne's own musical tastes – he listens to Schubert while driving through London or to Bach's Goldberg Variations while operating, but is equally partial to Miles Davis and John Coltrane (see *S* 77, 22, 68) – or his son Theo's musical prowess, when Henry thinks of Theo as part of a tradition of outstanding British blues musicians (see *S* 26, 132). In all these cases, the intertextual references situate the Perowne family within an intellectual framework that signals, particularly when it comes to Daisy and Theo, how well read and talented they are, at least in Henry's perception – the award of the University of Oxford's prestigious Newdigate Prize to Daisy seems to corroborate this view, though. The Perownes, it seems, are all highly educated and well-versed (quite literally, when it comes to Daisy and Grammaticus) in the cultural canon of a bourgeois elite[116], and the repeated references to representatives of high culture serve as constant reminders of this.

---

[116] The Perownes have frequently been described as a 'typical' middle-class family by critics (see for example Winterhalter 2010: 342; Schwalm 2009: 180) and reviewers (for an overview of such voices, see Ruge 2010: 69–71 and Ross 2008), but this assessment makes me wonder how many members of the middle class are set to inherit a château in southern France like the Perownes. I think it is hard not to arrive at a more sceptical view of the Perowne family,

6.2 "The Professional Reductionist": Perowne's "Metaphysics of Comprehension"

At the same time, particularly the uncountable literary references abounding in the novel also mark a contrast to Henry Perowne's role as a rational 'man of science', and to a broader undercurrent in the novel that seems to emphasise the discourses of rationality and science. At one level, then, *Saturday* investigates a frequently presumed rift between science and the arts, with Henry and Daisy Perowne as the standard bearers for their respective culture.[117] While this question is not the focus of my reading here, it is nevertheless related: My claim is that while Henry Perowne's views of science, elevated to a state of transcendence that effaces all alterity, dominate at the level of the novel's plot, the presence of the literary, specifically that of intertexts at the structural level, disavows the protagonist's tendency to subject all forms of otherness to his totalising matrix of knowledge.

Throughout the novel, Henry displays the desire to affirm his authority and gain control over all things that seem out of hand and therefore threatening to him. The primary threat to Henry consists in that which is unknown or irrational. This becomes clear from the very beginning of the novel, when he wakes up in the small hours of the morning, steps to the window and shakes off his dreams, which "don't interest him; that this should be real is a richer possibility. And he's entirely himself, he is *certain* of it, and he *knows* that sleep is behind him: to *know* the difference between it and waking, to *know* the boundaries, is the essence of sanity" (*S* 4; my emphases). Knowledge of 'the real' is not only Henry's only interest – his fixation on certainty and knowledge is made amply clear through the repetitions –, to him it is also a hallmark of sanity. This impression is reinforced when soon afterwards the first element that is out of control enters Henry's day: standing at the window he observes a burning plane descending over London. Significantly, after initially mistaking the plane for a comet, he

---

whose "almost comically formidable panoply of professional skill, literary and artistic distinction, and affluence" (Ross 2008: 77) would then have to be seen as ironical (for such a reading, see Ruge 2010) or at least as allegorical of the luxury and entitlement citizens of the 'first world' enjoy (such a reading has been suggested by McEwan himself in an interview with fellow writer Zadie Smith; see Smith 2005).

117 This chasm between the arts and science has perhaps been most prominently discussed by C. P. Snow in the context of his 'two cultures' paradigm. The novel's attitude towards this topic has received some critical attention, for instance by Dominic Head, who claims that "the 'two cultures' debate [...] assumes central significance" in *Saturday* (2007: 185), or by David Amigoni (2008), who points out the importance of intertextuality, such as the multiple references to Darwin, in the novel's negotiation of the 'two cultures'.

then realises that it is "less like a meteor or comet than an artist's lurid impression of one" and decides that the entire scenario is a "nightmare" he does not want to wake his wife up to (*S* 15). The burning plane is thus immediately associated with the irrational and unreal – the vision of a nightmare, painted in lurid colours, as if too bright to be real, a figment of an artist's irrational imagination. This threatening scenario that is entirely out of Perowne's control leaves him shaken and restless, seeking to regain some control by trying to understand what is going on. Immediately he recalls images of the 9/11 attacks and the familiar discourses of terrorism and assumes that the burning plane is a passenger plane that has been hijacked or bombed by terrorists (see *S* 16). These preconceived notions, the only 'knowledge' available to him at that moment, remain the 'truth' that governs his thoughts until he finally hears about the incident on the radio a good half hour later, when it is "made real at last" (*S* 35) and explained as an accident involving a cargo plane in which no one was injured – not the terrorist attack Perowne speculates about. Only at this point, through the establishing of knowledge, has the threat been diffused and Perowne is back in full control of his world.

What the plane incident already shows, however, is Perowne's tendency to reduce the world around him to familiar categories and reject everything that does not fit these categories, which is a consequence of his desire for knowledge and abhorrence of the unknown. In particular, this kind of categorical thought takes place on a meta-level, in that it seems impossible for Perowne not to think in schematic and necessarily exclusive categories – after all "to know the boundaries" is paramount to him. As Perowne is the focaliser through whom the entire narrative is filtered, this leads to the predominance of binary oppositions in the entire novel (see Nunius 2009: 239–246; 2011: 276–281). On the one hand, there appears to be nothing extraordinary or unethical about Perowne's initial reaction to the burning plane: it seems like the reaction most people might show when witnessing a potentially catastrophic event. On the other hand, however, his mechanisms of response that are triggered in this situation are indicative of a wider pattern in Perowne's perception, where his desire for knowledge means that all situations in which he encounters the unfamiliar are already governed by that which he knows, since it makes him attempt to immediately comprehend the world around him in familiar terms – for what else does *knowing* something mean.

The metaphor the novel uses to illustrate Perowne's schematic thought is that of Schrödinger's Cat. Shortly after first seeing the plane from his window, Perowne's mind turns to this thought experiment from quantum mechanics:

> [H]e remembers the famous thought experiment he learned about long ago on a physics course. A cat, Schrödinger's Cat, hidden from view in a covered box, is either still alive or has just been killed by a randomly activated hammer hitting a vial of poison. Until the observer lifts the cover from the box, both possibilities, alive cat and dead cat, exist side by side, in parallel universes, equally real. At the point at which the lid is lifted from the box and the cat is examined, a quantum wave of probability collapses. None of this has ever made any sense to him at all. [...] To Henry it seems beyond the requirements of proof: a result, a consequence, exists separately in the world, independent of himself, known to others, awaiting his discovery. What then collapses will be his own ignorance. Whatever the score, it is already chalked up. And whatever the passengers' destination, whether they are frightened and safe, or dead, they will have arrived by now. (S 18–19)

Originally intended to illustrate the problems arising from the conflation of observations at a microscopic scale with such at a macroscopic scale, the thought experiment, which centrally relies on the coinciding or superposition of opposite states, is at odds with Henry's desire for unilateral truth and therefore dismissed as nonsense. Intriguingly, he returns to the shunned hypothetical cat when after learning that the plane episode was merely an engine failure he bemoans his own "wild unreason" for speculating about terrorism: "He told himself there were two possible outcomes – the cat dead or alive. But he'd already voted for the dead, when he should have sensed it straight away – a simple accident in the making" (S 39). Notably, Perowne only chastises himself for jumping to the wrong conclusion, not for making a rash judgement. As Teresa Winterhalter observes, "although he is capable of moving beyond the fixity of one interpretation, he does *not* move beyond the need for a single reading to adjudicate the truth of his experience" (2010: 346). That is, while he admits that instead of the dead cat, he should have chosen the alive version, the mere thought of Schrödinger's simultaneously dead and alive cat is nonsensical to him. In a way, Perowne thus is very much a man of the Enlightenment, craving the "collapse of ignorance" and the attainment of an ultimate truth through scientific experiment, while lacking even a shred of Romantic 'negative capability' (see Root 2011: 71). What Perowne cannot accept is entertaining more than one truth or simply reserving judgement. The consequence is that his preconceived notions inform the way he sees the world around him and that the only way for him to encounter the unknown is to immediately subject it to his categories of knowledge – this is the prime, the only mode of perception *Saturday* presents to its readers, at least at the level of the novel's plot.

This is most clearly – and, from an ethical perspective, most problematically – the case in his encounters with Baxter, which are the most obvious encounters with otherness thematised in the novel. Perowne's mode of perception leaves no space for alterity. For him, from the beginning Baxter is never quite unknown, but always perceived in categories hostile to the neurosurgeon: Baxter represents an element of disorder and irrationality that crashes into Perowne's orderly life in a minor car accident. Even before their first face-to-face encounter, Perowne sees Baxter as an "intruder" (S 81) into his lane in the moment of the car crash and meets him with suspicion because Baxter has just left a lap-dance club (a "lawful pursuit", but not as reassuring an establishment as the "Wellcome Trust or the British Library", Perowne muses; S 83) and his car is "a vehicle he associates for no good reason with criminality, drug-dealing" (S 83). As Sabine Nunius points out, Baxter in the novel becomes a visible emblem of the fears entertained by the well-off, by the upper-middle class and its representative Henry Perowne (2011: 279): what Perowne perceives when he sees Baxter, both in their initial encounter and in the home invasion scene, is not his face in a Levinasian sense, but a grotesquely distorted image of the dangerous alien, of the terrorist threat, that is bundled in the person of Baxter. Perowne, then, projects discourses of a hostile and dangerous, anti-social otherness onto Baxter.

The effect is that from the beginning, for Perowne there is nothing truly alien, no alterity, about Baxter, whom he can only perceive in terms of his own preconceived categories as opponent in a "confrontation" (S 83). Henry interprets even Baxter's seemingly innocuous gesture of offering him a cigarette as a power game in which he is now "already one point down" for refusing to smoke (S 87). At the same time he perceives his adversaries in animal terms (S 84–85; see Wells 2010: 117–118) and observes in Baxter a "simian" appearance (S 88, 262), which reveals that he considers his adversary outright "sub-human" (Wells 2010: 118; see also Nunius 2011: 280).[118] While it is true that Baxter's aggressive behaviour does little to dispel Perowne's inhibitions, it is also notable that Perowne's disdain already originates before Baxter's aggression and that

---

118 This description of course implies a lack of culture and a retrograde evolutionary stage and uncomfortably echoes Social Darwinist and racist discourses of the late nineteenth and early twentieth centuries. Together with the overall absence of multiculturalism from Perowne's London (see Kowaleski Wallace 2007: 465) this passage may suggest that discourses that actively seek to purge alterity and their dangerous dehumanising reductionism lurk beneath the smooth surface of Perowne's perception and are the flipside of his "powers of detachment" (Hadley 2005: 93), his scientist's gaze that sees everything – and everyone – in the world around him as potential object of study. More generally, Perowne's attitude towards Baxter is part of what Nunius identifies as the novel's use of "difference for the production of affiliations" and its protagonist's instrumentalisation of differences "for the establishment of rigid boundaries both on an inter-societal and an intra-societal level" (2011: 276). This has also been picked up by critics who read *Saturday* in the light of postcolonial theories, such as Elaine Hadley (2005), Elizabeth Kowaleski Wallace (2007) and Lars Eckstein (2011; 2012/2013).

his overall reaction is one of establishing superiority by subjecting the other to his own discourses of knowledge.

This pattern of perception is closely connected to Perowne's profession as a neurosurgeon. His scientific background not only provides the order of knowledge he predominantly relies on, but it also serves to establish control and authority in situations that threaten to slip out of hand. When after the accident Baxter and his henchmen are behaving in an increasingly violent way, Perowne uses his trained medical eye to escape this dangerous situation: he spots a tremor in his prime assailant and without having any further confirmation he diagnoses Baxter off the cuff with Huntington's disease (see *S* 94). It is this sudden introduction of medical discourse into a situation in which he is threatened with a beating by three street gangsters that lets him escape because it allows him to assume authority, to establish the "magical" (*S* 95) superiority inherent in a doctor-patient relationship[119], and in the process to distract Baxter with a brief moment of hope for a cure for his illness (a hope that as Perowne himself knows is futile; see *S* 96–98). In a very similar way, Perowne exploits his medical knowledge to defend himself against Baxter's home invasion. In order to avert Baxter's threats of violence against his family, he makes up a story about a new drug that may cure Huntington's and is going on trial soon and promises to get Baxter a place on the trial (see *S* 215–216). Although Baxter initially shrugs off the suggestion and it takes another one of his mood swings, this time effected by the recital of "Dover Beach", for him to return to Perowne's invented drug trial, the hope for a reprieve from his illness is enough to lure him away from his henchmen so he can ultimately be overwhelmed and thrown down the stairs by Perowne (see *S* 224–228). In both encounters with Baxter, then, Perowne uses his medical training to re-gain control of situations that have got out of hand simply by re-inscribing scenarios that are dominated by Baxter's threats of physical violence, of irrationality and unruliness, with the rationality of medical discourse and thus re-assuming his mastery of the situation. Medical discourse, or more generally the discourse of science and rationality, allows Henry to detect his assailant's vulnerability and exploit it, to assume a position of control over that which is alien to these discourses, the irrational and (hence by definition) diseased, whose prime representative is Baxter.

---

[119] The novel's overt identification of medical knowledge with magic is also pointed out by Amigoni (see 2008: 162). Revealingly, Perowne associates magic with authority in general when in his heated squash match against his colleague Jay Strauss, at one point, after a turnaround in the players' fortunes, "the magical authority, and all the initiatives are Henry's" (*S* 104).

Crucially, this establishing of control for Perowne only works through reducing the unknown to what he knows and hence through the effacing of alterity. In particular in the moment of the (unasked for) medical diagnosis of Baxter's illness, "Perowne uses his material knowledge to define Baxter's character" (Adams 2012: 560), as from then on the illness is the only lens through which Baxter is perceived, the ultimate, genetic explanation for his deviant behaviour. Such a 'character definition' in the context of Levinasian ethics is, of course, highly problematic: it amounts to an eschewal of the face of the other, who is reduced to an ontological category within the remit of the self. When Levinas states that "the Other, in the rectitude of his face, is *not* a character within a context" (1985: 86; my emphasis), this points to the very impossibility of establishing an ethical relation through a process of 'character definition', which is a process in which inevitably alterity is extinguished. Henry Perowne, however, who at one point is described as "professional reductionist" (*S* 272), in his drive to subordinate the world to his categorical thought strives for precisely such scenarios in which otherness can be avoided.

This emerges most clearly during his operation on Baxter, when, looking down at Baxter's brain laid bare, his mind wanders:

> For all the recent advances, it's still not known how this well-protected one kilogram or so of cells actually encodes information, how it holds experiences, memories, dreams and intentions. He doesn't doubt that in years to come, the coding mechanism will be known, though it might not be in his lifetime. Just like the digital codes of replicating life held within in DNA, the brain's fundamental secret will be laid open one day. But even when it has, the wonder will remain, that mere wet stuff can make this bright inward cinema of thought, of sight and sound and touch bound into a vivid illusion of an instantaneous present, with a self, another brightly wrought illusion, hovering like a ghost at its centre. Could it ever be explained, how matter becomes conscious? He can't begin to imagine a satisfactory account, but he knows it will come, the secret will be revealed – over decades, as long as the scientists and the institutions remain in place, the explanations will refine themselves into an irrefutable truth about consciousness. It's already happening, the work is being done in laboratories not far from this theatre, and the journey will be completed, Henry's certain of it. That's the only kind of faith he has. There is grandeur in this view of life. (*S* 254–255)

Perowne's thoughts here do not only show an unquenchable optimism concerning scientific progress but simultaneously also his aversion towards all things that cannot be rationally explained, towards the enigma of alterity. What Perowne desires is the laying open of fundamental secrets and the establishing of an irrefutable truth. There is no space in his ideal world for anything that resists his categories of knowledge, for alterity.[120] This is so much the case that he elevates knowledge, in his case garnered through scientific discovery, to the state of a secular religion, "the only kind of faith he has". His quasi-religious reverence of the rational, then, betrays the way in which the neurosurgeon seeks to contain the world within that which he is certain of: Perowne subordinates everything to the kind of reductive ontology that Robert Eaglestone has described as "metaphysics of comprehension" (2004: 184; see ch. 3).

The metaphysical dimension of Perowne's epistemology with its privileging of scientific discovery is mirrored in his professional habit as a neurosurgeon and establishes a dual movement of control over and simultaneous effacing of alterity. As has been shown, his profession endows him with 'magical' authority, which he uses to defend himself against Baxter. In particular, the authority that is concomitant with Perowne's professional knowledge is thrown into sharp relief in the operating theatre, where his profession puts him into a position of control over life and death. Perowne is acutely aware of this, to the extent that he likens himself in his role as a surgeon to a god (see *S* 23, 246; see also Möller 2011: 158): his metaphysics of comprehension thus make him a secular god heralding a secular religion which is not built on divine omniscience, but on his ability to contain the unknown. This becomes clear when immediately after his 'confession of faith' in the very knowledge that enables him to be in the position he is in, i.e. still bent over the opened skull of his erstwhile adversary,

> Henry places his finger on the surface of Baxter's cortex. He sometimes touches a brain at the beginning of a tumour operation, testing the consistency. What a wonderful fairy tale, how understandable and human it was, the dream of the healing touch. If it could simply be achieved with the caress of a forefinger, he'd do it now. But the limits of the art, of neurosurgery as it stands today, are plain enough: faced with these unknown codes, this dense and brilliant circuitry, he and his colleagues offer only brilliant plumbing. (*S* 255)

Henry's gesture of placing a finger on Baxter's brain has no obvious use and no clear motivation – this is no tumour operation, the main operative action at this point is already over and there is not the slightest hint at any medical insight gained from placing the finger there. While it lets him fantasise about the "healing touch", itself a divine or magical feature, it also reminds him of the very real limitations of his profession and so highlights the neurosurgeon's odd position somewhere between the divine bringer of life and death and the mundane cere-

---

[120] This is not to say, it should perhaps be added here, that science per se endorses such an irrefutable truth: Schrödinger's Cat – shunned by Henry – may serve as a counter-example. More generally, it is not at all clear whether scientific search for knowledge is finite, i.e. directed towards an ultimate 'fundamental truth'.

bral plumber. What Perowne's gesture really is, then, is an expression of appropriation and of the power his metaphysics of comprehension allows him to wield. Even though his knowledge makes him neither altogether omniscient nor omnipotent, it has brought him into a situation where his opponent is quite literally under his thumb. From initially deterring Baxter, via luring him into a situation in which he can be overwhelmed, to now having his life at his mercy, Perowne has used his knowledge and professional status at each step of the way. At the same time, this progress of the plot comes with the reduction of Baxter's alterity (an alterity Perowne never seems poised to respect in the first place, of course) from unknown intruder into Perowne's lane to diseased thug to anaesthesised patient whose head can be looked into. Incidentally this is also a movement in which Baxter is increasingly, and unknowingly, passivised, made into an object of the doctor's comprehension.[121]

One way of reading *Saturday* – a rather naïve reading that, as I hope will become clear, turns a blind eye to one of the novel's central aesthetic features, its pervasive intertextuality – would then be as a literary celebration of precisely this metaphysics of comprehension. After all, Henry is, broadly speaking, successful with it. Not only is it tied to his professional status as a neurosurgeon and the lofty way of life that comes with that status, but it also allows him to defuse two threatening encounters with Baxter and escape them unharmed, in one case even without having to resort to physical violence himself. What is more, Henry is quick to exonerate himself from the ethical qualms he initially entertains for abusing his professional status (see *S* 111). The Perowne creed in the superiority of knowledge has thus seemingly won the day and led to the largely non-violent resolution of the conflict. Such a reading of the novel would then accept Henry Perowne's preference of the clarity and "irrefutable" correctness science may offer and find in *Saturday* a testament of the metaphysics of comprehension its protagonist adheres to.

---

[121] Perowne is nothing if not stringent in following through with his preference of comprehension and scientific observation in all domains of his life: in a reversal of the parameters that govern his encounters with Baxter, his position as a scientist is also what allows him to get to know his wife Rosalind. Himself a young doctor, he meets her as a tumour patient, is stunned by her beauty – "[h]e had yet to learn clinical detachment" (*S* 43) – and, in a pattern later recurring in the hoodwinking of Baxter, uses his position as a neurosurgeon to place himself at her bed as she wakes up after her operation (see *S* 45). All of this impacts on their courting and Perowne self-consciously reflects that "he knew more of her, or at least had seen more of her, than any prospective lover could expect" (*S* 25).

6.3 "A Yearning He Could Barely Begin to Define": Infinite Injections of Alterity

However, reading *Saturday* as an endorsement of totalising knowledge, or simply as the "privileging of scientific progress" it seems to be at the level of its plot (Head 2007: 187), runs the risk of entirely neglecting the novel's aesthetic structure and would in a way be tantamount to emulating Henry Perowne's premature declaration of the death of Schrödinger's Cat.[122] There is, I would like to argue, a strong undercurrent of the aesthetic that disavows such totalising tendencies by time and again injecting alterity into the discourse of the novel, predominantly through the encounter of intertexts and their infinite deferral of any irrefutable truth. At the level of this aesthetic counter-discourse, *Saturday* foregrounds the disruptive powers of the literary, and with its emphasis on processes of reading or encountering such intertexts, the novel investigates the power of literature to inject alterity into the rigid ontology of sameness – or, in Levinas's terms, it negotiates the capacities of literary texts to resuscitate saying from the fossilised said.

Initially, regarding the novel's aesthetics as a balancing force to Perowne's monologism may seem an odd claim. After all, the use of a covert heterodiegetic narrative voice, with Henry Perowne as the focaliser whose perception readers inevitably share and whose thoughts are the only explicit commentary on the goings-on, is certainly a central aesthetic choice and seems to further privilege Perowne's view of the world. It means the absence of a 'guiding', authoritative or even 'authorial' narrative voice that might set the record straight on Perowne's quest for the irrefutable truth. Likewise, there is no character-narrator whose involved, biased voice a reader might mistrust and suspect to be unreliable. Crucially, however, this absence leaves a blank for the readers to fill and forces them to implicitly position themselves towards the neurosurgeon and his views, or at the very least it "invites questions about what it is that draws us to [Perowne]" (Winterhalter 2010: 340).[123] In this sense, the novel's narrative per-

---

[122] Head arrives at a similar conclusion, when he observes that the emphasis on Perowne's point of view may well create the impression that "scientific discovery is lauded as having far greater social significance" than literature in *Saturday* (2007: 178), but points out that this is merely the protagonist's perspective, while the novel's aesthetics advocate the importance of literary imagination (see 2007: 187–196).

[123] Winterhalter seems to take a positive identification with Perowne for granted, since as a result of the focalisation, she argues, readers may identify with his thought processes. The consequence of this positive identification with Perowne is, according to Winterhalter, not one of unquestioningly adopting his viewpoints, but, ideally, one of self-critique on behalf of the read-

spective bestows a responsibility upon the reader to reflect on the protagonist and his views and in the absence of a narrator who overtly invites readers to take sides, the aesthetics of *Saturday* – that part of the novel which eludes Henry Perowne's control – become a vital counterbalance to the protagonist's monodimensional worldview.

When it comes to the narrative voice, the somewhat unusual use of the present tense throughout the narrative is a key element that contributes to implicating the readers in the narrative. Clearly, the consequence of the novel's simultaneous narrating is the creation of greater immediacy and a further blocking out of the narrator's voice.[124] Dominic Head argues that this is part of the novel's "bold attempt to engage with the immediacy of human consciousness" (2007: 192) and that McEwan's use of the present tense, by creating the illusion that the action coincides with the moment of reading, makes for a "style that gets very close to the experience of reading novels":

> Literary critics are in the habit of discussing novels in the present tense – that is, they concern themselves with what *happens* in a novel – and they do this because the substance of a novel, the experiences described, as well as the plot, comprise events and experiences in a sequence that *happen* each time a novel is produced through reading. In this sense, a novel captures a recurring present. [...] [T]he use of the historic present tense [...] might be said to be a stylistic attribute that comes closest to the experience of novel reading, a feature that McEwan exploits in *Saturday*. (2007: 193)

The immediacy of the present tense thus to some extent bridges the gap between perception and reception, as it eliminates the retrospection generally inherent in (literary) reception. It moves the reader closer to the action and a result of this is

---

ers. The narrative perspective is thus instrumental in making Henry Perowne a mirror of the readers, of their "self-justifying practices" and "bourgeois denial" that help them to, just like Perowne, withdraw into a bubble of domestic comfort, shutting out the complexity and diversity of the world at large (2010: 341).

124 Genette suggests that simultaneous narrating, i.e. narrating in the present tense, may have two opposing functions: it may on the one hand create a sense of heightened objectivity, as "the last trace of enunciating", the temporal distance inherent in a narrative presented in the more common past tense, is erased in such narratives, which then come across as objective presentations of the story (1980: 219). Conversely, Genette argues, the use of the present tense may also emphasise the discourse, as is the case in "narratives of 'interior monologue'", where the action is of secondary importance (1980: 219). *Saturday*, I would argue, is somewhere between those two extremes: Neither is the entire novel an interior monologue – there are plenty of 'exteriorised' passages, i.e. dialogues or straightforward, 'unthinking' action like the squash match between Perowne and Jay Strauss – nor is the narrative entirely objective, as the focalisation on Perowne renders any presumed objectivity moot.

that reading becomes part of the action precisely through the immediacy of experience Head describes. This 'action', however, is not only the action of the plot, but also the aesthetic unfolding of the narrative, in which readers become more directly involved through the simultaneous narrating. In this sense, there is a *performance* of reading implied in the novel's aesthetic structure and mirrored in its intertextual encounters.

Given the emphasis *Saturday* puts on the reading process through this indirect, aestheticised engagement with it, it seems necessary to briefly return to Henry Perowne's attitude towards the aesthetic, and the literary in particular, as these are the only such attitudes directly voiced in the novel. Despite his poet-daughter Daisy's best efforts to give him what he likes to call his "literary education" (S 6), Henry retains a good deal of scepticism towards literature. After all, "Daisy's reading lists have persuaded him that fiction is too humanly flawed, too sprawling and hit-and-miss to inspire uncomplicated wonder at the magnificence of human ingenuity, of the impossible dazzlingly achieved" – a capacity that Perowne is willing to concede to music, painting, sacral architecture and scientific achievement, however (S 68). His particular disdain is reserved for non-realist, or even anti-realist, narratives – Perowne thinks of the magical realists and alludes to Angela Carter's *Nights at the Circus*, Salman Rushdie's *Midnight's Children*, McEwan's own *The Child in Time* and Günter Grass's *Die Blechtrommel* (*The Tin Drum*) as examples of such fripperies (see S 67–68). They offend his tastes because of their alleged disrespect for "the material world, its limits, and what it can sustain – consciousness, no less" (S 67). Given Perowne's understanding that the knowledge of boundaries is the hallmark of sanity (see S 4), it is little wonder that his damning verdict on literature is, "[w]hen anything can happen, nothing much matters" (S 68).[125]

It is the novel's aesthetic structure that challenges Perowne's view. Firstly, the unquestionable prominence of the neurosurgeon's disparaging views on literature and his metaphysical devotion to science is, as Head points out, nothing

---

[125] Perowne's objections to the literary incidentally echo those made by Levinas in his early essays (see ch. 3.3): When Perowne claims that "the actual, not the magical, should be the challenge" he indirectly identifies the literary with the magical, for which he expresses his disdain (S 67). The irony in this – after all, the doctor-patient relationship and the assumption of authority are likewise branded as 'magical' in Perowne's stream of consciousness – seems lost on him. However, the thrust of the argument that is averse to the literary seems to be similar to Levinas's: it is grounded in a scepticism towards the imaginary or the rhetorical and a preference of the 'real'. After all, according to Levinas's early criticism of the literary, in literature "the reality that is sought will appear by magic. The truths or errors articulated are of no value in themselves" (Levinas 1989b: 161). Perowne's claim that "when anything can happen, nothing much matters" in the "magical" worlds created by literature is strikingly close to that.

less than paradoxical because "this view is being conveyed in the form of a novel, written by a writer widely held to be at the height of his powers" (2007: 187). This paradox serves to further highlight the role of the literary, which is already foregrounded in the debates between Henry and Daisy Perowne as well as through the many overt intertextual references in the novel. *Saturday*, then, quite directly "poses the question: what does literature do?" (Amigoni 2008: 161).

Intertextuality, I suggest, is instrumental in both asking and answering this question. The indisputable presence of other texts in *Saturday* must lead to the question of what is their function. At the same time, the striking clash between the protagonist's literary scepticism and the omnipresence of the literary in the narrative makes intertextuality a potent counter-discourse to Perowne's views, constantly challenging and undermining them. For the overt presence of intertexts in *Saturday* is so pervasive that it seems to be opening up a veritable horizon of literature within the novel. While Perowne religiously believes in the possibility, and eventual future discovery, of "an irrefutable truth about consciousness" (*S* 255), the presence of the literary at every instance within *Saturday* seems to resist such a truth. Whereas Perowne yearns for "uncomplicated wonder at the magnificence of human ingenuity" (*S* 68), the presence of the literary questions, and hence already complicates, the irrefutable truth supposedly to be marvelled at. It does so through its unmanageable plurality: precisely through the infinity of the intertextual, whose double logic inevitably introduces perspectives other than that of Henry Perowne, the one perspective that dominates the narrative of *Saturday*. Ultimately, the overt presence of the novel's countless intertexts thus introduces a form of textual alterity into the doctor's dogmatic discourse.

This, the novel's intertextual aesthetics, or more broadly speaking an awareness of the potential inherent in textual plurality, is just what Perowne is missing – or perhaps what he unwittingly realises but cannot, and will not, 'grasp' – in his chastising of the literary. He refuses to see literature as anything else but 'uncomplicated' representation, a manifestation of the said in which all traces of saying have been obliterated and subjected to his metaphysics of comprehension. In this, however, he summarily ignores the moment of literary reception and the dynamics inherent in encountering a text. It is characteristic of *Saturday*'s complex aesthetic structure that the encountering of (inter)texts takes centre stage at the very same time that the novel's protagonist brusquely brushes aside the literary. These textual encounters surface not only whenever one of the many intertexts present in the novel is directly mentioned – after all, each such reference is also the acknowledging of another voice and a different perspective – but also in a number of indirect allusions to intertexts that more or less overtly shape the plot structure of *Saturday*, and it culminates in the novel's climactic home invasion scene and the recital of "Dover Beach" there. This encounter with an intertext is not only the key moment in *Saturday*, it is also programmatic for the novel's wider theme of intertextual encounters and their ethical potential. For this reason, Baxter's home invasion warrants a detailed analysis. The key point is that in the conflict between Henry Perowne and Baxter, an awareness of alterity is created predominantly through the encounter with Matthew Arnold's poem.

The scene of this 'poetic' encounter is remarkable: it constitutes an interruption in a spiral of violence that has begun with the car crash and near-beating taken by Perowne in the morning and has quickly escalated in the attack on the home of the Perownes and hence is also an intervention at a moment of absolute vulnerability. For in the build-up to the recital of the poem, Henry Perowne is one-by-one stripped of all the protective layers that shelter his life: first his car, which has become an "intimate object" and "part of him" (*S* 76), is damaged, then the sanctity of his home is violated, his father-in-law is beaten and left with a bloodied nose, his wife is held at knifepoint, and now Baxter forces his daughter Daisy to undress, intending to rape her. Perowne himself is rendered utterly helpless in the process, but the focus in the scene is of course on Daisy, whose naked body is the starkest reminder of her vulnerability. It is certainly no coincidence that Henry at this moment thinks of her above all as "the vulnerable child" (*S* 218) and it is equally telling that this coercion uncovers what is perhaps her most intimate secret to that point, her pregnancy. This exposure is highly symbolic: Daisy's life-bearing, naked vulnerability is emblematic of that shared by all human beings, the (pre-)ontological condition that shines through in the face of the other as described by Levinas and later picked up by Butler in her account of precarious life. After all, nakedness and destitution, two terms that Levinas closely associates with the face (see 1989a: 83), are certainly embodied by Daisy at the instance she is forced to strip naked. It is this emblem of heightened vulnerability that Baxter shies away from: taken aback by Daisy's pregnancy he gives up on his plans to rape her and the spiral of violence is at least temporarily suspended.

While the discovery of Daisy's pregnancy thus already has an impact on Baxter, it also leads to the introduction of the poem as a substitute. Baxter espies the manuscript of Daisy's forthcoming collection of poetry – entitled *My Saucy Bark*, which is itself an intertextual reference to Shakespeare's Sonnet 80 and a matter of dispute between Daisy and Grammaticus (see *S* 199) – and suddenly decides to force her to "[r]ead one. Read out your best poem" (*S* 219). With the sudden shift of Baxter's attention from rape to recital, "Daisy's body of flesh and blood and her body of words and rhymes become interconnected" (Amiel-Houser 2011/2012: 139), and Baxter's violent attachment has been deferred from the physical to the literary body. After Daisy initially falters at the prospect, she chooses, prompted by Grammaticus, to recite not one of her own poems, but Arnold's "Dover Beach". A further deferral has taken place then, creating another interconnection and exemplifying the principle of intertextuality itself. When she finally speaks, Daisy's words thus overlap with Arnold's, she re-cites him, adopts his voice in a new context and so in her recital creates a new layer of the doubleness or multiplicity that according to Kristeva is inherent to poetic language.[126]

What is crucial about this secondary deferral of the poetic voice is that together with Daisy's very human vulnerability it may lead to the identification of the text with alterity. This is because firstly it blurs any referential specificity as to the origin of the voice and secondly it identifies Daisy's vulnerability with Arnold's text. When Amiel-Houser argues that Daisy's "appropriation" of Arnold attains, because of the situation of the naked recital, a "feminine, corporeal quality [... that] does not suggest a glorification of the English literary male tradition but rather its subversion" (2011/2012: 139), this illustrates both points. On the one hand, Daisy's recital of Arnold – a fictional poet, created by a real-world novelist, giving her voice to a real-world poet, who himself in "Dover Beach" refers to other writers before him, such as Sophocles or Thucydides (see Clark Hillard 2008: 191) – points towards the endlessness of intertextual referentiality. In particular, the specific reference to Matthew Arnold as the author is obscured when Daisy recites the poem in her own voice, a blurring of origins which is of course compounded by Henry's initial failure to recognise the source of the poem. In this sense, the disruption of the chain of attribution that Daisy's 'anonymous' recital of "Dover Beach" constitutes questions the metaphysics of origins that governs the search for the one original authorial voice and so points to the unlimited openness of literary texts. On the other hand, Daisy's nakedness and vulnerability become associated with the text she recites. The wordless plea of her naked body is thus echoed in the words of the poem, which take on the inscrutability of Daisy as the other encountered by both Baxter and her father here.

Indeed, as Amiel-Houser convincingly shows, "Daisy's communicative recitation of Arnold carries out that dimension of language that Levinas terms 'saying'" (2011/2012: 147). Amiel-Houser refers to Levinas's linking of maternity with responsibility for the other to corroborate this, and to further substantiate her claim I would like to show how the doubleness of the intertextual seems to

---

126 Similarly, Molly Clark Hillard in her analysis of the intertextual relation between "Dover Beach" and *Saturday* reasons that "McEwan presents Arnold's poem as a re-read text: that is, a text that allows other texts to walk free within it" (2008: 192).

endow the text with a performative power that disrupts both Baxter's and Henry Perowne's entrenched perceptions of the world – precisely with the power of Levinas's saying. According to Levinas, "Saying states and thematizes the said, but signifies it to the other, a neighbour, with a signification that has to be distinguished from that borne by words in the said. This signification to the other occurs in proximity" (1981: 46). This is precisely what happens in the recital of "Dover Beach": The words of the poem are received by both Baxter and Henry Perowne in proximity to Daisy's naked and pregnant body, to otherness. Yet what both men hear is not the content of the poem, not the said. Neither of them – certainly not Henry, who initially projects his daughter into the speaker role and thinks the speaker in "Dover Beach" is pregnant Daisy Perowne (*S* 220–221) and presumably not Baxter either, whom the poem reminds of where he grew up (*S* 222) – have an inkling of what the poem is 'about', in the sense of what its original Victorian cultural connotations would have been. This is mirrored in the novel's external communication system, for as a consequence of the focalisation, readers initially cannot know which poem Daisy recites. It is only when Daisy recites the poem a second time and some complete lines are now rendered verbatim (*S* 221) that the intertext becomes overt enough to be recognisable for those readers who are familiar with "Dover Beach". For readers who, like Henry Perowne, are not familiar with Matthew Arnold – "Arnold who?", Henry asks, making himself the target of Grammaticus and Daisy's laughter (*S* 230) – the uncertainty about the intertext is resolved only after the threat on the lives of the Perownes is averted (*S* 231–232). The implication is that *what* is being recited here is of far lesser significance than *that* it is being recited. The act of address outweighs its content.

Instead of evoking the specific situatedness of "Dover Beach", the poem thus becomes a projection surface for both Perowne and Baxter, who both attempt to comprehend the poetic text and thus to appropriate it to their own conceptual realms. This appropriation, however, precisely shows that Daisy's recital possesses the quality of saying, since saying is a form of passive, exposed address which is necessarily vulnerable to such appropriations:

> Saying is this passivity of passivity and this dedication to the other, this sincerity. Not the communication of a said, which would immediately cover over and extinguish or absorb the said, but saying holding open its openness [...], delivering itself without saying anything said. Saying saying saying itself, without thematising it, but exposing it again. (Levinas 1981: 143)

When Daisy recites "Dover Beach", the extreme passivity and vulnerability she exudes, standing there naked and threatened with immediate violence, extends to the words of the poem. They lose their communicative content, the said, while the openness of the text, its quality of pure address, its saying, is emphasised.

The consequence is that the words of "Dover Beach" as they are recited by Daisy develop a performative power that impacts on both Baxter and Perowne and, at least temporarily, leads to a change in both Baxter's behaviour and Perowne's perception of Baxter. While the change in Baxter's behaviour and his strong affective reaction to the recital are clear – he drops his rape plans and decides only to take the manuscript of Daisy's book – the precise reasons for this sudden "mood swing" (S 221) ultimately remain enigmatic. This is because the narrative situation with its focalisation on Henry Perowne restricts readers to the limited point of view of the neurosurgeon. The readers then experience the same puzzlement at Baxter's reaction as Henry, who tries to find the reason for it in Baxter's medical condition (S 223–224), but in the end arrives at the conclusion that

> Daisy recited a poem that cast a spell on one man. Perhaps any poem would have done the trick, and thrown the switch on a sudden mood change. Still, Baxter fell for the magic [...]. But Baxter heard what Henry never has, and probably never will, despite all Daisy's attempts to educate him. Some nineteenth-century poet – Henry has yet to find out whether this Arnold is famous or obscure – touched off in Baxter a yearning he could barely begin to define. (S 278–279)

The effect that the inability to comprehend Baxter's reaction to the poem has on Perowne is thus a disruptive one, questioning the "metaphysics of comprehension" that dominates his worldview. Acknowledging his own inability to 'define' the other man's yearning certainly marks a departure from the definition of Baxter's character as diseased and dangerous that Perowne makes throughout the novel. As Amiel-Houser argues, Baxter's reaction to "Dover Beach" makes him, finally, in Perowne's eyes "a unique individual, whose singularity cannot be reduced to Perowne's imaginative interpretations" (2011/2012: 138). Daisy's recital has therefore not only affected Baxter's behaviour, but also, indirectly challenged her father's monolithic thought patterns.

It would then seem that this episode illustrates what Derek Attridge has called the "workness" of literature. For Attridge, a work of literature is an event constituted in the act of reading – its "'workness' [...] lies in the effects it produces in a reader" (2016: 223). Only when a text, in the sense of a mere collection of signs, "a string of words" (2016: 222), is read in such a way that it becomes an event and produces an effect in the reader, that is, only when it is experienced and leads to some sort of response or reaction in the reader that goes beyond a mere extraction of information, does it become a work (see 2016: 223). Attridge describes this kind of reaction as "feel[ing] oneself taken into a new realm of thought and feeling, perhaps only fleetingly and temporarily, but occasionally with profound and long-lasting effects" (2016: 227).[127] Crucially, the reason why a work of literature can solicit such a response is that a work, both in its creation and in its reception, "introduces alterity into cultural and ethical norms, habits of feeling, frameworks of perception, mental associations, and so on" (Attridge 2016: 221). This is precisely what Baxter's reaction to the recital implies is happening in the climactic scene of *Saturday*. His affective reaction to the poem certainly unlocks a 'new realm of feeling' for Baxter and affords him, at least briefly, a hitherto unknown depth of character, revealing to Perowne, and with him to the readers, at least a brief glance at "the Other's enigmatic singularity" (Amiel-Houser 2011/2012: 139). What *Saturday* suggests, then, is that literature, in this case the recital of "Dover Beach", is capable of developing a performative power which is able to disrupt totalising patterns of thought and perception and that the source of the "workness" of literature need not necessarily lie in its contents, the said, but may equally, or even more effectively, be found in the performance of the text's address, in its saying.

The question that remains, however, is how far this power of the literary actually goes. Amiel-Houser suggests that it "catalyzes an ethical transformation" in Perowne, who at the end of the novel has become a "different" man, willing to operate on his assailant and feeling responsible for Baxter (2011/2012: 130, 148), an interpretation that is shared by Möller, who reasons that "Henry's forgiving behaviour towards the person who has threatened to kill his wife and rape his daughter can be explained through Levinas's concept of responsibility" (2011: 184). This view – and indeed the entire Levinasian reading of *Saturday* – has been challenged by Lars Eckstein, who casts doubt on any 'transformation' in Henry Perowne when he points out that right after the allegedly transformative recital, Perowne hoodwinks Baxter and pushes him down the stairs, causing him serious injury (2012/2013: 127). Similarly, the fact that Henry expresses his belief in the discovery of an "irrefutable truth about consciousness" (*S* 255), which at the same time is a refutation of alterity, only later during the operation on Baxter, would indicate that his "ethical transformation" leaves much to be desired. In this context, Tim Gauthier has argued that any "empathic gesture" on Perowne's

---

[127] This description is – if a slight digression along the lines of intertextuality is permitted in a reading that focuses precisely on the aesthetics of such intertextual encounters – reminiscent of the literary experience thematised in John Keats's "On First Looking into Chapman's Homer", where the speaker likens his feelings on the occasion of his first encounter with George Chapman's Renaissance translation of Homer's epics to those of "some watcher of the skies / When a new planet swims into his ken" (2012: 904). Literature, it seems, has the capacity to create workness from the experience of workness.

part is merely a "path to domination" over Baxter (2013: 26), whose otherness is eviscerated time and again when Perowne uses his epistemic superiority as a doctor to 'define' Baxter's character. Therefore, if the novel challenges its readers "to resist the temptation of over-interpreting Baxter's Otherness, and instead accept the limits of our rational knowledge of the Other's singularity, which is not reducible to comprehension and appropriation" (Amiel-Houser 2011/2012: 138), then Henry Perowne's behaviour is anything but exemplary in this regard. Indeed, far from being a contrite gesture of atonement, Henry's decision to operate on Baxter and his intention to make sure Baxter is not prosecuted can also be read as an ultimate act of re-establishing his authority (see Möller 2011: 158; Michael 2015: 232) that has been challenged by Baxter's violent intrusion: "By saving his life in the operating theatre, Henry also committed Baxter to his torture. Revenge enough. And here is one area where Henry can exercise authority and shape events. He knows how the system works – the difference between good and bad care is near-infinite" (*S* 278). The ambiguity of this passage, I would argue, leaves the evaluation of Perowne's behaviour to the reader, just like the answer to the question whether or not his decision to help Baxter is motivated by sincere ethical altruism or by a rather more sinister act of reappropriating authority.

Literature, then, ostensibly does not have the "magic" power Perowne finds in it in the end in a reaction typical of the neurosurgeon's essentialist approach (*S* 278), because there is little clear evidence of a permanent change in Perowne's way of thinking. Indeed, taking such a view of literature would render it a complement to (Perowne's view of) neuroscience, a magically irrefutable 'truth' that will inevitably and profoundly change humanity. This "Victorian fantasy of liberal agency" (Hadley 2005: 93), the idea that literature, by virtue of its cultural power, has a civilising function and morally improves its readers, constitutes merely the no less totalising inversion of Perowne's metaphysics of comprehension – only that this time a metaphysical concept of literature as a cultural product of "sweetness and light", as propagated by Matthew Arnold in *Culture and Anarchy*, another key intertext to *Saturday* (see Hadley 2005; Head 2007: 182–185), takes over from the neurosciences. In view of claims that *Saturday* embraces precisely such a form of "cultural imperialism" (Eckstein 2011; see 2012/2013; Hadley 2005), it seems necessary to stress that I do not think the novel dallies with any such kind of literary metaphysics.[128] Nevertheless, *Satur-*

---

[128] Eckstein argues that Amiel-Houser's Levinasian reading "gloss[es] over McEwan's liberal humanist leanings" (2012/2013: 131), because it does not acknowledge the problematic proximity to imperialist discourse in Arnold's poem and in his *Culture and Anarchy* that critics based in postcolonial studies, such as Elaine Hadley (2005) and Eckstein himself (2011), have pointed

day suggests that literature may develop a disruptive force, that encounters with literature may at least temporarily challenge the reader's perspective, even if they do not always lead to permanent changes in behaviour, and that they therefore may function as a vital counterbalance to any "metaphysics of comprehension".

This key role of the literary becomes clear not only from the "Dover Beach" episode, but from the novel's overall use of intertextuality as a central aesthetic principle that emphasises the novel's textual plurality. Apart from the many intertexts that are overtly mentioned (see above), *Saturday* recurs to a number of other intertexts that are only indirectly reflected in central aspects of its structural composition. On the one hand, the novel's plot loosely follows that of "Dover Beach": After waking up, Perowne comes to the window to take in the night air (*S* 3–4; the parallel to "Dover Beach" is also pointed out by Winterhalter 2010: 349, 354) and soon enough hears the "low rumbling sound" (*S* 14) of the damaged plane's engines rather than the "grating roar" of Arnold's pebbles in the sea spray (2012: l. 9). As his day unfolds, Perowne's reflection on the city's sounds, loosely paralleling the second and third stanzas of "Dover Beach",

---

out. While Eckstein's misgivings on "Dover Beach" are understandable, it would seem that his critique is very much rooted in the cultural context of the production of these particular Arnoldian intertexts, whereas the focus in *Saturday* is decidedly put on the moment of reception and even its immediate context of production is shifted from the Victorian Arnold to Daisy's naked body, as Amiel-Houser has shown. Of course it is possible to read this shift as a mere uncritical avoidance of the ideological overtones of Arnold's poem. Yet this seems to ignore that both Baxter and Henry Perowne, the two characters through whom the reception of the poem is predominantly filtered, are entirely ignorant of the poem's origins and hence also of its association with imperialist discourse. Eckstein somewhat polemically suggests that this ignorance on Henry's and Baxter's part only shows that "the cultured powers of 'sweetness and light' are more affecting if associated with an attractive pregnant woman in the nude rather than with a middle-aged Victorian with enormous whiskers" (Eckstein 2011: 9). However, to me it seems that this ignorance of any context shifts the focus onto the text, and in the conspicuous absence of the text itself a further shift of focus onto the reaction to the text, i.e. its reception, takes place. There the unknowability of the radically plural poetic text becomes apparent and it is this form of textual alterity, not the discourse of "Arnoldian Culture with a capital C" (Eckstein 2011: 9), that impacts on Baxter and Perowne. In other words, while all texts come with their own cultural, historical and ideological baggage, and "Dover Beach" perhaps more so than most, this baggage can be subverted by the radical plurality of the intertextual relation and in the context of *Saturday*, this is precisely what happens. The challenge that the intertextual relations of *Saturday* present, then, is *not* to embark on a quest for textual origins and their connotations, but to embrace the radical openness of the literary and its potential to rupture any 'metaphysics of knowledge'. For this reason, I think that Amiel-Houser's Levinasian reading is a perfectly viable approach to *Saturday*. Eckstein's convincing postcolonial critique of the novel is, however, a reminder that *Saturday* itself as a text is at least double.

only takes place later when he listens in on Theo's band practising (*S* 169–172) and acknowledges that music can have the power to "give us a glimpse of what we might be, of our best selves, and of an impossible world in which you give everything you have to others, but lose nothing of yourself" (*S* 171). This "Sea of Faith" (Arnold 2012: l. 21) evoked by his son's blues performance is almost verbatim linked to "Dover Beach" when Perowne reflects that "[h]e also heard it long ago" (*S* 172) at a school performance of his children (somewhat ironically Perowne usurps the place of Sophocles here; see Arnold 2012: l. 15–16). And like Arnold's poem, *Saturday* eventually turns more violent so that "[t]hrowing Baxter over the stairs [...] metaphorically reconstructs Arnold's night battle" (Clark Hillard 2008: 195).

On the other hand, *Saturday*'s setting, encompassing a 24-hour day in the life of its protagonist, inevitably places it in the tradition of two modernist masterpieces, James Joyce's *Ulysses* and Virginia Woolf's *Mrs Dalloway* (see e.g. Adams 2012; Groes 2009; Root 2011). Like "Dover Beach", both novels show a number of parallels to *Saturday*. In her detailed tracing of the intertextual relations between *Saturday* and *Mrs Dalloway*, Ann Marie Adams points out that both novels are

> recording the meanderings of a middle-aged, well-to-do member of society who marvels at the technologized splendors of the metropolis, ponders the effects of war, thinks about the growing independence of his/her children, and mentally justifies his/her choice of a spouse before having to restore an uneasy sense of normalcy after a tragic event that threatens to ruin a party. (2012: 553–554)

Beyond the parallel plot lines – Baxter's neurological disease can be seen to echo Woolf's shell-shocked World War veteran Septimus Smith (see Adams 2012: 556; Root 2011: 68) – the stylistic influence of Woolf's writing becomes clear, ranging from the use of free indirect discourse and a preoccupation with 'writing the mind' to more subtle parallels concerning the way cars and airplanes are woven into the fabric of both narratives that Groes uncovers in his perceptive reading (2009: 106–107).

At the same time, *Ulysses* provides yet another blueprint for *Saturday*. The meticulous description of Perowne's mundane, everyday routines, from making morning coffee to shaving and defecating (*S* 69, 57) mirrors Joyce's Buck Mulligan and Leopold Bloom, while the fraught relationship between Perowne and his mother bears similarities to Stephen Dedalus's situation (see Groes 2009: 105). For Winterhalter, these parallels continue on a more abstract level, since both novels are concerned with the "question of a redefinition of home" (2010: 351) and have their protagonists struggle with a fundamentally changed home (by Baxter's home invasion and Molly's marital infidelity, respectively).

Notably, *Ulysses* is indirectly present in *Saturday* from its very beginning, as McEwan's epigraph is taken from Saul Bellow's *Herzog*, itself a literary response modelled on Joyce's novel, which sets the tone for Perowne as modern individual partaking in city life (see Groes 2009: 105; Root 2011: 68).

Indeed, there are a number of further texts around which *Saturday* is structured or which it alludes to, mingling their voices with its own. Peter Childs sees Joseph Conrad's short story "The Secret Sharer" as a "key intertext" to *Saturday*, where Perowne becomes the sharer of Baxter's secret, his illness (2009: 28). Likewise, Robert Louis Stevenson's *Strange Case of Dr Jekyll and Mr Hyde* is a covert intertext to *Saturday*, and one that fits the novel's pattern of intertexts from the incipient modernity, i.e. the mid-to-late-Victorian period, up until high modernism.[129] For Perowne in many respects resembles the good doctor who tries to contain the atavistic 'creature' Baxter, whose description as "simian" (*S* 88) certainly evokes "ape-like" Hyde (Stevenson 2006: 20, 65, 66; see Bar-Yosef 2020: 2–3), and the antagonism between Baxter and Perowne certainly is similar to that between Jekyll and Hyde. But it is perhaps in particular the novel's framing scenes, which see Perowne stepping to his bedroom window in the small hours of the night and so establish circularity in the narrative, that are rife with intertextual references. Thus not only "Dover Beach" is evoked there, but also the beginning of Franz Kafka's novella *Die Verwandlung* (*The Metamorphosis*), which incidentally also marks the start of Henry Perowne's 'literary education' at the hands of Daisy (*S* 133). When Perowne wakes up, turns to the window, reflects on whether he is still dreaming and then thinks of his job, this resembles Gregor Samsa's thoughts after waking up transformed into a bug (see Lusin 2009: 146; Groes 2009: 103). At the same time, his pose at the window, lost in thoughts and surveying the square beneath him, summons up the end of Joyce's "The Dead", where Gabriel Conroy watches the snow "faintly falling" (Joyce 2016: 251) and is engulfed by a feeling of love for his wife in the bed next to him – just like Perowne at the end of *Saturday*, when "at last, faintly falling: this day's over" (*S* 279; see Clark Hillard 2008: 188; Groes 2009: 105; Root 2011: 74; and, in particular, Ganteau 2014).

It should have become clear at this point that *Saturday* is overloaded with intertextual references. Their presence is so ubiquitous and simultaneously such a conspicuous feature of the novel that the impression must ensue that these intertexts really form a limitless web transcending the boundaries of the

---

[129] I am indebted to Eva Ries for many enlightening discussions on *Saturday* and in particular for pointing out Stevenson's *Strange Case* as an intertext to me. On the parallels between the two texts, see Ries (2020), Bond (2017) and Bar-Yosef (2020).

novel itself. Thus, as Clark Hillard points out, there is an intertextual genealogy leading from "Dover Beach" via *Mrs Dalloway* to *Saturday* (see 2008: 200–201), where "Dover Beach" already is an intertext to Woolf's novel (see Childs 1997: 69–70). This lineage is expanded in *Saturday*, for the plot element of using a recital of "Dover Beach" to disrupt monodimensional thought itself establishes an intertextual link to Ray Bradbury's *Fahrenheit 451*, where protagonist Guy Montag commits the 'crime' of reciting a piece of literature – "Dover Beach" – to unsettle his wife's friends as a reaction to their unquestioning support for their totalitarian regime (Bradbury 2012: 96–97).[130] A similar line of referentiality extends from *Saturday* via *Herzog* to *Ulysses* and beyond, to Joyce's Homerian intertext. *Saturday* itself thus becomes a text which not only allows various intertexts to meet and intersect, but explicitly makes use of already established connections, expanding and reconfiguring them. Given the way these intertexts are contained and refracted in *Saturday* – overtly and with a clear sense of the iterability of the intertextual relation – the novel's intertextual constructedness may be understood as infinite via the Basic Metaphor of Infinity (see ch. 2.2.3 above).

The consequence of this unlimited overlapping of intertexts in the novel is that these texts and their many voices co-signify, generating a multiplicity of meaning entrenched in the novel's aesthetic structure that lets readers of *Saturday* face a similar indeterminacy of meaning as Baxter and Perowne do in Daisy's recital of "Dover Beach". If Henry Perowne can be seen as a literary revenant of, among others, Clarissa Dalloway, Leopold Bloom, Moses Herzog, Gabriel Conroy, Gregor Samsa, the unnamed speaker of "Dover Beach" and Henry Jekyll, all of whom themselves refer to long lines of textual tradition and carry with them the voices of other texts, then the ungovernable, indeed infinite, multivoicedness of *Saturday* becomes clear. Describing *Saturday* as "a novel by a man in which a woman recites a poem by a man that reflects a novel by a woman in which a woman recites a poem by a man" (Clark Hillard 2008: 201) therefore gives a good sense of the complex multiplicity of the intertextual relations – and of the iterability of the referential process – but does not by far come close to encompass all these textual traces (in fact, it only describes the relations between *Saturday*, "Dover Beach" and *Mrs Dalloway*). While it is of course possible to try to follow each single one of these intertextual traces and relate them to Henry Perowne's travails, it seems well-nigh impossible to find a reading that unites all these voices to a single interpretation that does justice to them all.

---

[130] While the effect of the recital is similarly catalytic, the immediate outcome in Bradbury's dystopian novel is more negative: the women react with disgust and start crying, Montag throws them out and threatens them and the last pretence of leading his life in conformity with the totalitarian state has collapsed.

For this reason, it seems that the point of the novel's excessive intertextuality is precisely to resist such a unifying interpretation and to challenge any reading that might posit itself with Perownian certitude as absolute. In this sense, the countless parallels with intertexts are not so much instrumental in furthering the plot as they are in constructing an aesthetic counter-discourse to Perowne's totalising thought patterns. The impact the literary may have is nevertheless already exemplified in *Saturday*'s central encounter with "Dover Beach" and in the way the poem disrupts both Baxter's and Perowne's thought. It continues with each of the many explicit references of other texts in the novel, since all of them imply voices directed against the neurosurgeon's essentialism. And finally, at the structural macro-level, the infinite plurality of voices attained by the overt intertextuality makes the novel resist any monodimensional reading. Instead, it leads to the radical openness of the literary text itself and makes it possible for *Saturday* to tentatively develop into a performance of saying, much like "Dover Beach" does in Daisy's recital.

This is reinforced by the way in which several of the intertexts are spread out across the novel, only occasionally puncturing the narrative. Jean-Michel Ganteau with regard to the references to "The Dead" asserts that this creates a "fleeting, phantom effect of *déjà vu* that may alert the reader to a presence and a familiarity even while dramatising its absence and building up the relational nature of the text around a feeling of impossible capture and loss" (Ganteau 2014: 226). Ganteau's analysis holds true in a similar way for many of the other intertexts *Saturday* relies on, for I would suggest that this impossible capture and loss does not only work at the plot level, but also at the level of textual determinacy. Indeed, the consequence of this 'phantom presence' of the intertext is, as Ganteau points out, that "[t]he epiphany of recognition seems to be for ever on the cusp of materialisation, a trace always already there and always already unattainable, making loss a paradoxical condition of apperception" (2014: 226). It is not a coincidence, I would argue, that Ganteau's wording here is strikingly close to a description of the condition of alterity, which is precisely rooted in a "paradoxical condition of apperception". As a consequence, the intertextual relation with "The Dead" infuses *Saturday* with a sense of vulnerability that is "a way to express an openness or more specifically a sensibility to the other rendered in Levinasian terms" (2014: 232). This vulnerability is then not only one that Henry Perowne becomes increasingly aware of towards the end of the novel, but one that is woven into the fabric of the entire novel, which it surreptitiously invades through its intertexts that are instrumental in creating openness at the textual level. Intertextuality in *Saturday* thus really produces "the introduction of alterity into the smoothly working machine of the same" that for Attridge characterises the "ethical charge of the literary work" (2016:

227). It is then through the novel's intertextuality and the infinite plurality it entails that any reading of *Saturday* also becomes an encounter with alterity.

This is the central claim of my reading of McEwan's novel: while *Saturday* readily engages with ethical conflicts, it does not profess to have unambiguous answers to them. Instead the novel is in the privileged position that perhaps only fiction can assume: it ultimately lets its protagonist 'do the right thing' (giving Baxter medical treatment), but does not cease to relentlessly question his motives and in the process denies itself any definitive closure of meaning. Only by resisting this sort of evaluative closure can *Saturday* be ethically engaging, which is why I would argue that the very point of the "workness" of *Saturday* is that Perowne's status in the end – ethically transformed or relapsed to monolithic thought patterns – remains unresolved. This is what places *Saturday* among the texts I like to call fictions of infinity. Where a recurring feature of such texts is the representation of the unrepresentable, what remains enigmatically unrepresentable in *Saturday* and yet at the same time key to its plot is the moment of encountering and responding to literature. In fact, since the novel's openness is both aesthetically and narratively encoded in the novel's overt intertextuality, which itself points towards the infinite plurality of fiction, *Saturday* might even be called a meta-fiction of infinity.

7 Infinite Perspective: John Banville's *The Infinities*

Given its title, my final case study, John Banville's 2009 novel *The Infinities*, may seem like an obvious choice for an analysis of the infinite in narrative fiction. While indeed there are several ways in which infinity is ingrained in *The Infinities*, such as the inability of the immortal gods to attain the one thing they cannot have, death (see *TI* 72, 79), or the intertextual references – in particular to Heinrich von Kleist's work and his aesthetic treatise "Über das Marionettentheater" ("On the Marionette Theatre"), which itself associates aesthetic grace with an infinite consciousness –, my focus here will be on the novel's investigation into infinity, alterity and narrative worldmaking. I will show that *The Infinities* does not only thematise the infinite at the story level, but that it also provides yet another example of a narrative construction of the infinite – this time through its unlimited narrative perspective. Overall, it is a strongly metafictional novel that uses its topic of infinite parallel universes and its narrator-god Hermes to reflect on the process of constructing narrative worlds as well as on the totality that necessarily forms a part of such narrative constructions, while its narrative infinity injects a form of textual alterity into the narrative that counterbalances the totality of the construction process.

The Infinities is a novelistic adaptation of Kleist's play *Amphitryon*, which Banville, who has a long-standing admiration for the German writer, also translated for the stage under the title *God's Gift* in 2000.[131] The Amphitryon myth, which tells the story of Zeus taking on the shape of the Theban general Amphitryon to spend a night with Amphitryon's wife Alcmene and beget Heracles in the process, has been made the topic of several comedies that exploit the comic potential of the doubling of Amphitryon as man and god, most prominently by Plautus and by Molière, whose version served as the inspiration for Kleist. Banville's *The Infinities* therefore looks back on a long intertextual tradition. While the novel keeps with the mythological side of Kleist's original and has the Greek gods Zeus, Hermes and Pan interfere with human affairs, it adds, presumably inspired by the double existence of Amphitryon and in keeping with Banville's interest

---

[131] Banville's interest in Kleist is traced by Mary Helen Dupree (2014; see also O'Connell 2013: 23). Besides his translations/adaptations of Kleist's plays *Der zerbrochene Krug* (*The Broken Jug*, 1994) and *Penthesilea* (*Love in the Wars*, 2005), Banville already recurs to *Amphitryon* in his 2000 novel *Eclipse*, in which the protagonist Alexander Cleave is an actor starring as Amphitryon in a production of Kleist's play (see Friberg-Harnesk 2010: 74–75). For a reading of *The Infinities* that focuses on the novel as an adaptation of Kleist, see Murphy (2014).

in scientist characters, the theme of multiple worlds (as well as multiple mythologies) and negotiates the ontological and epistemological consequences following from the existence of such multiple parallel worlds. This is what turns *The Infinities* into a metafictional novel which enquires into the status of fictional worlds, the capacity of fiction in worldmaking and the resulting ethical implications. In particular the protean narrative voice, which defies every (onto-)logical limit, serves to ironically question the process of narrative worldmaking and points towards the ethical demands that the encounter of a fictional world imposes on readers and writer alike: such encounters, the novel suggests, come with a challenge to avoid setting one's own perspective as absolute and total. Ultimately, the novel questions whether its eponymous infinities – whether incarnated as Greek gods, as Old Adam Godley's mathematical formulae, or as the potential infinity of narrative worlds implied by the story – are ever graspable or whether they must remain other to those who are trying to comprehend them and so becomes a sustained enquiry into fiction's ability to express alterity.

Banville's narrative is set on a single midsummer day[132] in Arden House, a stately country mansion, in a country and at a time that remain unspecified. Old Adam Godley, family patriarch with an aptly telling name and renowned mathematician, famous for his discovery of a formula that proves the existence of infinitely many parallel universes, lies in his bed paralysed after a recent stroke. His family, notably his second wife Ursula, his daughter Petra and his son Adam with his wife Helen, gather in the house, preparing for what seems like Old Adam's inevitably impending death. All of this is observed by two Greek gods, Hermes, who acts as the narrator for most of the time, and Zeus. Prompted by Zeus's longing for Helen, the gods, who are the most directly tangible representations of the novel's infinities, interfere with the mortals' lives. The novel begins in the early morning with a sleepless Adam junior wandering through the house. As Hermes reveals, he has been rendered sleepless by the god himself, who also halts dawn so that his father Zeus has time to take on Adam's shape and make love to Helen in the meantime. As the novel unfolds, there is little happening in terms of plot: Hermes observes the Godley family and their servants as they go about their daily routines and follows their thoughts as they reflect on their relationships with Old Adam, whose mind Hermes also visits repeatedly. It is only after the arrival of another god, Pan,

---

132 The single-day setting places *The Infinities*, like McEwan's *Saturday*, in the tradition of Joyce's *Ulysses* and Woolf's *Mrs Dalloway* – all novels that attempt "to fit the infinite into a single day" (Downes 2017: 25).

in the guise of Benny Grace, an old friend and colleague of the family patriarch, that further action ensues. Zeus has woken up from a brief slumber, still pining for Helen, takes on the shape of yet another mortal (with yet another comically telling name), Petra's reluctant boyfriend Roddy Wagstaff, and tries to kiss Helen, but this time is rejected. With Zeus sulking at his rebuttal, the further action unravels quickly into a happy ending orchestrated by Hermes: Adam Sr after a visit by Benny Grace raises from his sickbed and in the novel's final tableau-like scene gathers the entire household around himself, while Hermes promises the readers bright futures for everyone involved and as a last act of divine deliverance lets Adam junior know that Helen is pregnant.

7.1 "The Mystery of Otherness": Encounters with Perspective

In its presentation of this midsummer day's (in)action, *The Infinities* can be read as a sustained metafictional investigation of human perception, aesthetics and alterity. This shows both in the way the novel repeatedly links enigmatic otherness and aestheticised narration and in the way in which it mirrors Old Adam Godley's multiverse theory. In particular, *The Infinities* may itself be considered a multiverse narrative that reflects on the aesthetic and ethical consequences for narrative itself of the existence of an infinity of parallel worlds.

From the first page on, the novel presents readers with instances of looking at otherness, contrasting the encounter of the enigma of alterity with a totalising, frequently aestheticised, gaze at the other. *The Infinities* sets out with the narrator Hermes looking down at humankind waking up in the dawn twilight: "It is a spectacle we immortals enjoy, this minor daily resurrection, often we will gather at the ramparts of the clouds and gaze down upon them" (*TI* 3). This 'gazing down' not only implies a higher plane from which the gods observe the humans over whose lives they hold sway but also already connects this totalising gaze of the lofty beholders to the *theatrum mundi* metaphor. To the gods, the lives of the mortals are a mere "spectacle" for their diversion and the way this spectacle presents itself in *The Infinities* is strongly aestheticised, as becomes clear when the divine gaze zooms in on Adam Godley junior. Rendered sleepless, he is standing at the window wearing old, no longer fitting pyjamas, which are associated by Hermes with Adam's "tight-buttoned life, [which] fits him ill, making him too much aware of himself and what he glumly takes to be his unalterable littleness of spirit" (*TI* 4), and by Adam himself with childhood memories of being dressed up for Christmas and similar occasions in uncomfortable formal clothes. The metaphor of life as a pyjama lets two central ideas emerge: what is a question of aesthetics and properness of fit for the beholder, divine

Hermes, is an existential one for Adam, whose sense of being dressed up again recurs to one of the theatrical metaphors that pervade the novel. The gaze of the gods thus is shown to be a totalising one – the world before them, it becomes clear, is controlled by them, they are in a position of ontological mastery over the humans, who are merely players on the divine stage. When this god's-eye view beholds human beings as aesthetic objects whose pyjama-like lives may or may not fit, it denies humans any form of alterity in a Levinasian sense – after all, for Levinas it is the other who becomes the master in any ethical encounter with the self (see Claviez 2008: 125–131).[133] Instead of allowing their mortal others mastery in this way, however, the gods only project a totalising, evaluating stare from a position of absolute supremacy over the other.

As Hermes zooms in on Arden House, this divine gaze finds a complementary perspective in that of Adam Jr, who from a similarly elevated perspective encounters otherness as an enigma. For from his vantage point at the window, he looks down at a train stopping on the railway line next to the house – the scenario, of course, is a parallel to Hermes's vista on humankind in general – and observes the passengers in one of the carriages and their "bent heads" that look "like the heads of seals" (*TI* 6). As Adam Jr drifts in and out of his thoughts and recollections of a dream he just had, he becomes aware that

> [o]ne of the seal-heads has turned and he is being regarded across the smoky expanse of lawn by a small boy with a pale, pinched face and enormous eyes. How intensely the child is staring at the house, how hungry his scrutiny – what is it he is seeking, what secret knowledge, what revelation? The young man is convinced the young boy can see him, standing here, yet surely it cannot be – surely the window from outside is a black blank or, the other extreme, blindingly aflame with the white-gold glare of the sun [...]. Apart from those avidly questing eyes the boy's features are unremarkable, or at least are so from what of them can be made out at this distance. But what is he looking for, to make him stare so? (*TI* 7–8)

As opposed to Hermes's divine gaze, Adam's mortal perspective allows for doubt and self-questioning. Although this is not a direct, unmitigated encounter with otherness – the boy and Adam remain at a distance, separated by two windows

---

[133] Hermes's divine gaze – which because of its aestheticising and objectifying nature is not dissimilar to what feminist critics have dubbed the 'male gaze' – seems to serve as a case in point for Levinas's critique of art in general (see ch. 3.3). As Hermes's language that relegates human life to the level of a stage production makes clear, to the gods, who ostensibly exist on a different plane of being, the humans are not 'real' but, from the gods' perspective, take on a quality of the virtual, or even unreal, and it is precisely because of their 'unreal' status that they may never be encountered as the inscrutable others who are characterised by their infinite alterity.

(that of the house and that of the train carriage) and there is no interaction between them – Adam still becomes aware of the presence of the boy and in the boy's stare feels a challenge. Looking back at Adam, then, the boy captivates him and in this briefest of encounters a flicker of the ethical relationship in Levinas's sense, as a calling into question of the self by the presence of the other, can be found. Indeed, reflecting upon what just happened after the train has departed, Adam finds the boy's presence enigmatic:

> He thinks again of the child on the train and is struck as so often by the mystery of otherness. How can he be a self and others others since the others too are selves, to themselves? He knows, of course, that it is no mystery, but a matter merely of perspective. The eye, he tells himself, the eye makes the horizon. It is a thing he has often heard his father say, cribbed from someone else, he supposes. The child on the train was a sort of horizon to him and he a sort of horizon to the child only because each considered himself to be at the centre of something – to be, indeed, that centre himself – and that is the simple solution to that so-called mystery. And yet. (*TI* 8–9)

It is then because of the encounter with the other, reflecting the moment when his gaze falls on the boy's face and is met by the boy's intense, inscrutable stare back at him, that Adam questions his own place in the world, if only briefly.

The explanation – in this case quite literally borrowed from patriarchal discourse[134] – he seeks out to obliterate the mystery that is the presence of the other is nothing else but a reaffirmation of the established order of being. Indeed,

---

[134] The fact that Adam Jr readily adopts his father's explanation (see also *TI* 34) is relevant in that it traces back the impulse to explain alterity to Old Adam Godley's scientific mindset. Indeed, Old Adam, the scientific genius, is a character who is typical of Banville's investigation of solipsism that has informed much of his earlier work and is also central to *The Infinities* (see D'hoker 2004; O'Connell 2011 and 2013). As Elke D'hoker has argued, the investigation of a scientist protagonist's relations with the world around him is something Banville has repeatedly undertaken in his 'science tetralogy' (*Doctor Copernicus*, *Kepler*, *The Newton Letter*, *Mephisto*). In the tetralogy, she claims, "For the sceptical scientists, any form of emotional or physical dependence equals a loss of mastery, unity and self-containment, which they want to uphold at all cost. Or, put differently, entering into a relationship with other people is a sign of incompleteness, finitude and death, the reality of which they have always sought to avoid. In short, the protagonists' lack of intimate or significant thou-relations to other people is but another version of the same sceptical desire to transcend human finitude which put the scientists on their hubristic quests" (2004: 136). This observation certainly equally holds true for Old Adam, whose explanation, passed on to his son, integrates alterity into a solipsistic universe, relegating it to the level of "a kind of existential optical trick" (O'Connell 2011: 429). In his case, however, the awareness of finitude as a contrast to the infinite alterity of the other is one that permeates the entire novel: Adam Sr is about to die, whereas infinity is seemingly everywhere in *The Infinities*, from the gods to Adam's own scientific exploits.

Adam declaring himself to be the centre is the kind of ontological hierarchisation that Levinas criticises: "Heideggerian ontology subordinates the relation with the other to the relation with the neuter, Being", which leads to "an existence which takes itself to be natural, for whom its place in the sun, its ground, its *site*, orient all signification (1987b: 52). Crucially, in his endeavour to make sense of otherness, Adam immediately links the "mystery of otherness" to perspective and tries to contain it in the process. In his insight that "the eye makes the horizon", the homophony eye/I is not a coincidence: the perspectivisation of otherness means that the self defines what is other and in doing so already subjects the other to the self's ontology of knowledge, its horizon. When Adam tries to explain the presence of the other as the horizon to his own centre, this is precisely what happens; Adam's centredness is taken for granted and as the boy constitutes Adam's horizon, he signifies only in relation with, oriented towards this centre. The explanation Adam considers is therefore one that reaffirms the totality of ontology.

"And yet", as Adam himself realises, the boy's otherness remains a mystery which cannot be entirely done away with through such attempts at rationalisation. In Levinas's words, "the other alone can unsettle" the ontology of the self (1987b: 52) and the fact that Adam feels the intensity of the child's stare and begins to ask himself these questions, ending in the doubtful "and yet", would suggest that the absolute certainty of his "place in the sun" has been rattled by this glimpse of alterity. If then such a questioning of the ontological order takes place in the encounter with the boy, this must also be a questioning, implicit at least, of the god's totalising perspective and in particular of the mode of perception chosen by Hermes. Looking down from the ramparts of the clouds onto humankind, his divine gaze may find human life aesthetically pleasing, but he eschews the ethical challenge that an encounter with alterity represents. Adam's gaze, and especially the way he reflects on the encounter afterwards, therefore by thematising such encounters is also an implicit critique of the divine point of view.

In fact, *The Infinities* right at its beginning presents readers with a veritable mise en abyme structure of looking at the other. The god's gaze at Adam, Adam's gaze at the boy on the train and the boy's gaze back all present different perspectives and given the different states of elevation and knowledge of their respective positions (while Hermes sees all and Adam sees the boy, it remains unclear if the boy can actually see Adam), there is a hierarchical relation implied between them. Since in this 'visual', or perhaps ekphrastic, mise en abyme structure Adam Jr's gaze is met by the gaze of the boy and so Adam is contained in the field of vision of his own object of vision (regardless whether the boy can see him behind the window), it resembles most closely the "*réduplication aporistique*" (Dällenbach 1977: 51; see ch. 2.2.2) – with the caveat that the hierarchy implicit in an act of gazing (the beholder's 'control' over the object of their gaze) is different to that engendered by an act of narration (the narrator's control over the narration they create). While the situation Adam Jr finds himself in then is not a strictly aporetic condition[135], it is nevertheless in the gaze being returned that he becomes aware of the mystery that is alterity and therefore in a Levinasian sense entertains a thought that is just as elusive as infinity. After all, the thought of infinity "sketches the contours of a relation to something that is always in excess of whatever idea I may have of it, that always escapes me" and for that reason is structurally parallel to the relation with the other (Critchley 2007: 58). This excess of what can be grasped is encoded in Adam Jr's doubtful "and yet", which places the boy beyond the horizon of his explanations. What Adam Jr encounters then in the return of the gaze is what Levinas terms the 'face' of the boy. For the face "does not consist in figuring as a theme under my gaze, in spreading itself forth as a set of qualities forming an image", but rather "at each moment destroys and overflows the plastic image it leaves me, the idea existing to my own measure and to the measure of its *ideatum* – the adequate idea" (Levinas 1969: 50, 51) – in other words, it transcends the horizon of the self, as is the case with Adam.

Given the predominance of the spatial and visual in these initial encounters with alterity that the novel presents, it is particularly telling that Levinas himself has come up with a spatial metaphor to describe the ethical relation to the other. For this relation is characterised, he claims, by a "curvature of the intersubjective space [that] inflects distance into elevation" (1969: 291). As far as perspectivism is concerned, the consequence is that, as Critchley explains, "[w]hen I am actually within the ethical relation, I experience the other as the high point of this curvature. As such, the relation can only be totalized by imagining myself occupy-

---

[135] There is, however, a case to be made that the aporia of the ethical encounter here is reinforced by the allusion to a temporal paradox that is directly connected to Old Adam's theory of the infinity of parallel universes. Thinking of the train and of Arden House, Old Adam later remembers how, when he himself was a child, "the train used to stop here for no reason [...] and he would press his face to the window and look longingly at this house [...] and dream of living here" (*TI* 32). Both Merja Polvinen and Mark O'Connell therefore suggest that the boy on the train is in fact Old Adam's childhood version (see O'Connell 2011: 441–442; Polvinen 2012: 100), which would represent a temporal paradox that might be explained with an overlapping of two of the infinite parallel worlds of the novel's narrative multiverse. What is more, since Banville in an interview has hinted that this episode bears some autobiographical features (see O'Connell 2011: 442), it also constitutes an intersection of two mise en abyme structures (that of the gazes and one that pairs the writer with the narrator/protagonist and so transcends the borders of the text), which further underlines the complex but central role of this passage within the wider framework of the novel.

ing some God-like, third-person perspective outside of the relation" (2007: 59). *The Infinities*, of course, begins by presenting such a god-like and totalising view, but once the narrator-god's perspective is replaced by that of the human, Adam Jr, and Adam's gaze is met by the boy, this 'curvature' described by Levinas becomes apparent. The distance between Adam and the boy is that of alterity, that of the inexplicable "mystery of otherness", and although the inflection into elevation is perhaps not fully completed in this passage, Adam's astonishment at the boy's gaze suggests that the certainty he has of his own position (or his spontaneity, as Levinas has put it) has been called into question. "The Other measures me with a gaze incomparable to the gaze by which I discover him", writes Levinas (1969: 86). This is precisely what calls into question Adam's ontology, ultimately conceding to the boy the mystery of alterity.

7.2 "Another Kind of Elsewhere": The Metafictional Multiverse Narrative

Although this visual encounter on the first few pages of *The Infinities*, in which Adam's gaze already mirrors and questions that of Hermes while it is mirrored and questioned by that of the boy, is not central to the plot, it is nevertheless key to the novel's thematics (this scene or similar scenes are returned to several times, see *TI* 32, 95, 181), since it introduces the connection of perspective and alterity and reflects on the "importance of perception and its narrativization" (Puschmann-Nalenz 2016: 104). The motif of being or becoming aware of the other, be it in a totalising and frequently aestheticising way that superimposes the ontology of the self on the other or in a way that denies this primacy of the ontological, reverberates throughout the novel. At a far more abstract level, this is also thematised in the way in which *The Infinities* addresses narrative worldmaking and the perception of narrative worlds through Old Adam's theory of the existence of an infinity of parallel universes.

While Adam Godley Sr is incapacitated and in a coma as the story sets in, his life's work, his "theory of infinities" (*TI* 166), continues to impact on the narrative. The details that emerge over the course of the novel of Adam's big theory suggest that it has revolutionised physics and the scientific conception of time and space (see *TI* 164–173) and in particular that it has proven the existence of infinitely many parallel universes. In Benny Grace's (alias Pan's) words, the scientist has discovered "an infinity of infinities [...] all crossing and breaking into each other, all here and invisible, a complex of worlds beyond what anyone before him had imagined ever was there" (*TI* 170). The narrator-god Hermes's acknowledgement that there are infinitely many worlds beyond that in which the narrative is set (see *TI* 15) furthermore suggests that Adam's theory comprises the existence of a multiverse, although it is unclear with which, if any, of the prevalent real-world physical multiverse theories the narrative multiverse of *The Infinities* should be aligned.[136]

The world of *The Infinities* itself is gradually exposed as one among Old Adam's myriad of parallel universes that is distinct from the world of its readers. Although the novel's setting, with which Banville returns to the tradition of big house novels he has already repeatedly explored (for example in *Birchwood*, *The Newton Letter* or *The Book of Evidence*; see e.g. Berensmeyer 2000: 177–180), initially, were it not for its divine narrator, appears to be somewhere in the Ireland of our actual world, it becomes increasingly clear that this is not the case. Soon after the existence of parallel universes is first thematised by Hermes, a number of oddities, alternative scientific discoveries and seemingly ahistorical events make it clear that this is not a representation of the world readers of the novel find themselves in, but at best one of the stipulated parallel universes. Thus, there are English popes, cars are powered by salt water, cold fusion has been discovered, but a Thurn and Taxis postman delivers the mail on a pony, Goethe has almost been forgotten, but Kleist is considered sublime, Sweden is fighting war after war, Oppenheimer failed to build the atomic bomb and so on (see *TI* 23, 89, 103, 5, 161, 162, 171). Significantly, the history of science has taken different turns and as a consequence, Schrödinger, Einstein and Heisenberg are somehow blended into one person who came up with "Schrösteinberg's […] cat" (*TI* 35), the theory of evolution is named after Alfred Russel Wallace and has been overturned (*TI* 90) and thanks to Old Adam's research, the theory of relativity has been exposed as a "hoax" (*TI* 164). In short, readers may find themselves entertaining similar thoughts as Adam Jr, who during his early morning musings from his vantage point at the window realises, in one of the novel's many metafictional statements, that "the world looks like an imitation of itself, cunningly crafted yet discrepant in small but essential details" (*TI* 13).

Despite its preoccupation with multiple parallel universes and its setting in one such universe presumably parallel to ours, *The Infinities* can only be described as a minimal version of what Marie-Laure Ryan, recurring to possible

---

[136] For an overview of the various multiverse theories and their historical development in (Western) (meta)physics since antiquity, see Mary-Jane Rubenstein's *Worlds Without End* (2014). Max Tegmark provides a concise and accessible summary of multiverse theories deemed viable in modern physics, distinguishing four general types of multiverse by their broad characteristics (Tegmark 2003; see also Ryan 2006), while the articles in Bernard Carr's compilation provide in-depth discussions, mostly by physicists, of multiverse theories and related questions (Carr 2007).

worlds theory, has called a "multiverse narrative" (2006: 653). According to Ryan, "When we read a narrative, we are naturally inclined to regard its universe as centered around one, and only one, actual world, and it takes a deliberate effort on the part of the author to fight this tendency of the reader" (2006: 652). This may be achieved when, as is the case in *The Infinities*, the narrative claims "that its actual domain is made of a number of different worlds" (2006: 653). Although this kind of splitting up of the 'actual domain' of the narrative is not explicitly stated for the narrated world of Banville's novel, it is an implication that follows from the existence of multiple universes theoretically proven by Old Adam and the presence of the Greek gods at a different, 'higher' plane. There is, however, only one world in the narrative that is fully fleshed out, while the parallel universes are only ever hinted at, present in the ephemeral existence of the gods or by implication in the differences that distinguish the world of *The Infinities* from that of its readers. Ryan further claims that "[i]n a fully integrated multiverse narrative [...] characters either travel physically from branch to branch or know with certainty that other branches exist objectively. This knowledge affects their behavior and consequently alters the history of their own universe" (2006: 656). Again, this applies to *The Infinities*, but only in the narrowest sense. The only characters able to move between worlds are the gods, who are able to assume human shape and move among the mortals, which makes the border between the universes semi-permeable. The existence of the gods remains something the human inhabitants of the world are unable to verify, although Hermes says that Old Adam's belief in the existence of the gods is founded in a theoretical proof: "Since there are infinities, indeed, an infinity of infinities, as he has shown there to be, there must be eternal entities to inhabit them. Yes, he believes in us, and takes it that the hitherto unimagined realm beyond time that he discovered is where we live" (*TI* 146). Ryan's requirements for a multiverse narrative are thus met, but only in a minimal sense.

It would therefore seem that the way *The Infinities* employs its topic of the multiverse is different from those texts that Ryan identifies as the most typical kinds of multiverse narratives, namely narratives involving time travel, alternate history or the exploration of other worlds (see 2006: 656). In such texts, there is either a direct interest in the logical and physical consequences of the existence of parallel universes and the possibilities their existence opens up or a genuine interest in comparing the parallel world with the actual world, even though this may happen only indirectly by fleshing out a detailed, often fantastic parallel world, as is the case in *Harry Potter* or *The Chronicles of Narnia*, two examples of narratives of transworld exploration Ryan mentions (see 2006: 657). Nothing of this is at the centre of *The Infinities*.

Instead, the multiverse Banville's novel is interested in is that of the text itself. It is the multiverse of authorship and reception, of writing and reading, and of perceiving and being perceived. The multiverse itself is a plot device that mirrors the more far reaching questions raised about the way in which readers and writers engage with texts and ultimately expresses the fundamental plurality, an infinite plurality, inherent in each literary text. Instances in which perception is thematised function – like abstract, more (self-)reflective versions of the wardrobe in the *Narnia* books or platform 9¾ in the *Harry Potter* series – as hinges between the two modes of reading and writing that might be considered as the parallel worlds most comprehensively thematised in *The Infinities*. Furthermore, it is in these instances of heightened perception, such as in the scene with the boy on the train at the beginning of the novel, that the ethical dimension of perception shines through most clearly. Overall, then, the multiverse in *The Infinities* is above all a metaphor for literature and meaning in literature itself. *The Infinities* in this sense is a multiverse *meta*-narrative.

It follows that the multiverse is not only conceptually, but also aesthetically key to the novel. On the one hand, it allows for the strange, even fantastic (see Schwall 2010), yet oddly familiar world of the novel, which, as Merja Polvinen argues, combines "immersion and self-aware thematisation of the imagination" and so "emotionally engages readers even while the fictionality of the narrative is explicit", while it also "builds its argument concerning the nature of fictional representation on a concept of mimesis as simultaneously world-reflecting and world-creating" (2012: 96). On the other hand, the multiverse setting also provides the novel's infinities and an explanation for the presence of the gods and in particular of the divine narrator Hermes, whose role mirrors that of reader and writer alike and whose total, divine perspective is, as I hope to show, integral to the novel's self-questioning stance on perspective.

In both cases, the multiverse allows for reflections on authorship. The novel is interwoven with claims to creation. Hermes claims that the gods have created all the infinitely many worlds of the multiverse (*TI* 15) and that he has "contrived" all things in his narrative (*TI* 29). This focus on creation and his linking of the gods with storytelling – Hermes at one point admits that the gods offer the humans "nothing [...] except stories" (*TI* 91–92) – make of Hermes a "persona of the novelist who carefully crafts many different worlds" (Schwall 2010: 101; see also Puschmann-Nalenz 2016: 106). Meanwhile, Old Adam similarly sees his scientific discoveries as an act of creation through which, Godley doubling for the gods, he "made a world – worlds!" (*TI* 173). Creation and by extension authorship and writing are thus closely linked to the many worlds of the novel.

What is inherent in the claims to authorship by both the gods and Old Adam is an element of hierarchisation that again links to the question of perspective and, ultimately, actuality in the author's worldmaking. After all, the concept of authorship is tied to authority and control over what is created. In the case of the gods this control stems directly from their seemingly transcendental status as beings on a 'higher plane' that not only look down on the mortals but also are able to one-sidedly interact with them and so influence their lives. Conversely, when Old Adam comes up with his act of making worlds through his multiverse theory, the control exerted is on the level of cognition: by positing that he understands the universe (or multiverse), he imposes an ontology on his world and everyone in it. As Rebecca Downes remarks, "old Adam's attic perspective is an eminent conceit for the writer in command of his material, artfully inventing, marshalling the plot and mastering the flux of time into an ordered unity" (2017: 26). In the end, both Adam and the gods depend on their perspective in order to assume authorship. The only thing that counts in their claim to control is, somewhat solipsistically, their own point of view and understanding. As in Adam's explanation of the mystery of otherness, the eye/I makes the horizon.

This ties in with what in possible worlds theory has been discussed as the wider theoretical question of actuality.[137] According to possible worlds theory, the "universe is structured like a solar system: at the center lies a world commonly known as 'the actual world,' and this center is surrounded by worlds that are possible but not actual" (Ryan 2006: 644–645). These possible worlds are, broadly speaking, anything that can be imagined, as long as a couple of basic logical laws still apply. As a consequence, narratives in particular create new possible worlds all the time, whenever "a character contemplates or makes a decision", something that Ryan points out is very similar to the quantum-theoretical 'many-worlds interpretation' of the multiverse, which claims that every time we take a decision a parallel universe branches off in which the decision went the other way (2006: 644). The actual world, which clearly takes a position of ontological privilege in the universe of possible worlds, is either singled out by its physical existence (the "absolutist view") or, more pertinent to literary texts, according to the modal realist school of thought it is a question of perspective (see Ryan 2006: 645–646). According to modal realism, Ryan states, "all possible worlds are actual from the point of view of their inhabitants" – which makes actuality an "indexical notion" that precisely depends on the position of the beholder – and "our world, which we regard as actual, is a nonactual possible

---

[137] A very brief introduction to possible worlds theory can be found in Ryan (2006), on whom I mostly rely in this paragraph. For a longer introduction, see Fořt (2016). Book-length studies of the implications of possible worlds theory for literary theory have been conducted for example by Ryan (1991), Ronen (1994) and Doležel (1998).

world from the viewpoint of the members of those worlds that we regard as nonactual" (2006: 645, 646).

This ontological consideration of the status of actuality is one way in which the multiverse of *The Infinities* operates: on the one hand, the gods see themselves as at the centre of things, looking down on their creation, and so implicitly their world must be the actual one. On the other hand, Old Adam – whose proof that "[i]n an infinity of worlds all possibilities are fulfilled" (*TI* 116) reads like an echo of the modal realist interpretation of possible worlds theory, the status of 'fulfilled' implying actuality – posits a similar degree of actuality for his world, since he has mastered the equations of the multiverse. The belief in the actuality of their respective worlds, rooted in their positions as observers and self-proclaimed creators, then, is what endows the gods as well as Adam Godley Sr with what must appear as superior hierarchical positions. The crux of Banville's multiverse narrative is that it presents two worlds, that of the gods and that of the humans, or more specifically that of Adam Godley – the reflection on gazing and perspective at the beginning of the novel already hints that there may be as many worlds, or 'horizons', as there are characters –, which both stake a claim to totality and both found this claim on their respective 'authorship' of the multiverse.

At the same time, the very notion of the multiverse calls such claims to totality and to the privilege of actuality into question. In particular, given the frequency of metafictional comments and the conceptual proximity of particularly the gods to authorship, this calling into question of totality extends to the process of literary worldmaking in general, not just to the two worlds within *The Infinities*. It is in this context that the connection between the multiverse theories of physics and the literary worlds of possible worlds theory becomes particularly relevant, with the physical models providing a decentring counterweight to the totality inherent in claims to authorship. Ryan explains that the status of actuality is the key difference between multiverse theories from physics and possible worlds theory:

> The narratological application of PW theory supports the indexical theory of actuality, because it explains how fictional universes can be centered around their own actual worlds, even though, from the point of view of our world, they are nonactual creations of the imagination. To the reader immersed in a fiction, the center of the fictional universe functions temporarily as the actual world, and this reader relates to the characters as if they were flesh and blood human beings. Physics, on the other hand, has little use for the contrast between the actual and the nonactual and consequently for any definition of actuality – whether indexical or absolute. If parallel universes exist, they are collections of material objects, such as stars, planets, and galaxies, and they are not structured by the modal opposition between a single actual component and many nonactual possible ones. Within

parallel universes, all objects exist in the same ontological mode – the mode of actuality. (2006: 651)

If fictional worlds then imply the existence of a centre which is ultimately determined by the point of view taken by the readers, who may or may not immerse themselves in the fictional world and so make it temporarily actual, but physical models of the multiverse do not necessitate such a centre and even cast into doubt any such hierarchical ontological order, then what does that mean for fictional worlds like that of *The Infinities* that assume the existence of such physical multiverses? There is an obvious tension between the centredness of a fictional universe and the more 'egalitarian' ontology of the physical multiverse, a tension that multiverse narratives may exploit in order to question the perceptual habits that an ontological hierarchy implies.

This tension is once more rooted in the infinity of the multiverse and in the radical plurality that is inherent in the existence of infinitely many worlds of equal ontological status. In this light it is no coincidence that for physicists multiverse theories are a way to reject calls for the totality of an 'intelligent design' or theistic creation of the universe by arguing for sheer contingency: among an infinity of possibilities, a universe like ours is bound to come into existence (see Rubenstein 2014: 17). Thus, the astronomer Bernard Carr has claimed that "[i]f you don't want God, you'd better have a multiverse" (qtd. in Rubenstein 2014: 17). It indeed seems a logical conclusion that only the infinity of the multiverse can resist the imposition of the conceptual limit that a creator-god would constitute.

In fiction, as Banville's novel shows, the case is similar, but requires a more complex argument: Since we know that fictional texts have a creator, the author, and generally regard them as (more or less) well-crafted aesthetic works of art, their meaning – the literary critic's search for meaning really is the analogy to the astrophysicist's search for the origins of the universe – cannot be explained by mere contingency. While this is certainly true, texts like *The Infinities* (or any of the other novels discussed in this study) make a point of not just questioning, but actively denying any limits to their signification. In the novel, the multiverse is introduced, first by Hermes, then by Adam Sr, from the author's perspective of control, invoking the creator's total vantage point. However, it is the very notion of the multiverse that must cast this totalisation into doubt, since it denies the creator the privilege of (sole, unshared) actuality. In the novel, this is illustrated by the fact that there are two competing claims to creation and that the hierarchy implicit in the setting of a divine plane against a human one, as will be shown, all too often crumbles. Old Adam's reflections on his theory show this: "My equations spanned a multitude of universes", he muses, "yet they posited a single world of unity and ultimate order. Perhaps there is such a world, but if there is we do not live in it, and cannot know how things would be there" (*TI* 215). The "single world of unity and ultimate order" Adam attributes to his equations is precisely the totalising view of the author's meta-level that purports to be able to fully grasp and describe in its entirety, whether through words or more abstract equations, the universe beneath. Adam's doubt concerning the existence of such a monolithic point of view – akin to his son's "and yet", much earlier in the novel – is of a radical epistemological nature: a unifying position that imposes an "ultimate order" on the fictional universe may exist but cannot be known. The infinity of parallel universes of *The Infinities* is an infinity at the story level that, as I hope to show, continues at the discourse level, in the unbounded narrative voice, and beyond that, in signification: it suggests that it is impossible to find a single all-encompassing perspective that can give meaning to the infinite textual multiverse. With its multiverse, the novel thus not only casts doubt on its author-god and any claim to authenticity it might possess as a consequence of its divine creator (see Smith 2014: 147, 174), but also clearly suggests that what inheres in literature itself, and certainly its reception, is "a multiplicity which prevents totalization" (Smith 2014: 174).

This is the wider point about the literary that Banville's novel makes: there is no privileged position within a work of fiction and claims to totality must be viewed sceptically. Perhaps the most fitting image Banville finds for this, due to both its aesthetics and connection to the multiverse, is that of the soap bubbles Old Adam remembers making as a boy:

> The bubbles hesitated on the rim of the pipe-bowl, wobbling flabbily, then broke free and floated sedately away. They seemed to be rotating inside themselves, as if the top was always too heavy, and the iridescent surplus kept cascading down the sides. [...] They were made of an unearthly substance, a transparent quicksilver, impossibly fine and volatile, rainbow-hued. [...] They were another kind of elsewhere. (*TI* 66)

The making of these soap bubbles is a metaphor for the position towards the making of literary worlds the novel takes. The bubbles – incidentally an image that links to one kind of multiverse theory, called the 'level II multiverse' by Tegmark, in which the inflationary stretching of space causes the formation of bubbles that eventually burst in a big bang creating a new multiverse (see Tegmark 2003: 44–46) – are like the parallel universes in a multiverse and fictional worlds at the same time. They are "another kind of elsewhere", parallel worlds of their own, and simultaneously fragile, aesthetic entities – further related to storytelling through their "quicksilver" hue, where quicksilver, also known as mercury, alludes to Hermes's Latin name Mercury (see *TI* 261; see also Schwall 2010: 102) – that, crucially, once formed are beyond the influence of their creator.

As Hedwig Schwall, for whom the novel here highlights the "gap between signifier and signified" (2010: 101), observes: "Though one sees but one bubble, one 'sphere', they form a plural. As such they form an image of that chasm between word and world which even Hermes, [the] master narrator [...], cannot unify" (2010: 102). In a multiverse narrative that is all about worlds created by words, one could argue that the gap "between word and world" is a gap between worlds as much as a gap between words: the singular perspective of actuality, of the single, finely crafted sphere, is immediately undercut by the very same sphere's "unearthly", "rainbow-hued", or in other words ungraspably plural, appearance. Indeed, this is the same gap that readers encounter earlier as a gap in perception between Adam Jr's self-centred perspective and the inscrutable gazing back of the boy – it is a gap that calls into question any hierarchy of perception and creation. With their singular plurality, the bubbles thus embody the textual multiverse of *The Infinities*.

As such, the image of the soap bubbles also doubles for the novel's central image of the multiverse. What is inherent in both images is their indeterminate status between (echoing Levinas) totality and infinity. Just as each soap bubble seems a complete, self-sufficient entity, so the idea of the multiverse itself comes with the tacitly implicit suggestion of such a total perspective that may grasp the multiverse in its entirety: it is the perspective of the author/creator or that of the master scientist who claims to be able to describe the entire multiverse with her formulae. At the same time, the soap bubbles, just like the multiverse itself, present themselves to the beholder's gaze with an irreducible plurality, their fragile rainbow hue. Conversely, in the multiverse it is the sheer infinity of worlds of equal ontological status that physical theories posit that is at odds with the privilege of comprehension, which, following Levinas, ultimately is an ontological privilege. What establishes this privilege is, just as in the novel's initial reflection on gazes, the perspective under which the multiverse is viewed. Once this perspective considers itself absolute, the perspective of the author or creator, it already necessarily imposes a limit on the infinite plurality of the multiverse. At the same time, the metafictional multiverse of *The Infinities* is an aesthetic device that precisely resists such limits by its very nature, as a narrative multiverse that is infinite, boundless, and as such is resistant to any totalising gaze and must retain a measure of inscrutability.

7.3 "This Voice Speaking Out of the Void": Narrative Totality and the Protean Narrator

Given the way in which Banville's novel then carefully combines three at first glance disparate threads – perception, the multiverse and alterity –, returning again and again to questions of perspective, it is not surprising that the novel's narrative perspective plays a central role in the construction of this complex metafictional multiverse narrative. The narrative perspective becomes the most pertinent way in which both the gods and Old Adam lay claim to their authorship, their 'place in the sun', but at the same time it allows for the same interplay between totality and infinity that the aesthetic construction of the multiverse already suggests. The narrator's voice thus becomes perhaps the most striking feature of the novel's metafictional enquiry into the problem of alterity in narrative worldmaking. It becomes 'infinite' in its own way since it transcends all boundaries it encounters and does not maintain a stable shape, with the narrative voice switching back and forth between Hermes and Old Adam. However, although such an all-encompassing narrative voice suggests a (narrative) totality that eclipses alterity at every level of the narrative, *The Infinities* ironises the very omniscience and omnipresence a divine narrator might be expected to exude and so debunks any position of privilege such a narrator might occupy by foregrounding the inevitable incompleteness, the infinity, of any narrative.

When the story level begins with the totality of the divine gaze, this is emulated at the level of the narrative voice, which initially sets out to establish a narrative totality, embodied by the story-telling god Hermes, in which the readers are implicated from the very beginning. Thus, the garrulous primary narrator of *The Infinities* introduces himself, "this voice speaking out of the void" (*TI* 14), as the Greek god Hermes and, anticipating the reader's incredulity – "You don't say, you say" (*TI* 15) – explains that the gods, "who cannot but be everywhere" (*TI* 15), never ceased existing and unbeknownst to humans are still present in all the infinitely many worlds they created, and so firmly sets down the narrator's omnipresence and his divine omniscience. Hermes is quick to remind his narratee, who remains an anonymous, yet clearly mortal, 'you' throughout, in frequent direct addresses of his omnipotence and their own lack thereof. Such direct addresses are a "key device of omniscient authority" (Dawson 2013: 73) and used by Hermes to emphasise his position of superiority. Thus, he declares that he is reduced to speaking in "the language of humankind" (*TI* 16), since the language of the gods would be incomprehensible to mere mortals, or he boasts that "[t]his moment past, in the blinking of your eye, I girdled the earth's full compass thrice", for divine sport and "because I could and you cannot" (*TI* 16 – 17, 17). What is more, the frequency of the narrator's comments that directly address the narratee and the pronounced supremacy of the narrator over the narratee quite directly place the narratee under the narrator's control – a typical effect of such direct addressing of the narratee in omniscient narration (see Dawson 2013: 20). What Hermes strives to create, then, is a narrative totality, a storyworld in which everything is ordered, or ordained, by a narrative voice so all-encompassing that it leaves little room for uncertainty – or, for that matter, even for the narrative itself to develop without constant interruptions by its cocksure divine narrator. Indeed, Hermes insists on intrusively commenting on his narrative, with the comments ranging from the assertion of his narrative powers (*TI* 29) to a simple reminder – "in case you have forgotten me" (*TI* 99) – that the story-telling god is never absent from the action.

If the narrative voice is thus undoubtedly presented as 'total', as the divine epitome of omniscience and omnipresence, it also appears to take on the quality of 'infinity'. After all, in its most fundamental sense, this is a narrative voice that suggests that it is unbounded, not subject to restrictions of time, space, perception, or even identity – indeed, Hermes can halt dawn, access the parallel universes, is one of the all-knowing divine cast, and as such, like his father Zeus, is able to take on any shape he likes, which he demonstrates by posing as Duffy the cowman (see *TI* 75, 15, 80–88). Likewise, he can provide the perspectives of all the characters and even narrates a short passage in which the family dog Rex serves as focaliser (*TI* 198–201). It would seem that there is just no end to what this narrator can do. Given the novel's premise of an infinite multiverse – and hence of the existence of infinitely many perspectives the narrator might occupy – and the narrator's claim that he is indeed omnipresent the narrative perspective may thus be identified as infinite via the Basic Metaphor of Infinity: the various different perspectives are the discrete and minimal building blocks of an iterating process, with the iteration being the changing back and forth between different perspectives (see ch. 2.2.4). In this sense, the narrative perspective becomes a structural device that makes the text appear to be infinite.

At the same time, because of Hermes's claims that his perspective covers the entire narrative multiverse, this narrative infinity also becomes a central area for the novel's negotiation of narrative totality and infinity. For it is clear that this infinity of the omniscient and omnipotent narrative voice endows the narrator's control of the narrative with a totalising impetus: there is nothing alien, inexplicable or inscrutable to this narrating god and his striving for control does not allow any loose ends in the narrative. Therefore, at the end of the novel Hermes provides closure to all the narrative strands and characters involved, assuming – how else could it be? – the role of *deus ex machina* granting a "happy ending" (*TI* 293) and benevolently decreeing, "They shall be happy, all of them" (*TI* 299), before projecting the future lives of the mortal characters. It is because of the unlimited perspective, then, that Hermes, not surprisingly for a god, can speak from a position of totality. The future lives of the characters are projections of possible worlds compared to the god's position of actuality. As befits a god, the omniscient narrator here doubles as an author or creator of the human characters' fate, which is a typical feature of omniscient narration – Paul Dawson, for example, sees omniscience as "the rhetorical performance of narrative authority which simultaneously invokes and projects a historically specific figure of authorship" (2013: 19). In this way the divine narrator occupies the meta-perspective from which the plurality of the multiverse world – in this case the futures of the multiple inhabitants of Arden House – is orchestrated and in the process underlines the gods' superior hierarchical position in the world of the narrative.

However, even as this total narrative perspective is constructed, it is already subverted and its premise of omniscience is satirised. Firstly, the tone adopted by the narrative voice, veering between the conversational and the sardonic, creates an ironical distance and at times undercuts divine authority and hence also the narrator's own authority. Despite his general air of lofty disinterestedness, Hermes occasionally comments on the gods and their own shortcomings with some irreverence. His father Zeus is frequently described in derogatory terms, as "salacious old rip" (*TI* 50) or "old lecher" (*TI* 56), while Hermes highlights his own role as a trickster by describing himself as an "incorrigible prankster" (*TI* 81) and makes fun of other characters from Greek mythology, such as Heracles ("brave, but not the brightest"; *TI* 211), Athene ("that headache"; *TI* 212, a jocular reference to the mythological account of Athene's birth from the head of Zeus), or Pan ("the scamp"; *TI* 143). The way in which Hermes directs his narrative and comments on the characters, both human and divine, would make him an example of what Dawson in his study of contemporary cases of omniscient narration calls the "pyrotechnic storyteller", who is "typically humorous or satirical, employing a flourishing and expansive narrative voice, a garrulous conversational tone, to assert control over the events being narrated" (2013: 111). In this, the objects of his satire are humans and gods alike. As a consequence, the gods are humanised and the very authority they derive from being divine is undermined.[138] Since Hermes is one of the divine cast, this must extend to the narrator's own authority. Therefore, while the novel heavily relies on con-

---

[138] The fact that the novel presents gods, a polytheistic set with the very human character traits of the Greek gods, rather than the single, authoritative god of monotheism, certainly corroborates this. Similarly, when the novel's title refers to infinities rather than to one infinity (that has long been associated with divine authority), this is already disseminating the totalising potential of the infinite.

structing a position of authority for its narrator, this authority is called into question by the very way in which Hermes presents his narrative.

Secondly, not only the narrator's persona as one of the humanly flawed Greek gods, but also the very premises of the narrative totality, his divine omniscience and omnipresence, themselves are ironised and exposed as not quite so total as the conventions of omniscient narration would have the readers think (see Huber 2016: 83). This becomes clearest when Hermes is sent away by Zeus to look for Helen and complains that he will now miss out on the conversation between Benny and Ursula that takes place at the same time: "Now I shall not know what they do and will have to rely on hearsay. Only sometimes am I omniscient" (*TI* 188). And indeed upon his return, Hermes – and hence also the readers – does not know what happened in the meantime when he was "not there to invigilate" (*TI* 195). Both the narrator's omniscience and his omnipresence are thus exposed as limited.

Such limitations are of course a necessary feature of omniscient narration, since a narrator who knows everything is still not able to *tell* everything – the representational conundrum facing any attempt at representing infinity (in this case the narrator's perception) in a finite medium remains the same for omniscient narrators.[139] This becomes particularly evident when, as in *The Infinities*, the narrator is a god, since in this case the gulf between the god's absolute omnipotence and the limitations their narrative displays is thrown into sharp relief. As a consequence, a divine or supernatural narrator is a relatively rare feature of narrative texts that inevitably highlights these limits of narrative fiction. Such narrators by virtue of their transcendental status should be logically able to overcome any restriction of perspective, be it temporal, physical or spatial, and have an inherently non-linear perception. However, the narrative medium itself restricts this unlimited ('infinite') view to a finite and necessarily linear representation. This linearity ultimately arises from the linearity of language itself, since language is a concatenation of phonemes or graphemes along a monodimensional axis.[140] Therefore, language cannot mimetically express the absolute si-

---

139 Although the term 'omniscient narration' has long been in use in narrative theory, it has also faced severe criticism, most notably in recent years by Jonathan Culler (2004; see also ch. 2.2.4 above). For contrasting views on the issue, see for example Sternberg's (2007) reply to Culler, and Dawson (2013).

140 While poststructuralists foreground the pluri-dimensionality of language (e. g. Kristeva's intertextuality theory, see ch. 2.2.3), they also tend to focus on the creation of meaning, not on the production of signifiers in the first place – this representational act itself remains linear. And even if the polysemy of language and potentially of each single morpheme is taken into account, no single signifier can express absolutely everything at once – such a signifier would indeed be-

multaneity of different events – a speaker cannot produce two phonemes at the same time and a reader cannot read two graphemes at the same time. For a narrator who perceives *everything at once* – a feat which is humanly impossible but has long been considered a property of the divine (see ch. 2.2.4) – language, and hence the narrative itself, is then necessarily a limiting factor. Even a divine narrator's omnipotence fails when it comes to representing their own unlimited perception, and hence infinity – the task of representing infinity renders the omnipotent impotent.[141] In this sense, limitations are, somewhat paradoxically, part and parcel of narratorial omniscience, which has frequently been pointed out by narratologists (see for example Füger 2004: 287; Dawson 2013: 31).

In *The Infinities*, it is precisely this limitation of omniscience that is explored and used to satirise conventions of storytelling. For Hermes, the god who is and is not omniscient – part-time omniscience, much like being 'a little bit pregnant',

---

come a transcendental signifier and hence, paradoxically at the same time also a transcendental signified resisting depiction. There is thus no way to represent an actually infinite perspective with finite signifiers. Alan Moore's *Jerusalem* finds an interesting way of addressing this representational problem. When one of the angelic characters in the novel speaks, their speech is rendered in an extremely condensed way as what seems to be utter gibberish, an overlaying or co-inciding of the various phonemes and semes of a longer utterance that then 'unfolds' or 'unpacks' itself in the listener's mind – for example, "Wvyeo gaurl thik comnsd! Pleog chrauwvy ind tsef!" unfolds into a paragraph-long text in the focaliser's mind (2016: 557–558). However, even the most radical condensation of the narrative – that is, a condensation of a total, unlimited perspective into a single (or very few) morpheme(s) – can at best serve to highlight the representational aporia of infinity: such a condensed form, like the discourse of Moore's angels, is then necessarily unintelligible for a narratee or reader who cannot possibly share in the same unlimited perspective as the narrator.

Given that *The Infinities* addresses multiverse theories and hence indirectly also questions of quantum physics, it should be added that the linearity of representation is also directly connected with the linearity of time. Arguably a truly omniscient narrator-god should not only have knowledge of the future and past, but also of all possible futures, of which action will trigger what outcome. Narrating this infinity of infinities is impossible, as Ryan has shown, taking Jorge Luis Borges's short story "The Garden of Forking Paths" as her example. She states that such a narrative that would present all branches of a decision tree (and hence all possible future events) "cannot be written, because a narrative must limit itself to a subset of all possibilities and because its branches must be presented sequentially rather than simultaneously" (2006: 653–654). Hermes, of course, evades this problem by using his authorial power to decree which of the possible outcomes will indeed come to pass.

141 One might of course question whether this is then a limitation on behalf of the narrator, and hence a failure of their presumed omniscience and omnipotence, or whether it is rather the readers who are limited – as Hermes certainly argues when he claims he had to cast off "the voice of a divinity" and assume that of humankind in order to be understood by his narratee (*TI* 16). Pragmatically speaking, however, the representational problem remains the same either way.

is of course a contradiction in itself, since, as Meir Sternberg has pointed out, "omniscience, being a superhuman privilege, is logically not a quantitative but a qualitative and indivisible attribute" (1978: 282)[142] –, defies the logic of what is commonly, and certainly in classical narratology, expected of a narrator. If human standards are applied to the god, the narrative may be described to have zero focalisation. This is the case because although Hermes contradicts his earlier claim to omnipresence (*TI* 15) and describes his omniscience as an occasional rather than a permanent feature, he still has an omniscient narrator's insight into the thoughts and feelings of the human characters and so indeed does reveal more than a character could be expected to know. However, the specifics of Banville's narrative situation are apt to expose the limitations of the classical structuralist approaches to narrative. After all, Hermes is not just a narrator, but also a character in his own narration – hence a homodiegetic narrator – and Genette defines zero focalisation as a situation where "the narrator knows more than the character, or more exactly *says* more than any of the characters knows" (1980: 189). While Genette's model does not explicitly exclude the possibility of a homodiegetic narrator with zero focalisation, it does so implicitly, because such *narrators* would then have to 'know more' than they could possibly know as *characters*. This is precisely what seems to happen when it comes to Hermes, who as a narrator clearly becomes an oddity defying the logic of narratologists' attempts at structuralisation. Of course, the entire scenario of the storytelling Greek god may be read as a wry nod to Franz Karl Stanzel's 'authorial narrator', who is characterised as having an 'Olympian' knowledge of all things, i.e. omniscience (see 1955: 76). Yet as is the case with Genette's model, Hermes's presence in the storyworld would also rule him out as an authorial narrator in Stanzel's approach (see Fludernik 2001: 621). A narrator who is part of his

---

142 Culler has criticised this claim by Sternberg as too radical since it opens the doors to treating any narrator with unusual knowledge as omniscient (see 2004: 24–25). In *The Infinities*, however, on account of its divine narrator, many of Culler's arguments against omniscience, which are largely based on the necessity to distinguish between an author's or narrator's 'omniscience' and the theological omniscience of a god – a pertinent point in conventional types of narratorial 'omniscience', such as those found in eighteenth- and nineteenth-century fiction –, do not gain traction entirely, since the narrator here is just such a god. Even when it comes to omniscience Hermes is an untypical specimen. Sternberg and Culler both argue that the kind of divine omniscience that is associated with omniscient narration is a feature of the monotheistic Hebraic god rather than of the Greek gods, since the latter may have superhuman, but not unlimited knowledge (see Culler 2004: 26). Hermes, however, is at pains to demonstrate the boundlessness of his knowledge, as can be seen from his intrusive comments, the provision of a happy ending and his insistence on his supreme divine power, all of which puts him in the tradition of theistic omniscience and omnipotence as identified by Sternberg.

own story and at the same time omniscient is therefore certainly a challenge to the realist conventions of storytelling and Hermes's metafictional commentaries highlight the limitations not just of his own narratorial prowess but also of the way in which critics have traditionally tried to make sense of the narrator's voice as an instrument in narrative worldmaking.[143]

This becomes particularly clear, when the narrative voice crosses the only boundary that infinity logically speaking must have and becomes limited. This is the case when the narrative voice transcends the boundary of a stable identity, as happens when the role of the narrator seems to first switch back and forth between Hermes and Old Adam and then to indeterminately alternate between the two. It is at this point that the very notion of an 'infinite' narrative voice that underlies the totalising narrative perspective the novel seems to construct is finally exposed as paradoxical in itself – not surprisingly so, given that this is another attempt at the representation of infinity. Whereas for the first half of the novel, the narrator can clearly be identified as Hermes – the occasional deviation notwithstanding (see *TI* 33), Hermes is always referred to in the first person and Old Adam in the third person – this changes suddenly in the last section of the novel's short second part when the narrator presents Old Adam's memories in the first person (*TI* 155–173). A change of narrative voice from one autodiegetic narrator (Hermes) to the other (Old Adam) has taken place. While on the one hand the narrator's stable identity may be seen as a last boundary that needs to be crossed by a truly limitless, infinite narrative voice, the irony

---

[143] Formally, the least problematic approach to describing the unruly narrative voice of *The Infinities* seems to be viewing it as an example of an 'unnatural narrative'. Postclassical narratologists have defined unnatural narratives as narratives that "transcend real-world possibilities by projecting physically, logically, or humanly impossible scenarios or acts of narration", and so are in violation of their readers' common-sense expectations from the narration or contradict their pre-established cognitive frameworks (Alber, Skov Nielsen and Richardson 2012: 351, 352; see Alber 2016: 14–17 and Alber 2014). This certainly is the case in *The Infinities*, whose divine narrator by any standards is "humanly impossible" and whose shifting narrative voice may be seen to contradict the cognitive frameworks that are usually applied to narrative, in particular the expectation of a stable identity of the narrative voice, or at least of its clear identifiability. Unnaturalness may for example comprise "the disclosure of the contents of another character's mind (through interior monologue, free indirect discourse, or psychonarration)" (Alber, Skov Nielsen and Richardson 2012: 352). Indeed, for Alber the very concept of narratorial omniscience demands "superhuman qualities" in the narrator and "hence unnatural models of representation" (2016: 95), and "transgressive first-person narration", i.e. an omniscient first-person narrator like Hermes, is discussed by Alber, Skov Nielsen and Richardson (2012: 360–365). *The Infinities* thus clearly qualifies as unnatural narrative and this is largely due to the novel's attempt at emulating infinity in its narrative voice, since infinity itself is a concept that exceeds natural cognitive frames – "[i]n thinking infinity the I from the first *thinks more than it thinks*" (Levinas 1987b: 54).

here is that the very crossing of this boundary also means that the narrative voice, by passing over to Old Adam, retreats into finitude.

In the following scenes, *The Infinities* then foregrounds the uncertainties inherent in an infinite narrative voice that goes so far as to even transcend a stable narrative identity. At first, the original order with the divine narrator Hermes is restored in the next chapter, which begins with a startled Hermes who claims he "[m]ust have dropped off for a minute there" (*TI* 177). This marks the beginning of the third section of the novel and of a passage of the novel in which Hermes's omniscience is increasingly problematised and cast into doubt. After another switch of the narrative voice back to Old Adam's perspective (*TI* 215), the hitherto stable narrative identity begins to oscillate: Old Adam is thinking about his son and wife and seems to be able to observe them, from his sickbed, as they move about and talk in the kitchen (*TI* 234–235). This is of course logically impossible for a human first-person narrator, since it requires unlimited perspective (or at least the ability to see and hear through the house's walls). The perspective over the following pages imperceptibly switches back to that of Hermes, but remains both epistemologically and ontologically fluctuating. In a passage which seems to be narrated from Hermes's point of view, since it returns to his earlier shenanigans of impersonating Duffy the cowman, the narrator again thematises his limited knowledge – he realises things between Duffy and Ivy have not turned out as he had intended and asks himself what happened (*TI* 238–239) – and ends in negatively self-identifying: "My name must not be Hermes after all" (*TI* 239). Although this still seems to be Hermes speaking, it becomes increasingly unclear whose voice it is. This breakdown of the narrator's identity culminates soon after in the exclamation, "Who am I now? Where is my Dad? Enough, enough, I am one, and all – Proteus is not the only protean one amongst us" (*TI* 244). At this point, the narrative perspective has achieved what comatose Adam much earlier has already hinted at as a perceptual pattern (in this case with regard to the perception of time): "Everything blurs around its edges, everything seeps into everything else. Nothing is separate" (*TI* 71). Like an ouroboros, the narrative totality seems to have consumed itself.

It is despite, or perhaps rather because of, this narratorial assertion of authority and the insistence on the totality of the narrator's perspective ("I am one, and all") that the narrative perspective continues to shift back and forth between Hermes and Old Adam (see in particular *TI* 260–262, 286–292) before settling for the god's point of view for the last few pages of the novel. Incidentally, the insecurity over the narrative identity is not restricted to the first-person pronoun alternately referring to Old Adam and Hermes: at one point, when Adam thinks about his relationship with Benny Grace, he wonders whether Benny is his "bad self" but still arrives at the conclusion that "[h]e – I say he when

I think I mean I. I did great things" (*TI* 172). The complex and rather convoluted syntax of Adam's thought neatly illustrates the complexity arising from the protean narrative voice of *The Infinities*. Ultimately it suspends the grammatical category of person and as a consequence perhaps the oldest and most basic category of structural narratology, that of first- versus third-person narration, emphasising not only the transgressional character of this infinite narrative voice, but also its instability.

The unstable identity of the narrative voice thus makes it impossible to identify with certainty a dominant position within the narrative, which in itself erodes the totality of the narrative perspective: if there is no dominant narrating instance, then the narrative perspective can hardly be total. The repeated switching between the perspectives of Hermes and Old Adam precisely undercuts any attempts at identifying a narrator who truly is 'in charge'. This indeterminacy can be seen from the fact that critics have interpreted the narrative situation in quite contradictory ways. Mark O'Connell, for instance, argues that the dominant perspective is that of Old Adam, who then imagines himself as the god Hermes and rather than possessing unlimited knowledge takes control over the narrative by simply imagining everything that happens (O'Connell 2011: 439; see 2013: 200; for a similar argument, see Polvinen 2012: 109). Conversely, Barbara Puschmann-Nalenz sees "a clear hierarchy" of the narrative perspectives, with Hermes as "the intrusive, mostly omniscient, alternately hetero- and homodiegetic first-person narrator", and finds that "the narrating voice then shifts to Adam Sr." (2016: 103). These two diametrically opposed readings suggest that whatever hierarchy there may be is not quite as definite – and hence it would seem not a very strict hierarchy (see Downes 2017: 27, who likens the way the diegetic levels blend into one another to a Möbius strip). Instead, the narrator, or rather the narrative perspective itself, is protean and this polymorphous narrative at once serves to prove and subvert the supreme power of the narrator. For while the shapeshifting is on the one hand associated with omnipotence and a totality of perspective[144], with the narrator's absolutist "I am one and all", on the

---

[144] The connection between shapeshifting or polymorphic entities and totality is a topic the novel also plays with, when it comes to the initial on the ring Adam Jr has given to Helen. It bears, she claims, the initial A for *Amphitryon*, since she acts a part in the play (see *TI* 242–243), but when Petra later asks her about the ring, Petra reads the initial as Z and it is exposed as ambiguous – as Hermes suggests, this is a result of Zeus meddling with the ring (see *TI* 294). This doubleness of the sign is of course also key to the *Amphitryon* intertext, but Banville's version changes J (for Jupiter) to Z (for Zeus), thus letting the ambiguity express completeness (A to Z) while making an additional reference to the Christian moniker of "Alpha and Omega, the first and the last" (Rev 1.8) for the Christian God and hence for all-encompassing, total divine power.

other hand it cannot but stir up doubt in precisely this totality: it is unclear whether once the omniscient and omnipotent god's perspective has morphed into the limited[145] and decidedly impotent (Old Adam is in a coma after all) human point of view the narrative perspective has also shed its totality, or whether it only achieves totality in the first place because it allows itself such switches. Either way, paradoxically the consequence of the crossing of the identity threshold that would seem to make the narrative voice truly unlimited and hence let it achieve all-encompassing totality is a simultaneous disavowal of this narrative totality, as it is cast into ontological uncertainty. As Val Nolan puts it, "In *The Infinities* [...] the aesthetic certainties of a mechanistic, Newtonian universe are irrevocably unravelled" (2010: 40).

Overall, then, the omniscient narrative perspective in *The Infinities* is taken to its extreme – as a consequence, it is charged with indefiniteness and uncertainty rather than the certainty one might expect from such a narrative perspective. In its search for a surplus of epistemological certainty and total narrative puissance, the narrative ends up disseminating its own ontological status. The narrative perspective here mirrors the novel's overall movement from totality, the narrator-god's self-assured claims to omniscience, to infinity, the ultimate dissolution of narrative boundaries and hence of this absolute viewpoint. Ultimately, this calling into question of certainties may again be linked to modern physics: writing about Banville's preoccupation with theories of science in *The Newton Letter*, Ingo Berensmeyer with a nod to Heisenberg's Uncertainty Principle has pointed to the "impossibility, or at least the increasing difficulty, in modernity, of establishing and maintaining a definite and stable observer position" (Berensmeyer 2000: 180). Nolan directly connects this to the novel's narrative multiverse, where "reality itself, by virtue of being one amongst an infinity of equally viable realities, becomes just this 'supreme fiction'", an observation that leads to the question, "who is to say 'our' reality is any less fictional than those others beyond the veil of perception?" (2010: 42). The narrative perspective

---

[145] The narrative perspective remains so elusive that even the limitation of Old Adam's perspective is not entirely clear. If Old Adam is seen to possess an unlimited perspective as a narrator, then a strange case of variable zero focalisation might be assumed – which would raise the question whether two distinct infinite narrative instances may co-exist on the same narrative level, or, in other words, whether the novel presents readers with narratorial infinities. On the one hand, Old Adam and Hermes speak as two different entities, which would suggest that their narrative perspectives really are distinct infinities. On the other hand, this leads to the question whether the scopes of Hermes and Old Adam are infinities of a different magnitude – ultimately this asks whether the perspective of one of the two dominates over that of the other and can logically include it – or whether there really is just one narrator all the time, who is 'one and all', Hermes and Old Adam at once.

in *The Infinities* thus is another way in which the novel aestheticises infinity and in a self-questioning way poses it against positions of totality.

7.4 "Essence is Essentially Inessential": Reading Alterity

In view of the frequent metafictional comments in the novel, this construction of the narrative multiverse that meanders between the total and its other, the infinite, becomes particularly relevant because of the way in which it reflects on the status of literature and on acts of reading. In particular, it is acts of gazing, always connected to the question of perspective, through which otherness is encountered. As mentioned above, the novel introduces this topic at its very beginning with the 'mise en abyme' of gazes, where the gods look down on their creation and Adam Jr encounters the inexplicable otherness of the boy on the train. If the connection of perception to the novel's construction of a narrative multiverse and to its narrative voice is considered, then it becomes clear that perception is inextricably linked to both reception and conception of others, the universe as such and, of course, literature.

It is therefore fitting that in *The Infinities*, the gods double as figures of authorship and readership alike, and so do their human counterparts. While the gods are authors of the multiverse and one of them is the narrator, they are also spectators in their own *theatrum mundi*, and hence recipients, readers. Irmtraud Huber directly contrasts these two roles: "The gods' relationship to the world of humans [...] is very much like that of the omniscient narrator to the narrated world, or for that matter, like the position of the reader, facing a fictional world" (2016: 83; see also Polvinen 2012: 96). But conversely, she continues, it follows from the choice of narrator that "the reader's perspective on the events of the story is that of the gods" (2016: 83). As far as perspective is concerned, then, *The Infinities* implies that gods are readers and readers are gods. At the same time, if the gods are also writers of the human characters' fates, as Hermes repeatedly suggests, then this quality similarly transfers onto the readers. Indeed, an act of reading is also an act of interpretation and hence 'writing', as becomes clear in the gods' gaze down on their human creation that is instrumental to the entire act of narrating in the novel. In terms of the perspective taken, *The Infinities* suggests, reading and writing are not entirely dissimilar.

In a wider sense, then, the novel reflects on the way in which readers encounter texts. Here, *The Infinities* touches on a topic that is central to my entire interest in fictions of infinity and their ethical dimensions. In particular the self-conscious omniscience displayed by the narrator Hermes most starkly foregrounds the question of alterity that any narrative, any act of reading, implicitly is confronted with. In what way does narrative even afford space for alterity? Does narrative allow a direct access to the other, in this case to the fictional characters and their minds? This is often argued by proponents of an ethics of empathy in narrative, who claim that narrative is ethical because it allows us to see the world through someone else's eyes and so re-centre our own perspective. But if this direct access to the other through narrative really is the case, is a narrative act – every narrative act, but particularly those that describe a character's thoughts or feelings – not automatically an evisceration of alterity in its radical Levinasian sense? After all, authoring a narrative means writing characters into a fictional life, determining them, in the case of omniscient narration often down to their innermost thoughts and motivations. The answer suggested by *The Infinities* is tied to the novel's infinite narrative construction: while the totalising impulse of narrative is thematised, most clearly in the narrator's voice, it is at the same time also suspended and refracted in the infinity of the narrative multiverse. Literature, just as any act of speech, may thus at first seem to present itself as what Levinas calls the said, as an ontological fixity determined by the reader. Beneath this said of literature, however, there is, perhaps in every literary text, and certainly in *The Infinities*, an infinitely inscrutable moment of address – Levinas's saying –, in which the text speaks to the reader without allowing itself to be fully grasped. Between the saying and the said, "the ethical signifies through the oscillation, or alternation, of these orders" (Critchley 1992: 165; see ch. 3.2). This is what happens in *The Infinities* when the narrative voice transcends its own limits, or when the boy stares back at Adam. At these moments, the encounter with the literary text becomes (as Critchley has put it) infinitely demanding, in the sense that the text, like the idea of infinity itself, is here "grasping the ungraspable while nevertheless guaranteeing its status as ungraspable" (Levinas 1996b: 19; see Critchley 2007: 58).

However, the way to this grasping of the ungraspable is, as has already been shown, through the assertion of totality – the oscillating movement towards the said – that allows this comprehension in the first place, no matter whether this happens through Old Adam's claims that he understands the multiverse or through Hermes's unlimited omniscient perspective. These processes constantly raise the question of otherness in narrative, of how alterity can survive wedged between author-god and reader-gods. The narrative perspective is perhaps the most pertinent case in point: Hermes is able to look into the minds of all characters so that what ensues, presumably, is maximum transparency. The mode of omniscient narration itself lays claim to this absolute certainty, since it takes to the extreme a principle that is intrinsic to fiction in general: the readers get to *know* the characters, peering into the characters' lives and even into their minds, just like Banville's gods from the ramparts of their clouds. According to Jan Alber, "it is only in fictional contexts that we can gain *accurate* knowledge of the thoughts and feelings of 'others,' namely the characters. This knowledge differs qualitatively from the kind of knowledge that we can acquire in real-world contexts because it is epistemically reliable" (2016: 99). In other words, in a sense readers get to fully grasp the essence of the fictional personality on the page before them, rather than being reduced to coming up with "hypotheses and speculations about their interiority" (2016: 99), as is the case when it comes to encounters with others in the real world, where others are not (or only ever figuratively) open books from which their thoughts and feelings can be read. This epistemic certainty, which finds its culmination in omniscient narration, is nevertheless subject to the framework of fictionality and hence to the basic ontological indeterminacy that follows from the different ontological status of the fictional world as opposed to the real world. When Sir Philip Sidney claims that "the poet [...] nothing affirms, and therefore never lieth" (2012: 1068), the epistemic reliability (he "never lieth" – fiction is always true) is only a given because of the ontological status of non-actuality (he "nothing affirmeth" – fiction is never actual). The accurate and absolute knowledge of the fictional text a reader encounters, the complete grasping of its meaning that leaves no room for otherness – for that which has been grasped is no longer unknown or 'other' to us –, is thus dependent on the reader's awareness of the non-actuality of the fictional world and hence of their own ontological superiority.

What *The Infinities* does is to question these premises. The novel's movement towards infinity – the oscillating move towards the saying –, in its presentation of the multiverse as well as in its narrative voice, represents a challenge to the way that fiction is determined by reading (or, likewise, by writing), precisely because it leads to instances where the narrative remains indeterminate, or, to readers, indeterminable. The suggestion is that, like that of the gods, the readers' omniscience with regard to the fiction unfolding before them is itself a fiction, is never 'affirmed'. Indeed, the immortal gods in *The Infinities* are reduced to a state of not knowing when it comes to love and death. As Hermes remarks, these are "things our kind may not experience" (*TI* 72) and in particular love unfolds its fascination for the gods because it "is of their [the humans'] own making, the thing we did not intend, foresee or sanction" (*TI* 73). Crucially, both are experiences that are central to, yet must remain elusive in most, if not all literary texts. Likewise, both love and death are intricately linked with alterity – love is directed towards others (more pathological forms like narcissism aside) and death is that which cannot be experienced first-hand and spoken about afterwards and so in a sense always remains the ultimate unknown. When Puschmann-Nalenz comes to the conclusion that "*The Infinities* presents a fictional meta-discourse on the narrativization of love and death" (2016: 110), it should be added perhaps that this meta-discourse seems to be more about the impossibility of this narrativisation, which ultimately would require the reduction of alterity to sameness in the narrative.

It becomes clear once more that at its heart this is a representational problem as much as it is an experiential one – ultimately, the problem is again that of representing infinity. In one of the novel's more philosophical passages, where again a parallel between this representational problem and Old Adam's theory of the multiverse is drawn, Adam is critical of the way in which scientists before him have described the universe. Notably, he takes objection to their inept, "forged […] metaphors" (*TI* 144), that is, to the idea that an aestheticised representation of the world can ever be accurate. On the other hand, he, and certainly also Hermes, who narrates the passage, is aware of the pitfalls of any form of representation:

> Yet how else were they to speak that which cannot be spoken, at least not in the common tongue? He sought to cleave exclusively to numbers, figures, concrete symbols. He knew, of course, the peril of confusing the expression of something with the something itself, and even he sometimes went astray in the uncertain zone between the concept and the thing conceptualised; even he, like me, mistook sometimes the manifestation for the essence. Because for both of us this essence is essentially inessential, when it comes to the business of making manifest. For me, the gods; for him, the infinities. You see the fix we are in. (*TI* 144)

Speaking that which cannot be spoken – a turn of phrase reminiscent of Timothy Cavendish's map of the ineffable in *Cloud Atlas*, and certainly with similar conceptual implications (see ch. 4.2) – is perhaps the novel's clearest indication that the scientist patriarch's task in mapping the multiverse, just like that of the narrating gods or their readers, is that of grasping the ungraspable. Given the impossibility of representing, and hence also of reading and grasping, the textual multiverse, human otherness, the gods, or the novel's image for all this, the infinities, this grasping of the ungraspable is bound to fail and the status of the ungraspable is guaranteed. It is in this way, through its textual openness and the awareness that "essence is essentially inessential" in representation that *The Infinities* represents the idea of infinity in the aesthetics of the novel.

The overarching textual metatrope through which this is achieved is again that of the catachresis (see ch. 2.3 and ch. 3.4), with the difference that *The Infinities* in this passage and elsewhere actively reflects on its own catachrestic status. Like the other novels discussed above, *The Infinities* possesses textual features, such as its all-transcending narrative voice and the multiverse as a metaphor for the narrative itself, that may let its text appear infinite, making the text a strictly impossible, catachrestic, image of the infinite. Unlike the other novels, however, Banville's text seems to actively reflect on the impossible task that fiction takes up in its "business of making manifest" and to recognise that there is no way around what Levinas terms the "betrayal" in representation (see ch. 3.2). This betrayal is the ultimate catachrestic "cleavage in discourse" (Chrzanowska-Kluczewska 2011: 49) at the heart of representations of alterity. As *The Infinities* shows, infinity itself is the apt structural metaphor to illustrate this cleavage, since representations of infinity must, just like representations of alterity, inevitably fail: a representation of infinity cannot be infinite, just like a representation of alterity is no longer other to the reader who by reading has entered into a process of understanding and hence of reducing otherness to sameness. This is why for both infinity and alterity the concepts' "essence is essentially inessential" – in the sense that it cannot be grasped and reduced to the essence at the heart of any ontology. It is then the strictly illogical textual catachresis that in the end 'guarantees as ungraspable' the status of the ungraspable, in the idea of infinity as well as in alterity.

The catachrestic "cleavage in discourse" in *The Infinities* is thus a cleavage between otherness and sameness, saying and said, or totality and infinity and manifests itself, inessentially, in the openness the text attains at a meta-level. This openness, in which, in Critchley's sense, the main ethical appeal of *The Infinities* consists, is achieved precisely through the novel's oscillation between totality and infinity, between saying and the said. The back and forth movement between these two poles is then the reason why, for instance, O'Connell can read the protean narrative voice as the "closure of th[e] gap of otherness" (2011: 441), whereas Puschmann-Nalenz calls this reading an oversimplification and claims that, on the contrary, the narrative perspective "highlights otherness" (2016: 107). At a meta-level, the text here is doubly coded and while O'Connell focuses on the said, Puschmann-Nalenz's focus is on the saying. *The Infinities*, she concludes, "defends unending openness in the world of the text as well as in infinite parallel worlds. Using the power of textuality the writer evades closure" (2016: 109).[146] And yet, moving the pendulum back towards the said, the conclusion of the novel is, as has been shown, almost a textbook example of narrative closure, where all loose ends are tied up. Crucially, it is the "power of textuality", as Puschmann-Nalenz writes, already at a different level to the closure of the plot, that allows this "unending openness". In the narrative multiverse of the novel, closure and openness may coexist, and the closure at one level in a

---

[146] Meanwhile Downes argues that the many paradoxes in *The Infinities* "direct us away from the activity of sense-making and towards an immersion in the textual event", which renders the novel close to a "work of pure style" (2017: 30). Although Downes's reading does not rely on Levinas, what she describes seems to correspond to diagnosing an emphasis of saying over said in the novel.

sense is even a prerequisite for the overall multiplicity and openness of the novel.

It is then in this interplay of openness and closure that *The Infinities* establishes what Neil Murphy has aptly described as the "ontological confusion" that dominates its narrative and clearly hearkens back to the confusion that is central to the *Amphitryon* intertext that shapes Banville's plot (2014: 67). The consequence of this ontological confusion at the heart of "Banville's multi-textured fictional world", Murphy continues, "is the sense that existence itself is inherently mysterious in ways that extend far beyond the overt actions of characters" (2014: 67). In other words, it is precisely through erecting the multiple, confusingly complex, layers of its metafictional multiverse that the novel tries to capture the mystery of existence, which is also the "mystery of otherness". Murphy in this context points to a passage at the very end of *The Infinities* that seems to encapsulate the novel's stance on the role of fiction, and alterity in fiction, itself. The passage contains the last musings of the narrator-god Hermes on 'his' world – rather fittingly, since Hermes, as O'Connell points out, is not just the god of boundaries and of lies, but his name also is the etymological root of 'hermeneutics', the theory of interpretation (2011: 440–441):

> This is the mortal world. It is a world where nothing is lost, where all is accounted for while yet the mystery of things is preserved; a world where they may live, however briefly, however tenuously, in the failing evening of the self, solitary and at the same time together somehow here in this place, dying as they may be and yet fixed forever in a luminous, unending instant. (*TI* 300).

This, in short, is the world of fiction. *The Infinities* is a metafictional reflection on the multiverse that is fiction and on the way readers encounter the mystery of the "luminous, unending instant" of a narrative. Banville's novel thus really has "confusion and mystery at the core of its ontology" (Murphy 2014: 68) – it is the mystery inherent to representations of infinities.

Overall, *The Infinities* thus differs from my other case studies in that out of the four novels I have discussed it is the work with the strongest metafictional qualities. At its heart, *The Infinities* raises questions about perspective. In the novel, infinity, or *infinities* – whether the infinite alterity of the gaze of the boy on the train, the infinite worlds of equal ontological status of the multiverse, the truly infinite narrative perspective –, calls into question the observer's, and hence the reader's, claim to a stable centre of observation inherent in any perspective, whether that is a settled concept of self, the actuality of the observer's world as opposed to the non-actuality of all other worlds, or the Olympian bird's eye perspective of omniscience. With its aesthetics of the paradoxically protean omniscient narrator and the combination of the topic of the multiverse and the question of perspectivism and gazing at the other, it presents infinity both at story and discourse level and links the question of the infinite to that of otherness, with perception itself functioning as a hinge between them. It is the novel's decentring of this observer's perspective through the oscillation between totality and infinity, or said and saying, that amounts to a calling into question of the reader's spontaneity in assigning finality to the text and so constitutes the ethical impulse of *The Infinities*.

In this it is not unlike the other novels discussed here, albeit each of these novels uses different aesthetic means to express the infinite. Crucially, the aesthetic construction of an infinite text is different in Banville's novel than in my other three case studies in that it does not treat infinity as an unequivocally positive aesthetic quality, but rather *ex negativo*, as a dissolution of narrative (hence both epistemological and ontological) boundaries: its aesthetic approach to the infinite is not so much a narrative construction of infinity as a suspension of narrative finitude. Where *The Infinities* goes a step further than the other texts is in its metafictional discussion of the construction of narrative worlds. Narrative worlds, Banville's novel suggests, are always multiverses and the act of reading is at the same time one of creating a version of such a multiverse. The metaphor is apt: textual universes meet in textual encounters, such as intertextuality, self-referentiality, nested narratives and metalepses, but these are meetings that are ultimately dependent on the reader who must recognise and engage with them. *The Infinities* makes this point through Hermes, the narrator-god who is also a spectator in the novel's *theatrum mundi* and doubles for both writer and readers. It is from this doubling that the novel's ethics – grounded both in its metafictionality and its thematisation of infinity via perspective and the multiverse – can be derived most clearly. There is the danger in any act of reading to put one's own reading as absolute, to assume a totalising perspective. *The Infinities* presents Hermes's 'total' perspective – the author-narrator-reader-spectator god – and how this perspective is full of contradictions and must eventually crumble. It thus serves as a reminder that any perspective is just one out of an infinity of views on an infinity of possible narrative worlds generated in reading a text. In the end, what Adam Jr thinks about the appearance of the world before him in the dawn twilight is also true for reading itself: "*everything is different*" (*TI* 13).

8 Coda: And Beyond?

Infinity remains impossible to grasp, even at the end of a book-length study that, I hope, has shed some light on the way in which the idea of the infinite may enter literature, and specifically narrative fiction, and what role it may play there beyond aesthetic trickery. Perhaps inevitably, given the uncountable facets of the infinite, this study itself has not taken a singular approach, but has combined ethical criticism in a Levinasian tradition with a narratological investigation – again not restricted to a single narrative technique – of aesthetic practice. My aim was to show that narrative texts can attempt to embrace infinity and adopt various aesthetic strategies to become 'infinite' in their readers' perception, even though any such representation of the infinite must be beset with paradoxes. And precisely this paradoxical nature of the infinite and its representation is already – as any paradox – a challenge to the reader's cognition. Understanding a text to be actually infinite, an infinite 'thing', is only possible in a moment of catachrestic identification that makes the finite book an infinite text – an identification that can be explained with conceptual metaphor theory, and specifically with Lakoff and Núñez's Basic Metaphor of Infinity. By becoming infinite in this way such narratives then open up; they transcend the boundaries of the text and at the same time resist the reader's grasp. By extending, or rather overextending, in such a way, the finite book is asking 'too much' of its readers, it is asking them to, impossibly, grasp the infinity of the text, which cannot be grasped. This ungraspability of the infinite text is a direct reflection of the structure of the idea of infinity itself, which "consists in grasping the ungraspable while nevertheless guaranteeing its status as ungraspable" (Levinas 1996b: 19), which is why Levinas has associated the idea of infinity with the radical alterity that forms the basis of an ethical relation with the other. In presenting the reader with its ungraspability, the infinite text thus confronts them with something that is akin to alterity, with a language that cannot be subsumed under the finite category of sameness. This eschewal of the same is the way in which fictions of infinity disrupt the reading process, in which they call into question the spontaneity of the reader, i.e. their capacity to subordinate the text to the ontological category of the known, and so become ethical in Levinas's sense (see 1969: 43). It is in this way that what I have called fictions of infinity rely on the infinite to create a structure of ethical urgency that transfers onto the entire text, and, ideally, beyond the text onto the reader. Thus far my argument. And beyond?

    What the discussion of the four twenty-first-century novels that served as my case studies has certainly shown is that there is no single and unified 'aesthetics of the infinite'. Each of these novels employs different aesthetics to create a text that can then be identified as infinite, whether narrative structure, narrative voice or textual structures such as intertextuality and the establishing of a textual circularity. In this, the aesthetic devices that may endow a text with infinity need not even be experimental. While *Cloud Atlas*, *The Stone Gods* and *The Infinities* certainly are novels whose creative use of narrative embedding, circular structures within the narrative and the narrative voice respectively hearkens back to the even more radical formal experiments of the heyday of postmodernist fiction, *Saturday* employs an aesthetics that, at least where the narrative structure is concerned, has its roots in Woolf and Joyce rather than in Brooke-Rose and Barth. McEwan's use of unbridled intertextuality in a novel whose central moment is the encounter with a text in order to make such textual encounters an inescapable part of the overall narrative, while perhaps less conspicuous than the complex nested narrative of *Cloud Atlas*, serves a similar purpose: it insinuates that there is an infinite text beyond the words that fill the pages of the book. Like *Cloud Atlas* and *The Stone Gods*, *Saturday* achieves this infinity through the construction of a more or less explicit structure of iteration, the iteration of intertextual reference, as opposed to that of narrative embedding in Mitchell's novel and circular repetition in Winterson's. This iteration is the concrete basis for the conceptualisation of the abstract idea of the infinite, it is the source domain of the Basic Metaphor of Infinity that metaphorically endows these texts with completion in infinity. While this metaphorical identification by which readers can understand a text to be actually infinite underlies the aesthetic representations of the infinite in three of my four case studies, *The Infinities* realises an entirely different aesthetics of the infinite by presenting an absolute narrative perspective that is unlimited to the point where this boundlessness defeats itself and retreats into limitation. Its perspectival infinity, and hence its primary aesthetic device that aims at representing infinity, is thus characterised above all by the absence of limits, not, as in the other novels, by the presence of structural features that 'build up' to infinity. It is thus clear that where the aesthetics are concerned, like the protean narrator of *The Infinities*, narrative infinity also comes in many shapes.

Thematically, there is likewise little that unites the four novels, at least at the surface level of the story – and why should infinity restrict itself to a common thematic denominator? While *Cloud Atlas* and *The Stone Gods* both share an interest in human history at a grand scale, in "Big History" (Shoop and Ryan 2015), and both seem to aim, in an almost 'activist' and didactic way, at an immediate change of behaviour among their readership towards accepting a responsibility for the wider world – certainly the primary reason why both novels have been classified as cosmopolitan fiction –, they do so in different ways. Winterson emphasises love as the driving force that can intervene in all human actions for the better and links love to literature as a second motor of change, whereas Mitchell's novel focuses on the ethical appeal inherent in direct encounters with vulnerable others. Perhaps as a consequence of its much narrower temporal and spatial scope, *Saturday* is more introspective, thematising the workings of the mind and the way in which encounters with (inter-)texts may disrupt them. It also reduces the multiple disruptive encounters with otherness that Winterson's and Mitchell's novels present to the single but no less powerful encounter between Perowne and Baxter and the response to Matthew Arnold's "Dover Beach". Finally, *The Infinities* presents, paradoxically, at the same time the narrowest and widest setting among all four novels. It restricts itself to a single day, not even twenty-four hours, but from dawn till dusk, in a remote country house, withdrawing, it would seem, as far as possible from the 'wide world', and, for that matter, from narrative realism – a metaphorical setting seems to suffice for this particular presentation of infinity. One consequence is that Banville's novel does not possess any 'cosmopolitan' dimension in the sense that it is not overtly concerned with social or political questions, but turns the introspection that can already be found in *Saturday* to the extreme and back onto the text and literature itself. Simultaneously, however, it situates itself in an infinite multiverse that its divine narrator Hermes can access. It is this image of the textual multiverse that among a selection of texts that all contain strong metafictional elements makes Banville's novel the one that presents the most sustained enquiry into the interconnectedness of fiction and infinity. With its focus on the narrator's role in narrative worldmaking and the narrative multiverse one might almost say Banville's novel, as its title already suggests, puts the entire subject of this study into perspective. To some extent, this is a consequence of the fact that in *The Infinities* the text itself does not become 'infinite' in the same way as in the other novels. Instead, it reflects how the entirety of fiction itself is an infinite multiverse and so shifts my reading of fictions of infinity to another level. Again, then, there is little the four novels seem to have in common when it comes to story elements. Given the nature of the idea of infinity, this disparity may hardly come as a surprise, and it seems certain that other novels find yet different ways of embracing the infinite at their story level.

What unites all four novels, however, and what is certainly indicative of the wider phenomenon of what I have called fictions of infinity throughout this study, is the most basic function of such infinite texts: they serve to break open fundamental ontology, that of the text and that of the concepts these texts aim to criticise. When a reader conceptualises a text as infinite, the ontology of the finite book's text is superseded by the infinity of the text, which already destroys a first ontological certainty, that of the commensurability or graspability of the text. This is a central feature of poetic language according to Levinas – and also, although seen from an entirely different angle, according to Kristeva, who speaks of the doubleness or "transfinite" logic of poetic language (Kristeva 1986). Such a language is then already in itself disruptive because of what – borrowing a metaphor from John Banville – might be called its "iridescent surplus" (*TI* 66), not a surplus *of*, but a surplus *beyond* meaning. In the novels that form the backbone of this study, the disruptive moment of the poetic language that is engendered in the aesthetics of the infinite text spills over to the story level, where it then questions a number of basic assumptions and propositions which the texts themselves introduce in the first place but which also are representations of prevalent discourses in society. This is the case in *The Stone Gods*, where it breaks through the cycle of destruction that forms the narrative of human 'progress'; in *Cloud Atlas*, where likewise patterns of exploitation are disrupted by the text's infinite address to the reader; in *Saturday*, where the poetic is a challenge to Henry Perowne's reliance on rigid factual comprehension; and in *The Infinities*, where it turns back onto narrative itself and so becomes a form of poetic self-interruption. In all four novels, established orders that regulate the way in which the (diegetic) world is governed by the text and perceived by the reader are thus disrupted by the infinite text, which transcends these structures. In a way, then, fictions of infinity can be said to always be metafictional, in the sense that they go beyond (*meta-*) the confines that fiction typically is seen to have.

At the same time, the fictions of infinity in all my examples are also metafictional in the established theoretical sense of making the nature of fiction their own topic. One of the most pertinent, and perhaps surprising, qualities of all four of my case studies is the way in which the infinite is interwoven with processes of reading. This seems to be a logical consequence of my approach to these novels with a focus on the ethics of the infinite. Ethics, certainly as understood by Levinas, are not based on abstract rules, but are always rooted in an encounter with the other. Reading is the reader's encounter with the text. If the idea of infinity is what characterises the radical alterity of the other in an ethical encounter in Levinas's sense, then infinite texts likewise wait to be encountered in reading. Their textual infinity then becomes in the reading relation, which is by definition a cognitive relation of understanding and so would seem to be fundamentally different from any ethical relation in the Levinasian sense, a residual element that defies the final understanding of any "metaphysics of comprehension" (Eaglestone 2004: 184) that the ontology of the text otherwise evokes. This does not mean that such texts are at a par with the human other we encounter in the ethical relation. Such a claim would result in a lopsided, twisted ethics – or no longer ethics – that confuses the immediate, radical and infinite alterity of the other with the already mediated difference of the text.[147] It does mean, however, that the encounter with such infinite texts may have a similar impact on the reader as the encounter with alterity has on the subject in the ethical relation: a calling into question of their spontaneity. As the enigma of alterity is what causes this calling into question of my spontaneity and as this relation to the other is structurally akin to the perception of the idea of the infinite, it seems consistent that texts that emulate infinity in their structure should likewise challenge my spontaneity as a reader. Reading in this way then is a "perpetual questioning and interruption" that forms the backbone of an ethical criticism in a Levinasian tradition (Eaglestone 1997: 178; see 175–179). Seen from this angle, these fictions of infinity are all meta-hermeneutic in that they thematise (most clearly Winterson's *The Stone Gods*) and exemplify the unendingness of reading as an interpretive process – a process that, because it has no end prevents any fossilisation of meaning into the facticity of the said: as soon as such a meaning makes itself manifest in the infinite text, such a text also, because of its textual infinity, demands a re-reading and in this way again exceeds finitude.

Indeed, given the ethical dimension the reading process attains in this way, it seems as if this overflowing or transcending of their textual boundaries gives these texts an almost material quality in that it allows them to touch the reader. For this reason these infinite texts might also be called infinite *textures* and could be read, beyond what this study does, primarily with a focus on their material outreach with which they may affect their readers. Texture in this sense is a term that describes "the interface between text, reader, and world in its material, medial, and cultural dimensions" and encompasses the "dynamic interwovenness of material form and immaterial processes of signification by anchoring acts of reading in the differentiable layers of materiality and mediality in a given text" (Reinfandt 2016: 319). This can be linked to the affective quality that, according to Levinas, the infinite itself possesses, a quality which again is rooted in the basic structure of the idea of infinity as an idea that transcends the thought itself. In doing so, "[t]he Infinite affects thought by devastating it and at the same time calls upon it; in a 'putting it back in its place' it puts thought in place. It awakens it" (Levinas 1996c: 138). This is the outreach of

---

[147] The one decisive difference between texts and human others is that texts do not have a face. Their 'face' is only a typeface, an imprint of an ontology beyond the text. Where the face of the human other is "the nakedness and destitution of the expression as such, that is to say extreme exposure, defencelessness, vulnerability itself" and in this destitution "summons me, calls for me, begs for me" (Levinas 1989a: 83), a text, whose life is only ever metaphorical, cannot muster the same traumatic appeal.

the infinite which it also attains in the ethical appeal fictions of infinity may develop. It originates in precisely the impossibility of a representation of infinity, in the intimation of the idea of infinity *ex negativo*:

> The *in* of the Infinite designates the depth of the affecting by which subjectivity is affected through this "putting" of the Infinite into it, without prehension or comprehension. It designates the depth of an undergoing that no capacity comprehends, that no foundation any longer supports, where every process of investing fails and where the screws that fix the stern of inwardness burst. This putting in without a corresponding recollecting devastates its site like a devouring fire, catastrophying its site, in the etymological sense of the word. It is a dazzling, where the eye takes more than it can hold, an igniting of the skin which touches and does not touch what is beyond the graspable, and burns. It is a passivity or a passion in which desire can be recognized, in which the *"more* in the less" awakens by its most ardent, noblest and most ancient flame a thought given over to thinking more than it thinks. (Levinas 1996c: 139)

Levinas's language, it should be noted, becomes tactile here – loaded with the affective quality of the experience of infinity in a burning intensity. At the same time, since it is a "dazzling", this tactile quality, material to the touch, is implicitly linked to the "scintillation" (1989e: 156; see ch. 3.3) of the language of poetry. This means that infinity itself adds a material quality to the infinite text, a quality that would then seem to enable the narrative to "awaken" the thoughts of its readers. Where the infinite text thus overreaches its boundaries to get a hold on its reader, it may also be described as an infinite texture. When viewed in this way, the motif of infinity invites a critical approach that combines classical text-based criticism, ethical criticism in the wake of an "ethics of deconstruction" (Critchley 1992) and more recent theoretical approaches that take into account the material and affective dimensions of literature. A return to fictions of infinity under the auspices of the new materialism and/or affect studies with the aim of developing a new ethical criticism that is informed by these more corporeal approaches might therefore turn out to be fruitful.

Furthermore, throwing a glance beyond the aesthetic configurations of infinity in narrative texts and beyond their specific ethical impact – in as far as such a 'beyond infinity' is possible – there is also a more immediately political dimension of fictions of infinity that comes into view. In a political climate that is increasingly polarised all over the world, and quite certainly in the United States and the United Kingdom, the disruptive force of the infinite that has the potential to suspend the stark confrontation of binary oppositions seems to be needed perhaps more than ever. In this context it is not surprising that two of the four novels discussed here, *Cloud Atlas* and *The Stone Gods*, may indeed be said to have an outright political, cosmopolitan agenda of change and a third, *Saturday*, pursues similar goals in a slightly more veiled manner – *The Infinities* with its more philosophical discussion of the role of art and literature itself is again the odd one out. Fictions of infinity, it would seem, are apt vehicles to make the step from ethics to politics and promote a politics of change and openness. The reason may be that, although their infinite text is structured like the ethical relation to the other in Levinas's sense, it is still not quite the same: the reader's relation to these texts is not the same as that 'relationless relation' to the other on which Levinas's ethics is built – the ethical relation is always rooted in concreteness, in a direct encounter with the face of the other, while the reading encounter with a text is at a more abstract level. At this more abstract level of the text, the disruption that the infinite text constitutes is a disruption of the reader's network of relations, that is, of their situatedness in social discourse. As such, it is inherently political, where the politics such texts pursue can only be aligned with their rejection of totality and seek a form of unity in difference.

This potential of the infinite can be seen, for instance, in Judith Butler's more recent work and in particular in the political and ethical philosophy she wrote as a reaction to the 9/11 terror attacks, the as yet defining political event of the twenty-first century (see Butler 2004; 2005). Without specifically focussing on the infinite, Butler turns to Levinas and the ethical imperative that arises from encountering alterity: "To respond to the face, to understand its meaning, means to be awake to what is precarious in another life or, rather, the precariousness of life itself" (Butler 2004: 134), she argues and thus moves the pre-ontological Levinasian encounter with alterity into the realm of the social, into politics. Given this indebtedness to Levinas, it is little wonder that for her, "both our political and ethical responsibilities are rooted in the recognition that radical forms of self-sufficiency and unbridled sovereignty are, by definition, disrupted by the larger global processes of which they are a part, that no final control can be secured, and that final control is not, cannot be, an ultimate value" (2004: xiii). Infinity, as in forgoing the establishing of final control, rooted in an infinite indebtedness to others, in this sense does inform Butler's ethico-political philosophy. No wonder then that literature – and perhaps fictions of infinity would yield particularly good examples – therefore for Butler becomes "an exploratory site for re-imagining the human", resulting in her conception of what may be called the "catachretic [sic] human" – a notion of humanity that is engendered in "the dialectic between a normative ethics and a questioning of norms" (Arteel 2011: 85). This, it would seem to me, is likewise something fictions of infinity are prone to doing: they frequently perform a questioning of norms that are then tentatively replaced by an alternative ethical mode of behaviour, which again in itself is questioned, simply through the endless continuation of the process.

Of course, this more political side of the fictions of infinity leads to problems with regard to the politics of change itself: firstly, there is the question of whether literature can really make a difference; secondly there is an inherent danger that such a politics of change would merely replace one totalitarian ontological structure with another. On a more self-critical note, towards the end of this book it seems therefore reasonable to ask whether the view of literature and its potential to disrupt, challenge and make a difference that I have claimed again and again to be a central concern of fictions of infinity is not too optimistic or far-reaching. The notion that texts should have ethical agency seems quite radical – a Romanticising view of literature and its prowess – and proving any concrete (never mind lasting) effects on readers is a difficult, if not impossible task that would require long-term empirical studies to trace any changes in behaviour among the readership of such novels. Is the claim that fiction may develop an ethical appeal that readers may then perceive and react to itself then nothing more than the construction of a fiction? Yet this seems oddly beside the point the texts I have discussed are trying to make: change more often than not, or perhaps always, takes place at the micro-level and each act of reading carries the potential of such a change. Borrowing a central image from Mitchell's *Cloud Atlas* one might say that the novels I have discussed here and their ethical stances are just drops in an endless ocean of texts we are surrounded with every day. "Yet, what is any ocean but a multitude of drops?" (*CA* 509). Crucially, the novels I have identified as fictions of infinity here display a focus on literature's, and hence their own, capacity to make a difference. If reading these texts can disrupt the totality of perception, even just for a small part of the overall readership, then they have already succeeded in that goal.

Even more problematic is the question of where such reactions should be directed to, what the goal of any changes elicited by literature might be. Florian Kläger sees in both critical approaches and novels that promote literature's capacity to elicit change – *The Stone Gods* is one of his examples, but *Cloud Atlas* and *Saturday* might likewise qualify – a great deal of anthropological "hyperbole" that "partakes of a universalizing impulse" in contemporary fiction (2014: 292). There is a point to this criticism, which is directed mostly against the 'planetary' scope of cosmopolitanism or cosmodernism: the disruption caused by such texts may lead to new concepts that are again totalitarian or essentialist, such as what Kläger polemically calls the "Doomsday device of universal kumbaya-ification" (2014: 295). Such a danger may indeed exist where the disruptive power of such texts is read primarily with a view to its political potential and not – as in my approach here – to its ethics. If these texts are read as perpetually disruptive, then the formation of new ontologies is precisely what they seek to prevent; the only thing exempt from their disruptive power is the responsibility arising from the pre-ontological ethical encounter with alterity, that is, the moment of disruption itself. In this sense, the way I approach these novels is, I think, different from what Kläger criticises.

However, Kläger's lament goes on to take an even more fundamental form: "To inquire after the nonconceptual and inexpressible is to provoke hyperbolic answers. What is more, the question itself is of course hyperbolic, 'over-reaching', in its ambition for anthropological insight, and so are the sweeping claims made for the function of literature" (2014: 306). It would appear that this critique might also be levelled against fictions of infinity: the idea of infinity is certainly hyperbolic, since it is "nonconceptual and inexpressible" as well as "over-reaching" and, through the thematisation of reading, also makes a claim for literature's functionality. Yet this again seems to ignore the central idea of the texts I have discussed here: in enquiring after the infinite, after what resists expression or representation, fictions of infinity precisely disavow any pretence to "anthropological insight". Unless, that is, becoming aware of a fundamental ethical responsibility for the other were such an insight. If that is the case, then hyperbole is ethical – and indeed the Levinasian notion of the infinite may be described as excessive and hyperbolical (see Waldenfels 2008: 18–21).

As the cipher Levinas chooses for the ethical relation, infinity is then a hyperbolical demand, a demand in excess of those structures that organise thought and give it its categories, replacing these ontological categories with the extreme responsibility for the other. This impulse of the infinite is what fictions of infinity seek to emulate with their attempts at an aesthetic approximation of infinity. Infinity in this context has the function of providing the texts with their central aporias, the irresolvably paradoxical structures they are constructed around and that help them to aesthetically represent the complex ethical questions they address. Infinity also allows these infinite texts to develop an insistence, a sense of urgency that is fuelled by their very persistence: being infinite, they just won't go away. They never stop asking for a beyond the text.

Works Cited

Abbott, H. Porter. 2008. *The Cambridge Introduction to Narrative*. 2nd ed. Cambridge: Cambridge University Press.
Achtner, Wolfgang. 2011. "Infinity as a Transformative Concept in Science and Theology". In: Michael Heller and W. Hugh Woodin (eds.). *Infinity: New Research Frontiers*. Cambridge: Cambridge University Press. 19–51.
Adams, Ann Marie. 2012. "Mr. McEwan and Mrs. Woolf: How a Saturday in February Follows 'This Moment of June'". *Contemporary Literature* 53.3: 548–572.
Alber, Jan. 2014. "Unnatural Narrative". In: Peter Hühn et al. (eds.). *the living handbook of narratology*. Hamburg: Hamburg University. <http://www.lhn.uni-hamburg.de/article/unnatural-narrative> [accessed 2 May 2018].
Alber, Jan. 2016. *Unnatural Narrative: Impossible Worlds in Fiction and Drama*. Lincoln: University of Nebraska Press.
Alber, Jan, Henrik Skov Nielsen and Brian Richardson. 2012. "Unnatural Voices, Minds, and Narration". In: Joe Bray, Alison Gibbons and Brian McHale (eds.). *The Routledge Companion to Experimental Literature*. New York: Routledge. 351–367.
Allen, Graham. 2011. *Intertextuality*. 2nd ed. Abingdon: Routledge.
Amiel-Houser, Tammy. 2011/2012. "The Ethics of Otherness in Ian McEwan's *Saturday*". *Connotations* 21.1: 128–157.
Amigoni, David. 2008. "'The luxury of storytelling': Science, Literature and Cultural Contest in Ian McEwan's Narrative Practice". In: Sharon Ruston (ed.). *Literature and Science*. Essays and Studies 61. Cambridge: Brewer. 151–167.
Aragay, Mireia and Martin Middeke (eds.). 2017. *Representations of the Precarious in Contemporary British Drama*. CDE Studies 27. Berlin: de Gruyter.
Aragay, Mireia and Enric Monforte (eds.). 2014. *Ethical Speculations in Contemporary British Theatre*. Basingstoke: Palgrave Macmillan.
Aristotle. 1961. *Aristotle's Physics*. Trans. Richard Hope. Lincoln: University of Nebraska Press.
Arnold, Matthew. 2012 [1867]. "Dover Beach". In: Catherine Robson and Carol T. Christ (eds.). *The Victorian Age*. Vol. E of *The Norton Anthology of English Literature*. Gen. ed. Stephen Greenblatt. New York: Norton. 1387–1388.
Arteel, Inge. 2011. "Judith Butler and the Catachretic Human". In: Andy Mousley (ed.). *Towards a New Literary Humanism*. Basingstoke: Palgrave Macmillan. 77–90.
Attridge, Derek. 2016. "The Literary Work as Ethical Event". In: Martin Middeke and Christoph Reinfandt (eds.). *Theory Matters: The Place of Theory in Literary and Cultural Studies Today*. Basingstoke: Palgrave Macmillan. 219–232.
Auden, W. H. 1991. *Collected Poems*. Ed. Edward Mendelson. New York: Vintage.
Augustine. 1966. *The City of God Against the Pagans*. Vol. 4: Books XII–XV. Trans. Philip Levine. The Loeb Classical Library. London: Heinemann.
Badiou, Alain. 2011. "A History of Finitude and Infinity: Classicism". Talk given at the EGS. *YouTube*, 17 December. <https://www.youtube.com/watch?v=Lp7r6v169r8&list=PLeGESIHJQbKLOoJF9DsyeTwrOPGc83i_z&index=9>. Transcript available at: <http://www.egs.edu/faculty/alain-badiou/articles/a-history-of-finitude-and-infinity/> [accessed 3 June 2015].

Baldick, Chris. 2001. *The Concise Oxford Dictionary of Literary Terms*. 2nd ed. Oxford: Oxford University Press.
Banville, John. 2000. *God's Gift: A Version of* Amphitryon *by Heinrich von Kleist*. Loughcrew: Gallery Books.
Banville, John. 2009. *The Infinities*. London: Picador.
Baraitser, Lisa. 2009. *Maternal Encounters: The Ethics of Interruption*. London: Routledge.
Barnes, Julian. 1990 [1989]. *A History of the World in 10½ Chapters*. London: Picador.
Barrow, John D. 2005. *The Infinite Book: A Short Guide to the Boundless, Timeless and Endless*. London: Jonathan Cape.
Barth, John. 1988 [1968]. *Lost in the Funhouse*. New York: Anchor Books.
Barthes, Roland. 1977a [1971]. "From Work to Text". In: Roland Barthes. *Image – Music – Text*. Trans. Stephen Heath. New York: Hill and Wang. 155–164.
Barthes, Roland. 1977b [1971]. "The Struggle with the Angel". In: Roland Barthes. *Image – Music – Text*. Trans. Stephen Heath. New York: Hill and Wang. 125–141.
Barthes, Roland. 1977c [1968]. "The Death of the Author". In: Roland Barthes. *Image – Music – Text*. Trans. Stephen Heath. New York: Hill and Wang. 142–148.
Bar-Yosef, Eitan. 2020. "Dr. Perowne and Mr. Baxter: Gothic Resonances in Ian McEwan's *Saturday*". *ANQ: A Quarterly Journal of Short Articles, Notes, and Reviews*. <https://doi.org/10.1080/0895769X.2020.1742081> [accessed 15 May 2020].
Bayer, Gerd. 2015. "Perpetual Apocalypses: David Mitchell's *Cloud Atlas* and the Absence of Time". *Critique: Studies in Contemporary Fiction* 56.4: 345–354.
Beckett, Samuel. 2006 [1952]. *Waiting for Godot*. In: Samuel Beckett. *The Complete Dramatic Works*. London: faber and faber. 7–88.
Benjamin, Andrew. 1991. *Art, Mimesis and the Avant-Garde: Aspects of a Philosophy of Difference*. London: Routledge.
Berensmeyer, Ingo. 2000. *John Banville: Fictions of Order*. Heidelberg: Winter.
Berger Jr., Harry. 2015. *Figures of a Changing World: Metaphor and the Emergence of Modern Culture*. New York: Fordham University Press.
Bergo, Bettina. 1999. *Levinas Between Ethics and Politics: For the Beauty that Adorns the Earth*. Phaenomenologica 152. Dordrecht: Kluwer.
Bersanelli, Marco. 2011. "Infinity and the Nostalgia of the Stars". In: Michael Heller and W. Hugh Woodin (eds.). *Infinity: New Research Frontiers*. Cambridge: Cambridge University Press. 193–217.
Bode, Christoph. 2011 [2005]. *The Novel: An Introduction*. Trans. James Vigus. Malden: Wiley-Blackwell.
Bolten, Jürgen. 1985. "Die hermeneutische Spirale: Überlegungen zu einer integrativen Literaturtheorie". *Poetica* 17: 355–371.
Bond, Erik. 2017. "'Arrogant Fools with Blunt Instruments': Brain Surgeons, Novelists, and Metaphor in Ian McEwan's London". In: Joseph DeFalco Lamperez and J. Alexandra McGhee (eds.). *Urban Monstrosities: Perversity and Upheaval in the Unreal City*. Newcastle: Cambridge Scholars. 60–90.
Böttigheimer, Christoph. 2018. "Unendlichkeit als Gottesattribut: Von der Unmöglichkeit des begreifend-begrifflichen Erfassens Gottes". In: Christoph Böttigheimer and René Dausner (eds.). *Unendlichkeit: Transdisziplinäre Annäherungen*. Würzburg: Königshausen & Neumann. 169–180.

Boulter, Jonathan. 2011. *Melancholy and the Archive: Trauma, History and Memory in the Contemporary Novel*. London: Continuum.
Brachtendorf, Johannes, Thomas Möllenbeck, Gregor Nickel and Stephan Schaede (eds.). 2008. *Unendlichkeit: Interdisziplinäre Perspektiven*. Tübingen: Mohr Siebeck.
Bradbury, Ray. 2012 [1951]. *Fahrenheit 451*. New York: Simon & Schuster.
Bradway, Tyler. 2015. "Queer Exuberance: The Politics of Affect in Jeanette Winterson's Visceral Fiction". *Mosaic: An Interdisciplinary Critical Journal* 48.1: 183–200.
Breuer, Rolf. 1976. "The Solution as Problem: Beckett's *Waiting for Godot*". *Modern Drama* 19: 225–236.
Breuer, Rolf. 2002. "Zyklik, Zirkularität und Wiederholung bei Beckett". In: Martin Middeke (ed.). *Zeit und Roman: Zeiterfahrungen im historischen Wandel und ästhetischer Paradigmenwechsel vom sechzehnten Jahrhundert bis zur Postmoderne*. Würzburg: Königshausen & Neumann. 359–372.
Briggs, Caroline. 2007. "Winterson Novel 'Left at Station'". *BBC News*, 8 March. <http://news.bbc.co.uk/2/hi/entertainment/6430775.stm> [accessed 1 December 2018].
Brillenburg Wurth, Kiene. 2009. *The Musically Sublime: Indeterminacy, Infinity, Irresolvability*. New York: Fordham University Press.
Brits, Baylee. 2018. *Literary Infinities: Number and Narrative in Modern Fiction*. London: Bloomsbury.
Brogi, Susanna. 2008. "Kreis". In: Günter Butzer and Joachim Jacob (eds.). *Metzler Lexikon literarischer Symbole*. Stuttgart: Metzler. 189–191.
Brooke-Rose, Christine. 1958. *A Grammar of Metaphor*. London: Secker & Warburg.
Buell, Lawrence. 2000. "What We Talk About When We Talk About Ethics". In: Marjorie Garber, Beatrice Hanssen and Rebecca R. Walkowitz (eds.). *The Turn to Ethics*. New York: Routledge. 1–13.
Burke, Edmund. 1792. *A Philosophical Inquiry Into the Origin of Our Ideas of the Sublime and Beautiful*. Basel: Tourneisen. In: *Eighteenth Century Collections Online*. <http://find.galegroup.com/ecco/infomark.do?&source=gale&prodId=ECCO&userGroupName=dfg_ecco&tabID=T001&docId=CW117401693&type=multipage&contentSet=ECCOArticles&version=1.0&docLevel=FASCIMILE> [accessed 17 July 2017].
Butler, Judith. 2004. *Precarious Life: The Powers of Mourning and Violence*. London: Verso.
Butler, Judith. 2005. *Giving an Account of Oneself*. New York: Fordham University Press.
Butler, Judith. 2012. "Precarious Life, Vulnerability, and the Ethics of Cohabitation". *Journal of Speculative Philosophy* 26.2: 134–151.
Cantor, Georg. 1932. *Gesammelte Abhandlungen*. Eds. A. Fraenkel and E. Zermelo. Berlin: Springer.
Cantor, Georg. 1966. *Abhandlungen mathematischen und philosophischen Inhalts*. Hildesheim: Olms.
Carr, Bernard (ed.). 2007. *Universe or Multiverse?* Cambridge: Cambridge University Press.
Childs, Donald. 1997. "Mrs. Dalloway's Unexpected Guests: Virginia Woolf, T. S. Eliot, and Matthew Arnold". *Modern Language Quarterly* 58.1: 63–82.
Childs, Peter. 2009. "Contemporary McEwan and Anosognosia". In: Pascal Nicklas (ed.). *Ian McEwan: Art and Politics*. Heidelberg: Winter. 23–38.
Childs, Peter and James Green. 2011. "The Novels in Nine Parts". In: Sarah Dillon (ed.). *David Mitchell: Critical Essays*. Canterbury: Gylphi. 25–47.

Childs, Peter and James Green. 2013. *Aesthetics and Ethics in Twenty-First Century British Novels*. London: Bloomsbury.

Chiu, Melissa. 2017. Foreword. *Yayoi Kusama Infinity Mirrors*. Ed. Mika Yoshitake. München: Del Monico. 7–8.

Christiansen, Morten H. and Maryellen C. MacDonald. 2009. "A Usage-Based Approach to Recursion in Sentence Processing". *Language Learning* 59 (Suppl. 1): 126–161.

Chrzanowska-Kluczewska, Elżbieta. 2004. "Microtropes, Macrotropes, Metatropes". *AAA – Arbeiten aus Anglistik und Amerikanistik* 29.1: 65–80.

Chrzanowska-Kluczewska, Elżbieta. 2011. "Catachresis—A Metaphor or a Figure in Its Own Right?" In: Monika Fludernik (ed.). *Beyond Cognitive Metaphor Theory: Perspectives on Literary Metaphor*. New York: Routledge. 36–57.

Cirlot, C. E. 1971 [1962]. *A Dictionary of Symbols*. 2nd ed. Trans. Jack Sage. London: Routledge & Kegan Paul.

Clark Hillard, Molly. 2008. "'When Desert Armies Stand Ready to Fight': Re-Reading McEwan's *Saturday* and Arnold's 'Dover Beach'". *Partial Answers: Journal of Literature and the History of Ideas* 6.1: 181–206.

Clark, Robert. 2005. "Ian McEwan: Saturday". *The Literary Encyclopedia*, 12 April. <http://www.litencyc.com/php/sworks.php?rec=true&UID=16704> [accessed 4 March 2017].

Claviez, Thomas. 2008. *Aesthetics & Ethics*. Heidelberg: Winter.

Clegg, Brian. 2003. *A Brief History of Infinity: The Quest to Think the Unthinkable*. London: Robinson.

Connor, Steven. 1988. *Samuel Beckett: Repetition, Theory and Text*. Oxford: Blackwell.

Cook, James. 1772–1775. *Journal of Captain Cook's Voyage Round the World in HMS Resolution*. Manuscript. University of Cambridge Digital Library. <https://cudl.lib.cam.ac.uk/view/MS-JOD-00020> [accessed 1 November 2018].

Critchley, Simon. 1992. *The Ethics of Deconstruction: Derrida and Levinas*. Cambridge: Blackwell.

Critchley, Simon. 1994. "Eine Vertiefung der ethischen Sprache und Methode: Lévinas' 'Jenseits des Seins oder anders als Sein geschieht'". *Deutsche Zeitschrift für Philosophie* 42.4: 643–651.

Critchley, Simon. 2002. Introduction. In: Simon Critchley and Robert Bernasconi (eds.). *The Cambridge Companion to Levinas*. Cambridge: Cambridge University Press. 1–32.

Critchley, Simon. 2007. *Infinitely Demanding: Ethics of Commitment, Politics of Resistance*. New York: Verso.

Critchley, Simon. 2015. *The Problem with Levinas*. Ed. Alexis Dianda. Oxford: Oxford University Press.

Culler, Jonathan. 1981. *The Pursuit of Signs: Semiotics, Literature, Deconstruction*. London: Routledge & Kegan Paul.

Culler, Jonathan. 1997. *Literary Theory: A Very Short Introduction*. Oxford: Oxford University Press.

Culler, Jonathan. 2004. "Omniscience". *Narrative* 12.1: 22–34.

Currie, Mark. 2009. "The Expansion of Tense". *Narrative* 17.3: 353–367.

Dällenbach, Lucien. 1977. *Le récit spéculaire: Essai sur la mise en abyme*. Paris: Editions du Seuil.

Davis, Todd F. and Kenneth Womack (eds.). 2001. *Mapping the Ethical Turn: A Reader in Ethics, Culture, and Literary Theory*. Charlottesville: University Press of Virginia.

Dawson, Paul. 2013. *The Return of the Omniscient Narrator: Authorship and Authority in Twenty-First Century Fiction*. Columbus: Ohio State University Press.
Derrida, Jacques. 1992. *Acts of Literature*. Ed. Derek Attridge. New York: Routledge.
Derrida, Jacques. 1994. *Specters of Marx: The State of the Debt, the Work of Mourning, and the New International*. Trans. Peggy Kamuf. New York: Routledge.
Derrida, Jacques. 1995. "Deconstruction and the Other". In: Richard Kearney (ed.). *States of Mind: Dialogues with Contemporary Thinkers on the European Mind*. Manchester: Manchester University Press. 156–176.
Derrida, Jacques. 2000. "Hostipitality". Trans. Barry Stocker with Forbes Morlock. *Angelaki: Journal of the Theoretical Humanities* 5.3: 3–18.
Derrida, Jacques. 2005 [1967]. "Violence and Metaphysics". In: Jacques Derrida. *Writing and Difference*. Trans. Alan Bass. London: Routledge. 97–192.
Descartes, René. 2013 [1641]. *Meditations on First Philosophy: With Selections from Objections and Replies*. Ed. and trans. John Cottingham. Cambridge: Cambridge University Press.
D'haen, Theo. 2013. "European Postmodernism: The Cosmodern Turn". *Narrative* 21.3: 271–283.
D'hoker, Elke. 2004. *Visions of Alterity: Representation in the Works of John Banville*. Amsterdam: Rodopi.
Dickmann, Iddo. 2015. "Mise en abyme and Levinas's 'Infinite Responsibility'". In: Rita Šerpytytė (ed.). *Emmanuel Levinas: A Radical Thinker in the Time of Crisis*. Vilnius: Vilniaus universiteto leidykla. 131–137.
Doležel, Lubomír. 1998. *Heterocosmica: Fiction and Possible Worlds*. Baltimore: Johns Hopkins University Press.
Donne, John. 2010. *The Complete Poems of John Donne*. Ed. Robin Robbins. Rev. ed. Harlow: Pearson.
Donne, John. 2015. *John Donne*. Ed. Janel Mueller. 21st-century Oxford Authors. Oxford: Oxford University Press.
Downes, Rebecca. 2017. "Death and the Impersonality of Style in John Banville's *The Infinities*". *Nordic Irish Studies* 16: 21–36.
Duffy, Carol Ann. 2005. *Rapture*. London: Picador.
Dumbadze, Alexander. 2017. "Infinity and Nothingness". In: Mika Yoshitake (ed.). *Yayoi Kusama Infinity Mirrors*. München: Del Monico. 118–127.
Duncan, Diane Moira. 2001. *The Pre-Text of Ethics: On Derrida and Levinas*. New York: Peter Lang.
DuPlessis, Rachel Blau. 1985. *Writing Beyond the Ending: Narrative Strategies of Twentieth-Century Women Writers*. Bloomington: Indiana University Press.
Dupree, Mary Helen. 2014. "Kleist in Irland: Zur Kleist-Rezeption im Werk John Banvilles". In: Anne Fleig, Christian Moser and Helmut J. Schneider (eds.). *Schreiben nach Kleist: Literarische, mediale und theoretische Transkriptionen*. Freiburg: Rombach. 271–285.
Eaglestone, Robert. 1997. *Ethical Criticism: Reading After Levinas*. Edinburgh: Edinburgh University Press.
Eaglestone, Robert. 2004. "Postmodernism and Ethics against the Metaphysics of Comprehension". In: Steven Connor (ed.). *The Cambridge Companion to Postmodernism*. Cambridge: Cambridge University Press. 182–195.

Eaglestone, Robert. 2013. *Contemporary Fiction: A Very Short Introduction*. Oxford: Oxford University Press.
Eckstein, Lars. 2011. "Saturday on Dover Beach: Ian McEwan, Matthew Arnold, and Post-9/11 Melancholia". *Hard Times* 89: 6–10.
Eckstein, Lars. 2012/2013. "Against an Ethics of Absolute Otherness, for Cross-Cultural Critique: A Response to Tammy Amiel-Houser". *Connotations* 22.1: 125–136.
Edwards, Caroline. 2011. "'Strange Transactions': Utopia, Transmigration and Time in *Ghostwritten* and *Cloud Atlas*". In: Sarah Dillon (ed.). *David Mitchell: Critical Essays*. Canterbury: Gylphi. 177–200.
Elam, Diane. 1994. *Feminism and Deconstruction: Ms. en abyme*. London: Routledge.
Ellam, Julie. 2010. *Love in Jeanette Winterson's Novels*. Amsterdam: Rodopi.
Eve, Martin Paul. 2016. "'You Have to Keep Track of Your Changes': The Version Variants and Publishing History of David Mitchell's *Cloud Atlas*". *Open Library of Humanities* 2.2 (e1): 1–34. <http://dx.doi.org/10.16995/olh.82> [accessed 1 March 2017].
Ferber, Michael. 2007. *A Dictionary of Literary Symbols*. 2nd ed. Cambridge: Cambridge University Press.
First Vatican Council. 1869–1870. EWTN: Global Catholic Network. <https://www.ewtn.com/catholicism/library/first-vatican-council-1505> [accessed 28 May 2020].
Fludernik, Monika. 2001. "New Wine in Old Bottles? Voice, Focalization and New Writing". *New Literary History* 32.3: 619–638.
Fořt, Bohumil. 2016. *An Introduction to Fictional Worlds Theory*. Frankfurt a. M.: Peter Lang.
Foucault, Michel. 1970 [1966]. *The Order of Things*. New York: Pantheon Books.
Foucault, Michel. 1984 [1967]. "Of Other Spaces, Heterotopias". *Architecture, Mouvement, Continuité* 5: 46–49. Michel Foucault Info. <https://foucault.info/doc/documents/heterotopia/foucault-heterotopia-en-html> [accessed 26 January 2017].
Freiburg, Rudolf. 2016. Einleitung. "Unendlichkeit: Versuch einer asymptotischen Annäherung". In: Rudolf Freiburg (ed.). *Unendlichkeit*. Erlangen: FAU University Press. 5–33. <https://opus4.kobv.de/opus4-fau/frontdoor/index/index/docId/7462%20title> [accessed 17 September 2018].
Friberg-Harnesk, Hedda. 2010. "In the Sign of the Counterfeit: John Banville's *God's Gift*". *Nordic Irish Studies* 9: 71–88.
Front, Sonia. 2015. *Shapes of Time in British Twenty-First Century Quantum Fiction*. Newcastle upon Tyne: Cambridge Scholars.
Füger, Wilhelm. 2004. "Limits of the Narrator's Knowledge in Fielding's *Joseph Andrews*: A Contribution to a Theory of Negated Knowledge in Fiction". *Style* 38.3: 278–288.
Füredy, Viveca. 1989. "A Structural Model of Phenomena with Embedding in Literature and Other Arts". *Poetics Today* 10.4: 745–769.
Ganteau, Jean-Michel. 2005. "'Rise From the Ground Like Feathered Mercury': Baroque Citations in the Fiction of Peter Ackroyd and Jeanette Winterson". In: Susana Onega (ed.). *Intertextuality*. Spec. issue of *Symbolism: An International Annual of Critical Aesthetics* 5. 193–221.
Ganteau, Jean-Michel. 2014. "Ghosts, Texts, Phantom Texts: McEwan's *Saturday* and Joyce's 'The Dead'". In: Brigitte Johanna Glaser and Barbara Puschmann-Nalenz (eds.). *Narrating Loss: Representations of Mourning, Nostalgia and Melancholia in Contemporary Anglophone Fictions*. Trier: wvt. 223–238.

Garber, Marjorie, Beatrice Hanssen and Rebecca R. Walkowitz (eds.). 2000. *The Turn to Ethics*. New York: Routledge.
Gauthier, Tim. 2013. "'Selective in Your Mercies': Privilege, Vulnerability, and the Limits of Empathy in Ian McEwan's *Saturday*". *College Literature* 40.2: 7–30.
Genette, Gérard. 1980. *Narrative Discourse: An Essay in Method*. Trans. Jane E. Lewin. Ithaca: Cornell University Press.
Genette, Gérard. 1983. *Narrative Discourse Revisited*. Trans. Jane E. Lewin. Ithaca: Cornell University Press.
Genette, Gérard. 1997 [1982]. *Palimpsests: Literature in the Second Degree*. Trans. Channa Newman and Claude Doubinsky. Lincoln: University of Nebraska Press.
Gibson, Andrew. 1999. *Postmodernity, Ethics and the Novel: From Leavis to Levinas*. London: Routledge.
Gide, André. 1951. *Journal, 1889–1939*. Paris: Gallimard.
Gide, André. 1967. *Journals 1889–1949*. Harmondsworth: Penguin.
Gregory, Andrew. 2016. *Anaximander: A Re-assessment*. London: Bloomsbury.
Greisch, Jean. 1991. "The Face and Reading: Immediacy and Mediation". Trans. Simon Critchley. In: Robert Bernasconi and Simon Critchley (eds.). *Re-Reading Levinas*. London: Athlone. 67–82.
Groes, Sebastian. 2009. "Ian McEwan and the Modernist Consciousness of the City in *Saturday*". In: Sebastian Groes (ed.). *Ian McEwan: Contemporary Critical Perspectives*. London: Continuum. 99–114.
Grossman, Vasily. 1985. *Life and Fate*. Trans. Robert Chandler. London: Collins Harvill.
Haarkötter, Hektor. 2007. *Nicht-endende Enden: Dimensionen eines literarischen Phänomens*. Würzburg: Königshausen & Neumann.
Hadley, Elaine. 2005. "On a Darkling Plain: Victorian Liberalism and the Fantasy of Agency". *Victorian Studies* 48.1: 92–102.
Hart, David Bentley. 2011. "Notes on the Concept of the Infinite in the History of Western Metaphysics". In: Michael Heller and W. Hugh Woodin (eds.). *Infinity: New Research Frontiers*. Cambridge: Cambridge University Press. 255–274.
Head, Dominic. 2007. *Ian McEwan*. Manchester: Manchester University Press.
Heise, Ursula. 2015. "What's the Matter with Dystopia?" *Public Books*, 1 February. <https://www.publicbooks.org/whats-the-matter-with-dystopia/> [accessed 29 October 2018].
Heller, Michael, and W. Hugh Woodin (eds.). 2011. *Infinity: New Research Frontiers*. Cambridge: Cambridge University Press.
Henke, Christoph and Martin Middeke (eds.). 2009. *Literature and Circularity*. Spec. issue of *Symbolism: An International Annual of Critical Aesthetics* 9.
Herrick, Robert. 1996. "Upon Julia's Clothes". In: Margaret Ferguson, Mary Jo Salter and Jon Stallworthy (eds.). *The Norton Anthology of Poetry*. 4th ed. New York: Norton. 323.
Hicks, Heather J. 2010. "'This Time Round': David Mitchell's *Cloud Atlas* and the Apocalyptic Problem of Historicism". *Postmodern Culture* 20.3. <http://www.pomoculture.org/2013/09/03/this-time-round-david-mitchells-cloud-atlas-and-the-apocalyptic-problem-of-historicism/> [accessed 22 September 2016].
Hicks, Heather J. 2016. *The Post-Apocalyptic Novel in the Twenty-First Century: Modernity Beyond Salvage*. Basingstoke: Palgrave Macmillan.
Hofstadter, Douglas R. 1979. *Gödel, Escher, Bach: An Eternal Golden Braid*. New York: Basic Books.

Holmqvist, Kenneth and Jarosław Płuciennik. 2008. *Infinity in Language: Conceptualization of the Experience of the Sublime*. Newcastle upon Tyne: Cambridge Scholars.
Hopf, Courtney. 2011. "The Stories We Tell: Discursive Identity Through Narrative Form in *Cloud Atlas*". In: Sarah Dillon (ed.). *David Mitchell: Critical Essays*. Canterbury: Gylphi. 105–126.
Horace. 2002. *Odes* III. Trans. David West. Oxford: Oxford University Press.
Hoskins, John. 1935 [1599]. *Directions for Speech and Style*. Ed. Hoyt Hudson. Princeton: Princeton University Press.
Huber, Irmtraud. 2016. *Present-tense Narration in Contemporary Fiction*. London: Palgrave Macmillan.
Huber, Werner, Martin Middeke and Hubert Zapf (eds.). 2005. *Self-Reflexivity in Literature*. text & theorie 6. Würzburg: Königshausen & Neumann.
Irigaray, Luce. 1986 [1983]. "The Fecundity of the Caress: A Reading of Levinas, *Totality and Infinity*, Section IV, B, 'The Phenomenology of Eros'". Trans. Carolyn Burke. In: Richard A. Cohen (ed.). *Face to Face with Levinas*. Albany: State University of New York Press. 231–256.
Iser, Wolfgang. 2000. *The Range of Interpretation*. New York: Columbia University Press.
Jennings, Hope. 2010. "'A Repeating World': Redeeming the Past and Future in the Utopian Dystopia of Jeanette Winterson's *The Stone Gods*". *Interdisciplinary Humanities* 27.2: 132–146.
Johns-Putra, Adeline. 2017. "The Unsustainable Aesthetics of Sustainability: The Sense of an Ending in Jeanette Winterson's *The Stone Gods*". In: Adeline Johns-Putra, John Parham and Louise Squire (eds.). *Literature and Sustainability: Concept, Text and Culture*. Manchester: Manchester University Press. 177–194.
Jori, Alberto. 2010. *Das Unendliche: Eine philosophische Untersuchung*. Norderstedt: Books on Demand.
Joyce, James. 2016 [1914]. *Dubliners*. Ed. Keri Walsh. Peterborough: Broadview.
Kaleva, Wilfred. 1995. "The Cultural Context of Mathematics Education Development in Papua New Guinea". *Papua New Guinea Journal of Education* 31: 143–149.
Kant, Immanuel. 2000. *Critique of the Power of Judgment*. Ed. Paul Guyer. Trans. Paul Guyer and Eric Matthews. The Cambridge Edition of the Works of Immanuel Kant. Cambridge: Cambridge University Press.
Kearney, Richard. 1995. *Poetics of Modernity: Toward a Hermeneutic Imagination*. New Jersey: Humanities Press.
Kearney, Richard. 1999. "The Crisis of the Image: Levinas's Ethical Response". In: Gary B. Madison and Marty Fairbairn (eds.). *The Ethics of Postmodernity: Current Trends in Continental Thought*. Evanston: Northwestern University Press. 12–23.
Keats, John. 2012 [1816]. "On First Looking into Chapman's Homer". In: Deirdre Shauna Lynch and Jack Stillinger (eds.). *The Romantic Period*. Vol. D of *The Norton Anthology of English Literature*. Gen. ed. Stephen Greenblatt. New York: Norton. 904.
Kennedy, Juliette. 2011. "Can the Continuum Hypothesis Be Solved?" Institute for Advanced Study. <https://www.ias.edu/ideas/2011/kennedy-continuum-hypothesis> [accessed 20 July 2018].
Kerler, David Ramón. 2013. *Postmoderne Palimpseste: Studien zur (meta-)hermeneutischen Tiefenstruktur intertextueller Erzählverfahren im Gegenwartsroman*. text & theorie 12. Würzburg: Königshausen & Neumann.

Kermode, Frank. 1967. *The Sense of an Ending: Studies in the Theory of Fiction*. Oxford: Oxford University Press.
Kläger, Florian. 2014. "Here Comes Everybody: Anthropological Hyperbole in Some Recent Novels". *Zeitschrift für Anglistik und Amerikanistik* 62.4: 291–308.
Kline, Morris. 1972. *Mathematical Thought from Ancient to Modern Times*. New York: Oxford University Press.
Korte, Barbara. 1985. *Techniken der Schlußgebung im Roman: Eine Untersuchung englisch- und deutschsprachiger Romane*. Frankfurt a. M.: Peter Lang.
Kövecses, Zoltán. 2002. *Metaphor: A Practical Introduction*. Oxford: Oxford University Press.
Kowaleski Wallace, Elizabeth. 2007. "Postcolonial Melancholia in Ian McEwan's *Saturday*". *Studies in the Novel* 39.4: 465–480.
Kristeva, Julia. 1980 [1969]. "The Bounded Text". In: Julia Kristeva. *Desire in Language: A Semiotic Approach to Literature and Art*. Ed. Leon S. Roudiez. Trans. Thomas Gora, Alice Jardine and Leon S. Roudiez. New York: Columbia University Press. 36–63.
Kristeva, Julia. 1986 [1969]. "Word, Dialogue and Novel". Trans. Alice Jardine, Thomas Gora and Leon S. Roudiez. In: Toril Moi (ed.). *The Kristeva Reader*. Oxford: Blackwell. 34–61.
Lakoff, George and Mark Johnson. 1980. *Metaphors We Live By*. Chicago: University of Chicago Press.
Lakoff, George and Mark Johnson. 1999. *Philosophy in the Flesh: The Embodied Mind and Its Challenge to Western Thought*. New York: Basic Books.
Lakoff, George and Rafael E. Núñez. 2000. *Where Mathematics Comes From: How the Embodied Mind Brings Mathematics Into Being*. New York: Basic Books.
Lakoff, George and Mark Turner. 1989. *More Than Cool Reason: A Field Guide to Poetic Metaphor*. Chicago: University of Chicago Press.
Lausberg, Heinrich. 1990. *Handbuch der literarischen Rhetorik: Eine Grundlegung der Literaturwissenschaft*. 3rd ed. Stuttgart: Franz Steiner.
Levinas, Emmanuel. 1969 [1961]. *Totality and Infinity: An Essay on Exteriority*. Trans. Alphonso Lingis. Pittsburgh: Duquesne University Press.
Levinas, Emmanuel. 1974 [1967]. *En découvrant l'existence avec Husserl et Heidegger*. Paris: Vrin.
Levinas, Emmanuel. 1981 [1974]. *Otherwise Than Being Or Beyond Essence*. Trans. Alphonso Lingis. The Hague: Martinus Nijhoff.
Levinas, Emmanuel. 1985 [1982]. *Ethics and Infinity: Conversations with Philippe Nemo*. Trans. Richard A. Cohen. Pittsburgh: Duquesne University Press.
Levinas, Emmanuel. 1986 [1963]. "The Trace of the Other". Trans. Alphonso Lingis. In: Mark C. Taylor (ed.). *Deconstruction in Context: Literature and Philosophy*. Chicago: University of Chicago Press. 345–359.
Levinas, Emmanuel. 1987a [1948]. "Reality and Its Shadow". In: Emmanuel Levinas. *Collected Philosophical Papers*. Trans. Alphonso Lingis. Dordrecht: Martinus Nijhoff. 1–13.
Levinas, Emmanuel. 1987b [1957]. "Philosophy and the Idea of Infinity". In: Emmanuel Levinas. *Collected Philosophical Papers*. Trans. Alphonso Lingis. Dordrecht: Martinus Nijhoff. 47–59.
Levinas, Emmanuel. 1989a [1984]. "Ethics as First Philosophy". Trans. Seán Hand and Michael Temple. In: Seán Hand (ed.). *The Levinas Reader*. Oxford: Blackwell. 75–87.
Levinas, Emmanuel. 1989b [1947]. "The Other in Proust". Trans. Seán Hand. In: Seán Hand (ed.). *The Levinas Reader*. Oxford: Blackwell. 160–165.

Levinas, Emmanuel. 1989c [1949]. "The Transcendence of Words". Trans. Seán Hand. In: Seán Hand (ed.). *The Levinas Reader*. Oxford: Blackwell. 144–149.
Levinas, Emmanuel. 1989d [1947]. "Time and the Other". Trans. Richard A. Cohen. In: Seán Hand (ed.). *The Levinas Reader*. Oxford: Blackwell. 37–58.
Levinas, Emmanuel. 1989e [1966]. "The Servant and her Master". Trans. Michael Holland. In: Seán Hand (ed.). *The Levinas Reader*. Oxford: Blackwell. 150–159.
Levinas, Emmanuel. 1995 [1981]. "Ethics of the Infinite". Interview. In: Richard Kearney. *States of Mind: Dialogues with Contemporary Thinkers on the European Mind*. Manchester: Manchester University Press. 177–199.
Levinas, Emmanuel. 1996a [1984]. "Peace and Proximity". Trans. Peter Atterton and Simon Critchley. In: Emmanuel Levinas. *Basic Philosophical Writings*. Eds. Adriaan T. Peperzak, Simon Critchley and Robert Bernasconi. Bloomington: Indiana University Press. 161–169.
Levinas, Emmanuel. 1996b [1962]. "Transcendence and Height". Trans. Tina Chanter et al. In: Emmanuel Levinas. *Basic Philosophical Writings*. Eds. Adriaan T. Peperzak, Simon Critchley and Robert Bernasconi. Bloomington: Indiana University Press. 11–31.
Levinas, Emmanuel. 1996c [1975]. "God and Philosophy". Trans. Alphonso Lingis, Richard Cohen, Robert Bernasconi and Simon Critchley. In: Emmanuel Levinas. *Basic Philosophical Writings*. Eds. Adriaan T. Peperzak, Simon Critchley and Robert Bernasconi. Bloomington: Indiana University Press. 129–148.
Levinas, Emmanuel. 1996d [1951]. "Is Ontology Fundamental?" Trans. Peter Atterton, Simon Critchley and Adriaan T. Peperzak. In: Emmanuel Levinas. *Basic Philosophical Writings*. Eds. Adriaan T. Peperzak, Simon Critchley and Robert Bernasconi. Bloomington: Indiana University Press. 1–10.
Lingis, Alphonso. 1981 [1974]. "Translator's Introduction". In: Emmanuel Levinas. *Otherwise Than Being Or Beyond Essence*. Trans. Alphonso Lingis. The Hague: Martinus Nijhoff. xi–xxxix.
Llewelyn, John. 2002. "Levinas and Language". In: Simon Critchley and Robert Bernasconi (eds.). *The Cambridge Companion to Levinas*. Cambridge: Cambridge University Press. 119–138.
Lusin, Caroline. 2009. "'We Daydream Helplessly': The Poetics of (Day)Dreams in Ian McEwan's Novels". In: Pascal Nicklas (ed.). *Ian McEwan: Art and Politics*. Heidelberg: Winter. 137–158
Lyotard, Jean-François. 1984 [1982]. "Answering the Question: What Is Postmodernism?" Trans. Régis Durand. *The Postmodern Condition: A Report on Knowledge*. Manchester: Manchester University Press. 71–82.
Lyotard, Jean-François. 1988 [1983]. *The Differend: Phrases in Dispute*. Trans. Georges Van Den Abbeele. Theory and History of Literature 46. Minneapolis: University of Minnesota Press.
Lyotard, Jean-François. 1991 [1983]. "The Sublime and the Avant-garde". Trans. Lisa Liebmann, Geoff Bennington and Marian Hobson. In: Jean-François Lyotard. *The Inhuman: Reflections on Time*. Cambridge: Polity. 89–107.
Machinal, Hélène. 2011. "*Cloud Atlas:* From Postmodernity to the Posthuman". In: Sarah Dillon (ed.). *David Mitchell: Critical Essays*. Canterbury: Gylphi. 127–154.

Machinal, Hélène. 2015. "The Poetics of the Human in J. Winterson's *The Stone Gods*". In: Maylis Ropside and Sandrine Sorlin (eds.). *The Ethics and Poetics of Alterity: New Perspectives on Genre Literature*. Newcastle upon Tyne: Cambridge Scholars. 158–174.

Madison, Gary B. and Marty Fairbairn. 1999. Introduction. In: Gary B. Madison and Marty Fairbairn (eds.). *The Ethics of Postmodernity: Current Trends in Continental Thought*. Evanston: Northwestern University Press. 1–11.

Maor, Eli. 1986. *To Infinity and Beyond: A Cultural History of the Infinite*. Stuttgart: Birkhäuser.

Marvell, Andrew. 1996. "The Fair Singer". In: Margaret Ferguson, Mary Jo Salter and Jon Stallworthy (eds.). *The Norton Anthology of Poetry*. 4th ed. New York: Norton. 438.

McCulloch, Fiona. 2012. *Cosmopolitanism in Contemporary British Fiction: Imagined Identities*. Basingstoke: Palgrave Macmillan.

McEwan, Ian. 1995 [1994]. *The Daydreamer*. London: Vintage.

McEwan, Ian. 2001. "Only Love and Then Oblivion: Love Was All They Had to Set Against Their Murderers". *The Guardian*, 15 September. <https://www.theguardian.com/world/2001/sep/15/september11.politicsphilosophyandsociety2> [accessed 4 April 2017].

McEwan, Ian. 2006 [2005]. *Saturday*. London: Vintage.

McHale, Brian. 1987. *Postmodernist Fiction*. New York: Methuen.

McMorran, Will. 2011. "*Cloud Atlas* and *If on a Winter's Night a Traveller*: Fragmentation and Integrity in the Postmodern Novel". In: Sarah Dillon (ed.). *David Mitchell: Critical Essays*. Canterbury: Gylphi. 155–175.

McNally, Lisa. 2014. *Reading Theories in Contemporary Fiction*. London: Bloomsbury.

Mellet, Laurent. 2015. "The Political Ethics of Alterity in Ian McEwan's Film Adaptations and Screenwriting". In: Jean-Michel Ganteau and Christine Reynier (eds.). *Ethics of Alterity, Confrontation and Responsibility in 19th- to 21st-Century British Arts*. Montpellier: Presses Universitaires de la Méditerranée. 221–232.

Mertens, Mahlu and Stef Craps. 2018. "Contemporary Fiction vs. the Challenge of Imagining the Timescale of Climate Change". *Studies in the Novel* 50.1: 134–153.

Mezey, Jason Howard. 2011. "'A Multitude of Drops': Recursion and Globalization in David Mitchell's *Cloud Atlas*". *Modern Language Studies* 40.2: 10–37.

Michael, Magali Cornier. 2015. *Narrative Innovation in 9/11 Fiction*. Amsterdam: Brill.

Middeke, Martin. 2005a. "Self-Reflexivity, Trans-/Intertextuality, and Hermeneutic Deep Structure in Contemporary British Fiction". In: Werner Huber, Martin Middeke and Hubert Zapf (eds.). *Self-Reflexivity in Literature*. text & theorie 6. Würzburg: Königshausen & Neumann. 211–222.

Middeke, Martin. 2005b. "Intertextualität/Transtextualität: Funktionen und hermeneutische Tiefenstruktur". In: Hans Vilmar Geppert and Hubert Zapf (eds.). *Theorien der Literatur: Grundlagen und Perspektiven*. Vol. 2. Tübingen: Francke. 225–242.

Middeke, Martin. 2009. "On Circles and Spirals: Time, Repetition, and Meta-Hermeneutics in Literature". In: Christoph Henke and Martin Middeke (eds.). *Literature and Circularity*. Spec. issue of *Symbolism: An International Annual of Critical Aesthetics* 9. 103–128.

Miller, J. Hillis. 1987. *The Ethics of Reading*. New York: Columbia University Press.

Mitchell, David. 2004. "David Mitchell – The Interview". *bbc.co.uk*, February. <http://www.bbc.co.uk/nottingham/culture/2004/02/david_mitchell_interview.shtml> [accessed 9 August 2016].

Mitchell, David. 2005. "Genesis". *The Guardian*, 16 April. <http://www.theguardian.com/books/2005/apr/16/featuresreviews.guardianreview23> [accessed 11 July 2016].
Mitchell, David. 2012 [2004]. *Cloud Atlas*. New York: Random House.
Möller, Swantje. 2011. *Coming to Terms with Crisis: Disorientation and Reorientation in the Novels of Ian McEwan*. Heidelberg: Winter.
Moore, Alan. 2016. *Jerusalem*. New York: Norton.
Moore, A. W. (ed.). 1993. *Infinity*. Aldershot: Dartmouth.
Moore, A. W. 2001 [1990]. *The Infinite*. 2nd ed. London: Routledge.
Moraru, Christian. 2011. *Cosmodernism: American Narrative, Late Globalization, and the New Cultural Imaginary*. Ann Arbor: University of Michigan Press.
Mückenheim, Wolfgang. 2011. *Die Geschichte des Unendlichen*. Augsburg: MaroVerlag.
Murphy, Neil. 2014. "John Banville and Heinrich von Kleist: The Art of Confusion". *Review of Contemporary Fiction* 34.1: 54–70.
Neidhart, Ludwig. 2007. *Unendlichkeit im Schnittpunkt von Mathematik und Theologie*. Göttingen: Cuvillier.
Neumann, Uwe. 1998. "Katachrese". In: Gert Ueding (ed.). *Historisches Wörterbuch der Rhetorik, Band 4: Hu–K*. Tübingen: Niemeyer. 911–915.
Ng, Lynda. 2015. "Cannibalism, Colonialism and Apocalypse in Mitchell's Global Future". *SubStance* 44.1: 107–122.
Nicklas, Pascal. 2009. "The Ethical Question: Art and Politics in the Work of Ian McEwan". In: Pascal Nicklas (ed.). *Ian McEwan: Art and Politics*. Heidelberg: Winter. 9–22.
Nietzsche, Friedrich. 1891 [1883]. *Thus Spake Zarathustra*. Trans. Thomas Common. EBSCOhost eBook Collection. Raleigh: Generic NL Freebook Publisher. <http://search.ebscohost.com/login.aspx?direct=true&db=nlebk&AN=1085963&site=ehost-live&ebv=EB&ppid=pp_COVER> [accessed 6 February 2017].
Nietzsche, Friedrich. 1968 [1883]. *Also sprach Zarathustra*. Vol. VI.1 of *Nietzsche Werke: Kritische Gesamtausgabe*. Eds. Giorgio Colli and Mazzino Montinari. Berlin: de Gruyter.
Nixon, Mignon. 2012. "Infinity Politics". In: Frances Morris (ed.). *Yayoi Kusama*. London: Tate Publishing. 176–185.
Nolan, Val. 2010. "The Aesthetics of Space and Time in the Fiction of John Banville and Neil Jordan". *Nordic Irish Studies* 9: 33–47.
Nunius, Sabine. 2009. *Coping with Difference: New Approaches in the Contemporary British Novel (2000–2006)*. Münster: LIT.
Nunius, Sabine. 2011. "Difference and Ethics in Ian McEwan's *Saturday*". In: Alexandra Böhm, Antje Kley and Mark Schönleben (eds.). *Ethik – Anerkennung – Gerechtigkeit: Philosophische, literarische und gesellschaftliche Perspektiven*. München: Fink. 269–284.
O'Brien, Flann. 2001 [1939]. *At Swim-Two-Birds*. London: Penguin.
O'Connell, Mark. 2011. "The Empathic Paradox: Third-Person Narration in John Banville's First-Person Narratives". *ORBIS Litterarum* 66.6: 427–447.
O'Connell, Mark. 2013. *John Banville's Narcissistic Fictions*. Basingstoke: Palgrave Macmillan.
O'Donnell, Patrick. 2015. *A Temporary Future: The Fiction of David Mitchell*. New York: Bloomsbury.
Onega, Susana. 2009. "Circularity and the Quest in the Novels of Jeanette Winterson". In: Christoph Henke and Martin Middeke (eds.). *Literature and Circularity*. Spec. issue of *Symbolism: An International Annual on Critical Aesthetics* 9: 193–216.

Onega, Susana. 2011. "The Trauma Paradigm and the Ethics of Affect in Jeanette Winterson's *The Stone Gods*". In: Susana Onega and Jean-Michel Ganteau (eds.). *Ethics and Trauma in Contemporary British Fiction*. Amsterdam: Rodopi. 265–298.

Opałka, Roman. 2017. *Roman Opałka: Official Website*. <http://www.opalka1965.com> [accessed 20 September 2018].

Oppy, Graham. 2006. *Philosophical Perspectives on Infinity*. Cambridge: Cambridge University Press.

Oppy, Graham. 2011. "God and Infinity: Directions for Future Research". In: Michael Heller and W. Hugh Woodin (eds.). *Infinity: New Research Frontiers*. Cambridge: Cambridge University Press. 233–254.

Organ²/ASLSP: John-Cage-Orgel-Kunst-Projekt Halberstadt. N.d. <www.aslsp.org> [accessed 2 June 2016].

Parker, Jo Alyson. 2010. "David Mitchell's *Cloud Atlas* of Narrative Constraints and Environmental Limits". In: Jo Alyson Parker, Paul A. Harris, and Christian Steineck (eds.). *Time: Limits and Constraints*. Leiden: Brill.

Pascal, Blaise. 1958 [1670]. *Pascal's Pensées*. Trans. W. F. Trotter. New York: E. P. Dutton. <http://www.gutenberg.org/files/18269/18269-h/18269-h.htm> [accessed 1 April 2017].

Pascal, Blaise. 1976 [1670]. *Pensées*. Ed. Léon Brunschvigg. Paris: Garnier-Flammarion.

Pfister, Manfred. 1985. "Konzepte der Intertextualität". In: Ulrich Broich and Manfred Pfister (eds.). *Intertextualität: Formen, Funktionen, anglistische Fallstudien*. Tübingen: Niemeyer. 1–30.

Pier, John. 2014. "Narrative Levels (revised version; uploaded 23 April 2014)". In: Peter Hühn et al. (eds.). *the living handbook of narratology*. Hamburg: Hamburg University. 13 May. <http://www.lhn.uni-hamburg.de/article/narrative-levels-revised-version-uploaded-23-april-2014> [accessed 29 September 2016].

Pier, John. 2016. "Metalepsis (revised version; uploaded 13 July 2016)". In: Peter Hühn et al. (eds.). *the living handbook of narratology*. Hamburg: Hamburg University. 14 July. <http://www.lhn.uni-hamburg.de/article/metalepsis-revised-version-uploaded-13-july-2016> [accessed 6 October 2016].

Polvinen, Merja. 2012. "Being Played: Mimesis, Fictionality and Emotional Engagement". In: Saija Isomaa et al. (eds.). *Rethinking Mimesis: Concepts and Practices of Literary Representation*. Newcastle upon Tyne: Cambridge Scholars. 93–112.

Puschmann-Nalenz, Barbara. 2009. "Ethics in Ian McEwan's Twenty-First Century Novels: Individual and Society and the Problem of Free Will". In: Pascal Nicklas (ed.). *Ian McEwan: Art and Politics*. Heidelberg: Winter. 187–212.

Puschmann-Nalenz, Barbara. 2016. "'Et in Arcadia ille – this one is/was also in Arcadia:' Human Life and Death as Comedy for the Immortals in John Banville's *The Infinities*". *Anglistik: International Journal of English Studies* 27.1: 99–111.

Rauff, James. 2013. "The Chicken Went Into the Bush and Never Came Back: A Note on Infinity". *BSHM Bulletin: Journal of the British Society for the History of Mathematics* 28.2: 97–100.

Reichl, Susanne. 2017. "Only Time Will Tell: The Temporal Poetics and Politics of Martin Amis's *Time's Arrow* and Jeanette Winterson's *The Stone Gods*". In: Winfried Eckel and Anja Müller-Wood (eds.). *Die Macht des Erzählens: Transdisziplinäre Perspektiven*. Remscheid: Gardez! Verlag. 245–261.

Reinfandt, Christoph. 2016. "Reading Textures". In: Martin Middeke and Christoph Reinfandt (eds.). *Theory Matters: The Place of Theory in Literary and Cultural Studies Today.* Basingstoke: Palgrave Macmillan. 319–334.
Ricardou, Jean. 1967. *Problèmes du nouveau roman.* Paris: Editions du Seuil.
Richter, David H. 1974. *Fable's End: Completeness and Closure in Rhetorical Fiction.* Chicago: University of Chicago Press.
Ridout, Nicholas. 2009. *Theatre & Ethics.* Basingstoke: Palgrave Macmillan.
Ries, Eva Katharina. 2020. "Precarious Flânerie – Towards the Formation of an Ethical Subject". In: Oliver Bock and Isabel Vila-Cabanes (eds.). *Urban Walking: The Flâneur as an Icon of Metropolitan Culture in Literature and Film.* Wilmington: Vernon Press. 1–28.
Riffaterre, Michael. 1978. *Semiotics of Poetry.* Bloomington: Indiana University Press.
Rimer, Sara. 1994. "Cavendish Journal; Shielding Solzhenitsyn, Respectfully". *New York Times*, 3 March. <http://www.nytimes.com/1994/03/03/us/cavendish-journal-shielding-solzhenitsyn-respectfully.html> [accessed 6 January 2017].
Rine, Abigail. 2011. "Jeanette Winterson's Love Intervention: Rethinking the Future". In: Ben Davies and Jana Funke (eds.). *Sex, Gender and Time in Fiction and Culture.* Basingstoke: Palgrave Macmillan. 70–85.
Robbins, Jill. 1999. *Altered Reading: Levinas and Literature.* Chicago: University of Chicago Press.
Robbins, Jill. (ed.). 2001. *Is It Righteous to Be? Interviews with Emmanuel Levinas.* Stanford: Stanford University Press.
Robbins, Bruce. 2015. "Cosmopolitanism in Time". *Journal of English Language and Literature* 61.1: 3–18.
Rolf, Eckard. 2005. *Metaphertheorien: Typologie, Darstellung, Bibliographie.* Berlin: de Gruyter.
Ron, Moshe. 1987. "The Restricted Abyss: Nine Problems in the Theory of *Mise en Abyme*". *Poetics Today* 8.2: 417–438.
Ronen, Ruth. 1994. *Possible Worlds in Literary Theory.* Cambridge: Cambridge University Press.
Root, Christina. 2011. "A Melodiousness at Odds with Pessimism: Ian McEwan's *Saturday*". *Journal of Modern Literature* 35.1: 60–78.
Rösch, Gertrud Maria. 2010. "Schlange". In: Günter Butzer and Joachim Jacob (eds.). *Metzler Lexikon literarischer Symbole.* Stuttgart: Metzler. 324–325.
Ross, Michael L. 2008. "On a Darkling Planet: Ian McEwan's *Saturday* and the Condition of England". *Twentieth-Century Literature* 54.1: 75–96.
Rotman, Brian. 2011. "Mathematics". In: Bruce Clarke with Manuela Rossini (eds.). *The Routledge Companion to Literature and Science.* London: Routledge. 157–168.
Rubenstein, Mary-Jane. 2014. *Worlds Without End: The Many Lives of the Multiverse.* New York: Columbia University Press.
Rucker, Rudy. 1982. *Infinity and the Mind: The Science and Philosophy of the Infinite.* Stuttgart: Birkhäuser.
Ruge, Enno. 2010. "Seize the Saturday: Re-viewing Ian McEwan's *Saturday* and Re-reading the Novels of Saul Bellow". *Anglistik: International Journal of English Studies* 21.2: 69–81.
Ryan, Marie-Laure. 1991. *Possible Worlds, Artificial Intelligence, and Narrative Theory.* Bloomington: Indiana University Press.

Ryan, Marie-Laure. 2006. "From Parallel Universes to Possible Worlds: Ontological Pluralism in Physics, Narratology, and Narrative". *Poetics Today* 27.4: 633–674.
Sandford, Stella. 2002. "Levinas, Feminism, and the Feminine". In: Simon Critchley and Robert Bernasconi (eds.). *The Cambridge Companion to Levinas*. Cambridge: Cambridge University Press. 139–160.
Sargent, Lyman Tower. 1994. "The Three Faces of Utopianism Revisited". *Utopian Studies* 5.1: 1–37.
Scheffel, Michael. 1997. *Formen selbstreflexiven Erzählens*. Tübingen: Niemeyer.
Schleiermacher, Friedrich. 1977. *Hermeneutics: The Handwritten Manuscripts*. Ed. Heinz Kimmerle. Trans. James Duke and Jack Forstman. Missoula: Scholars.
Schoberth, Wolfgang. 2016. "'Alles Ding währt seine Zeit': Theologische Überlegungen zu Unendlichkeit und Ewigkeit". In: Rudolf Freiburg (ed.). *Unendlichkeit*. Erlangen: FAU University Press. 85–104. <https://opus4.kobv.de/opus4-fau/frontdoor/index/index/docId/7462%20title> [accessed 17 September 2018].
Schoene, Berthold. 2009. *The Cosmopolitan Novel*. Edinburgh: Edinburgh University Press.
Schwall, Hedwig. 2010. "An Iridescent Surplus of Style: Features of the Fantastic in Banville's The Infinities". *Nordic Irish Studies* 9: 89–107.
Schwalm, Helga. 2009. "Figures of Authorship, Empathy, & the Ethics of Narrative (Mis-)Recognition in Ian McEwan's Later Fiction". In: Pascal Nicklas (ed.). *Ian McEwan: Art and Politics*. Heidelberg: Winter. 173–185.
Shakespeare, William. 2006. *Hamlet*. Eds. Ann Thompson and Neil Taylor. Arden Shakespeare, Third Series. London: CENGAGE Learning.
Shakespeare, William. 2007. *Shakespeare's Sonnets*. Ed. Katherine Duncan-Jones. Arden Shakespeare, Third Series. Rpt. London: CENGAGE Learning.
Shoop, Casey, and Dermot Ryan. 2015. "'Gravid with the Ancient Future': *Cloud Atlas* and the Politics of Big History". *SubStance* 44.1: 92–106.
Sidney, Philip. 2012 [1595]. *The Defense of Poesy*. In: Stephen Greenblatt et al. (eds.). *The Sixteenth Century and the Early Seventeenth Century*. Vol. B of *The Norton Anthology of English Literature*. 9th ed. Gen. ed. Stephen Greenblatt. New York: Norton. 1044–1083.
Smith, Eoghan. 2014. *John Banville: Art and Authenticity*. Bern: Peter Lang.
Smith, Zadie. 2005. "An Interview with Ian McEwan". *The Believer* 26. <https://believermag.com/an-interview-with-ian-mcewan/> [13 September 2017].
Spitzer, Leo. 1957. "Language of Poetry". In: Ruth Anshen (ed.). *Language: An Enquiry into Its Meaning and Function*. New York: Harper and Brothers. 201–231.
Staehler, Tanja. 2010. *Plato and Levinas: The Ambiguous Out-Side of Ethics*. New York: Routledge.
Stanzel, Franz K. 1955. *Die typischen Erzählsituationen im Roman*. Wien: Braumüller.
Stanzel, Franz K. 1984. *A Theory of Narrative*. Trans. Charlotte Goedsche. Cambridge: Cambridge University Press.
Sternberg, Meir. 1978. *Expositional Modes and Temporal Ordering in Fiction*. Baltimore: Johns Hopkins University Press.
Sternberg, Meir. 2007. "Omniscience in Narrative Construction: Old Challenges and New". *Poetics Today* 28.4: 683–794.
Stevenson, Robert Louis. 2006 [1886]. *Strange Case of Dr Jekyll and Mr Hyde*. In: Robert Louis Stevenson. *Strange Case of Dr Jekyll and Mr Hyde and Other Tales*. Ed. Roger Luckhurst. Oxford: Oxford University Press. 1–66.

Stewart, Ian. 2017. *Infinity: A Very Short Introduction*. Oxford: Oxford University Press.
Sutton, Gloria. 2017. "Between Enactment and Deception: Yayoi Kusama's Spatialized Image Structures". In: Mika Yoshitake (ed.). *Yayoi Kusama Infinity Mirrors*. München: Del Monico. 138–155.
Tannery, Paul. 1904. "Pour l'histoire du mot apeiron". *Revue de Philosophie* 5: 703–707.
Tegmark, Max. 2003. "Parallel Universes". *Scientific American* 288.5: 40–51.
Trogovnick, Marianna. 1981. *Closure in the Novel*. Princeton: Princeton University Press.
Vergil. 1900. *Bucolics, Aeneid, and Georgics Of Vergil*. Ed. J. B. Greenough. Boston: Ginn. In: *Perseus Digital Library*. <http://www.perseus.tufts.edu/hopper/text?doc=Perseus%3atext%3a1999.02.0055> [accessed 11 January 2017].
Vilenkin, Naum Yakovlevich. 1995. *In Search of Infinity*. Trans. Abe Shenitzer. New York: Springer Science+Business Media.
Waldenfels, Bernhard. 2008. "Aporien des Unendlichen". In: Johannes Brachtendorf et al. (eds.). *Unendlichkeit: Interdisziplinäre Perspektiven*. Tübingen: Mohr Siebeck. 3–22.
Waldenfels, Bernhard. 2012. *Hyperphänomene: Modi hyperbolischer Erfahrung*. Berlin: suhrkamp.
Wallace, David Foster. 2010 [2003]. *Everything and More: A Compact History of Infinity*. New York: Norton.
Wallhead, Celia, and Marie-Luise Kohlke. 2010. "The Neo-Victorian Frame of Mitchell's *Cloud Atlas*: Temporal and Traumatic Reverberations". In: Marie-Luise Kohlke and Christian Gutleben (eds.). *Neo-Victorian Tropes of Trauma: The Politics of Bearing After-Witness to Nineteenth-Century Suffering*. Amsterdam: Rodopi. 217–252.
Weidle, Roland. 2009. "The Ethics of Metanarration: Empathy in Ian McEwan's *The Comfort of Strangers, The Child in Time, Atonement* and *Saturday*". In: Pascal Nicklas (ed.). *Ian McEwan: Art and Politics*. Heidelberg: Winter. 57–72.
Wells, Lynn. 2010. *Ian McEwan*. Basingstoke: Palgrave Macmillan.
Wharton, David. 2008. "*Sunt Lacrimae Rerum*: An Exploration in Meaning". *The Classical Journal* 103.3: 259–279.
Wiemann, Dirk. 2017. "David Mitchell, *Cloud Atlas* (2004)". In: Cristoph Reinfandt (ed.). *Handbook of the English Novel of the Twentieth and Twenty-First Centuries*. Berlin: de Gruyter.
Winterhalter, Teresa. 2010. "'Plastic Fork in Hand': Reading as a Tool of Ethical Repair in Ian McEwan's *Saturday*". *Journal of Narrative Theory* 40.3: 338–363.
Winters, David. 2015. *Infinite Fictions: Essays on Literature and Theory*. Winchester: Zero Books.
Winterson, Jeanette. 2008 [2007]. *The Stone Gods*. London: Penguin.
Wolf, Werner. 2008. "Mise en abyme". In: Ansgar Nünning (ed.). *Metzler-Lexikon Literatur- und Kulturtheorie*. 4th ed. Stuttgart: Metzler. 502–503.
Womack, Kenneth. 2015. "Ethical Criticism and the Philosophical Turn". In: Julian Wolfreys (ed.). *Introducing Criticism in the 21st Century*. Edinburgh: Edinburgh University Press. 81–100.
Wyatt, Thomas. 2005. "They fle from me that sometyme did me seke". In: H. R. Woudhuysen (ed.). *The Penguin Book of Renaissance Verse: 1509–1659*. Rev. ed. London: Penguin. 181–182.

Wyschogrod, Edith. 2002. "Language and Alterity in the Thought of Levinas". In: Simon Critchley and Robert Bernasconi (eds.). *The Cambridge Companion to Levinas*. Cambridge: Cambridge University Press. 188–205.

Yoshitake, Mika (ed.). 2017. *Yayoi Kusama Infinity Mirrors*. München: Del Monico.

Zellini, Paolo. 2010 [1980]. *Eine kurze Geschichte der Unendlichkeit*. Trans. Enrico Heinemann. München: C. H. Beck.

Zimmermann, Michael F. 2018. "Unermesslichkeit der Natur – Unergründlichkeit des Subjekts: Caspar David Friedrichs *Mönch am Meer* (1809–10) und die visuelle Poetologie des Subjekts der Moderne". In: Christoph Böttigheimer and René Dausner (eds.). *Unendlichkeit: Transdisziplinäre Annäherungen*. Würzburg: Königshausen & Neumann. 305–378.

Index

absolute infinity   10f.
actual infinity   7–12, 15, 19f., 27, 30, 32, 35–37, 50f., 54, 64–66, 152, 204, 217f.
actuality   7f., 11f., 195–197, 199, 202, 212, 215
affect   13, 124, 140, 142, 144f., 153, 155, 175f., 221f.
Anaximander   6
apeiron   6f.
apocalypse   38, 98, 103, 106, 111, 114, 121f., 125, 128, 132
aporia   4–6, 18, 45f., 64, 74–76, 78, 80, 85, 90, 95, 128–131, 190, 204, 225
Aristotle   7–10, 12, 19, 32, 34–36, *see also* actual infinity, potential infinity
Arnold, Matthew   157f., 172–175, 177–179, 219
– *Culture and Anarchy*   177
– "Dover Beach"   157f., 164, 172–176, 178–182, 219
Auden, W. H.   141
Augustine of Hippo, Saint   11f.

Bakhtin, Mikhail   53, 88
Banville, John   2, 24–26, 29, 61, 184f., 188, 190, 192–194, 196–198, 200, 205, 208f., 211, 213, 215f., 219f.
– *Doctor Copernicus*   188
– *Eclipse*   184
– *God's Gift*   184
– *Kepler*   188
– *Love in the Wars*   184
– *Mephisto*   188
– *The Broken Jug*   184
– *The Infinities*   2, 20, 24–26, 29, 31, 61, 184–216, 218–220, 222
– *The Newton Letter*   188, 192, 209
Barnes, Julian   39–42
– *A History of the World in 10½ Chapters*   39
Barth, John   26, 41f., 49, 218
– "Frame Tale"   41, 49
– *Lost in the Funhouse*   26

Barthes, Roland   54f., 57, 139
Basic Metaphor of Infinity   2, 20, 27f., 33–42, 49–52, 54–59, 61f., 64f., 85, 97, 100, 105, 125, 130f., 181, 201, 217f.
Beckett, Samuel   19, 26, 44, 47
– *Waiting for Godot*   44, 46, 50
Bellow, Saul   180
– *Herzog*   180f.
betrayal (Levinas)   27, 73–76, 79, 81–83, 90–92, 94, 97, 114, 118, 214
bible   11, 111, 128, 143, 147
Blanchot, Maurice   83f.
Borges, Jorge Luis   19, 24, 26, 63, 204
Bradbury, Ray   140, 181
– *Fahrenheit 451*   140, 181
Bruno, Giordano   9
Burke, Edmund   12f., 34
Butler, Judith   80, 82, 84, 91, 116, 156, 172, 223

Cage, John   16f.
Calvino, Italo   99
– *If on a Winter's Night a Traveller*   99
Cantor, Georg   9–12, 19f., 31, 88
caress (Levinas)   28, 144–149, 152f.
catachresis   20, 27f., 32, 62–66, 80–82, 84f., 87–93, 95, 109, 118, 123, 125, 131, 213f., 217
circularity   10f., 20, 24, 27f., 32, 38, 41–43, 47, 49, 93, 96f., 100, 107–109, 118f., 122, 124–128, 130–134, 136–139, 141f., 146, 151f., 154, 180, 218, 220
closure   22, 38, 46, 48f., 51f., 54, 72, 75, 85, 90, 92f., 96, 99f., 102–106, 113f., 117, 119, 122–125, 128, 132, 136, 183, 201, 214f.
cohabitation   96, 116, 151
conceptual metaphor   2, 19f., 22, 32–37, 49–52, 55, 62, 64f., 130, 217
Conrad, Joseph   180
– "The Secret Sharer"   180
Cook, James   126, 129, 134f., 140

244 — Index

cosmodernism   25, 224
cosmopolitanism   25, 96, 116, 124, 218f., 222, 224
Critchley, Simon   22, 66–68, 70, 72f., 75, 92, 95, 110, 140, 143f., 148, 150, 190, 211, 214, 222
Culler, Jonathan   57, 60, 89, 203, 205
cycle, cyclicality   *see* circularity

de Man, Paul   20, 22, 81
deconstruction   22f., 75, 110, 122, 137, 222
Derrida, Jacques   20, 25, 72, 75, 78, 90–92, 122, 137, 150
Descartes, René   56, 67–69, 82, 85
Donne, John   103f., 134, 142
dystopia   28, 124, 126, 132f., 139–141, 143, 155, 181

epistemology   2, 10, 19, 25f., 31, 96, 123, 166, 185, 198, 207, 209, 216
Escher, M. C.   15
eternal recurrence (Nietzsche)   41, 97, 100, 104, 106–109, 111, 119, 131f., 134
eternity   5, 12, 15, 17, 38f., 41f., 108f., 139, 151
ethical criticism   22f., 66, 78, 217, 221f.
ethical responsibility   21–23, 66, 70f., 74, 78, 83, 87, 90, 95, 105, 112, 114, 116, 122f., 147, 158, 169, 173, 176, 223–225
ethical turn   2, 22f.
excess   12–14, 18, 20f., 29, 38, 65, 76, 82, 87, 182, 190, 225

face (Levinas)   27, 69–71, 73f., 77–84, 90–92, 94f., 112, 116, 163, 165, 172, 190, 221, 223
feminism   38, 67, 86, 143f., 150, 187
Fielding, Henry   60
– *The History of Tom Jones, a Foundling*   60
Foucault, Michel   63
frequency (narrative)   40f.
Friedrich, Caspar David   16

Genette, Gérard   40f., 47, 52, 55–58, 60, 100, 169, 205
Gide, André   43–45

god   5, 7, 10–13, 19f., 29, 36, 58, 60f., 67f., 101, 104, 117, 149, 166, 184–189, 191–194, 196–198, 200–213, 215f., 219

Heidegger, Martin   66, 72, 81, 115, 189
hermeneutics   28, 55, 123, 136–138, 152, 215, 221
heterotopia   63f.
Hofstadter, Douglas   3, 46, 100, 106, 130
Homer   56, 105, 140, 176, 181
– *Iliad*   83, 105
– *Odyssey*   56, 140
Hopper, Edward   16
Horace / Quintus Horatius Flaccus   15, 17
horror infiniti   9f., 31
hyperbole   13f., 18, 224f.

indefinite   4, 15, 34–43, 46–51, 54, 58f., 61, 64f., 97, 106, 120, 130f., 136f., 209
infinite regress   7, 47, 50, 54, 57, 86
infinity   *see* absolute infinity, actual infinity, potential infinity
intertextuality   19f., 22, 24, 27, 29, 32, 38, 52–58, 86–90, 92f., 96f., 103–105, 125, 130, 133–136, 142, 147, 157–160, 167f., 170–174, 176–184, 203, 208, 215f., 218
Irigaray, Luce   143, 150
Iser, Wolfgang   136f.
iteration   27, 34–43, 47, 49–51, 53–55, 58f., 61, 64f., 96, 106, 130f., 137, 142, 181, 201, 218, *see also* repetition

Joyce, James   26, 42, 56, 159, 179–181, 185, 218
– *Finnegans Wake*   26, 42
– "The Dead"   159, 180, 182
– *Ulysses*   26, 56, 159, 179–181, 185

Kafka, Franz   180
– *The Metamorphosis*   180
Kant, Immanuel   12–14
Keats, John   176
Kleist, Heinrich von   184, 192
– *Amphitryon*   184, 208, 215
– "On the Marionette Theatre"   184

Kristeva, Julia   53–58, 87–89, 93, 142, 173, 203, 220
Kusama, Yayoi   16–18

Lakoff, George   2, 20, 27, 32–38, 49–51, 54, 61, 64, 97, 130f., 217, *see also* Basic Metaphor of Infinity
Levinas, Emmanuel   2, 5, 14, 20–23, 25, 27f., 53, 56f., 66–95, 97, 109f., 112f., 115f., 118, 120f., 123, 140–148, 150, 152f., 157f., 163, 165, 168, 170, 172–174, 176–178, 182, 187–191, 199, 206, 211, 214, 217, 220–223, 225, *see also* betrayal, caress, face, said, saying, scintillation
love   28, 124–126, 128, 133, 135f., 143–147, 149–153, 155, 212, 219
Lyotard, Jean-François   13, 81

mathematics   1, 3, 5, 7, 9–11, 14, 20, 31, 33f., 36f., 47, 88, 185
McEwan, Ian   2, 8, 25f., 29, 97, 156–158, 160, 169f., 173, 177, 180, 183, 185, 218
– *Saturday*   2, 24, 26, 29, 31, 58, 97, 156–183, 185, 218–220, 222, 224
– *The Child in Time*   170
– *The Daydreamer*   8
medium   14, 16, 18, 27, 31f., 40–42, 46, 49, 64, 78, 95, 111, 118, 203
metafiction   45, 56, 104, 107, 113, 127, 130, 149, 154, 183–186, 192, 194, 196, 199f., 206, 210, 215f., 219f.
metaphysics   5, 7, 10, 14f., 36, 67, 91, 123, 149, 166f., 170f., 173, 175, 177f., 220
Miller, J. Hillis   23, 94
mise en abyme   18, 20, 24, 27–29, 32, 38, 43–52, 54, 63, 85–89, 93, 96f., 99f., 102, 105–108, 122, 128f., 131, 189f., 210
– *réduplication à l'infini* (Dällenbach)   27, 45, 49, 51f., 64, 87, 97, 100, 109, 129
– *réduplication aporistique* (Dällenbach)   45, 129, 189
– *réduplication simple* (Dällenbach)   45, 51
Mitchell, David   2, 25f., 28f., 96, 99, 103–108, 110, 114, 118, 121, 123f., 152, 218f., 224

– *Cloud Atlas*   2, 24–26, 28, 31, 42, 52, 96–124, 131, 152, 213, 218, 220, 222, 224
Möbius strip   41, 49, 107, 208
Moore, Alan   26, 59, 61, 204
– *Jerusalem*   26, 59, 61, 204
morals, morality   23, 77, 123, 177
multiverse   24, 29, 186, 190, 192–201, 204, 209–216, 219
– multiverse narrative   186, 190, 193, 196f., 199–201, 210f., 213

Nancy, Jean-Luc   116
negativity   4–6, 8, 20, 216, 222
Nietzsche, Friedrich   97, 100, 104, 106–109, 111, 123, 131f., *see also* eternal recurrence
Núñez, Rafael E.   2, 20, 27, 32–38, 49–51, 54, 61, 64, 97, 130f., 217, *see also* Basic Metaphor of Infinity
Nussbaum, Martha   23

O'Brien, Flann   26, 45
– *At Swim-Two-Birds*   26, 45
– *The Third Policeman*   26
omniscient narration   27, 32, 38, 58–61, 93, 200–206, 208–212, 215
One Thousand and One Nights   100
ontology   2, 7f., 10, 21f., 27, 30f., 41, 45, 49f., 66f., 69–73, 75–78, 81–83, 85, 87, 90f., 95, 100, 103, 107, 110, 115, 119, 121, 129, 140, 142, 146f., 149–151, 153, 165f., 168, 172, 185, 187, 189, 191, 195–197, 199, 209, 211f., 214–217, 219–221, 223–225
Opałka, Roman   16f.
ouroboros   108, 127, 132, 207

paradox   1–6, 11, 16, 18, 21, 32, 35, 40, 46, 68, 71, 74, 81f., 85, 94, 107, 125, 129, 132, 142, 171, 182, 190, 206, 214, 217, 225
Pascal, Blaise   5f.
Plato   7, 76–78
plurality   20, 29, 53, 55, 92, 116, 136f., 141f., 144, 146, 149–152, 157, 171, 178, 182f., 194, 197, 199, 202

possible worlds theory   193, 195f.
postmodernism   13, 26, 41, 85, 99, 106, 218
poststructuralism   19, 22, 54f., 58, 75, 137, 203
potential infinity   7–10, 12, 16, 19, 25, 31, 34–36, 41, 44, 48–53, 130f., 185
precariousness   21, 69, 71, 80, 90, 94, 172, 223

queerness   28, 126, 143, 145–147, 152, 155

recursion   28, 35, 46–50, 52f., 97, 100, 102, 105, 109
religion   5, 7, 11f., 20, 148, 166
repetition   15, 17, 27–29, 32, 34f., 37–43, 45, 47f., 50–52, 55, 65, 83, 93, 118, 124–127, 129, 131–134, 136–140, 142, 145, 147, 151–154, 218, *see also* iteration
responsibility   *see* ethical responsibility
Rushdie, Salman   26, 170
– *Midnight's Children*   26, 170

said (Levinas)   27, 72–76, 78f., 81–84, 90–94, 110, 114, 121, 140–142, 148, 168, 171, 174–176, 211, 214, 216, 221
saying (Levinas)   27, 72–76, 78, 81–84, 90–92, 94, 110, 112, 121, 140–142, 148, 168, 171, 173–176, 182, 211f., 214, 216
Schleiermacher, Friedrich   136f.
Schrödinger's Cat   161f., 166, 168
scintillation (Levinas)   83–86, 91, 109f., 123, 222
Shakespeare, William   15, 17, 135, 146, 172
– *Hamlet*   43, 45, 51f., 146
– sonnets   15, 17, 135, 172
Sidney, Sir Philip   77, 212
Snow, C. P.   160

Solzhenitsyn, Alexander   103
– *The Gulag Archipelago*   103
Stanzel, Franz Karl   58, 60, 205
Sterne, Laurence   24
– *Tristram Shandy*   24, 26
Stevenson, Robert Louis   180
– *Strange Case of Dr Jekyll and Mr Hyde*   180
strange loop   46, 97, 100, 106–108, 130f.
structuralism   19f., 22, 55, 58, 205
sublime   12–18, 34, 111

texture   221f.
theatrum mundi   186, 210, 216
theology   1, 3, 7, 11f., 14, 36, 205
transcendence   2, 11f., 15, 19f., 61, 93, 114, 153, 160, 195, 203f.
transfinite   9–11, 19f., 88f., 142, 144, 220
transtextuality   55–57

Vergil / Publius Vergilius Maro   104f.
– *Aeneid*   56, 104f.
vulnerability   21, 28, 69f., 73, 80, 90, 94, 111f., 116, 147, 156, 164, 172–174, 182, 219, 221

Waldenfels, Bernhard   4–7, 12–14, 225
Wallace, David Foster   3, 5, 26
– *Infinite Jest*   26
Warhol, Andy   15
Winterson, Jeanette   2, 25f., 28f., 124f., 127f., 132–136, 138–140, 142–144, 146, 150–155, 218f., 221
– *The Stone Gods*   2, 24–26, 28, 31, 42, 124–155, 218, 220–222, 224
Woolf, Virginia   159, 179, 181, 185, 218
– *Mrs Dalloway*   159, 179, 181, 185
workness (Attridge)   29, 175f., 183
worldmaking, narrative   29, 184f., 191, 195f., 200, 206, 219

www.ingramcontent.com/pod-product-compliance
Lightning Source LLC
Chambersburg PA
CBHW030538230426
43665CB00010B/941